Writ
Wome

M000281803

Writing Queer Women of Color

Representation and Misdirection
in Contemporary Fiction
and Graphic Narratives

MONALESIA EARLE

McFarland & Company, Inc., Publishers
Jefferson, North Carolina

LIBRARY OF CONGRESS CATALOGUING-IN-PUBLICATION DATA

Names: Earle, Monalesia, author.
Title: Writing queer women of color : representation and misdirection
  in contemporary fiction and graphic narratives / Monalesia Earle.
Description: Jefferson, North Carolina : McFarland & Company, Inc.,
  Publishers, 2019. | Includes bibliographical references and index.
Identifiers: LCCN 2019028628 | ISBN 9781476674544 (paperback : acid free paper) ∞
Subjects: LCSH: Comic books, strips, etc.—History and criticism. |
  Graphic novels—History and criticism. | American fiction—Women authors—
  History and criticism. | Canadian fiction—Women authors—History and criticism. |
  Minority women in literature. | Lesbians in literature. | Race in literature.
Classification: LCC PN6714 .E37 2019 | DDC 809.399287—dc23
LC record available at https://lccn.loc.gov/2019028628

BRITISH LIBRARY CATALOGUING DATA ARE AVAILABLE

ISBN (print) 978-1-4766-7454-4
ISBN (ebook) 978-1-4766-3681-8

Front cover illustration by Volha Rumiantsava (Shutterstock)

Printed in the United States of America

McFarland & Company, Inc., Publishers
  Box 611, Jefferson, North Carolina 28640
  www.mcfarlandpub.com

Table of Contents

*Between pages 130 and 131 are 8 color plates
containing 13 photographs*

Acknowledgments

This book would not have happened without the support of many people. I would like to thank Layla Milholen, my editor at McFarland. Her guidance and support has been so greatly appreciated. I would also like to thank Jenny Prince-Chrisley for her wizardry with all things Word. She pulled off some incredible magic tricks when absolutely nothing else worked. And special thanks to Amber Djemal for translating some of the Turkish phrases for me in *Snapshots of a Girl*. I think she has now become a big fan of graphic narratives.

In the early stages of my research I was also lucky enough to have known some of the most amazing scholars in the Department of English and Humanities at Birkbeck, University of London. My appreciation goes out to several of those women whose ideas about all manner of things kept me thinking outside the box. They know who they are.

I am also fortunate to have a wonderful circle of friends who offered encouragement during the long journey of bringing this book to fruition. A big thanks goes out to my "brutha" Russell Derek Campbell, an incredible man with whom I have shared so many laughs and tears and everything in between. He is my chosen family and I cannot imagine my life without him. And to my lesbian "family" here in the UK—many thanks for the love, the passionate political discussions, the annual quiz nights, the occasional long weekends away, but most of all for welcoming me into your circle. My life is much richer for having met such incredible women. A special thanks also goes out to Afi Adjei and Suzanne Elwick, both of whom were so good about listening to me chirp on and on about my research. And to Cath Yankson, whose quirky humor and "sistah" wisdom is always appreciated.

My gratitude also goes out to the artists who granted me permission to use their illustrations in this book and also to those who worked with me to create original pieces. Their generosity and enormous talent is very much appreciated.

And finally, to the memory of Patricia, who left me (and so many others) with an abiding memory of her unconditional love. She was the best sister ever. This book is dedicated to her.

Introduction

The question I seek to answer in this book through various theories, strategies, and queer subject positions is, "How are queer women of color represented in contemporary literary fiction and graphic narratives?" I first approached this query from an overly optimistic belief that because women of color had in many ways established a strong presence in the field of literary fiction, then it stood to reason that bookstores, libraries, newspapers, and even oral histories would offer up a wealth of representations of us in graphic narratives. I was already deeply immersed in the literature of the Harlem Renaissance; the "Womanist" literature about which Alice Walker wrote with such eloquence and passion; the Africana Womanism espoused by Clenora Hudson-Weems; and the Afrofuturism that aimed to unlock the minds, spirits, and earth-bound souls of a colonized people.

Like many people around the world, I had read comics in my youth, but as I grew older and moved on to more intellectual pursuits, I lost interest. It was not until I came across Alison Bechdel's graphic narrative *Fun Home* (2006) that I realized the potential of graphic narratives to open up ever more windows into the imaginative worlds I was already familiar with through literary fiction. My initial feelings were that the visual-textual language of graphic narratives came closest to matching the expansive cultural and creative frameworks I admired in the stories of Walker, Hudson-Weems, and other significant figures in black literary movements. In fact, as Neil Cohen pointed out in a 2005 essay, comics are "an artifact bound to its socio-cultural context."[1] Put another way, each person brings their own social and cultural experiences to how they read and interpret comics.

As I delved more deeply into graphic narratives, naively expecting a wide choice of titles and subjects that reflected my image and experiences back to me, the comparative lack of work by or about queer women of color both intrigued and troubled me. This in turn gave rise to more probing questions that I began to formulate about why, even in graphic narratives and comic books, our humanity, and even our visibility, seemed dependent upon

1

validation from a mostly Eurocentric point of view. I quickly realized that unless people of color were portrayed in graphic narratives and comics as hyper-sexualized African savages in grass skirts (as popularized in the controversial work of Robert Crumb and Hergé, the Belgian cartoonist), or as the "Yellow Menace" portrayed in political cartoons produced from the 1920s to the 1940s by Theodor Seuss Geisel (popularly known as Dr. Seuss), or as illiterate and bumbling sidekicks to handsome, heroic white men in spandex tights, we seemed to have never appeared inside of the spatiotemporal frame as our truly authentic selves. Moreover, queer women of color were so far out of the frame that the conspicuousness of our absence was telling.

Considered by many of his contemporaries as the pre-eminent authority in the field of sequential arts, Will Eisner was one of many cartoonists whose racist tropes were part and parcel of his early work. One character featured in Eisner's *The Spirit* comic strips was Ebony White, a man drawn with exaggerated racial features who spoke with an over-the-top "black" dialect. And while Marvel Comics featured the character Whitewash Jones, yet another sidekick to a superhero in spandex tights, DC Comics trotted out Steamboat, the servant to Captain Marvel. Both were drawn as caricatures of blackness: thick lips, bulging eyes, shuffling gait and garbled speech. Although these characters featured quite prominently in the comic frame, it was primarily to advance the narrative of whiteness as the only legitimate symbol of virtue and patriotism.

Contemporary scholars and cultural critics have revisited the early work of comics' illustrators from the early twentieth century, some asserting that Robert Crumb and his contemporaries were simply expressing the sentiments of the times in which they lived, while others saw demeaning visual tropes being perpetuated from a privileged white-centric point of view.[2] Even the more contemporary—and some might suggest less stereotypical representations of people of color in political cartoons of today—have a whiff of racism about them. One need look no further than the cover of the July 2008 *New Yorker* magazine, depicting former president Barack Obama and first lady Michelle Obama as militant Muslim interlopers intent on turning America into a country where terror cells flourish under wrong-footed and potentially dangerous leadership. The editor of the *New Yorker* defended the cover as political satire but to the president and his wife, and to many other people of color, it was a visual reminder of our conditional belonging, no matter that Obama had just been elected to the most powerful position in America.[3]

More recently the *Herald Sun* in Melbourne came under fire for what many interpreted as another grotesquely racist illustration of a person of color. The image of Serena Williams having a tantrum as a result of penalties that saw her lose a chance at winning her 24th Grand Slam title to Naomi Osaka at the 2018 U.S. Open finals was revealing. She is drawn in the most offensive manner imaginable, with all of the physical characteristics commonly seen in racist drawings of people of color. The irony here is that the artist drew Naomi Osaka as a white woman with blond hair, perhaps to set forth an even starker visual contrast to Serena's raging black woman persona and Naomi's relatively calm one.[4] This visual interplay of the angry black woman and her self-composed rival simply underscores how deeply embedded racism is.

While the oversized, muscular body of Serena Williams is in the foreground and takes up much of the frame, Osaka, who is Japanese and Haitian but given blond hair, light skin, and a petite, non-threatening physical body, is located off to the side. She is at once the "model minority" as well as a representative of the false construct that whiteness equates to goodness. As Gary Younge rightly points out in his incisive commentary regarding this crude illustration, "cartoons work best when they push boundaries, challenge perceptions," and "create an image that text would struggle to conjure."[5] It is obvious in this case that Younge is speaking to the better nature of man rather than the grim place that Mark Knight's illustration takes us to, yet the impulse of Knight to (mis)direct our gaze in this way demonstrates how stereotypes of women of color persist in the popular imagination.

There have been far too many examples of how prominence in the spatiotemporal frame does not necessarily equate to visibility or equality for people of color, primarily because racial stereotypes have been so normalized and ingrained in the collective psyche. And while there has recently been what could be seen as a black renaissance in film and comics (the well received *Black Panther* comics and subsequent film, for instance), queer women of color are still often nothing more than props in the over-representational world of whiteness or even black masculinity.

Having come away disappointed in what I had hoped would be a surfeit of queer women of color graphic narratives on offer, I realized that in order to put forth a convincing argument regarding the complexities of what it means to be a queer woman of color who is—by circumstance, law, religion or custom—rendered perennially invisible, I needed to turn a negative into a positive by using the hybrid structure of graphic narratives, together with the interstices and Third Spaces in literary fiction, to challenge the primacy of the Eurocentric, heteronormative gaze. As Sherene Razack puts it, "If we pay attention to the interpretive structures we use both to tell stories and to hear them, we quickly find ourselves having to thread our way through a number of relations at once."[6] Razack was referring to activism in education and how the line between upholding the rights of the disenfranchised, and unintentionally slipping into the trap of oppressing those very same groups, can sometimes get blurred.[7] Nevertheless her argument is fundamental to my own, in that how queer women of color lay out our stories through existing political and social structures, and how we tie these stories into the structures we learn to create for ourselves, is essential to positioning us in more generative spaces.

Although queer women of color have established a strong presence through online comics and zines, and these cultural productions reach untold numbers of queer girls and women of color who might otherwise eschew popular mainstream works that do not fully capture the reality of our lived experience, this still locates us at the margins of popular culture that continues to privilege a white-centric norm. But there are always exceptions to any rule, most notably in the graphic narratives created by Mariko and Jillian Tamaki, Elisha Lim, Ariel Schrag, Melanie Gillman, Keshni Kashyap, and Amruta Patil. But these representative works are still too few and the graphic narrative market continues to be dominated by heterosexuals from various ethnic and cultural backgrounds, by white lesbians whose stories fit more recognizably into mainstream narratives about belonging (even if their belonging is in terms of the advantages afforded to them by the color of their skin), and by men of color (straight or otherwise) who are creating work that is representative of their experiences.

Not quite certain how to approach the problem of an abundance of contemporary literary fiction written and produced by women of color on the one hand, and a conspicuous absence of queer women of color representation in graphic narratives on the other, I decided to create a bridging dialogue between graphic narratives and literary fiction that would bring into sharper critical focus the reality of the visually dispossessed. I wanted this dialogue to be predicated upon what hegemony has historically perceived as "lack" when casting its Eurocentric gaze out into the world. By filling in this discursive lacuna with the richness of queer temporalities that come to the fore through misdirection, literary fiction and the multimodal structure of graphic narratives, my contribution to articulating an expanded approach to queer women of color representation considers two central ideas.

The first idea looks at the twin categories of heteropatriarchy and religion from a place of empowerment rather than from a strictly deficit model. Operating from a place of creative strength that capitalized on the very interstices and gaps where intersecting oppressions have historically conspired to keep the masses in a constant narcotized state allowed me to drill down into the "physical" structure of heteropatriarchy by visualizing a system of what I refer to in my analysis of Ann-Marie MacDonald's book as "phallocentric rings." This in turn opened up a different critical pathway to interpreting how interlocking oppressions encircle and bind women and how using misdirection (the second central idea in this book) to break free of these phallocentric entrapments might enable us to reimagine ourselves as agents in our own creative spaces.

I then considered the broader issue of queer women of color representation and decided that a careful selection of both literary fiction and graphic narratives would allow for different angles to how we look at and process information. The idea was to gain a fuller understanding of the shifting contexts in which queer women of color representation has been subsumed into literary and cultural critiques that have historically made little or no allowance for difference. In this way, each text in this book approaches representation differently, although to varying degrees trauma, in all its many forms, is the unifying theme throughout.

The texts in this book range in scope from historical fiction and graphic narratives to gender-bending stories that challenge and disrupt entrenched hetero and homonormative paradigms. They cover overlapping and intersecting moments in history where multi-issue politics started to take on greater significance in feminist discourse. Yet what joins these texts together is an implicit assertion that patriarchy can be challenged and destabilized through radically queer(ed) epistemological and performative frameworks. Thus, by utilizing the hybrid elements of graphic narratives to deepen critical engagements with literary fiction, this book goes some way in setting out a self-representational strategy that is most provocatively expressed through misdirection and its complex signifying semiotics. It argues for radical disruptions to hegemonic paradigms that situate "difference" and "normativity" in terminal opposition to each other, and in an effort to redress disparities in representational narratives that privilege the white heteromormative gaze, this book also engages with multiple and intersecting theories and reading strategies to illuminate that which hides in the shadows. Ultimately, my attempt in this book is to understand how queer women of color who have been historically underrepresented in graphic narratives and comics can take up pen and ink to insert our images and our stories more prominently (and authentically) into the spatiotemporal frame.

By inserting ourselves into spaces and frames where we are not recognized, valued, or validated, the work here is to use these very same spaces to renounce the idea of an unassailable truth constructed around a white-centric norm. If we use the unseen spaces that are located in between the dominant spaces policed by those who wish to keep us marginalized, the ambiguity this then creates allows for a more sustained challenge to the status quo. It is indeed through the signifying structure of comics, working in tandem with the signifying semiotics of misdirection, that the invisible and oppressed have the potential to change the dominant constructions of "difference."

Although each work in this book—from Ann-Marie MacDonald's exploration of racism, gender, religion, class and sexual orientation in the late nineteenth to early twentieth centuries to Jaime Cortez's "graphically" rendered account of transgender activist Adela Vázquez's journey from Cuba to Florida during the 1980 Mariel Boatlift—addresses different historical periods, all turn on the idea of representation and erasure and how these paradoxical positions become inscribed upon the queer(ed) subaltern body. Crucially, this book recognizes the potential of comics/graphic narratives as a transformative medium through which misdirection can be enacted and used to contest the "Othering" of queer women of color. Moreover, in writing this book and formulating ideas about misdirection and what I wanted the term to convey, it occurred to me that there needed to be a unifying *structure* that allowed two different mediums (comics and literary fiction) to communicate across discursive boundaries.

To facilitate this work, conventional literary frameworks and the hybridity of graphic narratives have been repurposed to develop the idea of misdirection not only as semiotics, but also as a methodology. In this way, the illegitimacy of interlocking systems of oppression that have historically conveyed an almost casual disavowal of responsibility for the subjugation of women of color is brought into sharper relief. Furthermore, through a peeling back of the multiple layers of oppression that have ensnared the queer subaltern in a tangle of heterosexual and homonormative imperatives, this book offers new ways of deconstructing the codes that privilege one form of representation over another.[8]

Underpinned by theories arising from the dialectics of often unresolvable, yet passionately held beliefs in the right of women to shape our own realities, all seven texts in this book can be read as indictments on the historical sublation of the queer female body. Taking both an intertextual and interdisciplinary approach, this book advocates for interdiscursive platforms that advance critical thinking beyond the boundaries of genre, space, form, and even time. By drawing on graphic narratives to open up pathways into a deeper understanding of representation and its increasingly important significance in bringing difficult subjects to the fore, this book is uniquely positioned to place into the hands of the dispossessed, the tools with which oppressive and exclusionary practices can be challenged.

Ruth Ronen captures this sometimes awkward balancing act in her own work on literary theory when she writes about "possible worlds" and "fictional worlds," which in effect is what I attempt to do here. She writes: "Since possible and fictional worlds interact both in the philosophical discipline and in the domain of literary theory, my conceptual exposition switches constantly between discourses of both."[9] I admit that there are, in my own weaving together of literary fiction and graphic narratives, conceptual leaps that are perhaps stretched a bit too far beyond the boundaries of conventional literary practices. But how else are we to navigate the inhospitable roads back to our queer black selves, if not through charting our own course? And in charting new roads, this book picks up on the excavation work started by many who have gone before and those who are just arriving.

The authors and artists whose work I engage with in this book identify as Canadian, American, Cuban, Turkish, and Japanese. Each in their own way weaves powerful stories that shine a light on queer women of color representation and the historical injunctions that work to diminish or completely erase our voices. Three of the seven texts fall into the category of graphic narratives while the others come under the heading of literary fiction. The focus on such a wide range of texts can be explained very simply by personal preference (I admire the work of each author) and practical considerations (there is still an underrepresentation of graphic narrative memoirs being written by queer women of color, which is not the case with mostly North American literary fiction, which features more prominently in this book). Considering this disparity, the aim of this book is to create a literal and metaphorical joining together of these texts as a way of offering multiple entry points through which readers can engage with the difficult themes of sexual violence, emotional trauma, and disenfranchisement. Specifically, this book considers how the hybrid structure that is the stock in trade of graphic narratives/comics, combined with the semiotics of misdirection, can open up possibilities for more critical readings of literary fiction and by extension a more nuanced and generative approach to queer women of color representation.

Classic approaches to writing and interpreting literature are often framed through deconstructionist, formalist, gender, queer, feminist or psychological criticism, or a combination of one or more of these approaches. This book puts forth the idea of misdirection as both a reading strategy and a methodology that builds on multiple theoretical and creative approaches. Misdirection also works as a multimodal strategy that enriches the voices and actions of the characters in the texts critiqued here, as well as the writers whose personal experiences often drive the plot.

Misdirection offers a way for writers and readers to unravel questions of agency and to "take up the challenges of these queer times by claiming intellectual kin where we find them."[10] This is important because as I use it in this book, misdirection "speaks to, with, and through discourses appropriate to the conversation rather than those merely expected by convention, while reaching back to foundational works and projecting our imaginations forward."[11] In other words, misdirection is a language, a performance, a strategy and a methodology that compels us to think differently about representation. It is a signifying strategy that operates through the interstitial (or "gutter") spaces in both graphic narratives and literary fiction to support what Allen advocates for as more "insurgent rereadings" of familiar texts.[12] Moreover, because of similar structural elements in graphic narratives and literary fiction that facilitate misdirection's intervention where race, gender, and sexual orientation intersect, queer women of color have alternative ways of speaking through structural and methodological frameworks that ultimately promote the reclamation and reconfiguring of our own space.

I attend to the idea of misdirection more fully later on in this book, but note here that the basic premise is that as a methodology, and in developing my own definition of the term, misdirection is a signifying strategy defined by the contexts through which it seeks to effect perceptual shifts. Its potential application as a tool with which multiple creative readings of queer women of color representation can be introduced is central to this book. By using the hybrid language of graphic narratives side by side with the reading of literary fiction, misdirection intervenes in discursive debates to advocate for more fluid and creative engagements. Thus, this book is interdisciplinary in that it does not fit neatly into just one theory or model or methodology. Moreover, where the structure of graphic narratives and literary fiction serve as complementary elements that work to disrupt the intersecting oppressions experienced by queer women of color across multiple contexts, misdirection functions as a signifying strategy that allows for multivalent creative and methodological approaches.

Before moving on I want to briefly explain the meaning of the term "gutter" and how it is used throughout this book. It is a common term that is shared in both comics and literary fiction. In comics it is usually the white space that separates panels, whereas in the actual production of books of any kind, it refers to the margin between the typed page and the binding. Yet the gutter space in comics does not necessarily denote absence or blankness, even though it is still sometimes thought of in this way because it is usually signaled by white space. Jason Fabok and Richard Ortiz, among others, have used black (and even gold and blue) gutters in their comics to great effect.[13]

Michael Nicoll Yahgulanaas's interpretation of the gutter also represents more than white space that is statically rendered and dependent upon the reader's active engagement and imagination to infuse it with meaning. As Richard Harrison notes, Yahgulanaas creates work in the tradition of Haida Manga, a combination of the traditional Haida form that is "painted or carved into wooden masks, stand-alone sculptures and reliefs, with the dynamics of the manga that Yahgulanaas first saw when he was a guide for Japanese tourists visiting Haida Gwaii."[14] His use of thick black, red, and blue bands interspersed throughout irregularly drawn panels speak to what Harrison describes as a "*presence* [italics mine] that surrounds the panel, shaping it, confining it, drawing it out or narrowing it down."[15] Thus where a traditional work of literary fiction uses commas, periods, colons and semi-colons to signal various pauses and stops, the gutters in comics—be they the conventional white spaces that separate panels, or Yahgulanaas's "framelines" that are interspersed throughout the story itself—are the spatiotemporal punctuation marks that pace, guide, and shape the graphic narrative.

Christopher Green notes that Yahguanaas's take on turning oral history into a "fluid, nonlinear reading experience" by side-stepping "comic-book conventions," meaning there are no "gutters, square borders, or empty spaces," and his work sets up a "fluid push and pull between the meandering framelines and the spaces they circumscribe."[16] Yahgulanaas does not make the gutter a primary structural element or focus in his work, likely seeing the separation of panels as an artificial boundary that interrupts the fluidity of a good story. His work demonstrates that how stories unfold—be they visual or text-bound—is crucial to understanding the complex, layered and intersecting identities that cannot be fitted into just one cultural, political, or social framework. He offers inventive ways of using the gutter to mine the gutter, showing us how to reclaim a cultural relevance and visibility that has long been suppressed through historical misrepresentations.

The stories of queer women of color cannot be told from one place, or through one voice, or via one method. This is largely the reason why this book does not rely just on the language of comics to the exclusion of literary fiction, or literary fiction to the exclusion of comics, to explore and illuminate the idea of representation. Indeed, the gaps, gutters, and interstitial spaces in graphic narratives offer crucial insights into that which influences and shapes how we see ourselves and how we come to be seen by others. As Bacchetta, El-Tayeb, and Haritaworn have noted, "much work remains to be done to account for the racialized absent presences that have haunted writings on queer space from the beginning."[17] Here space relates to geographical space, specifically cityscapes where queer people of color represent a disruption to the "dominant temporality of the nation."[18] Yet whether these spaces are literal, imagined, or the interstitial spaces/gaps/gutters in graphic narratives, they are ultimately discursive spaces where dominant homo- and heteronormative realities can be radically contested and remapped. One need only look to Joe Sacco's work or the subversive political comics of Amir Soltani and Khalil, or the wonderful anthology *Drawing the Line: Indian Women Fight Back* (2015), created in reaction to the gang rape of a medical student in New Delhi in December 2012, to understand that even "racialized absent presences" can speak through a medium that cannot be fully controlled by social customs, political pressure, marginalization, or censorship.

Before proceeding I would like to briefly explain my usage of a few terms in comics studies that appear throughout this book and may cause confusion for the reader. Wherever possible I use "sequential art" as a term that speaks more precisely to my interest in the *structure* of comics and how this structure can be used to facilitate a signifying movement across multiple platforms. The terms "autographics" and "graphic narratives" also feature in this book, although my focus on the structure of comics refers specifically to the "gaps," "gutters," speech balloons, panels, frames, and captions that progress a story. These structural elements also allow for more nuanced readings and interpretations of racial, cultural, sexual, religious, and political differences. I use the term "graphic narrative" to describe book-length comics told as autobiographical or nonfiction accounts, although not all book-length graphic narratives are autobiographical. There are also occasions when I use all of these terms interchangeably, although I have attempted to keep this to a minimum. Nevertheless, to offer a bit more explanation of these terms it may be useful for readers to bear in mind Will Eisner's definition of sequential art. Eisner used the term to describe an "art and literary form that deals with the arrangement of pictures or images and words to narrate a story or dramatize an idea."[19] He further noted that

> in its most economical state, comics employ a series of repetitive images and recognizable symbols. When these are used again and again to convey similar ideas, they become a language—a literary form, if you will. And it is this disciplined application that creates the "grammar" of Sequential Art.[20]

It may also be useful to consider Scott McCloud's extension of Eisner's definition, whereby he proposed that sequential art is comprised of "juxtaposed pictorial and other images in deliberate sequence, intended to convey information and/or to produce an aesthetic response in the viewer."[21] Graphic narratives, on the other hand, are "book-length comics that are meant to be read as one story,"[22] although in many ways it functions as a catch-all term for collections of stories in genres such as mystery, superhero, or supernatural, that are meant to be read apart from their corresponding ongoing comic book storyline; heart-rending works such as Art Spiegelman's *Maus*; and nonfiction pieces such as Joe Sacco's journalistic work, *Palestine*.[23]

Therefore, this book explores book-length nonfiction stories produced in the graphic narrative form to make an argument for the potential of visual language and literary fiction to support alternative methods for "reading" queer women of color subjectivities in more affirmative ways. In so doing, this book also makes a contribution to scholarly work in queer, feminist, postcolonial, and gender studies. For example, it stands alongside such thought-provoking work as Qiana Whitted's "'And the Negro thinks in hieroglyphics': Comics, Visual Metonymy, and the Spectacle of Blackness."

Whitted's work aligns particularly well with many of the arguments I make in relation to how comics "destabilize the meanings that blackness has traditionally signified in the comics form and develop new sequential frames of reference between the self and the racial other."[24] Whitted follows this by noting John Reider's consideration of elements of the colonial gaze that "'distributes knowledge and power to the subject who looks, while denying or minimizing access to power for its object, the one looked at.'"[25] What Whitted goes on to explain, as I do in this book, is that comics also have the ability to "restore the agency of a black speaking, seeing subject."[26] Nevertheless, I take the idea of seeing and being seen in comics and literary fiction one step further by exploring how the intersecting, and not wholly unrelated, ideas of semiotics and signifying in both comics and literary fiction are brought to life through misdirection. What I mean by a signifying language is that as a vernacular commonly associated with African American culture (although not exclusively) in its most basic form, and as I use it in this book, it can be seen as a close kin to misdirection. Both do the work of shifting perceptions of how one is seen and/or heard by others.

Perhaps the most formalized or "high brow" version of signifying can be seen in debate clubs where verbal dexterity and extensive knowledge of a particular subject positions a winning team or an individual as the signifier, and the loser as the signified. Perhaps a more relatable example of signifying being used to challenge and disrupt the status quo was in the film *The Great Debaters*, the true story about Melvin B. Tolson, a professor at a historically black college in East Texas who inspired his students to enter into a debate competition against white students from Harvard.

Set in the 1930s when Jim Crow laws were still on the books, the film was a dramatization of how largely disenfranchised black students from a Texas university were able to win a difficult competition against better funded, better educated, and purportedly better prepared white students. The black college students mastered the art of formal debate by out-signifying the white students. Turning the semiotics of difference on its head through a masterful signifying performance, the black students symbolically "read" the white students and by doing so prevailed. Gates expertly illustrates the tension between these black and white signifying practices when he explains that signifying is not just a rhetorical device specific to black culture, but rather a multilayered and coded form of instruction that black parents teach their children from an early age. He makes reference to "linguistic masking," which he essentially describes as the life lessons/survival strategies that black parents teach their children from an early age.[27] In a very real sense, signifying is a multilayered and coded form of discourse that instructs black children in how to "manipulate language" when navigating the boundaries between white and black worlds.[28]

Signifying, in the terms just discussed, align with what Qiana Whitted has described as the "creative strength and ingenuity of black vernacular culture" that has "depended upon the proposition that words could be more valuable when they acted like pictures."[29] Claudia Mitchell-Kernan indirectly sets out a path for pushing this notion even further when she writes about the "total universe of discourse," where those being signified upon (for lack of a more nuanced phrasing on my part) are "constrained to attend to all potential meaning-carrying symbolic systems in speech events."[30] She goes on to note—and this is where misdirection, semiotics, and the structural relationship between comics and literary fiction come back into play— that the "context embeddedness of meaning is attested to by both our reliance on the given context and, most important, by our inclination to construct additional context from our background knowledge of the world."[31] Mitchell-Kernan's observations about context and what we do with it in turn takes us closer to Whitted's view that when pictures, signs, or the hieroglyphics that Whitted discusses act like words; when they stand in for or represent something other than a questionable truth promulgated through the lens of a white-centric norm, then comics can function as a portal through which more authentic signifying representations can be expressed.

Following on from the aforementioned observations, this book is appropriately positioned alongside such works as Sheena C. Howard's and Ronald L. Jackson's *Black Comics: Politics of Race and Representation* (2013); Monica Chiu's *Drawing New Color Lines: Transnational Asian American Graphic Narratives* (2014); Joseph J. Darowski's *X-Men and the Mutant Metaphor: Race and Gender in the Comics Books* (2014); Frances Gateward and John Jennings's

The Blacker the Ink: Constructions of Black Identity in Comics and Sequential Art (2015); and Deborah Elizabeth Whaley's *Black Women in Sequence: Re-Inking Comics, Graphic Novels, and Anime* (2016). All of these works point to recent critical developments in comics scholarship.

Gateward and Jennings use the metaphor of ink as representative of black subjectivity, arguing that "the ink used in comics is not only physically and formally perceived to be the neutral of black; it is also the reification of 'Blackness' in the modern sense."[32] The connection between social perceptions of the black body and art forms that mirror these perceptions on both an aesthetic and subversive level speak to the complex layers of "Otherism" through which the black body continues to be read.

Monica Chiu borrows the title of her book from Frederick Douglass's "The Color Line" (1881) to demonstrate how even in our more contemporary times we "grapple with issues of pluralized color lines."[33] By acknowledging the commonalities that people of color from different geographical, historical, and cultural backgrounds share, Chiu makes the connection between racism reflected in comics and the real life issues we are faced with. And finally, Deborah E. Whaley's observations on the dearth of black women in the field of comics reflect my own frustrations in locating work that affirmatively describes the multiple and intersecting layers of queer women of color subjectivity.

Though all of these works speak eloquently to the gains made by women of color in literature, politics and the arts, they also underscore the difficulties that remain in bringing to the fore the authentic voices and stories of the queerly dispossessed. The theories and themes that I draw upon throughout this book support the development of misdirection as a type of defamiliarization that facilitates the stripping away of the comforting "veil of familiarity" that often separates society from its most difficult truths.[34] I explore how the multiple discursive pathways that misdirection opens up for rigorous interrogation might support a "break with" the "hegemonic modes of seeing, thinking, and being that block our capacity to see ourselves oppositionally" or that allow us to "imagine, describe, and reinvent ourselves in ways that are liberatory."[35] In other words, this book considers the "representational limitations of the text-based narrative form"[36] to argue for more affirmative and creative readings of queer women of color representation and embodiment through graphic narratives. I show that the theoretical framework upon which the arguments in this book turn support critical interventions at the site of the very foreclosures that prohibit an emergence of the "Other" as desirable or even visible.[37]

Unmasking the Literary Canon: In Search of Our Queer(y)ing Sisters

The following brief literature review examines the contribution that writers of color in the early to late twentieth century made to the development of a queer black canon and what this has come to mean in contemporary terms for queer women of color representation. Turning, as Thelma J. Shinn rightly argues, to "Other American novelists for the other parts of our common story" is crucial to establishing a meaningful context for who we are.[38] Shinn asserts that women novelists who celebrate "the meronymic perspective that sees the shadow in its double, that knows every boundary to be a threshold," practice an

> art of style and structure that begins to heal the fragmented tradition of the novel and to encompass its seemingly endless labels in a common, maturing form that yet offers seemingly endless variations.[39]

Shinn's analysis of the contemporary novel underscores the other aim of this review, which is to briefly highlight work that sets the stage for a broader interrogation of race, gender, and sexuality. Furthermore, by reviewing literature that takes as its double the thresholds and boundaries of misdirection as performance, the "seemingly endless variations" that Shinn points to become new methodological tools developed in this book.

This review sets out three interconnected questions that form the narrative arc of this book. The first asks in what ways we "read" the queer woman of color body across multiple and changing contexts. The second considers what benefit is derived from using the structural elements of sequential art and the autobiographical storyline in graphic narratives to critique how queer women of color are represented in contemporary literary fiction. And the third question considers the part that misdirection plays in tying together these questions throughout the book, particularly in facilitating a deeper analysis of the issues raised in the seven texts that are critiqued.

But narrowing a review of the literature to creative works that touch on or incorporate themes and methodologies specific to the study of queer women of color representation sets out an immediate, although not necessarily insurmountable, problem. Is there a single methodology sufficient in scope to address not only a multiplicity of intersecting identities, but to also capture the nuances of queer black female lives that have been shaped by a history of physical and psychological enslavement? To answer this question I turn briefly to Sheena C. Howard's *Black Queer Identity Matrix: Towards an Integrated Queer of Color Framework* (2014), which argues for an integrated framework from which more in-depth analyses of queer black lives can be explored. And while Howard's work touches on the ability of images to "provide powerful and objective insights into the complexities of one's life," in what she terms "photo feedback analysis," she is speaking mainly of photographs rather than sequential art.[40]

Howard's matrix is underpinned by Afrocentricity, standpoint theory, and the matrix of domination. These support her intersectional approach to black queer female identity.[41] My argument for a methodology that seeks to answer similar questions as those posited by Howard turns more decisively on images (sequential art), misdirection (as a signifying strategy), and the frameworks through which queer women of color can express different, but no less important, realities. Nevertheless, I agree with Howard when she writes:

> We are in desperate need of paradigmatic inquiry around the intersections of gender, sexual orientation, and race-ethnicity. Current literature around queer studies does not adequately acknowledge the complexities of racial-ethnic identity coupled with gender in negotiating identity.[42]

Susy Zepeda also argues for a more generative methodology that intervenes in, and works to alter, the restrictive landscape through which queer women of color identities are represented. In "Mapping Queer of Color Methodology," Zepeda—not unlike Howard and myself—explores the need for a queer methodology that, in citing the work of Mujeres y Cultura Subterránea, a collective of filmmakers from Mexico City, "actively disrupt[s] mainstream and state representations that assert a crafted narrative of the authentic truth."[43] Thus this review begins in a modest way to chart the circuitous path that writers and artists of color have taken in the quest for visibility and legitimacy.

Challenging the Privileged Narrative

Michael Bennett and Vanessa D. Dickerson's aptly named book *Recovering the Black Female Body: Self-Representations by African American Women* (2001) encapsulates the fundamental tensions in narratives that persistently write the black female body as unworthy or hyper-sexualized and "seldom" perceive it "as the body of the 'damsel in distress.'"[44] Thus, how we read the queer woman of color body across multiple and changing contexts seems to turn on what her body is not. It is not on a level footing with the white female body, especially when we consider that whereas white women can be largely confident that their rights (and bodies) will be rescued or protected by the state, the inverse is true of black female bodies in that "Western culture" does not deign these bodies to be "rescuable" (or, I might add, *representable*).[45]

Attempting to address the pathologizing assemblage of stereotypes that "fix" the black female body as always and forever "Othered," Bennett and Dickerson underscore the problem of racial and gender inequities that persist to this day. It is in this way that this book advocates for an extension of discursive platforms that link representation to misdirection as a signifying method of reinvention and intervention. In fact, the benefit derived from reimagining and even re-reading the queer woman of color body through the structural elements of sequential art moves us on to the third question in this review: exactly what part does misdirection play in tying together seemingly unconnected narratives and facilitating a deeper analysis of the issues they raise?

The work involved in building a multiplicity of counter-narratives that rescue black bodies from historical and cultural irrelevance is a task predicated on understanding how the of color experience has been shaped. The assertion in this book, which at once requires a recognition of the past in order to create new epistemological frameworks in contemporary times, requires the use of language that is comprised of many voices and multiple perspectives. This polyphonic heteroglossia described by Mikhail M. Bakhtin as the "social life of discourse" is, in my view, crucial to those whose very lives often depend upon the mastery of both visual and linguistic misdirection.[46]

Bakhtin argued that when living discourse is overlooked in favor of "individual and tendentious overtones of style" it is effectively "cut off from the [...] social modes in which discourse lives."[47] Subsequently, discourse is rendered socially ineffective, although stylistically it may be advantageous to those whose aim is to appropriate and control the production of language and, by extension, knowledge. Bakhtin's contribution toward developing a methodology to reading and critiquing the novel, as well as to discourse that is publicly performed, has been influential in contemporary interpretations of prose writing. Indeed, this line of analysis allows here for a much broader application and interpretation of the texts this book examines. Thus my aim in this review is to illustrate how specific periods in the development of North American literature, as well as in the work of the writers of color whose roots are in Cuba, Turkey, and Japan, contribute to a fuller understanding of misdirection as counter-performance to white Eurocentric constructions.

Multiple and Changing Contexts

Through the acts of passing, masking, signifying, lifting the veil, or enacting a queer liminality, this review synthesizes creative and scholarly works from the past to the present in order to highlight the unique issues queer women of color continue to face. This in turn informs methodological frameworks that support alternative interpretations of queer women of color representation in contemporary contexts. This review as well as the texts covered in this book "speak through and about the mythologies of blackness that we inherit as a culture that bears the historical mark of slavery and the privileging of whiteness in American society."[48] It also exemplifies the need for reading strategies that are fluid, hybrid, and multi-modal. To the greatest extent possible this review places into context how women of color who write about race, gender, and sexual orientation in the past have contributed to discussions regarding the challenges of expressing multiple identities in the present moment. In this regard I turn briefly to the work of Nella Larsen, whose skill as a writer during the Harlem Renaissance has come to exemplify the

> trope of passing to examine how her female protagonists depend[ed] upon performances of identity to constitute their subjectivity and to resist representation as objects to be looked at.[49]

Quicksand (1928) and *Passing* (1929) function as textual representations of race, class, sexual transgression and identity in an American context. Taking on multiple and complex meanings, Larsen's work challenged cultural norms in ways that cast an uncomfortable light on America's conflicted relationship with race and sexual expression. As spectators whose representations of themselves were reflected back in the most distorted and stereotypical of ways, Larsen's characters were at once seduced and repelled by the "white myths of American life."[50] Although women writers of the Harlem Renaissance and beyond developed work that "offered" opportunities "for self-expression, visibility and creation of new images of themselves and their futures,"[51] their secondary status as black women often placed them several rungs below even the least heralded black male author. The exceptions were writers such as Zora Neale Hurston, Gwendolyn B. Bennett, Georgia Douglas Johnson, Helene Johnson, playwright May Miller and Anne Spencer, author of the poem "White Things."[52]

Larsen, as well as poet and novelist Jessie Redmon Fauset, wrote powerful stories from a perspective that called into question the instability of racial constructs and the very myths typified by an all-pervasive white arrogance.[53] The crucial difference between the two novelists is that where Larsen

wrote about racial and sexual "passing," Faucet's *Plum Bun* (1929) looked primarily at the singular (though no less complex) issue of race relations.
Dorothy West was also recognized for her observations on race relations in
America, although *The Wedding* (1995) was not written until three years
before her death at the age of ninety-one.[54] Other writers producing allegorical prose that interrogated race as a social construction were predominantly
men whose racially ambiguous protagonists were often women. The female
protagonist in William Dean Howells' *An Imperative Duty* (1891) is mixed
race but passes for white. Mimi Daquin, the female protagonist in Walter
White's 1926 novel *Flight*, also passes for white. And tackling race from the
scientific angle, George S. Schuyler's *Black No More* (1931) was an Afrofutur-
istic novel set in a sanatorium where technology was used to turn black people
into whites.[55]

These influential and visionary works gesture toward the cruel irony of
a system too long in the business of constructing racial categories based on
so-called "scientific" proof of racial origins that were often no more rigorous
than visual observations of a person's mannerisms, speech or physical attributes. As Claire's husband proclaims in Larsen's novel, "'I draw the line at that.
No niggers in my family. Never have been and never will be,'" the irony being
that by virtue of his marriage to her, his wife was clearly successful at passing
for white.[56] Research shows that cultural critiques of race, gender, and sexual
orientation have progressed from what Harrison-Kahan argues as "ambivalent
performances" that "destabilize the gaze," although "performers" such as
Larsen's characters "still remain objects to be looked at, even if they are self-
creating objects."[57] Yet controlling the gaze through misdirecting performances is quite different from being objectified.

The performances that Larsen masterfully set up for readers were not
so much about ambivalence as Harrison-Kahan suggests, as they were powerful counter-narratives in response to the inherently destructive constructions of "Otherness." Indeed, this book expressly focuses a critical lens on
how identity that continues to be performed under the relentless gaze of
whiteness in many ways draws upon the misdirection and sleight of hand
used to such great effect in nineteenth- and early twentieth-century writings
by women of color. On a conceptual level Larsen's novel is not just a story
about oppression and doing whatever it takes to survive in hostile environments. Its approach also serves as a provocative literary technique that disrupts how race, sexual orientation and gender are interwoven in hegemony's
morass of Eurocentric imperatives.

The foregoing section of this review has taken as its impetus Larsen's
satirical look at "white obsessions with 'racial integrity'" and serves as one

of several entry points to the dialogic and methodological bridge this book seeks to create.[58] Although Larsen died seventeen years before the publication of *The Dialogic Imagination* (1981), she clearly understood that dialogue is most often effective in concert with the fullness of the writer's imagination and in-the-world experiences. Her ability to infuse her writing with the very hybridity that this book applies throughout speaks to the importance of bridging the links between past and present.

The Souls of Queer Folks

The long period of so-called "protest writing" showcased the work of some of the finest black scholars, prose and poetry writers in American history. From slave narratives, to the insurrectionary antebellum poetry of Frances Ellen Watkins Harper and Paul Laurence Dunbar, through to the Harlem Renaissance, the Black Arts Movement and beyond, writers of color used the power of words and performance to expose the hypocrisy of life in America.[59] One of the most critically acclaimed works published in 1903 was W.E.B. DuBois' *The Souls of Black Folk*. Du Bois' incisive meditation on the burden of a double consciousness borne by black Americans eventually led to a "critical-emancipationist analytic program" better known as "critical race theory,"[60] which holds that the "problem of the color line," which DuBois saw as a twentieth-century problem, was a failure of social theory to develop

> an explicit and sustained analysis of racial injustice, a pernicious problem that, then and as now, is deeply entrenched in the very foundations—the everyday thought processes, practices, and institutions—of U.S. society.[61]

Writing about race and politics in different historical periods and contexts, yet with the common purpose of illuminating the plight of dark-skinned races, both DuBois and Fanon spoke of a double consciousness that divided a person's sense of self from that reflected back to them through the "misrepresentations of the outside world."[62] Critical race and postcolonial scholars building on the work of W.E.B. DuBois, Franz Fanon and others developed new critical responses to the intractable social problems experienced by historically marginalized groups. The central focus of critical race theory is in its intonation of critical forms of expression that turn on the voices and experiences of people of color. Crucially, it "directs attention to the ways in which structural arrangements inhibit and disadvantage some more than others in our society."[63] While there is little doubt that DuBois's early work compelled more nuanced and broader interpretations of race relations in America, what took far longer to achieve was the development of critical theories that adequately tended to the souls, and increasingly to the complex subjectivities, of queer women of color. Yet critical race theory can build even further on developing ways in which institutional practices that oppress certain individuals and groups can be dismantled or at the least disrupted.

If we take the same structural arrangements that have historically disadvantaged certain individuals and groups to instead think about misdirection as a contesting structural arrangement operating both from within and outside of the center, we can see its usefulness as a critical perspective that helps marginalized groups mount more nuanced challenges to oppressive systems. If we accept that the novels and poems published by early twentieth-century writers of color worked to contest the essentializing white gaze, we can also understand the way they informed how contemporary writers (such as Ann-Marie MacDonald and others whose works I critique) have been able to expand upon the idea of "multiple significations" and also "text[s] that resist containment."[64] To varying degrees these early works crossed their own stylistic and dialogic borders, coming together in contemporary times as imbricating formations of queer self-representational counter-stories. A central feature of critical race theory, counter-stories have

> produced a community of discourse with a plethora of metaphors (e.g., the border), typologies (e.g., Black gay/butch-trans, double minorities), concepts (e.g., race-d, intersectionality, structural determinism), and methods (e.g., perspectivalism), all of which provide us with a better understanding of the multi-dimensionality of racism in America that heretofore had not been possible.[65]

The literature reviewed here underscores the importance of the numerous counter-stories that Larsen and others have so masterfully coaxed from the seams and liminal spaces of history. It advocates for a more fluid discourse that has the potential to reinvent itself and stand unmolested by fear or by failure of the imagination. In reframing how the queer subaltern body continues to be read and inscribed, visual-textual counter-narratives introduce to the reader what Susan Sontag described as the "insuperable power" of images/photographs to "determine what we recall of events."[66] While Sontag was referring to the violence of war and of government resistance to televising images of flag-draped coffins being returned to American shores, comics and graphic narratives have also served as a form of cultural reportage that is not easily controlled. The comics journalism of Sarah Glidden, Joe Sacco, Josh Neufeld, and Sam Wallman are examples of this, although it must be said that comics have also been used quite effectively as government propaganda.

During World War II comics were used by the Writers' War Board (WWB) to stir up patriotic fervor.[67] Captain America, the Shield, and even

Wonder Woman were cast as crime fighting superhero patriots who encouraged readers to support the war effort by remaining vigilant and helping their government push back against foreign threats to our national borders.[68] Yet what we know is that even under the most repressive regimes, how we interpret or make sense of images on television or through comics cannot always be controlled through censorship. Indeed, underground comics of the mid-sixties radicalized the way comics were read, using raunchy and irreverent drawings to subvert (and misdirect) the dominant hegemonic gaze that sought to police every aspect of our lives.

The underground comics movement went some way in acting as a gateway into self-representation possessed of "an oppositional gaze that reverses the scenario of white voyeurism"[69] or power. In fact, Frantz Fanon's take on the power of an oppositional gaze to effect change is expressed as an obligation of the artist to speak truth to power. He notes that the first duty of the "colonized poet is to clearly define the people," insisting that unless we recognize our alienation, we will not be able to go forward. We must, he stated, "focus on that zone of hidden fluctuation where the people can be found."[70]

The "zone of hidden fluctuation" can certainly be interpreted to signify the gaps and interstitial spaces in Larsen's discourse on passing. Yet we can also locate these zones in the discourse on "double consciousness" in critical race theory, through LatCrit, queer-crit and critical race feminism. In its more contemporary form, passing can be reinterpreted through literary fiction and graphic narratives as misdirection, which is a more precise term that captures the complex performances enacted by queer women of color.

(Re)inscribing Queer Women of Color

This book begins with a brief chapter on how misdirection as an organizing principle in queer women of color representation functions across different literary genres and critical contexts. My approach to the use of misdirection is based on close readings, discourse analysis, intertextuality and, to a lesser extent, "deviant historiography."[71] The overarching theoretical grounding supporting my articulation here of misdirection as methodology turns on critical race feminism, gender, postcolonial and queer of color theory. I focus on how the representation of "Otherness" in each of the texts is in fact an example of how misdirection performs through multiple contexts and theoretical constructs to expose the hypocrisy of racial, political, sexual and gender inclusiveness. It is also of note that although MacDonald's novel is the only text in this book not authored by a queer person of color, my focus is not so much on the writers themselves as it is on the varied and complex notions of queer women of color representation they each address in their respective works.

As a critical approach that underscores and contests how systems of representation are constructed, misdirection not only offers alternative ways of knowing, it also opens up a way of reading that speaks truth to power. Yet misdirection cannot function in isolation from signification and semiotics, which is why these concepts appear together throughout this book. Misdirection is in fact dependent for its own voice upon the structures and contexts that it encounters, as will be seen in critiques of the themes from the individual texts that comprise this book. By drawing on multiple intersecting concepts, theories, art forms and cultures to put back together the pieces of our lives that have largely been excised from historical records, misdirection becomes the subject, the framework, and the methodology of this book. I offer a summary here of how misdirection is expressed and operationalized in (and through) different literary contexts.

Ann-Marie MacDonald's historical fiction turns on the idea of patriarchy and how it is comprised of "phallocentric rings," a term I have coined to explain not only how the oppression of women is bound up in interlocking rings of power, but also how misdirection deconstructs these interlocking systems to contest the false premises upon which they turn. In MacDonald's novel, misdirection is expressed through the voices of her characters who live during a historical period in which race, gender, and religion formed an unholy trinity that held powerful sway over women's lives. To varying degrees each character in the novel uses misdirection as either a strategy of domination or as a form of protest. The novel explores themes of forbidden desire between women, rape, incest, religion, culture, and race.

Bad Habits is Cristy C. Road's love story told through the lens of punk subculture. The stark imagery that she employs in her work compels the reader/observer to use various cognitive strategies to unpack themes that visually position race, gender, and sexuality as ideological contradictions. Adding to this, Road also explores the ideological clash between white and *of color* DIY punk subcultures. Furthermore, her bisexuality and cultural and ethnic representation as a Cuban-American speak to her personal struggle to hold firm to a Cuban heritage that is not reflected back to her through predominantly white male punk subcultures. Road creates a canvas of images and words that focus on male and female genitalia, DIY punk, drugs, and the wild excesses of youth. Representation is signified in her book through the double-voiced/double-sexed/transcultural reality of her punk avatar.

Examples of misdirection also abound in *Bad Habits*, most notably just

over halfway through the book where the reader is offered a visual representation of Road as part woman and part machine. This is perhaps an unintentional reference to Donna Haraway's influential book *Simians, Cyborgs,
and Women: The Reinvention of Nature* (1991), but it works well to highlight
queer representation that can be expressed quite powerfully through the
hybrid form of sequential art.

In considering the implications of representation shaped by dominant
narratives that have historically privileged the hegemonic center over the
margins, and how developing a framework of opposing and more affirmative
responses must begin with the re-appropriation of our minds and bodies,
Gloria Naylor's novel exemplifies how differences that are played out in
socially insular communities become a cautionary tale of disempowerment,
rage, black masculinity, and, ultimately, a crisis of individual and collective
identity. Misdirection in *The Women of Brewster Place* is enacted through
the physical structure of the alley where Lorraine, the lesbian partner of
Theresa, is gang-raped. This structure, which is analogous to the gutter spaces
in comics, turns on misdirection and its semiotics, which I explain in more
detail in the chapter and elsewhere. Naylor's novel looks at the psychic and
physical trauma of rape; the issue of queer women of color who are triply
marginalized by gender, race, and sexual orientation; the trope of black hyper-
masculinity and the complicated relationship this has with stereotypes of
black women as matriarchs of the community but also as secondary to men;
and finally, the complex issues of belonging and identity.

Chapter 5 continues the theme of women's oppression, racism, poverty
and the subversive power of misdirection, with an analysis of the representation of women and madness. The lesbian protagonist's love for a married
woman, as well as their shared Chicana culture that demands acquiescence
to a heteronormativity that is itself derived from an inauthentic morality, is
filtered through a "mad" fugue-state that draws the reader into what Benita
Roth refers to as "nested contexts."[72] Faced with choices that extend only as
far as the boundaries of the cotton fields her brown-skinned family and
friends are hired to tend, the Chicana lesbian protagonist (and the madness
her lesbianism signifies) becomes a commentary on the hypocrisy of a world
out of touch with its own madness. Thus the thematic pulse of this book
takes up its strongest challenge at the place where representation and misdirection align to deconstruct reductionist narratives that characterize the
racialized queer(ed) body as threatening, diseased, sub-human, or simply
lacking.

Chapter 6 turns to Jaime Cortez's graphic novel about the life of Cuban
exile and transgender activist Adela Vázquez. It looks through the contem-

porary political lens to problematize hetero and homonormative notions of queer representation distilled through the narrow frame of Cuban politics immediately preceding and following the 1980s Mariel Boatlift. Shining a light on issues of gender identity, transphobia, exile, racism, AIDS, and sex work, the protagonist becomes multiply determined by forces over which she has little control. It is ultimately through misdirectional performances that Adela and others like her who seek to transcend gender norms are able to "pass" into womanhood on their own terms.

Chapter 7 looks at Belden Sezen's *Snapshots of a Girl*, a graphic memoir that traces her life as a young girl from a Turkish background to her "coming out" in her twenties as a lesbian. Unsurprisingly, her "coming out" is fraught with the cultural expectations of her family but also complicated by her own lack of understanding of any other way for women to express their sexual desire. Drawn in black and white and sans the intricate detail that marks out the work of such illustrators as Jillian Tamaki, Sara Gomez Woolley, Nina Bunjevac, or Emil Ferris, Sezen's uncomplicated sketchbook style allows for a more focused study of the narrative arc of her story. Nevertheless her strategic use of lines, borders, splash pages, captions and various symbolia add just as much complexity to her work as illustrators who deploy more technical (and sometimes inaccessible) approaches. In fact, Sezen's use of symbolia throughout much of her book functions as a type of misdirection that offers an alternative point of view through which to express a more positive and meaningful interpretation of "Otherness." Her narrative strategy is also deceptively simple, yet touches on the "expressive potential" that even a single line (or word) on the page transmits to the reader.[73] In this chapter, then, misdirection sits squarely alongside *ayip*,[74] the Turkish concept of shame, to unpack the culturally coded spaces of a queer Turkish girl.

And finally, Chapter 8 explores Kabi Nagata's manga memoir, *My Lesbian Experience with Loneliness*. It tells the story of Nagata's struggle with depression, loneliness, self-harm, and a sexual awakening that is fraught with confusion and anxiety. The reader is drawn into the visual depths of a personal angst that is so disturbingly real that the overly large eyes looking out at us become mirrors reflecting back our own emotional vulnerabilities. Using the hybridity of Nagata's *shōjo yuri* manga,[75] this chapter explores the idea of loneliness through the lens of Paul Ricoeur's hermeneutics.

None of the texts in this book are discussed in chronological order, yet the themes they each introduce interconnect and overlap across time and space. This allows for a more fluid analysis of the structural oppressions and ruptures in queer women of color representation that were in play between the decades spanning the 1980s to the mid–2000s, not the least of which was the AIDS epidemic that cast a spotlight on an already queer-phobic nation. Thus as Keniston and Quinn note, "while we read texts from beginning to end, literature also complicates chronology through flashback, anticipation, and other strategies."[76] Moreover, in looking to contemporary scholarship to track the transformation of the queer(ed) *of color* body from abjection to complex subjectivity, but most especially in freeing subaltern bodies from the indeterminate yet charged spaces that Gayatri Chakravorty Spivak argues are embodied within imperialist narratives, a rupturing of this historical stranglehold is necessary and inevitable.[77] To varying degrees this book explores these critical ruptures, focusing in some way on dubious narratives that continue to shape and influence cultural debates regarding how "difference" is perceived and negotiated.

Chapter 1

Misdirection
Situating the Subversive Voice in Critical Context

Words, signs, symbols, and gestures are fundamental components to communication. How we perceive the world and how the world in turn perceives us shapes our understanding of who we are and where we belong. Yet when communication is filtered through a system of laws that are crafted to protect the vested interests of the powerful few, those furthest away from the center of power must find ways to bypass, disrupt, subvert, or create alternative forms of communication through which hegemony can be discursively challenged. In this chapter I argue that through misdirection, marginalized voices can form new lines of communication situated within a more relevant and contemporary epistemological framework.

As a queerly performed signifying strategy that crosses literary, spatiotemporal, and structural boundaries, misdirection interrogates "politically coded"[1] spaces that are designed to preserve a particular set of social norms. Yet when these norms (or the historically faulty premise upon which they have been constructed) are perceived to be under attack from without or within national borders, intolerance in its usual guise of patriotism is trotted out and used to crush dissent. Misdirection in literature, art, comics, theater, music, film, or global citizen uprisings is a way of pushing back against the narcotizing rhetoric of political demagoguery. It flourishes, and indeed is at its subversive best, when it operates through semiotic frameworks that position it alongside scholarly and cultural critiques that problematize enduring tropes of "Otherness."

Opening up pathways into what Susanna M. Morris calls "black people's futurist cultural productions,"[2] misdirection presents as a futurist signifying creation firmly located in a tradition of African American and brown/red/yellow resistance. Underpinned by a queer semiotics, the application of misdirection in this book serves as a lens through which queer women of color subjectivity triggers a paradigm shift that radically disrupts hetero and homo-normative expectations. Furthermore, by taking an interdisciplinary approach in linking together the semiotics of graphic narratives and literary fiction, this book demonstrates that misdirection is a useful tool that turns on the "simultaneous mobilization" of a multiplicity of alternative systems of "codes" and theories.[3] Indeed, Karin Kukkonen's connection between the "cooperation between different modes in narrative"[4] and Thierry Groensteen's explication of graphic narratives that are built on multimodal systems reflect my own movement towards developing misdirection as a critical methodology capable of breaking through and contesting rigidly coded spaces.

I want to first take a moment to consider the significance of semiotics in relation to misdirection and its many signifying forms. At its most basic, Charles S. Peirce's theorizing on semiotics holds that it is comprised of three interdependent and interrelated components: the *representamen* (the form that the sign takes or its "sign vehicle"); the *object* (something to which the sign refers or that which it represents); and the *interpretant* (the effect produced by the sign or the *sense* made of it).[5] Bronwen Martin and Felizitas Ringham describe semiotics as a theory of signification that is applied to numerous fields of study. They point out that in literature, as well as a tool for analysis, semiotics is guided by four principles summarized here: meaning is not inherent in objects, objects do not signify themselves; semiotics views the text, any text, as an autonomous unit, that is, one that is internally coherent; semiotics posits that story structure or narrativity underlies all discourse, not just what is commonly known as a story; and a text must be studied at [...] different levels of depth and not just at the surface level as is the case with traditional linguistics.[6]

As I note later on in this chapter when offering an analysis of several images that illustrate the potential of misdirection as a signifying strategy, semiotics works well in supporting the complexity of misdirection at different levels: discursive, narrative, the contract, and the deep or abstract.[7] In literary terms one might say that these levels are congruent with the definition of diegesis, an analytic expression which functions at the diegetic, extradiegetic and hypodiegetic levels. However, for my purposes here, the most useful explanation of semiotics as I advance the term in this book takes up aspects of Martin and Ringham's work, as well as the social semiotics advanced by Theo van Leeuwen and Gunther R. Kress.

Bringing his work into alignment with M.A.K. Halliday's, who asserted that the "grammar of language is not a code, not a set of rules for producing correct sentences," but instead a "resource for making meanings,"[8] Theo van

Leeuwen locates semiotics firmly in the cultural realm where there is unlimited potential for making meaning.[9] In the early work of Charles S. Peirce, certain rules had to be followed, and in mastering those rules, the signifiers and signifieds decide how meaning is made.[10] In other words, the "rules rule[d] people," and those who set the terms of the debate were typically the ones most resistant to collaborative thinking.[11] However, in social semiotics it is the other way around, and this makes all the difference in how meaning is made. But van Leeuwen sounds a cautionary note when he points out that not everyone is in a position to change the rules, although he concedes that just as there are different kinds of rules, there too are different ways to effect change.[12] This is an assertion exemplified in Nella Larsen's novel, which I discussed in the introduction, but want to briefly revisit here.

The central characters in Larsen's novel are Irene Westover Redfield, her childhood friend Clare Kendry, and Clare's husband John (Jack) Bellew. Clare is of mixed race but easily passes through life as a white woman. As her skin darkens with age, her husband gives her the nickname of "Nig," purportedly a term of endearment and unconnected to any suspicions he might have about his wife's true racial origins. But for Clare, the insulting phrase only underscores the deception she has perpetrated throughout her marriage. It becomes a trickery that she ultimately performs to the death, her life ending in questionable circumstances almost immediately after her husband discovers the truth of who she is.

Larsen's novel brought to the fore difficult conversations about the construction of race in early twentieth-century America. She created characters like Clare and Irene to represent the fraught relationship America has always had with her black sons and daughters. Although subtext and trickery underpinned these fraught relationships between blacks and whites, due to inequalities built into the legal system, there were vastly different outcomes. As we know from Larsen's novel, for people of color, the art of misdirection was usually a temporary shield protecting one from discovery. What we also know from Larsen's work is that the strands of deception we weave in an effort to neutralize or divert the hostile white gaze are inextricably linked to the object(s) it attempts to deceive. For one side of this two-headed coin, misdirection is a matter of survival. For the other side it is simply another tool in an already vast arsenal of unfair laws and onerous social proscriptions.

In *Passing*, Clare Kendry represents the trickster whose ability to move between worlds enabled her to hide in plain sight. Nevertheless, her negotiation of the semiotics of whiteness did not prepare her for the ever-changing rules of the game and in the end we came to understand that the rules ruled her. Furthermore, the accidental discovery of Clare's race by John Bellew "generate[d] an additional layer of meaning" which in turn created "a sign field substantively different from" the codes she mistakenly thought she had mastered.[13] The misdirection that had shielded Clare from discovery for so long had finally failed her, and in so doing it revealed the complex layers of meaning inextricably bound up in America's long standing and poisonous racial contract with the dispossessed.[14] Ultimately what Larsen was able to communicate to readers was the irony of performing behind a mask in order to be our authentic (or in Clare Kendry's case) our inauthentic selves. Larsen's novel demonstrates that misdirection can operate in a myriad of ways, sometimes to the detriment of those who rely on its signifying performance to divert the unwelcoming white gaze. Yet examples abound of another type of misdirection that is used to ensure that power remains in the hands of the few to the detriment of the many.

In his critically acclaimed book on the illegal re-enslavement of black people after emancipation, Douglas A. Blackmon exposes the contractual sleight of hand that gave rise to profit making prison systems. Writing about the hypocrisy of a system that on the one hand reluctantly acquiesced to the emancipation of slaves, while on the other invented new laws that effectively re-enslaved them, Blackmon said newly freed blacks were at risk of arrest for the slightest infractions. I call attention to Blackmon's book because of the parallels to misdirection in Larsen's novel. In Blackmon's telling, white southerners believed they had been betrayed by the emancipation of slaves, which for them meant a loss of free labor and profits. Thus, in plotting for the return of what they saw as their rightful property, whites used what William R. Freudenburg and Margarita Alario refer to as "diversionary reframing" to intentionally circumvent federal laws. This is the ideological opposite of misdirection, in that diversionary reframing is mostly recognized as a political tactic that diverts public attention away from illegitimate policies and laws.[15] Although disinformation is nothing new, and diverting attention away from truth has been routinely trotted out by virtually every administration since George Washington took office in 1789, it has become particularly egregious in modern day politics.

The expediency of telling lies rather than being inconvenienced by truth is the hallmark of diversionary reframing. I mention it here because when queer women of color attempt to speak truth to power, losing sight of how power often disguises itself in seemingly inclusive ways, rather than as a series of interlocking diversions that keep us off balance, works to our detriment. In other words, where misdirection in this book is a signifying strategy operationalized through the frameworks of queer, gender, postcolonial, comics studies, and feminist theory, diversionary reframing usually starts from a position of entitlement and requires no additional mechanism beyond social media, advertising, or television to facilitate the delivery of its homogenizing message. Furthermore, misdirection deployed as a form of tricksterism operates through the liminal spaces of sequential art and literary fiction to lessen the distance between truth and lies, whereas diversionary reframing seeks to increase and exploit this distance. Granted, even within the comparatively inclusive genre of comics, there are exceptions and differing interpretations to these rules. Nevertheless, I believe the comparison is important to make because each strategy, although seemingly similar to the casual observer, aims to achieve vastly different outcomes. Misdirection (in the context of queer performance) is meant to give agency, whereas diversionary reframing is meant to take it away.

I also mention these distinctions in the context of Nella Larsen's novel, where we see Clare Kendry's use of misdirection to distract notice from her true racial background, whereas her husband relies on diversionary reframing (in the legal context) to preserve his white entitlement. These two ideas are perpetually in tension, setting out rules of engagement that always seem to privilege those who hold the power.

As a tool of empowerment, misdirection is most often described as a technique designed to mislead or manipulate audience perceptions. In placing the phrase squarely in the tradition of black autobiography, M. Clay Hooper, for example, might describe it as a form of tricksterism that is "a historically embedded practice of discursive cunning and agility" designed to "evade, redirect, or otherwise subvert the techniques" of a dominant "cultural discipline."[16] Throughout this book the semiotics of sequential art, coupled with the subversive coding embedded in many American cultural and literary productions, particularly African American writing, support a more fluid definition of misdirection that allows for a broader application of its unique properties.

Gustav Kuhn and Luis M. Martinez concede that misdirection is "rather difficult" to define, yet they generally agree that its literal meaning of "pointing out the wrong way" is one way to approach it.[17] In one of the few sustained critiques of misdirection that I have come across, James V. Morrison puts forth a mostly classical definition that is largely predicated upon the notion that misdirection works as a series of false predictions that are "integral [to] […] the poet's presentation of the story of the *Iliad*."[18] According to Morrison, Homer "uses misdirection to draw the audience closer to the central problem faced by characters in the *Iliad*: mortal expectation and miscalculation."[19] It is with a somewhat related purpose in mind that I apply misdirection to the task of disrupting audience expectations where the outcome (based on dominant hetero-normative values) is assured.

Although misdirection has its most recognizable corollaries in magic, crime fiction, cartoons, warfare and masquerade, Morrison asserts in his study of the narrator's role in Homer's *Iliad* that misdirection also occurs when a prediction is given, persuasive, false or in some way misleading.[20] This aligns neatly with his definition of the term as a narrative that is structured "in such a way as to upset or disappoint the audience's expectations in some way [...]."[21] One of the main turns the arguments in this book takes up is to position misdirection in such a way that it is enacted through a semiotic framework, thereby allowing it to function on multiple levels to effect meaningful change for queer women of color. This is where my own definition and development of misdirection reframes and extends it as a signifying strategy defined by the contexts through which it seeks to effect perceptual shifts. Indeed, as Kuhn and Martinez note, misdirection can also be defined by focusing on its function. The idea is to deploy a technique that disguises the method of delivery that brings about a desired effect.[22] In this way both the disguise and the delivery can take multiple forms. A useful example of this process can be seen at figure 1.

The relationship between the reader (who is outside the panel) and the comic strip figure who "bursts the frame" by walking off the page into the reader's world is one of signified and signifier. The signifier (in this case the figure bursting from the frame) aims to misdirect the signified (the audience) away from what is happening in the background. The delivery—or the perceptual shift that brings about the desired effect—is referred to colloquially as "Sheena-ing" in comics and in both theater and film as "breaking the fourth wall."[23] In narratology this action is also known as metalepsis, and when it "occurs in literature, film or other media, the boundaries of a fictional world are glanced, travelled or transported across."[24] Put another way, metalepsis breaches the boundaries of real and imagined worlds, therefore by walking off the page and alluding to a patriotic duty to support America by purchasing

Figure 1. Bringing Up Father" by George McManus (copyright © 1945 by George McManus. Reprinted by permission of King Features Syndicate, Inc.).

war bonds, the comic strip character demonstrates a self-referential aware-ness.

The fictional character's awareness of himself, and indeed of the type of audience he is reaching out to, is based on two important elements in the layering of meaning: "denotation" and "connotation."[25] I will not go into detail here on Roland Barthes's theory of visual semiotics, as others have written at great length on the subject. I simply make brief reference to this aspect of his work because it supports the overall theme of my own analysis of queer representation and what this means across different and changing contexts.

In the Barthian system of semiotics, denotation is the first layer that asks: "what, or who, is being depicted [...]?" The second layer of connotation asks: "what ideas and values are expressed through what is represented, and through the way in which it is represented?"[26] In other words, the conceptual leaps we routinely make as cultural consumers can serve as dialogic bridges that reveal the "critical blind spots" in discursive frameworks.[27] This is where the frame within the frame in McManus's drawings, as well as the "Sheena-ing" or breaking through the fourth wall, visually illustrates how individuals who hold multiple viewpoints are able to take in more complex systems of meaning making, thereby enabling them to traverse back and forth between different cultures, realities, and media.

The sub-text of McManus's work is difficult to miss on a number of levels where meaning is made. The largely undisturbed first frame in figure 1 sig-nifies control through a system of containment, although we see that Jiggs is clever enough to exploit its weakest point.[28] By bursting through this area of literal or metaphorical containment—be this in the case of people trapped in poor inner city communities, or locked away in prisons where people of color are disproportionately represented, or warehoused in psychiatric hos-pitals where the "queer" and infirm languish—the trickster finds ways to insert himself/herself into the larger narrative.

What I am aiming for in this book is to use the semiotics of misdirection that run throughout graphic narratives and literary fiction as a way to inter-rogate and disrupt the "subtextual fragmentedness" that continues to render queer women of color invisible and mute.[29] In this regard, Eve Kosofsky Sedg-wick's insistence that we keep faith with "promises to make invisible possi-bilities and desires visible"[30] supports a focus on misdirection as a way to circumvent and ultimately transcend the politics of those who are unable or unwilling to accept the layered and complex subjectivities that comprise "dif-ference" in all its forms. I seek to bring queer women of color squarely back into the larger narrative frame by deploying misdirection to "combine mul-tiple semiotic resources"[31] that combined or intersected succeed in giving voice to that which is "unspeakable," that which represents the "unrepresentable" in relation to what literature can sometimes only "gesture toward."[32]

Hinting at a kind of existential panic lurking at the periphery of white-centric discursive formations, Sedgwick (and by extension Darren L. Hutchinson and Jonathan Kemp) suggests that we must "smuggle queer representation in where it must be smuggled and [...] challenge queer-eradicating impulses frontally where they are to be so challenged."[33] In taking up this advice as it relates to the experiences of queer women of color whose rights are multiply abridged in deference to the patriarchal white-centric norm, misdirection allows for self-representational narratives that are not so much bound by a discourse of sameness, but rather predicated upon how we negotiate the differences that comprise our reality. To this end, I want to briefly draw a comparison to the tasks that I identify later on in this chapter as essential functions and defining concepts of misdirection, with Gloria T. Randle's interpretation of how space (in its physical and metaphorical sense) operates as a form of protection (and, indeed, misdirection) in Harriet Jacobs's *Incidents in the Life of a Slave Girl, Written by Herself* (1861).

Randle makes the connection between the constant threat of violence to enslaved black bodies as a method of control deployed by slave owners and Jacobs's "ability [...] to construct sites of temporary refuge where none exist."[34] This ability to create limited places of safety, no matter that they are often "inevitably flawed and grossly inadequate,"[35] occurs through various strategies of misdirection that are applied in direct proportion to perceived levels of threat. For queer women of color who are multiply disenfranchised on the basis of race, gender, ethnicity and sexual orientation, misdirection in its most injurious form has played a large part in Eurocentric chicanery. Compelled to perform a hyper-normativity not typically required or demanded of white heterosexuals, or even white lesbians and gay men, queer women of color have been expected to conform to a set of unrealistic standards of beauty, femininity, motherhood and (hetero) sexuality. To contest these rigid proscriptions, and to give voice to that which remains unsayable, misdirection is applied in this book to create more affirmative methods of representing the queer woman of color body.

The Semiotics of Misdirection

In an attempt to broaden my discussion of how misdirection works to reframe current debates regarding queer women of color subjectivities, I offer an unlikely comparison to several points made by John Arthos, Jr., in his critique of the misdirecting rhetoric of Louis Farrakhan. Describing misdirection as "an adroit manipulation engendered by a history that crushed open confrontation,"[36] Arthos positions Farrakhan in the role of a master trickster whose skillful exploitation of white anxiety exemplifies a basic tenet of misdirection, which is a "misattribution of motive through the ambiguity of the sign that permits the open display of subversion" by the disenfranchised.[37] The art of black (queer, subaltern, female, transgender, the list goes on) survival turns on this crucial point. Handed down from generation to generation, trickery (or signifying misdirection) plays out "along a number of divergent conceptual directions that have to do with boundary marking and boundary breaking."[38] Thus, for those with the power to construct boundaries that separate people through social, cultural or legal classifications (the signifier), there is often an equivalent response that attempts to subvert and rewrite those master narratives (the signified).

Homi K. Bhabha's exposition on the destructive and residual effects of colonialism in self-representational contexts is equally applicable in discourse relating to the suppression of queer of color voices. Indeed, performances of resistance enacted by queers of color as strategies designed to protect against further harm can be located within the hybridity of the sign. As Bhabha notes:

> Hybridity is the revaluation of the assumption of colonial identity through the repetition of discriminatory identity effects. It displays the necessary deformation and displacement of all sites of discrimination and domination. It unsettles the mimetic or narcissistic demands of colonial power but reimplicates its identifications in strategies of subversion that turn the gaze of the discriminated back upon the eye of power.[39]

Brief consideration here of the process of signification (its constituent terms being hybridity, multimodality, and semiotics) is necessary. As pointed out previously, semiotics is a study of "signs and their meanings in all their different material realisations."[40] This opens up a wide path through which the hybrid form of misdirection finds its critical footing. Taking its methodological cues from postcolonial, critical race feminism, queer and gender theory, misdirection is most effectively deployed through the gutters, gaps and interstitial spaces of discourse. It is here, then, in the coded spaces of contemporary colonizing projects, that signifying as performance relies upon misdirection to position the performer (or the trickster) within a signifying frame in order to prevail over or convince the signified of something.

These terms (misdirection and signifying) are inextricably linked and bound up in African American traditions. Signifying derives in part from African American literary tradition as well as the Yoruba system of what Henry Louis Gates, Jr., explains as *Èsù-'túfunààlò*, or "bringing out the interstices of the riddle,"[41] or, as he notes in *The Signifying Monkey*, the "Esu's double voice."[42]

Whereas misdirection simultaneously obscures and even impertinently performs the trickery behind the riddle, "signifying" (as I use it here) exposes the contradictions inherent in cultural productions of "difference" by locating those very contradictions through a signifying frame of black representation.[43]

Gates, in citing J.L. Dillard, the American linguist, writes that Dillard "defines Signifyin(g) as 'a familiar discourse device from the inner city [which] tends to mean communicating (often an obscene or ridiculing message) by indirection.'"[44] I want to note here that Dillard's usage of the term "indirection" is part of the continuum of signifying, in that, as Gates points out, signifying has multiple meanings "because so many black tropes are subsumed within it."[45]And while the standard dictionary definition of "indirection" is closely aligned with my usage of the term "misdirection," it is not a like-for-like relationship as I explain below.

A significant part of Marcyliena H. Morgan's primary research into language usage in African American communities is her discussion of indirectness as a "counterlanguage" deployed by black people which "functioned to signal the antisociety (e.g., ideological black audience) and provided a means for a speaker to reveal a social face [...] that resisted and contested the practice of racial repression."[46] My application of misdirection draws not upon the study of linguistics per se, but rather upon the structural elements of comics and literary fiction to operationalize misdirection as its own unique signifier in queer women of color representation. In general, misdirection often requires an agreement between the audience and performer. The agreement is that what is happening or being proposed will shift the terms of engagement or the broader narrative upon which our worldview is based. These agreements are sometimes explicit, but if they are implied they are often obscured or masked through coded language. This is where the term "indirection" comes into closer alignment with misdirection.

Pauline Greenhill argues that "in the context of complex audiences in which some members may be competent and willing to decode the message," some will also be "monocultural" and thus assume "that its own interpretation of messages is the only one possible."[47] Greenhill goes on to note: "the second group, living in two cultures, may recognize a double message."[48] The double message, double voice, or double consciousness that is an inescapable feature of many queer(ed) black subjectivities speaks to (and finds ways to challenge) the "circulating currents of contradiction" (and codes) that inhere in white hegemonic paradigms.[49] Turning on ambiguities that are coded into identity discourse, misdirection effectively destabilizes our notions of who we are or who we *think* we are. Moreover, what we see, hear, smell, touch or intuit forms the basis of our individual (and sometimes collective) reality.

Scott McCloud notes that we all "perceive the world as a whole through the experience of our senses," but crucially "our senses can only reveal a world that is fragmented and incomplete."[50] In other words, none of us can actually see or know the entire world, but through acts of faith and drawing together fragments of what we know from past experience, we can achieve what McCloud refers to as closure. Although we observe the parts as McCloud suggests, we can only achieve closure by perceiving the whole.[51] While McCloud does not explicitly equate this stitching together of fragments as misdirection, I frame his approach in a way that places the conventions of misdirection within what Hortense J. Spillers has described as "nested semiotic readings."[52] In other words, there are levels upon levels of codes in what we see and in what we read, but we must be conversant in the language of signs and symbols in order to decipher what is truly being communicated.

We must also understand that "metaphors" of difference "reveal as much as they conceal"[53] and that oppressed groups must use this to their advantage by embracing "the hybrid figure" of the trickster, queers, transgender individuals, people of color, who "open up [...] space[s] of cultural uncertainty and instability."[54] It is through these openings, in the spaces where the hybrid body is misaligned against "normative" constructs of embodiment and identity, that misdirection begins its semiotic performance. To this end, Ashley Manchester's incisive observations on the usefulness of comics as a pedagogical tool in teaching queer theory and its attendant conceptualizations and re-working of "Otherness" is useful for also understanding the value of misdirection in contesting hyper-mediated hegemonic representations of cultural norms. She writes:

> Systems like compulsory heterosexuality perpetuate through their visibility, rendering non-normative genders or sexualities virtually unimaginable and restricted from view. Paradoxically, normative sexuality continues to be constructed as naturalized, making it insidiously invisible in the social world while queer sexualities become hyper-visible as "deviant." These seemingly contradictory ways of being in the world are intertwined with the politics of visuality, and teaching comics in the [...] classroom as a queer process can allow students the ability to *actively* and *visually* challenge the sociocultural codes embedded into comics and other visual systems.[55]

The imagery that we have learned to equate with "normative" sexual expression is ubiquitous and permeates every facet of our lives. From religious iconography reminding us of our duty to God and man, to bridal shops peddling fantasies of marital bliss, to soft porn music videos streamed to our tablets, our phones, and our television screens, heterosexuality, it would seem, is the basis from which all else flows. Therefore, it is important for scholars and educators to promote interdisciplinary projects that draw on visual and written language to create opportunities for more expansive representational practices within and outside of the classroom. My contribution to "un-dis-appearing" the queer subaltern body is introducing misdirection as a dynamic tool that, like a jazz composition, creates fusion with the structural notations of literature and comics.

Queering the Ga(y)ze Through Misdirection

I offer here a brief example of how the historical misalignment between the hegemonic and subaltern gaze sets up a confrontation that is fraught with reminders of the ongoing legacies of racism, but which might—through col-laborative engagement with scholarship from various disciplines—be resolved through a new system of reverse-coding. This system manifests materially and discursively at the intersection where the images shown below at figures 2 and 3 bring into stark relief the limits and contingencies of identity while also setting up paradigm shifts that in turn raise questions about the inherent instability around social constructions of race, gender, and sexual orienta-tion.

The image in figure 2 is by London-based artist Kat Williams.[56] It com-pels us to ask the question "What is it that defines a person?" I extend this query to argue that on both a diegetic and extradiegetic level—borrowing once again from the "nested semiotic readings" that Hortense Spillers dis-cusses—the mask represents three things: what is in plain sight, what is hid-den, and what has been subsumed into wider nationalist agendas. Here the reader must find a referent, a familiar thing that puts into context what they see or know about themselves, based on what they have been socialized to believe they are or who they can become. Setting aside for a moment the controls imposed upon gender non-conforming, ethnic and racial minorities, Freudenburg and Alario rightly note that even the most intuitive and aware people are "capable of 'seeing' only in the direction in which they are pointed."[57] But through the semiotics of misdirection, the aim in this book is to unveil new paradigms through which a reorientation of queer women of color embodiment gestures toward a more affirmative interpretation of who we are, rather than who we are not.

In Kat Williams's drawing, the critical spectator behind the mask mis-directs the nullifying gaze, thereby indirectly challenging and destabilizing the systems around which identity and representation have historically been fixed. The layered meanings evoked through the iconic image of the mask comes through in both comics and literary fiction where, as bell hooks put it in terms of film, "conventional representations have done violence" to the black "image."[58] This is nowhere more evident than in Rahana Daria's drawing at figure 3, where the black woman stares into a mirror and sees a white woman gazing back at her. The black woman has been conditioned to *not* see herself, to imagine herself out of existence, whereas the white woman sees a black person looking at an image that has been constructed as the ideal. Now imagine that the black woman is a lesbian and the visual semiotics shift to an entirely different level of meaning and complexity.

Left: **Figure 2. Illustration by Kat Williams, UK-based artist (see C•1 for larger image).** *Right:* **Figure 3. Illustration by Rahana Daria, UK-based artist (see C•2 for larger image).**

Where together literature and images intercede to unpack these representational conundrums by offering a historicizing frame on the matter of representation and abjection, bell hooks' chapter "Representing Whiteness in the Black Imagination" eloquently expresses this conundrum.

> In white supremacist society, white people can "safely" imagine that they are invisible to black people since the power they have historically asserted, and even now collectively assert over black people accorded them the right to control the black gaze.[59]

Indeed, numerous postcolonial scholars have written at length about social constructions of "difference" and how this impinges upon nearly every facet of life, from employment to housing to sexual orientation to gender to politics to identity. That which is mirrored back to us is shaped by how we are perceived by others, which in turn influences how we see ourselves and whether or not we accept or reject these abstractions. For queer women of color, these disquieting reflections never fully resolve, no matter from which angle we are positioned. In this regard Penelope Ingram's call for a "language of physical signification," or, more precisely, the enactment of a signifying language, is useful.[60]

Ingram sets up her argument of the signifying body based in part on Heidegger's "authentic Being-in-the-world" and Franz Fanon's polemical writings on corporeality and race.[61] However, I am drawn more to Ingram's framing of the signifying body as constructed and read through Lacan's mirror stage. In this regard the illustrations at figures 2 and 3 of the racialized subject can be understood as "subjectivity [...] founded on" a "form of alienating specularity."[62] Moreover, Lacan's "theory of a mirror stage suggests that a subject's identity is founded on a paradoxical recognition/misrecognition" in that "it recognizes an image of itself in the mirror and at the same time misrecognizes that image as itself."[63] It is this very paradox that Ingram points to which supports my discussion throughout of misdirection as both a representational and oppositional strategy. Making queer/black/gender marginalization about something other than the machinations of corrupt political systems has recently been seen to chilling effect through the Trump administration's response to Colin Kaepernick's "taking of the knee." Rather than acknowledging the gesture as a symbolic protest against police brutality in America, the Trump administration used "diversionary reframing" to make it about overpaid black athletes' unpatriotic stance against people serving in the military.[64] It is in this way that a queer(ed) misdirection must be deployed as a counter-response to the practice of "diversionary reframing" by corrupt political regimes.

Graphic Incursions and Misdirection

In order to enact change, to problematize the interstices where queer women of color have been at once rendered invisible and silent, yet also seen as guardians of our ancestral memories, literature must evolve apace of ever-shifting cultural and transnational contexts. In arguing for bodies of work that illuminate the complexities of representation across multiple hierarchies, geographies, and intersecting realities, there must be an attendant recognition that representation is not a singularly defining concept that engages all marginalized groups or issues in identical ways or through identical modes or methods. In this regard, critical engagement in literary productions must vigorously contest not just the "cultural rhetorics of silencing" that Pramod K. Nayar, for example, discusses in the review of the wordless graphic novel *Hush*, but also its underlying impulse.[65]

Given that there is a "shared historical assignment to invisibility faced by" queer women of color "in literature,"[66] what is equally true is that "through the multiple voices that enunciate [...] complex subjectivity, the woman writer not only speaks familiarly in the discourse of" misdirection, for instance, "but as Other she is in contestorial dialogue with the hegemonic dominant and subdominate or 'ambiguously (non)hegemonic' discourses."[67] This is where (if used to its fullest potential), and in tandem with literary fiction, the semiotics of graphic narratives can intercede in, and negotiate, the politically coded spaces between representation and invisibility. With their combined visual and textual elements, graphic narratives (rather than fiction alone) can effect a more meaningful incursion into dominant hegemonic paradigms by making visible the intersecting and over-lapping oppressions that have masked over the experiences of queer women of color. Whereas fiction relies exclusively on text to convey complex subjectivities, Hillary Chute and Marianne DeKoven argue that the graphic narrative's ability via its most basic make-up of frames and gutters to call "reader's attention visually and spatially to the act, process, and duration of interpretation"[68] is central to a fuller understanding of representation and how this is constructed in the wider cultural imaginary.

Through the use of frames, panels, gutters, captions and other visual/textual devices in graphic narratives, stories are propelled forward sequentially so that readers remain engaged and can understand unfolding events. The difference for Chute and DeKoven between fiction and graphic narratives, it seems, is in the graphic narrative's ability to absorb and redirect "the ideological, formal, and creative energies of contemporary fiction."[69] Indeed, these are precisely the synergies that I seek to harness by bringing together queer women of color representation in fiction and the visual power of graphic narratives. By drawing on the notion of misdirection to reorient or redirect these ideological, formal, and creative energies for which Chute and DeKoven advocate, I attempt to draw out a more nuanced interpretation of queer women of color lives.

I end this chapter on misdirection by returning briefly to the importance of the trickster as a semiotic figure capable of traversing multiple physical and metaphorical borders. I do so by drawing on Gloria Anzaldúa's coinage of the word "Nepantleras" to offer further analysis of how misdirection operates in a multimodal way that is facilitated by coded spaces in graphic narratives and literary fiction. Anzaldúa describes the Nepantleras as a "threshold people" who "move within and among multiple, often conflicting worlds" and who resist alliances that would fix their beliefs to narrowly defined ideologies.[70] They are "visionary cultural worker[s]" who face all the risks that other marginalized people experience for being too different or individualized.[71] Yet the rewards result in the Nepantleras being able to "use their movements among divergent worlds to develop innovative, potentially transformative perspectives."[72] In effect, these movements can be said to mimic the spatiotemporal properties of graphic narratives in that these incursions into "normative" paradigms work to realign our worldview. The following chapters take up all of the foregoing arguments to build upon the transformative performances of queer(ed) "threshold people" who exist between the words, spaces, gaps, and gutters of history.

Chapter 2

Women of Color
in Queer(ed) Space
Ann-Marie MacDonald's
Fall on Your Knees *(1997)*

What is queer but a familiar thing estranged, lost in the field
of the other?[1]

Ann-Marie MacDonald's novel charts the lives of the Piper family in
nineteenth-century Nova Scotia, tackling such issues as incest, physical abuse,
xenophobia, patriarchy, and class. Replete with all manner of subversive
meanings, religious symbolism, horror, trauma, hauntings and illicit sexual
desires, the Gothic aspects of the novel lend themselves particularly well to
an analysis that illuminates the secrets that the narrative works so hard to
hide.

James and Materia Piper are an interracial couple who met, fell in love,
and eloped. Materia's father disowns her and after the birth of her first child
she eventually comes to understand that she is trapped in a loveless marriage
with James. The Pipers have three children together, all of whom are born
with fair skin and fine features. Kathleen is her father's favorite, the one he
grooms for stardom on the operatic stage and who eventually becomes the
object of his sexual desires. Mercedes is the next oldest, the one who grows
up to find solace in religion, and upon her mother's death decides that she
is the de facto parent to Kathleen and Frances. Frances is the youngest and,
by any measure, the most rebellious. Sexually molested as a young child by
her father, she acts out by putting herself in dangerous situations with men
and by defying her father at every opportunity. Lily Piper's birth is the result
of Kathleen's rape at the hands of her father. Because of all that Lily symbolizes, she replaces Kathleen as the favorite daughter/granddaughter to James.
She is sweet and innocent, has a deformed foot, and is loved by everyone.

43

This chapter examines how the Piper girls mount both overt and covert challenges to their father's authority. Peering through the Gothic lens to problematize questions regarding the oppression of women of color, this chapter considers two pivotal moments in the novel when MacDonald's adroit use of language works to

> distinguish our own experience in the world of real things from that represented in the framed narrative and to move us toward that framed, (hypo)diegetic experience through a narrative space that is neither the reader's world nor the world of the framed story.[2]

It could be said that the above statement parallels the diegetic and extradiegetic spaces in comics. Pascal Lefèvre describes the diegetic space as the "fictive space in which the characters live and act" and the extradiegetic space as "material space that surrounds the individual panels: not only the whites between the panels, but also the real space in which the reader is located."[3] The first pivotal moment in MacDonald's novel "narrates" the attic as a liminal space open to those courageous enough to lift the veil separating the living from the dead. The second pivotal moment occurs in New York's Central Park where Rose and Kathleen come together as "signifier and signified [...] into a sign that depends simultaneously on the layer" of what could be said to be their internalized imagery "and the layer of words to represent the effect of a coherent subjectivity."[4] My aim here is to bring seemingly disparate signifiers into critical conversation with each other by using the semiotics of the Gothic form, as well as the interstitial spaces in sequential art, to better "negotiate complex, hybrid identities by embodying this hybridity in both structure and form."[5] What I mean by this is that Rose (who is visibly racialized and therefore rendered invisible) and Kathleen (whose white skin protects her from a similar erasure) interrupt this narrative by using the signifying language of desire to both embody and transcend their differences.

Stephanie Cawley's intriguing examination of comics in relation to post-colonial feminism helps to locate this chapter in liminal spaces where misdirection plumbs the depths and fissures of subalternity and representation to explore how aspects of both Gothic and comics might facilitate "a discussion of the problematics of narrating the Other."[6] Where Julia Round, for example, seeks to "bring together some of the narrative strategies of Gothic and comics and [...] use them to reflect on each other" by applying "gothic criticism to re-approach and reconsider comics theory,"[7] I use the structural elements of comics and the semiotics of misdirection to reconsider approaches to queer women of color representation in the interstices of Gothic fiction. As a multimodal system made up of "a complex combination of elements, parameters, and multiple procedures,"[8] both comics and misdirection can be complementary methodologies in the analysis of historical misrepresentations.

Fall on Your Knees is set primarily in Nova Scotia, Canada, during the late nineteenth to just past the twentieth century. Most of the early action takes place at 191 Water Street where the Piper family lives, but shifts back and forth between New York and Cape Breton later on in the novel. The opening lines, "They're all dead now," alerts readers to a story that is told from the end to the beginning.[9] This flashback technique is reminiscent of Toni Morrison's provocative lead-in to *Paradise* (1999) where she writes: "They shoot the white girl first. With the rest, they can take their time."[10] Both openings, spare and foreboding, beckon to ghostly actors whose scripted lines foreshadow momentous and often tragic events.

Morrison's work has become well known for its innovative engagement with "a world filled with signs, visitations, and ways of knowing that encompassed more than concrete reality."[11] The cultural moments she examines in her work illuminate the uneasy relationship between dominant hegemonic paradigms and the struggle for recognition by women of color living on the periphery.[12] To some extent, MacDonald follows in the vein of Morrison, although from a historical perspective *Fall on Your Knees* is not so much an excavation of forgotten cultural and historical moments in the shaping of racial identities as it is a tragic love story shaped by the fissures and temporal dissonances of changing social and political realities. At the diegetic level where the main story unfolds, the reader's understanding of "normative" behavior is reinforced through white Eurocentric signifiers of gender, femininity, masculinity, and race. Yet when these signifiers are interpreted and decoded at the extradiegetic level, *Fall on Your Knees* can be read as a novel that speaks convincingly—though perhaps unwittingly—in the African American literary tradition. That is to say, in African American literature there is almost always a narrative within a narrative, a story that reveals its truth through codes, parody, and misdirection. An example of this double-coded language comes at the beginning of MacDonald's novel where the secret marriage between James Piper and Materia transgresses the rules of their respective cultures.

Realizing too late that they are ill-suited in marriage as well as in temperament, each in their own way seek refuge in memories past. Materia spends time in the attic, her longing for home triggered by the rich smell of her hope chest, which is made of cedar. Her husband assumes she has nothing to put in the chest, but the real reason she keeps it empty is so that "nothing could come between her and the magical smell that beckoned her into memory."[13]

Materia recalls the language of her childhood, which is rich and layered with levels of meaning that are in contrast to her husband's narrow view of the world. In order to understand the levels of meaning in Materia's story, readers must be able to traverse the spaces between dreams and reality. This "fictional and paradoxical transgression of the border between mutually exclusive worlds that cannot be transgressed in our actual world"[14] effectively describes the Gothic tale as a "metonym for […] cultural critique […]."[15] In other words, where social norms may suppress the questioning of hegemonic systems by marginalized groups, the Gothic (and comics as its framing narrative) becomes a device through which criticism, dissent, fear of the unknown, forbidden desire and longing take on the guise of something else.

Although Materia does not appear to be as quick thinking as her increasingly controlling husband, she has learned how to navigate in between the spaces characterized by James as empty and therefore harmless, as places where her foolish hopes and dreams would rightly be locked away in a cedar chest, in the family attic, in the dead spaces of the past. Yet if we are able to construct "[…] diegetic space in various ways: both by elements that appear inside the frame of a panel and by elements that remain unseen,"[16] we can treat the pages of a book, or the outer edges of a cedar chest, or the doorways of government institutions that separate rich from poor, as frames or panels that are semiotically and diegetically related. In other words, in the spaces where meaning is made and where I have previously described misdirection as a signifying strategy defined by the contexts through which it seeks to effect perceptual shifts, both the cedar chest and the attic operate through "narrative elements that 'work with' the space between image and words."[17] The feminist analysis that Elizabeth Marshall and Leigh Gilmore bring to the importance of the interstitial or "gutter" spaces in comics is particularly apt here.

Marshall and Gilmore note that even though "Roberto Innocenti and Aaron Frisch's *The Girl in Red* and Phoebe Gloeckner's *A Child's Life and Other Stories* are steeped in different histories of production and reception," there are "meaningful convergences" that "enable" the authors to "chart the politically divergent work of their creators."[18] Where Innocenti and Frisch's treatment of the gutter as a place where child rape happens out of the frame, as it were, Gloeckner's unflinchingly graphic rendering of child sexual abuse turns the space of the gutter into "a source for generating ethical witness through the elicitation of feminist affect."[19] Thus where James Piper believes his wife has nothing to put into the hope chest and certainly nothing to say, and that she is disturbingly and unappealingly childlike, she has learned to draw comfort from its smell and the memories that those smells bring forth.

Materia's thoughts flow uninhibited from the outer dimensions of the chest, signifying the first and second levels of her story, which are the equating of cedar with Lebanon, her mother's hands, and the dark elixir of her language which she will soon be forbidden to teach to her own children. What emerges then from the depths of the hope chest are memories of a young girl's life peeking through the fissures, spaces, and gaps of time. As is the case regarding the fictional attic in Thornfield Hall, the attic in Cape Breton is an important and recurring theme in MacDonald's novel.[20] Certainly one of the main thrusts of postcolonial feminism has been its persistent interrogation of race and the racialized body and how this continues to be pathologized as a way to regulate "non-normative" expressions of identity and its rhetoric. This is why scholars such as Franny Howes remind us that we are "constituted by the multiplicity of stories we tell about ourselves."[21] However, these stories—in the form of oral traditions, drawings, songs, and dancing—must first be reclaimed and recognized as legitimate records of our individual and collective histories. In her analysis of visual rhetoric and the importance this has in the excavation and preservation of pre–Western traditions, especially in looking at alternatives to the rhetorical tradition "as the locus of the history of writing"[22] (and, I daresay, representation), Howes picks up on the urgency of this work by imagining

> comics studies as a place where decolonial work can happen to constellate our field as broadly as possible, and to draw productively from as many places as possible, to craft a truly interdisciplinary field of study that does justice to visual rhetorical traditions practiced by people throughout space and time.[23]

Thus by recognizing the structural relationship between comics and fiction, and using this to subvert historical mischaracterizations of the "Other," the "'space between' presents itself as a solution for the inadequacy of words or images" alone "to the task of representation of the self."[24] In this way I also borrow from Thierry Groensteen's brief recognition of the similarities in fiction and comics, as the dynamics of these complex intersections of representation opens up rich discursive territory that would benefit from further enquiry.

Of the comic panel, Groensteen writes that it is "a condition of reading that [...] panels are physically isolated from each other or cognitively isolatable, of the sort that they can be *read* [italics belong to Groensteen] separately."[25] What Groensteen is getting at, and bearing in mind that this is a relatively insignificant point to his way of thinking, yet central to my argument here, is that the panel frame functions much like punctuation marks in language. The white space between panels is described as "the elementary sign that [...] separates [...] words," essentially inserting the necessary breaks and pauses that help readers make sense of the text.[26] Mario Saraceni offers his view of the relationship between comics and other textual forms when he suggests that the "language of comics has many similarities with the language we use every day," specifically regarding "functional" and "content" words.[27] As I have pointed out elsewhere, on the diegetic level fiction and comics operate in slightly different, yet also functionally related, ways. Where the diegetic space in comics represents the fictional world of the characters, the extradiegetic space is described as actual physical space surrounding panels and extending to the space comprising the world of the reader.[28]

The Ties That Bind

The Pipers are working class people living in a coal mining company town. Kathleen is the eldest child born to her Lebanese mother, Materia, and her Scots-Irish father, James. Mercedes, Frances, and Lily come next, along with Lily's dead twin brother who was their father's son *and* grandson. The family's very difficult beginnings—Materia eloped on the night of her thirteenth birthday with eighteen-year-old James Piper and her father never forgave her—anticipate the fraught and violent relationships that tie them together. As James slowly comes to the realization that he no longer loves the girl whose "summer skin" and the "darkest eyes he'd ever seen"[29] once intrigued him, he begins to focus his attention on Kathleen, his white-skinned daughter. The one he eventually rapes and locks away in the attic. She dies in childbirth and it is through the mostly unreliable memory of Frances (the narrator) that a picture slowly emerges of a family in crisis.[30]

By focusing on the novel's play with the conventions of the Gothic genre, I examine dominant narratives that run throughout the story. This includes issues of ethno-cultural difference and racial hierarchies, as well as the idea of "knowing" and whose knowledge is legitimated or, conversely, discounted. I problematize these representations by filling in the elliptical cultural moments in the lives of MacDonald's female characters, doing so by framing my explorations within interdisciplinary readings and applications of critical race, feminist, standpoint, semiotics, misdirection, gender, and queer of color theory. The aim is to demonstrate how *Fall on Your Knees* cleverly redefines *agency* in contested spaces. To this end, three main issues are examined through the Gothic frame: the heterosexual imperative—or "phallocentric rings"—by which private/public spaces are shaped; the queering of intimate relationships and how this "troubles" heteronormative conventions; and the racial imperative or the way in which racial hierarchies become entrenched.

"Gothic texts," as Eugenia DeLamotte notes, are "documents in the history of racial formation [...] that might give us a better sense of what the construction of whiteness involved, and in particular," she goes on to state, "of the white terrors it worked both to express and produce."[31] Put another way, if Gothic acts as a mirror into the collective psyche, with one's most intimate thoughts comprised of a series of self-affirming fears about the "Other," the task must then be to identify the source of those fears in order to challenge them.

In the final section of this chapter I show that the recuperation of female space is subject to similar conditions upon which issues of gender are determined. I suggest here that the way women "see" and are seen (what Patricia Hill Collins refers to when discussing black feminist epistemologies as "similar angles of vision") derives from women experiencing similar challenges in reclaiming their lost selves/voices/identities.[32] In her reading of *Fall on Your Knees*, Hilda Staels looks at "the female characters' liberating encounter with the alienated other within themselves."[33] I would add that women who have no clearly defined geographies, and whose safety is not inside the homes of their fathers or husbands or sons, must invent their own self-affirming geographies and ways of seeing. Therefore I focus on the intimate relationships in the novel and how this plays out for women of color, the spaces they inhabit, and the stories they tell. Going forward, I briefly outline the theoretical debates that inform my reading of MacDonald's novel before engaging in detail with the text and how it complicates the issues at stake.

Women of Color in Queer(ed) Space

These two terms, "women of color" and "queer space," have not always been treated as coterminous in that the *queering* of space has been historically associated with white gay and lesbian movements.[34] Historically women of color have either been deconstructed into various irreconcilable parts (black/invisible, female/incomplete, aggressive/helpless) or subsumed into hetero and homonormative narratives that ignore differences by conflating multi-issue struggles into one broad platform.[35] Yet "queer" is also a term used to describe strange and unusual things. Eve Sedgwick refers to the term as an "open mesh of possibilities, gaps, overlaps, dissonances and resonances [...]."[36] As a descriptor with a fraught relationship to the entrenched messages of heteronormativity, Sedgwick further argues that the term is also about the "lapses and excesses of meaning" that occur "when the constituent elements of anyone's gender, of anyone's sexuality aren't made (or *can't be* made [italics belong to Sedgwick]) to signify monolithically."[37] My use of the term in this chapter serves two functions: to underscore the peculiarities of hegemonic systems that "queer" racial and gender differences to the detriment of certain groups of people and as the adjective "queering" to suggest a reclaiming of identity/space/knowledge. I also use the terms "queer(ed)" space and "gay(ze)" as discursive tools for expanding, and also reformulating, narratives that are more reflective of the lived realities of women of color.

Patricia Hill Collins's work on black feminist standpoint theory and E. Patrick Johnson and Mae G. Henderson's scholarship in queer black studies troubles historical assumptions that on the one hand valorize white episte-mological discourse and on the other derogates the epistemes comprising the black experience. Each in their own way unearth various cultural and historical markers relevant to the black experience, as well as the historical dissimilitude between dominant hegemonic systems and the legitimacy of queer people of color realities. Relatedly, Churnjeet Kaur Mahn discusses the "inadequacy of labels such as 'gay' and 'lesbian' in non–Western contexts,"[38] specifically in South Asian diasporas, where these limited Western descriptors fail to account for a more nuanced and inclusive "reading" that the term "queer" allows.

Taking the idea of "queering" to another level, Mahn draws on Gayatri Gopianth's *Impossible Desires: Queer Diasporas and South Asian Public Cultures* (2005) to make the point that "critical revision[s]" are needed "that can allow narratives of desire to emerge that cannot be catalogued and mapped by the existing parameters of Anglo-American liberal and bourgeois ideologies."[39] To those whose point of reference has historically been outside the white hegemonic center, Mahn's argument is central to understanding how *difference* continues to inform and shape global narratives, suggesting that hierarchies of difference (examples of which are abundant in *Fall on Your Knees*) must be continually challenged.

Ultimately, there must be a re-articulation of language, such as that suggested by Burkhard Scherer, who locates the etymology of the word "queer" in the German word *quer*, "meaning transverse, cross, oblique," or its fuller usage of *Querkopf*, which is defined as someone who "thinks outside the box."[40] Karen Tongson takes no less of a critical run at the term when she notes: "queer-of-color critique is [...] about *critique* [italics belong to Tongson] in its multifaceted sense [...]" functioning as

> a method of criticism that draws from an expansive and variegated critical tool kit, including psychoanalysis, Marxism, deconstruction, or other so-called white theorizations of the subject.[41]

Queer incursions into the white hegemonic center is nothing new, and while Tongson's observation resonates on many important levels, I would add that through the variegated tool kit she mentions, the semiotics of misdirection is crucial to queer women of color representation because it draws upon its own signifying theorizations of resistance. While Ann-Marie MacDonald's novel is based partially on the argument that the lives of its female characters and the spaces they inhabit derive from dominant/subordinate paradigms historically tied to the patriarchal center, and we are made to understand these paradigms early on in the novel when Mr. Mahmoud "raises the forefinger of his left hand slightly, and his wife replenishes his teacup,"[42] what is equally true is the powerful human impulse to break the chains of psychological and/or physical enslavement.

How space is occupied and negotiated in the above example is representative of male power and the commodification of women. There is an expectation that women will respond to, and indeed wait for, cues telegraphed to them by men. The spaces that women are *permitted* to occupy, and through which they serve men, is determined by their roles as wives, girlfriends, sisters, mothers, or prostitutes. Entry into her husband's space confers no special status upon Mrs. Mahmoud. She is automatically defined by the raised forefinger on her husband's left hand, and although given no symbolic meaning in the text, in some Muslim countries the left hand is considered unclean and it is impolite to point or beckon with the index finger.[43] Therefore, not only has Mrs. Mahmoud been relegated to subservient status by cultural and historical practices that elevate the needs of men over those of women and children, but by signaling to her with his forefinger rather than speaking to her, Mr. Mahmoud has communicated that his wife has little worth.

This pathologizing of women and the reification of female stereotypes is directly related to Adrienne Rich's influential chapter on "Compulsory Heterosexuality and Lesbian Existence." Drawing on the work of British anthropologist Kathleen Gough, Rich argues that men have the power to (and I paraphrase just a few of Rich's renderings of Gough's original categories) deny women sexuality or force it upon them; command or exploit the labor/work of women as a way of controlling what they produce; and control women and/or rob them of their children. Rich used these observations to critique how male power is "manifested and maintained," often through the use of emotional and physical aggression.[44] *Fall on Your Knees* similarly critiques this troubling dynamic.

The storyline in MacDonald's novel hinges quite significantly on Gough's point that men have the power to control women or to rob them of their children. This is accomplished via enforced sterilization, using the courts to remove children from their mothers, or through "systematized infanticide," to name just a few of the methods noted in Gough's point.[45] This method of control is illustrated when James locks a pregnant Kathleen in the attic, thereby setting up a contrapassio or counter-suffering that is perhaps reflective of his own emotional imprisonment. As her father, and also as the man who raped her, James has full legal rights over his daughter and the twins who are born almost at the moment of her death. The narrative arc of Mac-Donald's novel points to a historical record that must be carefully rewritten, retold, and re-inked. This is accomplished through the voice of Frances Piper, the mostly unreliable narrator of the family history, yet the only one courageous enough to find, and then keep, her own powerful voice.

"Seeing"—from Where We're Standing: Intimate Relationships in Fall On Your Knees

In order to understand the intimate relationships in *Fall on Your Knees*, it is important to move beyond prosaic formulations of "seeing" as a purely mechanical function, through to what the more revelatory idea of *second sight* reveals about the construction of race, identity, and intimacy. It is this more nuanced way of seeing that underpins the complex meanings laid out in MacDonald's novel, particularly as this relates to sexual intimacy and the masquerading of queerness. What I mean by this is that as a Gothic tale, masquerade (which is in effect a type of misdirection) becomes the performance through which truth gains its foothold. In this way the links that I have drawn between the unseen yet intuited spaces in comics, alongside the diegetic levels in fiction, once again come to the fore through the story of the Pipers.

Lily Piper is the youngest in the family. Physically disabled at birth and, along with her twin brother, almost accidentally drowned by Frances, she is sweetly naïve and trusting. She is alternately taunted and protected by Frances and seen by James Piper as his "consolation."[46] Upon her father's/grandfather's death, and after digging up the tiny remains of her dead twin brother, Lily is sent away on a quest. She has a special pair of red boots that were made for her by James to make less noticeable her uneven gait, money pressed upon her by Frances, who is the one forcing her out of the nest, and possession of her dead mother's/sister's diary which will eventually lead her to Rose Lacroix. It is long after she has taken up her new life with Rose that her nephew—the mixed-race son of Frances who was spirited away at birth by Mercedes and placed in the "Novia Scotia Home for Coloured Children"—also arrives in New York seeking answers to impossible questions.[47]

Though not explicitly named as such in the novel, the "veil"—most commonly known in African American spiritual literature by its appellation "second sight"—works to hide that which is in plain sight. It is a metonym for subterfuge, protection, liminality and misdirection. Alternately obscuring and revealing truths, it almost always has some mystical properties associated with it, investing the chosen with the ability to see or divine things that others cannot.[48] Yet while Lily knows *how* to see, she is too young to fully understand *what* it is that she sees and experiences. Mercedes—whose "visions" are fancifully self-induced through endless tedious rituals of penitent prayer—thinks she is able to interpret Lily's experiences. On a clandestine outing to locate Frances, their ever-wayward sister, Mercedes believes she knows that Lily "is being guided," although there is no proof or further illumination of this in the novel.[49] But later on Mercedes says to Frances, "You know […] one thing looks pretty much like another."[50] Her comment is made while she and Frances are observing Lily in the garden. Frances decides that Lily is praying but Mercedes is not convinced. It is in this way that misdirection works. Through manipulation, subtle suggestion, or even overt trickery, it aims to recalibrate our thinking in order to destabilize (or reinforce) our most cherished beliefs. This double way of "seeing" (and/or being *seen*) is evident throughout this Gothic novel and it opens up discursive pathways that encourage divergence from the patriarchal center.

Betrayal

Kathleen Piper's character is set up as emblematic of the type of society where playing by the rules is the default position for women. For men, the rules are there to be changed, amended, flouted. Kathleen happens to be her father's favorite daughter, destined, he hopes, for stardom on the operatic stage, but her happiness is nevertheless conditional upon his benevolence. He loves, and is also *in love* with Kathleen, whom he sees as representative of a new kind of woman.[51] But he is shocked when he discovers that the "New Woman" he had in mind when he envisioned Kathleen's future was apparently not the same one he had sent off with such high hopes to New York. Even after he rapes Kathleen and she eventually dies after giving birth to twins, James has convinced himself that someone else sullied her reputation. Blaming himself for allowing her to go to New York on her own, he believes he could have prevented her from falling under the spell of "Other" forces, from getting pregnant, from sullying her reputation.[52] One can only infer that he means *he* never would have raped his own daughter. That Kathleen was beginning to live out her father's dreams for her in ways he never could have imagined leads to her complicated relationship with Rose Lacroix.

When Kathleen first meets Rose at the studio of her voice teacher, Rose is dressed primly "in a pale pink dress perfect for a dear little thing with an open face and a trusting nature, and therefore all wrong on Rose."[53] While there is acknowledgment that Rose is an accomplished pianist, Kathleen is so enamored of her own special talents that only grossly incompetent piano accompaniment would draw her attention.[54] She sees Rose as nothing more than background support to her developing musical career. Yet when Kathleen does deign to consider Rose, she sees her through her choice of dress rather than as a complex human being whose style of dress deliberately misdirects others from getting too close or from making assumptions about who she is as a black woman.[55]

Outwardly Kathleen and Rose are worlds apart yet they share a mutual love of music. By day Rose plays classical compositions as Kathleen's accompanist but by night she lives another life, far different from any that Kathleen has ever known, or, more precisely, different from anything Kathleen has consciously acknowledged. Having become exceptionally skilled in the art of misdirection (her innocent manner of dress, the living she makes from playing classical music, her standoffish behavior, which could be interpreted as "knowing her place"), Rose is thus able to create an easy narrative for her white observers that does not impinge upon their limited view of the world.

My reading of Kathleen and Rose Lacroix's relationship is based on questions about how we see and interpret the complex lives of women of color whose identities often hinge on *how* or *if* they are seen by others and/or how they see themselves. With the exception of Materia, the Piper women appear to be largely protected by their white skin. Yet in reality, their outwardly white appearance (or what they want other people to see) has caused them to unconsciously distance themselves from their Lebanese heritage. They are unable to think beyond the whiteness of their skin to who they really are, so instead they choose to exist under false pretenses. They press up against, and sometimes even manage to push through, these fictions, but mostly they are trapped in their own distorted reflections.

Kathleen and Rose's eventual sexual relationship begins and evolves with Kathleen as the initiator and pursuer. In a beautiful scene set not too long after Kathleen and Rose first become sexually intimate, both are acutely aware of their growing attraction to each other. They are also mindful of the need for caution, as there is no defined space they can inhabit which acknowledges their kind of relationship. They are forced to push against, and also subvert, the boundaries established by heteronormative rules and they do this—like so many others before and since—by locating a public/private space where they can express their forbidden love.

There is a scene where Rose and Kathleen stroll through New York's Central Park, which at the turn of the century was still known as Seneca Village, an established area that just happened to be "one of the principle black settlements in New York City."[56] The irony of course is obvious. Both Rose and Kathleen are mixed-race, yet it is 1918 New York, a time when it would have still been quite unusual for blacks and whites to be seen socializing together in public. Even though Kathleen and Rose are two women out for a seemingly innocent walk, the fact of their gender (and outwardly different races) places them in opposition to how public/private space is regulated. As Nancy Duncan notes in "Renegotiating Gender and Sexuality in Public and Private Spaces," the "public-private distinction is gendered."[57] In fact, it would have been unusual for a woman to engage in public sex with another woman during this time period, as cruising was still very much a male activity.[58] If there was any crossing of geographical or sexual boundaries at all, this often took the form of "slumming" and both men and women engaged in this activity.[59]

As they stroll through the park, Kathleen and Rose eventually happen upon a secluded place, "a thicket that you enter like a rabbit."[60] And having planned ahead, they bring a blanket and "choke-cherry wine."[61] To reach this secluded spot, they have to enter the thicket on hands and knees before they reach a point where they can stand upright, and the reward is that there is nothing but the stars looking back at them.[62] But what is hidden in plain sight—the thicket as a visually coded space, the whiteness of Kathleen's skin, and perhaps even a presumption that dark-skinned Rose is her chaperone or trusted servant—turns on misdirection. It is based on the notion that as long as what we see is close enough to our own sense of reality, then we do not have to acknowledge the "strange" within the parameters of the familiar.

Both women, emboldened in this liminal space between truth and illusion, are undeterred by the danger of discovery, for neither are strangers to the desire that consumes them. The thicket (and the opening—like that of a woman's sex—to its deeper recesses) work as interconnecting signifiers that at once describe the prohibitions against lesbian love, yet at the same time offer protection from discovery. As a metaphorical bridge between two diegetic levels, the thicket represents a temporal space that can be conceptually linked to the sub-textual aspects of women's sexual and social agency. Furthermore, by being with a woman in ways that only another woman can be, we see that Kathleen has a chance to reclaim parts of herself that she does not consciously realize have been lost.

Crawling into the thicket requires a conscious process of decision-making for both women. For Kathleen, a young woman whose entire life has been shaped by the hand of her father, her desire for another woman disrupts every social convention drilled into her from birth. For Rose, whose inability to "pass" through the cover of night or the light of day as anything other than a servant to the wishes of others, her defiance of social and sexual mores frames the thicket as a reminder of her daily struggle to make herself small and inconspicuous. Thinking at first that each sexual encounter with Rose would make her "calmer" and "surer,"[63] it could be said that Kathleen instead experiences an imbalance of her psychic equilibrium. Unable to figure out the connection between her desire for Rose and her opposing physical reaction of nausea, Kathleen only knows that what she feels can only be reconciled through intimate contact.[64] In unpacking the symbolism in this particular scene, it would be difficult to separate the physical feelings described here from the social conventions that would brand both women as sexual deviants. Being discovered would have devastating consequences for both women.

The consolation that Kathleen experiences while pressed against the length of Rose's body is in conflict with the relatively privileged upbringing her outwardly white skin affords her. Loving Rose in such an intimate way, even if no one can see them in the space they inhabit, introduces two clear dynamics. One is around race in public/private spaces, and the other around forbidden sexual desire. These dynamics are in turn a mirror reflecting back the complex issues queer women of color face not only in this novel, but also in real life, outside of contemporary fictional works. By hiding her blackness in "plain sight," Kathleen's public/private self doubles back on her and one has to wonder who, or what, she is hiding from.

In this next scene, the dual consciousness that Kathleen experiences while making love to Rose represents her internal struggle to reconcile the competing messages she feels compelled to separate into hierarchies of acceptable and unacceptable behavior. By imagining that she is healing Rose, as one might were her lover "a soldier fallen in" a "field," Kathleen has unconsciously characterized their forbidden trysts as an act of mercy.[65] Yet when her "fingers slide against beautiful Rose, when they swell her to a sweet unfolding and she puffs out like a sail,"[66] the scene becomes a prelude to Kathleen and Rose's *Stretto*, their overlapping sexual fugue playing out in closely staggered rhythms. The metaphor of a fallen soldier being healed by touch, as well as the image of a head tilted at an angle, appears in different places in the novel in seemingly unconnected ways, as if it is a loop of music catching up with itself at strategic locations along a notational score. The text effectively sets Rose's character up as counterpoint, as a steady melodic refrain to Kathleen's newfound lyricism.

The desire that makes Rose's body respond so surely to Kathleen's touch is born of the queer musicality of what they are creating together. These private moments shared by Kathleen and Rose are a sort of counterpoint to the treatment of jazz itself within the narratological *fugue*[67] that Trish Salah deploys to situate her argument at the juncture of music, race, and sexual orientation—fugue in this sense acting as a type of contrapuntal composition *with* narratology. Salah suggests that *Fall on Your Knees* "[...] codes ethno-cultural and sexual identity through the metonymic figure of music."[68] What she does not fully draw out, however, or at least not in a way that adequately problematizes the conflation of race, music, and sexual expression in regards to Rose's character, is how abjection acts as foreclosure to the life Rose deserves to have as a talented pianist and also as a lesbian.

The only roles made available to Rose were first as a reluctant enabler of her white mother's drug habit and then as a male cross-dresser taking on the disguise of heteronormativity. She did this so that Kathleen's desire to immerse herself in black music—and perhaps reclaim her own black self—could be satisfied. She was also the wounded daughter coming to hard realizations about her mother's possessiveness, and finally she was "Doc Rose," the "male" jazz musician whom Lily finds at the end of her pilgrimage.[69] It could be said that the masks donned by Rose, either for protection or as artifice, represent the inadequacy of a single system of language to describe many and multiple things. Here, Trish Salah seems to suggest that where social conventions restrict or curtail the free expression of one thing (sexual orientation, ethnicity, knowledge), music can give voice to a language otherwise forbidden or forgotten in service to higher linguistic, semiotic, or *narrative* conventions.[70] And while I agree with Salah to some extent, I contend that the jazz and blues references in the novel alternately act as a series of complex narrative notations that happen to be set to music and also as a fugue of loss that will never be recovered or resolved. Music has at once opened up new vistas for Rose and Kathleen, but it has also become the vehicle through which Rose remains mired in grief over a lover who will literally be ripped from her arms.

The cultural and ethnic roots of the characters, as well as realities that are reworked as fugue-induced-psycho-musical-narratives, place Rose and Kathleen in closer psychic alignment to each other than they had thought possible. We see this when Kathleen, overcome by a type of music that she has only ever heard before from her mother, enjoys her first fully unguarded moment with Rose. The piece begins at a slow tempo but then quickly builds to "a big thumping tune" similar to what Kathleen had heard streaming out of the windows of the church Rose attended.[71] Whirling and dancing and then just jumping up and down to the increasingly fast pace of Rose's playing, Kathleen mimics the dance style she had "seen the hep cats do," believing she had "brought Mecca into the classroom!"[72]

This brief and joyous reconnection to the part of herself she has lost or never really known allows Kathleen to use her body as a conduit for the language her father has forbidden her Lebanese mother to speak. Through her fugue-state she brings Mecca into the room, calling up ancient words for the music Rose Lacroix is coaxing out of the piano. And in words her sisters had known were only to be spoken "between them and Mumma," like "*Ya aa'yni, te'berini*" and "*bezzella*" and "*roz*," Kathleen's unself-conscious dancing is not so unlike her mother's own remembered "*dabke*," languid movements that Materia had learned from her own mother.[73]

Performed in separate unguarded moments by mother and daughter, their memory-fugue is indicative of the unexpected liberatory refrains at work in the novel. It is a movement that retraces cultural markers that have been lost to the dominance of white hegemonic paradigms. It is the Piper women's memory-fugue, their woman-dance bringing them together over distances created by what they have each been made to believe is foreign within themselves. There are no men to watch or judge, no rules except those that keep them moving, no punishment, banishment, or mockery. Even in death, which is where their story begins, the seductive master narratives of racial and class superiority will not see them silenced.

Phallocentric Rings: The Heterosexual Imperative in Private/Public Space

The ruptures in and buckling of space generated by what Hilde Staels suggests is the "patriarchal domination resulting from man's fear of the other sex, specifically his anxiety about women's transgression within dominant bourgeois society's sex-gender system"[74] is at the crux of the problems in the Piper family. They can be understood in terms of the "phallocentric rings" I mentioned earlier on, which I use here as a term that seeks to illustrate the stratification between men and women as portrayed in MacDonald's novel. The basic concept as I use it here is based both on Lacan's notion that the "phallus is the privileged signifier" and also on Derrida's argument that what he terms "phallogocentrism" elevates the masculine (or phallic) point of view in the construction of meaning and social relations.[75] My own coinage of "phallocentric rings" extends Derrida's notion in line with Irigaray's famous feminist intervention to argue that *Fall on Your Knees* introduces questions that are inextricably linked to phallocentrism and the "ownership" of bodily and emotional "knowing."[76] Ultimately, Irigaray invites us to move beyond didactic critiques of phallocentrically-oriented systems by considering that

> [...] what is important is to disconcert the staging of representation according to *exclusively* [emphasis belongs to Irigaray] "masculine" parameters, that is, according to a phallocratic order. It is not a matter of toppling that order so as to replace it—that amounts to the same thing in the end—but of disrupting and modifying it, starting from an "outside" that is exempt, in part, from phallocratic law.[77]

In heeding Irigaray's call to disrupt and modify the "phallocratic order,"[78] I approach phallocentrism from a different angle by critiquing the construction of interlocking "rings" of phallocentric systems, and how these rings are weakened through the subversive acts of the women of color in *Fall on Your Knees*. I contend that the phallocentric point of view (incorporated into laws, religion, and social customs) illustrates how women of color are particularly bound up in heterosexual imperatives and how re-shaping and re-naming phallocentric spaces and epistemologies via the signifying sign of misdirection can introduce new and more affirming realities.

If we can visualize phallocentrism as a series of interlocking "rings" that are comprised of religiosity, reproduction and race, we can begin to understand the complex work involved in undertaking subversive literary strategies that seek to uncover and legitimize alternative lived realities. This homologous structuring of phallocentrism as "rings" which are comprised of signifiers that reinforce and support hierarchical paradigms is important to an understanding of power and how it is used to oppress and divide those outside the patriarchal center. Thus, this section establishes where the center is in *Fall on Your Knees* and what happens at the outer edges.

A prime example of power imbalances between the male and female characters in the novel is illustrated mid-way through when, after receiving an anonymous letter suggesting that Kathleen has been taken in by the most unsavory elements of the big city, James rushes to New York to force her to return home. That he catches her *in flagrante delicto* with her black lover makes his disappointment and rage all the more dangerous. He sees Kathleen's "spray of red-gold hair upon the pillow," her hands caressing the back of her black lover and "disappearing beneath the waistband" of the trousers that Rose wears.[79] Incensed, he hears his daughter's moans of pleasure and watches her lover moving between her thighs. Mistaking Rose's gender-bending pinstripe trousers and exposed black skin as belonging to a man, James snatches her up by her small frame and hurls her out of the room. This violent rupture of the queer(ed) space that Kathleen and Rose Lacroix have made together is all the more disturbing because the text sets up cues that trigger a visceral response in the reader. That response—be it one of sympathy, rage, disbelief—is, however, contingent upon the reader's understanding of the risks involved in creating one's own safe haven.

The violent acts that James directs towards Rose and Kathleen reflects the contestation of the public/private divide. This is important, because as Nancy Duncan notes in "Renegotiating Gender and Sexuality in Public and Private Spaces," the political and spatial dimensions of the public and private dichotomy are "frequently employed to construct, control, discipline, confine, exclude and suppress gender and sexual difference preserving traditional patriarchal and heterosexist power structures."[80] In other words, and as underscored by Gough's eight characteristics of male power, space is heavily regulated. This is illustrated in the text when James arrives in Greenwich Village and finds his elderly cousin's apartment door unlocked and slightly ajar. He enters, immediately describes one of the rooms as an "old-lady parlour,"[81] hears laughter, discovers Kathleen and Rose, and takes control by putting his masculine mark on what he is conditioned to perceive as *unregulated* women's space.

James had sent Kathleen off to New York for professional voice lessons and eventual stardom on the classical stage, and he did so with the confidence that his spinster cousin would be an appropriate chaperone to his most prized possession. Thus, it could be said that in the way he perceived his cousin's celibate life, he also mistakenly assumed that her apartment would be a sexually neutral zone. In this way the cleverly phrased "code" words in the anonymous letter James had received turned on morality and a responsibility to maintain racial "purity" in a world that was rapidly being taken over by undesirables.[82]

The invasion of women's space and the dissonance MacDonald creates by describing Kathleen's "spray of red-gold hair upon the pillow," followed almost immediately by a description of her (white) "hands travelling over a black back," is deployed in an almost metastatic way, as if to initially draw the reader unthinkingly into and quickly beyond the familiarity of heteronormatively produced spaces, but then shock us with the force of James Piper's rage at seeing his daughter's whiteness—and, upon later reflection, her heterosexuality—violated.[83]

These ethno-hetero-cultural signifiers produce two very specific responses from James. He must reassert his authority; first as a father protecting his daughter and second as a white man upholding the racial order against a presumed "black threat," which is made clear in an earlier exchange that James has with Leo Taylor, a young black teenager (who is later tricked by Frances into impregnating her) he has hired to chauffeur Kathleen to and from school. James is at once protecting his "property" by hiring a driver for Kathleen, but also reminding Leo of the fate that awaits him if he crosses the line. "I don't want you talking to her," James tells Leo. "Don't touch her," he goes on to admonish. "I'll kill you," he finally says.[84]

James understands only too well that to witness another "man" (especially a black one) inscribe a different heteronormative "code" onto his daughter's white flesh in a presumptively white space cannot go unchallenged. Kathleen's transgression against her father is also—in James's mind—a transgression against nature, against the laws of God and decency, and a violation against patriarchy itself. That Kathleen has finally, through her thoughtless rejection of her father's sacrifices, opened herself up in his mind for the sexual desire he has held back for so many years, compels him to brutally rape her, drag her back to Cape Breton, and lock her in the attic where another chapter of her life both begins (she has twins) and ends (she dies in childbirth). James thus *re-encircles* Kathleen in the phallocentric rings of ownership guaranteed to him by law.

This dominant positioning, and reassertion of patriarchal authority, echoes Hélène Cixous's observations on the historical censorship of the female body and voice in literature. In "The Laugh of the Medusa," Cixous challenges women to take up the pen and write themselves back into existence, to resist patriarchal codes of what a woman can or should be, and to never again be "kept in the dark" or "led into self-disdain by the great arm of parental-conjugal phallocentrism."[85] But Kathleen had misread these patriarchal codes. She grew up smug in the belief that the rules holding the patriarchal center together did not apply to her, and so she was unprepared for the violence visited upon her by the very man who had allowed her to nurture this belief in the first place.

Raised by James to expect the best in life, to pass for something she was not, to be his creation, his triumph, his legacy, Kathleen becomes no more than a favored pet living inside a gilded cage. The space she inhabits was never traversable, never truly hers. It was instead a quagmire, a misdirecting performance enacted from the patriarchal center. It was a performance that she became accustomed to, one that she chose to believe, and one that eventually resulted in an indictment of her queerness, her unclaimed blackness, and her gender. Yet while James is raping his daughter, while he allows his obsession with her to consume him, he fails to notice how she resists. By allowing the space that she and Rose created together to buckle in on itself and disappear in the silent life she will adopt from that point forward, her silence becomes her resistance. By ignoring her father's entreaties that she allow him to protect her, to tell her "*after* [italics mine] how much he loves her,"[86] she has foreclosed his *after* by going mute.

The voice her father has come to love, to nurture, to listen for during his every waking hour is no longer his to shape or coax forth. "She has stopped screaming [...]," her voice denying him the full access to a place that he has craved almost from the moment she was born.[87] By ignoring her father's pleas for her to submit to him, Kathleen has refused to participate in his reclamation of *her* space as phallocentrically defined. Symbolically, she has weakened the first phallocentric "ring" and de-stabilized the center upon which the heterosexual imperative relies. It is this imperative that eventually becomes her father's contrapassio, as noted in the following passages.

The reader is told that James has broken through the locked attic door where Kathleen has given birth, once again violating women's space to assert his authority. His wife stands over her daughter's lifeless body, holding "two dripping infants trussed by the ankles, one in each hand, like a canny shopper guesstimating the weight of a brace of chickens."[88] It is here that the ekphrastic phrasing in the following scene brilliantly captures the moment when James acknowledges, and finally accepts, his own self-imprisonment.

> This is not a gauzy Victorian death scene. No fetishized feminine pallor, no agnostic slant of celestial light, no decorously distraught husband. This portrait is in livid colour. A crucified Christ hangs over a metal-frame single bed. On either side of the crucifix are two small pictures: one is of the Virgin Mary exposing her sacred heart aflame, the other is of her son Jesus, his heart likewise exposed and pierced to precious blood by a chain of thorns. They look utterly complaisant, Mother and Son. They have achieved a mutual plateau of exquisite suffering.[89]

This key scene in the novel at once contrasts and synthesizes the excesses of its violent patriarchial intimacies. It draws on the conventions of the Gothic narrative by describing suffering as a kind of theater of the surreal, while at the same time elevating religious pain/death over that of the secular. Death becomes an event replete with thorns, crucifixes, and blood. But neither the secular nor the religious is complete without reference to the other, for both represent staged excess. Thus it is in this way that James is struck through with the gravity of what he has done. No longer able to explain away or romanticize the rape of his daughter, the horror he is confronted with is Gothic's ultimate staging.

If the ghoulish scene of Kathleen's last moments "were really a painting, there would also be a demon peering out from under the lid of the hope chest at the foot of the bed, looking to steal the Young Mother's Soul."[90] But the reader already knows that Materia called up the demon long ago, when Kathleen was still an infant. She made a bargain that if "the demon [...] limit[s] itself to one daughter," she would sacrifice Kathleen when the time comes.[91] One has to wonder if this demon conjured up from the depths of despair also struck a Faustian bargain with James, for how else does one explain the evil lurking in the hearts and souls of men who lust after their own children. But James wants to be rid of the image he has seen, the one he had a hand in creating. He thinks that if he can bury his memories there will be some reprieve, realizing of course that it is an unworkable solution because "you can't stuff a memory of a moment into a real-life hope chest as if it were a family heirloom."[92] He momentarily believes that he is looking at "an old portrait that he hid in the hope chest many years ago and stumbled upon again."[93] However, what he comes to understand is that his "temporary confusion is a premonition; it tells him that he will never get over this sight [...] it will be as fresh fourteen years from now, the colours not quite dry, just as it is today."[94] Although Kathleen is dead, by retelling and reshaping her story with the mortar of their own particular memories, the Piper sisters are able to send their sister, once more whole, into the afterlife.

Rosaries and the Glory of God

Religion plays a major role in MacDonald's novel. It is at once instructive (leading those who adhere to its tenets to an awareness of something larger than themselves), but also tautological in that it is a self-reinforcing belief practiced by the already converted. Mercedes is one of the faithful. She is the second oldest daughter in the Piper family, the pious one who is joined to God in her lonely and plain life. She discovers at an early age that acquiescence to God, and to her father, are the two safest options available to her as the self-appointed rescuer and peacemaker in the family. Even before she could speak her "little white-gloved hands" were "folded around her very own rosary beads."[95] Yet as she gets older and gains awareness, her alternately obsequious and conniving actions turn out to be the things that both endanger, and protect, her sisters.

Mercedes is the one who first witnesses her father's molestation of Frances, although she was too young at the time to understand exactly what it was that she saw. When she is older, and upon her mother's death, which is followed closely on the heels of the almost simultaneous birth of the twins and Kathleen's death in childbirth, the surviving twin (Lily) is baptized at home. When considering the promise that godparents will step in if anything happens to the parents, Mercedes tells herself, "I'm the mother now."[96] This silent promise is taken to the extreme years later when justifying her decision to place Frances's newly born mixed-race son in an orphanage, and this naïve sense of duty plays out in the form of blurred boundaries. Mercedes has convinced herself that "once Frances has a child" she "will no longer need a mother."[97] In many ways, the violation of boundaries acts as the narrative bridge in the novel, connecting seemingly random events together. It seems right then that Mercedes is introduced thusly: "this is a picture of Mercedes, holding her opal rosary, with one finger raised and pressed against her lips. She's saying 'Shshsh.'"[98] Symbolic of the most recognizable type of acquiescence to phallocentrism, it can be said that rosaries (and even Mercedes's "Shshsh"ing) represent interlocking rings that foreclose questions or access to the negotiation of (bodily) space or personal choices. If we extend the symbolism of the rosary to that of an unquestioned commitment to Christ, whose teachings are often misinterpreted and used to prop up and sustain phallocratic societies, we understand Mercedes's limited options as a woman.[99] Indeed, if we place her love of God and her prayers to Him via the symbolism of the rosary as a devotional act, we can understand the power of what the Church calls Christocentric prayer, or that which centers theologically on Christ. Viewed through the lens of gender, feminist and queer theory, the rosary can also be interpreted as symbolizing the ultimate phallocentric ring or "chain"[100]—a primary ring, I contend, that must be weakened in order for the rest to give way.

Perhaps it is also accurate to say that not only is it the indeterminacy or ambiguousness of the "Shshsh" that is at once reflective of Mercedes's role as inept protector of her younger siblings, but also a nod to the deeply buried secrets of the Piper family. Thus in a larger sense, the "Shshsh" is an exhortation for women to become complicit in their violation, as we come to understand so well when James is raping Kathleen. She is limp in his arms and her face is bruised and swelling. And although her father has raped her she is the one who is "racked with shame," pleading with him to allow her to get dressed, to cover herself.[101] But her father's focus remains on his sexual needs, his power over his young daughter, in exhorting her to "Shshsh," to acquiesce, to believe that everything will be fine. "Shshsh" precludes a knowing of anything except what is presented as the truth, as reality, as the price to be paid for the space women inhabit. Therefore the question here must be which of the Piper women had an awareness of their own power as a disruptive force? I argue that it was Frances, the one who was most often the object of her father's rage, the one who most directly challenged patriarchal conventions by standing her ground and refusing to be broken. She refused the "Shshsh," the exhortations to be good, the power of men over her body, and in this way she became symbolic of radical female resistance.

Resistance in Eighths and Half Notes

In this section I examine the complex interplay between subtle acts of resistance in male-dominated spaces and overt defiance that often results in the violent suppression of women. I contend that agency is, or can be, as Toni Morrison suggests, "[...] knowledge transformed from invasion to conquest to revelation and choice."[102] Of all the Piper women, Frances seems to be the one who understands the intricacies of power better than the others. She contests the authority of her father in ways that few men would attempt, introducing a destabilizing effect on his position as family patriarch, which eventually results in his displacement as the figurehead of the family.

Frances's character is enigmatic. She is promiscuous, unpredictable, defiant, unreadable, self-destructive, calculating, and smart. Throughout the novel, her actions exemplify contestations of heterosexual space described by Gill Valentine as a performance that "in a way [...] produces (an)other space."[103] She sneaks behind her father's back to take a job in a speakeasy, and her mission in life seems to be to disrupt, tear down, and then recalibrate space according to her own interpretations of form and function. She engages in these subversive recalibrations by adopting an over-the-top, rough-hewn, and world-weary sexual persona during her performances at the speakeasy, as we see when she "wriggles out of her" school "uniform and down to her skivvies" while doing the "highland fling cum cancan" to the tune of "Coming thru' the Rye."[104] After her first impromptu performance lands her the job at the speakeasy, she eventually begins charging money for the hand jobs she gives to inebriated men around the back of the club. However dangerous this particular revenue maker is for her, she never forgets to don the "special glove she wears, left over from her first communion."[105] It is indeed a fitting gesture given the crimes of the flesh that men commit in the name of God.

By using the relative power attached to her father's name to gain entry into an illegitimate way of life, Frances has openly defied social norms by rewriting the rules of engagement. Where the limits of her gender have been determined by the spaces controlled by men, and in which women are expected to perform in certain ways, she has managed to reclaim this space through her mockery of it. In those moments when she wiggles and dances and shimmies, expertly directing the male gaze exactly where she wants it, she alone determines how she will be seen. She changes the angle of the male gaze, situating it at the periphery of the central space she has momentarily claimed as her own.

Ironically, and towards the end of her father's life, Frances is the one who becomes his confidante and his confessor. But during his life she is the one he brutalizes the most. In an extremely disturbing act of violence that James directs towards Frances, we are made to believe he is punishing her for displaying the only photograph that remains of Kathleen. In reality, I submit that he is punishing himself for having violated sexual boundaries. That Frances is actually taking the blame for Mercedes, who—up to this point— has never stood up to her father on behalf of Frances, makes the beating all the more disturbing. The brutal assault in the following passage is constructed as a type of macabre dance performance. The assault is set to measured beats that underscore the deliberateness of James's violent control over his children. The setting is a shed, a male space, where the physical punishment he metes out to Frances has a "thump now and then like a bass drum with a foot-pedal at work inside it keeping the beat."[106]

The "performance" referred to above is an ancient rite passed down from father to son. It is a heterosexual imperative, a legal and social mandate to preserve order, to subdue the "Other," be they real or Gothically imagined. MacDonald's structuring of these scenes as a form of dance makes it all the more horrific to take in because there is an implied beauty in music that is wholly absent in acts of violence. James is methodical in his brutality, grabbing Frances by "her neck till she's on point" and thrusting "her back against the wall [...]."[107] The sexual undertones of this dance are unmistakable. Just as one might delight in the fulsomeness of an embrace that leads to the sweetness of a lingering kiss, so too is James's violence measured out in "eighth-notes" at the head and "half-note[s] [...]" lighting "up her pale face."[108] This is at once the *acciaccatura*,[109] contained in the wordless struggle between James and his daughter, for they are locked in Prudontius's *psychomachia*,[110] with James playing the role of the (good) father who feels it is his duty to impose rules upon his (evil) daughter. He does this, one might surmise, to save her from destruction. Yet this uneasy and brutal relationship breeds contempt, not acquiescence. Nevertheless, James fails to sense this shift and he continues, oblivious to his own emotional imprisonment.

Between breaths James says to Frances, "What right have you, you have no right, no right to even speak her name, who's the slut, tell me who's the slut!"[111] But she does not answer him and so the "performance" continues from the first and "into the second movement," a do-si-do where James swings Frances "from the wall into the workbench," followed by a "*staccato* across the face..."[112] Here, the musical theme is overtly linked to issues of (un)speakability, the forbidden, and also violence. Indeed, James's assertion that "I don't want to hear you speak her name" is intended to remind Frances of his power to deny her the memory of her own sister.[113] This scene reflects on the loss of Kathleen to both James and Frances, but it also depicts James in his endless revisions of the real nature of his relationship with Kathleen, as well as his fruitless efforts to blame Frances for reminding him of that which he has destroyed. He does not know how to deal with defiance, except by trying to force acquiescence. He asks Frances if she understands him, but what he is really admitting is that she has chosen *not* to understand him. Thus it is what is described in the last two passages that clue the reader into not only the deadliness of James's resolve, but Frances's control of the very space in which he assaults her. Her resistance to what the shed denotes (male space, power) also points to her control over him.

The performance of violence, this chilling tête-à-tête between father and daughter, obscures the boundaries between parental discipline and rage. When James announces to Frances that he will extract the ultimate price for her impertinence by cutting out her tongue, she challenges him by actually sticking out her tongue.[114] By mocking her father's authority with so simple an act, Frances has not only reconfigured the grids of power, she has also destabilized the phallocentric order. And because of Frances's refusal to submit, she has, in a sense, disrupted what Alison Blunt and Gillian Rose describe as the "power relations of gendered identity."[115] Not only has Frances subverted her father's personal space, but she has also broken his hold over her.

An example of Frances's escape from her father's authority is when she sets out to get expelled from school so that she can take the job at the speakeasy. Her father finds out, but as he stands over her and "raises his hand," she "doesn't wince" or "look up [...] she [...] just reaches for Lily's fork and starts eating."[116] He suddenly realizes he is tired and that violence will no longer work as a way of controlling Frances. He drops his hand, telling her not to bring whatever she is involved in home. Thus the second phallocentric "ring" has been weakened.

The Racial Imperative: Race and Self-Loathing

Perhaps more than her sisters, Frances signifies everything that is uncontrollable in her father's world. She is, he believes, intent on bringing into the light his most shameful transgressions, his hypocrisy, and his inconsequential life. She is the "blackness" that rebukes him, the "Otherness" of which he is most fearful, the invisible stain that threatens his desperate claims to whiteness and, conversely, to the very blackness that he abhors. Yet there was a time when his Lebanese wife was capable of making him sing her a "Gaelic lullaby which made him cry because, if such a thing was possible, he loved her more in his mother tongue [...]."[117] But almost too soon in the marriage

James begins to think of Materia as "bovine"[118] and as someone whose "dark body and soft mind allowed him to enjoy her in an uncomplicated way."[119] Materia exists to respond to her husband's wishes, to take care of *his* children (for he has forbidden her to lay claim to, or call up their Lebanese heritage), and to ask no questions.

By reducing his wife—whom he once thought of as beautiful—to the level of a ruminant animal who "eats her own supper, then eats Kathleen's," and who is "stooped over her plate, masticating slowly," James's thinking underscores two tropes that fuel and perpetuate racist stereotypes.[120] The first is the old fallacy of biological determinism that claims that blacks are not as evolved as whites. The second is what writer Richard Hardack suggests as the black body being set up as a "site of" an "endless dialectic hierarchy."[121] This question of race, lineage, and belonging appears repeatedly in the novel. For example, although Kathleen classifies herself as white, her classmates are happy to remind her of who she really is: "She may be peaches and cream," one of her classmates says to another, "but you should see her mother … black as the ace of spades, my dear."[122] Kathleen knows how her classmates feel about her and she wants nothing more than to be accepted by them, but race is the ultimate equalizer, and Kathleen's white skin affords her no protection from those who know her true background. She is Irish on her father's side and Lebanese on her mother's.

The Irish have a long and troubled history of being defined by their religion, cultural practice, and/or ethnicity. Noel Ignatiev points out in *How the Irish Became White* (1995) that as Catholics the Irish were known by such derogatory names as "Celts" or "Gaels" and "frequently spoke of themselves as a 'race,' rather than a nation."[123] Furthermore, race and class hierarchies in the eighteenth century were such that "penal laws imposed upon" the Irish a "caste status out of which no Catholic, no matter how wealthy, could escape."[124] Specifically, penal laws forbade the Irish from inter-marrying, holding political office, or serving in the military. Their religious worship was also restricted, although usually applied only to those who refused to take an oath of allegiance that would effectively have them deny their own identity.[125] In this regard, it would seem that the distance between the persecution of the Irish and blacks in the eighteenth century was noticeable only in the fine print of laws enacted that were specific to the American colonies and those coming from the English government in Ireland.

The Gothicization of race—replete with violence, omens, scandals, visions, and hauntings—has been served up to chilling effect by numerous writers, many focusing on the Victorian era.[126] Contemporary writers draw on elements of the genre to articulate larger narratives of social, ethnic, gender, religious, and political oppressions. Gothic formulations about "dark forces" (read: the black body), noble struggles (the white phallocracy), and particularly the Gothic as a tool of resistance by the oppressed[127] also help us understand how lesbians of color inhabit and survive in unwelcoming heteronormative spaces.[128] Thus the context in *Fall on Your Knees* can be understood in one of the lengthier exchanges Rose Lacroix and Kathleen Piper engage in shortly after their first real conversation on the fire escape in Rose's neighborhood.

Kathleen and Rose have just finished supper at the apartment Kathleen shares with her elderly cousin, Giles. This passage, an adumbration of the truth, is delivered by Kathleen to not only maintain her own illusion of who she believes herself to be, but also as an unconscious reinforcement of racial codes that are meant to keep blacks and whites separate. This is interesting because Kathleen is beginning to have feelings for Rose, although she cannot quite bring herself to fully accept what those feelings may be telling her about herself.

Kathleen waits for Rose to spot the photo of her parents that she keeps on the dresser in her bedroom. Rose asks who the people in the picture are and Kathleen identifies the man as her father.[129] This prompts Rose to ask about the woman in the photo, and Kathleen matter-of-factly identifies the woman as her mother, to which Rose expresses incredulity. Rose cannot believe that the woman in the photo is Kathleen's "natural mother," but Kathleen assures her that she is.[130] The conversation that ensues reveals Kathleen's willful ignorance about her own racial and cultural heritage, particularly regarding her mother's ethnic origins. Kathleen insists that her mother is Canadian and Lebanese, claiming that Lebanese people are "more Mediterranean, more European [...] not like Arabs."[131] But when Rose continues to express skepticism and comments that Kathleen's mother looks like she "musta come from inland," and that you "coulda fooled me," Kathleen takes umbrage by claiming she is not trying to fool anyone.[132] Rose responds by saying, "You look pure white," to which Kathleen replies, "I am pure white. My mother is white." "Not quite," Rose quips. "Well, she's not coloured," Kathleen asserts.[133]

By distancing herself from her Lebanese heritage, Kathleen rationalizes the loss of that part of herself by *naming* James as her father, thereby laying claim to her whiteness through him. Her naming is an act of situating herself on the "normative" side of race, yet it actually works to position her at a disadvantage with Rose. Her silence on identifying the woman in the picture as her mother until she is prompted to do so by Rose's question imbues her with the power (through her white father) to "un-name" her mother. Rose confronts

Kathleen on this by pointing out her dishonesty and the obvious embarrassment she feels about her mother's Lebanese heritage.

By introducing the specter of racial "Otherness" into the newness of their friendship, Kathleen's character calls up all of the fears and self-doubts she has internalized. Her ridiculous belief that she is "pure white," and contrary to all evidence that she shares genetic material with her dark-skinned Lebanese mother, Kathleen insists on claiming a different racial history. Her representation of herself aligns with the Euro-centric views of her father, no matter that both she and Rose are mixed race women. The difference, however, is that Rose is the inverse of Kathleen, in that her blackness is on the outside, whereas Kathleen's is on the inside where it is undetectable. Were Rose tempted to *claim* her whiteness as Kathleen has done, her dark skin would suggest that she is not only as delusional as Kathleen, but even more so because of her inability to shrug off one layer of identity for another.

The spectral qualities of race are also at work throughout the novel. Frances wakes one night to "a black woman staring down at her."[134] The woman (who turned out to be her mother escaped from the coal cellar where her husband had locked her) "reaches out and lightly strokes Frances's forehead. She does the same to Mercedes, and then leaves."[135] The apparition that Frances saw, or that she believed she saw, could be said to represent a subconscious acceptance of her racialized self. As the only obvious woman of color in the Piper family, the symbolism of Materia being covered in soot, indeed in blackface, should not go unremarked.

Materia's body has been colonized by history and also by her husband, who has stopped *seeing* her humanity. In an exchange he has with one of Materia's cousins, with whom he has some illegal business interests, James reflects on his feelings about the racialized "Other." He is perturbed that the illegal line of work he has reluctantly engaged in with Jameel requires him to come into contact with someone whom he believes to be so obviously inferior in both appearance and manner. When he looks at Jameel, all he sees is a man with "short black whiskers against a yellowish complexion" and "oily jet hair and the fussy smell of fried bread."[136] James positions Jameel under the category of "Otherness" by describing his ethnicity and racial features in negative terms. This allows him to renegotiate the value of their business exchange. What I mean by this is that by virtue of his whiteness, James has been programmed to believe in, and assert, a racial superiority over darker skinned people. This hierarchy of racial purity impacts on, and often determines, the outcome of any number of social and private interactions.

The above point is further illustrated when Leo Taylor's sister is fired for allegedly stealing items from Mr. Mahmoud's home. Although Frances was in fact the one who stole the items, Teresa is wrongly implicated and her reputation is tarnished. Even after the thefts from his home continue, and Mr. Mahmoud realizes he has made a mistake in accusing Teresa, she does not get her job back. In both his and James Piper's view, black skin places the "Other" in the default position of never being fully trustworthy. Even with his own dark skin, and a daughter who is married to Jameel, Mr. Mahmoud soothes himself with the thought that "the Jameels are Arab" and the Mahmouds are "more Mediterranean [...] closer to being European, really."[137] This self-negation, the denial of one reality in pursuit of another, is an affliction the characters in this novel seem particularly struck by. It is of note that Mr. Mahmoud's rationalizations echo those of Kathleen, the white-skinned granddaughter he has never really known. Both are culpable in their own erasure, yet neither has the insight to understand the psychic damage they are inflicting on themselves and on those they claim to love.

When James conflates his dealings with Jameel into his increasing alienation from his wife, he is unable to see anything beyond the small sphere of his own whiteness. Everything he says and does is predicated upon the value of white skin or the inherent power of whiteness itself, neither of which can penetrate the confusing darkness of the "Other." Perhaps this is why James did not see his wife hiding near the furnace in the coal cellar. He did not *have* to see her. Being of no racial or social value, Materia was simply a pair of restless eyes with no recognizable landscape upon which to alight. This disappearance of a once vibrant woman, dragged into the muck of the racial imperative, is significant because of its historical intractability. By classifying nearly everyone he comes into contact with by their race, culture, religion or social status—"Compared to Materia's family, the Luvovitzes seemed downright white"—James sets the stage for the numerous temporal ruptures this novel leads us into.[138]

James Piper's feelings about Materia, his incredulity at how he ended up married to her, how he had become "[...] ensnared by a child"[139] is justified by further marginalization of his wife as someone he cannot relate to. He makes her out to be the one who seduced him into the marriage, convincing himself that "normal children did not run away with men."[140] Putting it down to what he believes to be a flaw in her racial background allows James to absolve himself of any responsibility for the decisions they both made to elope. Racial privilege/rupture becomes a convenient way for James to divert attention away from the crimes he perpetrates against his dark-skinned wife, his daughters, and the *darkness* he senses in himself. By utilizing intersecting spheres of religiosity, reproduction, race and social order/politics to validate his transgressions, James can simultaneously erase and lay claim to

Kathleen, the object of his desire. Yet the weakening of the final phallocentric ring comes after a disagreement James has with Jameel over how their illicit business dealings should be handled and who James should take on as a new driver now that Leo Taylor has quit. This is news to James, who initially takes it in stride, but Jameel decides he has had enough of James's attitude and decides to taunt him by revealing what Frances has been up to.

"Fuck you Piper, you fuckin uppity sonofabitch, did you know you're supplying my place with Piper pussy, eh boy? And she's fuckin your precious spade, Leo Taylor?"[141] What is of note here is that Jameel, whose ethnicity and dark skin mark him as an outsider, just as much as the Pipers' Irish background brands them as different, is precisely the inescapable truth that haunts James. His wife is related to Jameel, and, by extension, so too are his beautiful white-skinned daughters. Thus it is no wonder that James is incensed, and upon arriving home slightly drunk, he retrieves the bayonet he had brought back with him from the war. Alarmed, and fearing that her father is going after Frances, no matter that he tells her he is "after the man who's been at her [...]," Mercedes places her hand over Lily's eyes, and when James turns to head down the stairs, she gives him a shove.[142] When she later douses James with ice-cold water to bring him back around, helping him to the couch where he promptly passes out again, the long ago memory of Frances being molested advances "steadily towards the front of her mind."[143] Later on, when Mercedes rouses her father again and he asks after Frances, she orders him to sit back down.

James is surprised by her tone of voice but does not move. She lies to him, telling him that she caught him trying to molest Lily and had to pull him off of her. He is sickened by this news, staggers to a half-crouch and leaves the house. Mercedes justifies her lie by thinking that she has "[...] rescued Frances. Finally."[144] But it would seem that it has been Mercedes who has been rescued from colluding in her own erasure. She has lived most of her life wrapped in the protective cocoon of religion and ignorance and was taught never to question authority. Her self-appointed role as the default mother in the household overrode her usual meekness, and she saw no other way to save Frances or herself than by retracing her own faltering steps towards a different truth.

Fall on Your Knees sets up useful insights into how representations of queer women of color are inextricably linked to the white-centric patriarchal center and how through acts of misdirection those links can be effectively disrupted. Situated firmly in the Gothic tradition, MacDonald's novel illustrates how agency for queer women of color is dependent upon careful negotiation of multiple realities and spaces that have been shaped by a history of racial oppression and sexual violence. These realities are often based upon complex and interlocking systems that center whiteness, religion, and patriarchy as definitive markers of unimpeachable morality in relation to the assumed immorality of the "Other." The tension between these long established terms of patriarchal privilege, and the enactment of misdirection through subversive acts of racial and/or sexual "passing," opens up alternative ways of "seeing" and being in the world. For the Piper women, breaking the "phallocentric rings" that had bound them to a false representational narrative, was the ultimate act of defiance.

Chapter 3

Queer(y)ing
the Punk Aesthetic
Reading Race, Desire
and Anarchism in Cristy C. Road's
Bad Habits *(2008)*

Stripped of identity, the bastard race teaches [us] about the
power of the margins...[1]

The previous chapter examined how Ann-Marie MacDonald's Gothic
novel cast a critical light on intersecting systems of oppression that have historically elevated whiteness and patriarchy to the material and psychological
detriment of the "queer(ed)" subaltern. Informed by visionary literary frameworks such as those developed by Nella Larsen and other writers of the
Harlem Renaissance, race and sexuality in MacDonald's novel are read as
alternately "fixed" categories, yet also unstable ones that can be challenged
through the enactment of subversive misdirecting performances.

In this chapter I turn to Cristy C. Road's auto(bio)graphically inspired
graphic novel to extend these arguments through the more contemporary
frame of DIY punk. I am interested here in how queer women of color in
DIY punk culture are represented, how they challenge the white nullifying
gaze from within and outside of the punk movement, how "queer" and "of
color" are discursively "performed" in punk culture, and how the ways in
which the visual/textual elements of the graphic narrative can facilitate alternative interpretations and understandings.[2]

Road's candid revelations about her life as a bisexual Cuban punk rocker
allow for wider interpretations and applications of punk beyond its own self-
reflexive borders. Utilizing misdirection in this chapter as a performative
tool located within the semiotic frame of auto(bio)graphic DIY punk, I show

that *Bad Habits* extends its conceptual reach through the indeterminate spaces where *of color* counter-narratives force a paradigm shift in our understanding of the queer(ed) subaltern. The character in this graphic narrative is Road's avatar. She is portrayed as a drug using, partying, sexually uninhibited punk who breaks every norm women are expected to uphold. She has sexual relationships with both men and women, searches for love and acceptance from her peers, rails against the two political systems that would have her deny or minimize one culture for the other, and eventually comes to understand that her truth does not turn on someone else's version of who she should be. Navigating the boundaries that tie her firmly to her Cuban heritage, but also to her adopted American identity, Road's character struggles to find a place where she truly belongs.

Road builds her story from a place of what Michael A. Chaney refers to as "autobiographical authority" in comics, a place, he insists, that is "constituted within, against, and sometimes between pictures and words."[3] There is a logical tie-in here to Chaney's description of autobiographical authority in comics and the authority that queer women of color express from the in-between spaces of their lived lives. From these spaces, Road expresses her *self* through a kind of scarification of the page, using inks, brushes, and pens to tell (and show) her personal truth. She makes no apologies for her choices or for the ambivalence she feels of trying to fit somewhere into mainstream culture while also embracing her outsider status.

Road was born in Miami, Florida, and her interest in punk culture (or, more specifically, in her favorite band, Green Day) first took shape through her publication of *Green'zine*, the fanzine she published from 1996 to 2004. In 2006 she turned to rendering her own life on the page with the publication of *Indestructible*, the first of her three graphic novels. It was followed by *Bad Habits* in 2008 and *Spit and Passion* in 2012. All three books chronicled her life as a punk rocker, a bisexual Cuban woman, an activist, and an artist. Relying almost exclusively on interior splash panels, two-page spreads, a few captions, and the occasional speech bubble, both *Indestructible* and *Bad Habits* are notable for the large number of text pages Road uses to progress her storylines. In contrast, *Spit and Passion* falls more solidly into the category of sequential art, in that it focuses more on the temporal and spatial techniques one typically finds in comics.[4] Black and white drawings feature in all three of her books. Cross-hatching is used liberally throughout to suggest shading and shadows, while the facades of buildings, newspaper headlines, posters, and the covers and spines of books contain words and symbols that, while not central to the storyline, provide important meaning to the overall narrative.[5]

As a prominent member of DIY punk subculture, Road has contributed her artwork and her voice to anthologies, readings, panel discussions, exhibitions, and zine fests. She has toured with Sister Spit, the lesbian-feminist spoken-word and performance art collective based in San Francisco, California. She also plays guitar and sings in The Homewreckers, her own pop-punk band whose lyrics are about "lost love, cultural gentrification getting in the way of the perfect date, Cuba, cops, gender, depression, the fight against slut-shaming, and reclaiming our sex organs."[6] Road's music and autobiographical confessions are, I contend, reflective of punk's *bricolage* of style, culture, and politics. Dick Hebdige asserts that bricolage is a useful term to "explain how subcultural styles are constructed."[7] The term does not, however, explain punk's own inherent gender and racial hierarchies that even within its purportedly anarchist framings often mimic the very binary and exclusionary systems it purports to reject. In her own words, Road is concerned "with maintaining the spirit of punk that made it a haven for angry girls and angry queers" and even for "angry straight guys who experience some kind of disenfranchisement and maybe have tough as nails mothers and a basic respect for women."[8] Yet Road also expresses conflicting emotions about DIY subcultures. On the one hand, she states that "punk" is "fucked up," and on the other she admits to being obsessed with it.[9]

This ambivalence is certainly not uncommon in subcultural movements or, for that matter, in adolescent angst, but when overlaid with racist and misogynistic constructions of difference, it can take on similarly oppressive practices to that which it rails against. Therefore when Road's character uses "throwing shit" as a euphemism for empowerment, for "overthrowing double standards that persist as blockades to keep us from moving forward," what she is describing has its source in complex gender, sexual, and racial hierarchies that derive power from who/what is excluded or different.[10] Her visual and written expressions construct a powerful argument against sexual, gender, racial, cultural, and political homogeneity, while at the same time advocating for the right to maintain vital connections with one's community.

Cristy confesses that she grew up "in a neighborhood so Cuban I thought white people were fictional characters on film and television."[11] Yet through acculturation, and "unlike my siblings," she states, she loses her accent because of her tendency to be a "loner [...] with no Cuban companions to influence my developing epiglottis and vocal folds."[12] But in a bid to recuperate strands of her identity, she dredges the muddy rivers of a fractured past for clues to that which has been pulled under and smoothed over by ever-changing tides. What she sets in motion through the language of a queer(ly) punk aesthetic is the "cultural coherence" of self representation.[13] In fact, the imagery in *Bad Habits*, explicit in its depiction of chaos spilling into and out of Cristy's body, is representative not only of anarchy tearing away at layers of uncomfortable historical truths, but of punk rock's own questionable legitimacy around identity, gender, sexual orientation, ethnicity, and race. While Road's character might be afforded entry into the inner circles of a culture still largely dominated by white males, her Cuban heritage makes that entry conditional. Tied to a history of complex truths that are linked to every note she sings and every image she draws, the protagonist effectively takes up the banner of resistance and re-appropriates an array of voices that have been subsumed into larger postcolonialist narratives.

Cristy recalls the time when she was "entering" into a "more fragile, baffled state of existence" where "nothing was right—class, race, war, gender, men, women, animals, law."[14] She describes one of her male lovers as "both a buzz kill and a redeemer,"[15] and figure 4 shows the two of them on either side of a sign that warns of chemical hazards. Much like Fernando Ortiz's description of different ethnic groups being "torn from" their "native moorings" and "faced with the problem of disadjustment and readjustment, of deculturation and acculturation,"[16] this visual metaphor represents intersecting yet conflicting subjectivities. Another panel in the book (not included here) shows Cristy's body physically turned away from her boyfriend. Her face is tilted up, her mouth open, and her right arm outstretched as if she is performing the very mating ritual she describes. There is a cutaway of her beating heart that she holds in her left hand, which is the one nearest to Randall. The ventricular musculature can be seen, and it is a version of the drawing on the cover of the book. Her semi-open-bodied stance signifies not just "two young [...] tortured souls who questioned society and authority before questioning one another," but also a recognition of the past as well as some ambivalence towards the future.[17]

Touching on issues of sexual and cultural identity, self-expression and displacement, Cristy asserts that "the human heart beats to a sick [...] world" and that "being Latin, bisexual, and sexually unkempt was clearly undesirable."[18] In an intricate and perhaps undifferentiated display of cathexis, Cristy exemplifies what it means to reject societal norms as they pertain to women's life choices. In the personal journey she embarks on, her actions serve to amplify the underlying inequities in what is deemed to be acceptable notions of sex, gender, race, and artistic expression for both men and women. Through her art, a disdain, yet also a longing for love and acceptance, is communicated. Indeed, her statement that she "reinvested in Cuban music and literature to relearn where the fuck my natural idiosyncrasies even came

Figure 4. Panel from p. 28, *Bad Habits: A Love Story* (copyright © 2008 by Cristy C. Road. Reprinted by permission of Counterpoint Press. All rights reserved).

from"[19] speaks more broadly about the long journey from marginalization to love and punk and finally to self-representation.

Road states that she is motivated in her work by one concern: that people of color "have to fend for our story to be heard." She believes that "our stories aren't as present in communities we overlap with."[20] Her observation is certainly uncontested in queer of color feminist scholarship, where Elisa A. Garza, for example, questions entrenched hetero and homosocial customs and discourse that continue to have a deleterious impact on minority groups. With its particular focus on the lives of Hispanic and Latina lesbians, and the central role that family plays in the construction of identity, Garza draws upon the work of Cherríe Moraga and Gloria Anzaldúa to underscore the complexity of identitary narratives. She notes that Moraga and Anzaldúa have "made a deliberate effort to push their writing beyond a simple articulation of identity based on race, gender, and sexuality."[21] Garza goes on to make the point that Moraga and Anzaldúa's "intentions to write from and define multiple identities and multiple oppressions create the need to both redefine and critique their culture in the process."[22] This is similarly echoed in the *Curve* interview where Road speaks of the struggle for recognition of her work, noting that although she has "felt honored to be able to tell [her] story," she has also put a great deal of time and energy into self-publication, "putting it out into the world whether or not people wanted to see it."[23] Her argument is based on "being shut down by predominantly white communities who didn't want race to put a damper on their 'radical punk' or 'radical queer' circles."[24]

Taking this type of approach to art and writing that allows Road's own frustrated voice to emerge, while at the same time advocating for a community of inclusiveness, she uses the fissures arising from these contradictions to explain that as a Latina she does not want to "give the middle finger to the culture that attacked my identity. I want to fix that fracture" and goes on to acknowledge that it is "difficult and takes a lot of work and it's a less romantic route to queer acceptance."[25] An acceptance informed by, and flowing out of, hierarchical systems that are ultimately controlled by whites.

Road often describes herself in collective terms: "as QPOC" (Queer People of Color), or "getting to meet other queer people of color," or in oppositional terms to white hetero and homonormative systems when she declares:

> I got tired of feeling like the smelly punk as opposed to the sassy Latina—I found that feeling balanced, without compromising any of my identities, required this rigid critique of mostly-white queer communities, as well as mostly-male punk rock communities.[26]

What comes to the fore is the inherent instability of racial equality's curious misanthropic yearnings. Indeed, gaining an understanding of the layers of difference that bind punk rockers together (on picket lines, in mosh pits, through zines, and music) while also pushing them apart (racism, sexism, homophobia) is central to a fuller understanding of the punk aesthetic, its incoherence, and the limits of its own activism. What is particularly instructive here is Stephen Duncombe and Maxwell Tremblay's assertion that when counterculture's efforts at solidarity "takes the form of racial fetish, it relies upon and perpetuates the very privileges accorded by the dominant culture it is attempting to subvert."[27] Dick Hebdige similarly argues that at the very core of punk "lies this frozen dialectic between black and white cultures" and this interplay of contradictory philosophies, he asserts, is "beyond a certain point (i.e., ethnicity) incapable of renewal."[28] Furthermore, he explains that the dialectic "becomes trapped, as it is, within its own history, imprisoned within its own irreducible antinomies."[29] For my purposes here, a more pivotal argument lies in the intersecting—yet conflicting—dialectics that open up new questions about the constricted pathways lesbians of color have had to traverse just to see ourselves even partially materialized in the spillover of punk's (or hip hop or rock-n-roll's) existential nihilism. This takes my argument back to self-representational truths that are often informed by how we are seen by others.

Auto(bio)graphics

Representational (or self-referential) narratives plot the trajectory of a life bound up in memory, the passage of time, class, race, culture, gender, sexual orientation, and even cognitive functioning. In order to weave together an accounting of a life well lived, or one that has perhaps been irreparably changed by traumatic events, autobiography requires a reliable narrator. Yet the pitfall in attempting to retrospectively represent one's own life in truthful or accurate ways, be it through the visual medium of graphic narratives or through conventional autobiography, is an argument that has been explored by numerous scholars approaching the topic from many different angles.[30] Elisabeth El Refaie writes that "authenticity in autobiographical comics inevitably involves an element of performance and is produced jointly by the artist and the audience in a process of constant renegotiation."[31]

Autographics, on the other hand, support an unpacking of the complexities of difference for those whose lives have remained unseen, unheard, and unremarked.[32] In "Autographics: The Seeing 'I' of Comics," Gillian Whitlock reframes into a more contemporary context the term "autographics" to describe graphic novels that are multimodal, in that they rely upon an interplay between various textual, visual, and technological forms to engage autobiography at multiple interpretive and discursive levels.

In 2008 Whitlock co-authored an essay with Anna Poletti that described autographics as "life narrative fabricated in and through drawing and design using various technologies, modes, and material."[33] *Bad Habits* is such a fabrication, as it is inspired by Road's own life, which she situates within a wider critique of race, sexual expression, and gender in punk subcultures. The graphic narrative form lends itself particularly well to Road's concerns with making both visible and speakable the experiences of queer women of color. Through images and text that skillfully utilize the outer limits of the graphic narrative form to construct alternative perceptions of queerness, culture, belonging, and truth, *Bad Habits* plays an important part in how both mainstream and subversive counterculture representations are interpreted and enacted. And it is by no means unreasonable to state that graphic narratives by women have reached an unprecedented cultural presence since the success of Alison Bechdel's *Fun Home* (2006). We have seen exceptional works by both self-identified queer women (Bechdel, Ariel Schrag, Julie Maroh, Diane Obomsawin) and by heterosexual women of color (Marjane Satrapi, Miné Okubo, Zeina Abirached, and Margeurite Abouet). However, this remains a genre where queer women of color are noticeably underrepresented, an unfortunate reality that is only recently beginning to shift with the publication of works by Cristy C. Road, Erika Lopez, Jennifer Crute, Sara Farizan, Amruta Patil, and Tee Franklin. And while there is no shortage of web comics and comic books being produced by queer women of color, there are still inroads to be made in graphic narratives.

Whitlock's use of the term "autographics" is helpful in unpacking the issues at stake in Road's work. I look specifically at the relevance of the term for understanding the cultural politics of race, sex, and gender representation, as well as the countercultural stylings of the DIY punk aesthetic. Whitlock notes: "there is no essential or singular reading or reader of [...] cartoon[s]."[34] In her analysis of Leigh Gilmore's work on autobiographics, Whitlock suggests that autobiography "introduces a way of thinking about life narrative that focuses on the changing discourses of truth and identity."[35] Yet autographics as "self-portrait and [...] self-representation" that utilizes multi-modal approaches to the articulation of the self also "deliberately signals its progenitors within itself: biography, autobiography, autobiographics."[36] It "implies an interpretation of self-portraiture that deliberately attends to textuality and texture" and it "frequently involves the 'graphic' in the sense of explicit and confronting images of bodies in pleasure and pain."[37] It is in this way that *Bad Habits* opens up much needed avenues of investigation into the relative lack of representation of queer women of color in subcultural movements.

I argue that *Bad Habits* provides alternative responses to the "multiple hierarchies" and "structures of dominance" which, according to Maxine Baca Zin and Bonnie Thornton Dill, "links gender to other forms of domination."[38] In this regard Road's novel engages multiple angles from which to consider alternative and contradictory subject positions.[39] Yet it seems that the expression and twinning of such cultural tropes as rage and punk, queerness and camp, and anarchy and radical feminism is often the luxury of those who are most able to mitigate—either through gender, politics, or skin color—its opposite, though no less frenzied response, from hetero and/or homonormative forces.

Effectively utilizing the outer-boundaries of the graphic narrative and the punk aesthetic to explore the outer-boundaries of race, gender, sexual orientation, and identity, Road draws on her own truths and experiences which straddle multiple and intersecting cultural and sexual realities. She uses visual misdirection (most notably in the illustration of herself as a cyborg, which I go into in some detail later on) to subvert the expectations of both her counterculture peers, as well as the dominant culture that anchors her to her Cuban roots. Telling (and drawing) her punk love story with remarkable candor, Road in her work echoes the sentiments of writers such as Catrióna Rueda Esquibel who link together Chicana lesbianism and its "complex relationship to Chicano nationalism."[40] In identifying common struggles facing queer women of color—no matter if they are Mexican, Brazilian, Cuban, Puerto Rican, African American, Muslim, Catholic, or Protestant—Road's work mounts its most decisive response to Esquibel's assertion that inherent in the challenges to nationalist agendas/institutions, self-representation is often articulated through the very structures it seeks to destabilize.[41]

However, the irony in re-articulating the self through an appropriation of the systems that work to suppress alternative modes of expression is that oppression/poverty/exclusion is simply repackaged, turned into kitsch-rage, and sold as "authentic" urban experiences. Bona fide self-representation most often occurs through independently produced works that circumvent established institutional processes, thereby mounting their most strenuous challenges from the outside. These projects (pirate radio stations, off-the-grid clubs, queer web comics and punk art, to name just a few) use technology to either hide in plain sight or to offer alternatives to underground projects that have become increasingly mainstream. No group reflects this more than queer punks of color who create spaces on their own terms and who resist the allure of commercial success (and commodification) in order to nurture and preserve the unique characteristics of their queerly subcultural voices. *Bad Habits* epitomizes this resistance by extending queer realities beyond the limits of punks' self-affirming whiteness. Along these lines, Julia Downes—writing in *Riot Grrrl: Revolution Girl Style Now!* (2007)—invites us to consider how the suppression of gender difference in punk during the 1970s, while purportedly creating "asexual space," in reality "prevented a confrontational exploration of resistant femininities and sexualities within punk."[42] Lauraine Leblanc makes a similar point in her book, *Pretty in Punk: Girls' Gender Resistance in a Boys' Subculture* (1999).

Leblanc has argued that "although punks may appear to be sexually deviant, their sexual relationships conform to many of the mainstream cultural standards governing adolescent relationships," in the sense that they mirror gender and sexual binary formations and experience the same relationship problems as their non-punk counterparts.[43] Setting aside for a moment Leblanc's seemingly casual use of the term "sexually deviant," and the negative connotations this holds for queers of color in mainstream, as well as countercultural contexts, the fact remains that punk does not necessarily or automatically equate to alternative expressions of gender and sex. This is clear in Road's own push-back against a largely male-dominated subculture that fails to acknowledge its complicity with mainstream culture in the silencing and/or commodification of women.

Graphic Beginnings

Writing in her graphic novel with the fervor of an adolescent girl whose intelligence shines through in ways that lend her admitted imperfections a rough kind of charm, Road's punk "anthem" is filled with vividly drawn images that depict the wild excesses of youth. Serving as a rebel call to queer women of color who also happen to love punk, but who are often just as marginalized in punk subculture as they are in the dominant one, the book's cover art shows the main character (Cristy) in figure 5 holding her bleeding and crudely extracted heart aloft in her left hand. Part of her rib cage is visible through the tear in her blouse, which reveals the gash in her chest from which her heart was ripped out. There are patches of blood on her blouse, her fingernails are painted black in the classic punk style, and her trousers ride low on slender hips. Underneath the image of her bloody heart are the words "A Love Story." On the page for the first chapter are the words "The first step is always disillusionment."

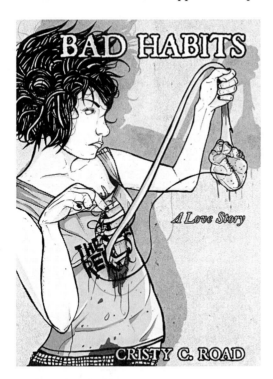

Figure 5. Cover Art, *Bad Habits: A Love Story* (copyright © 2008 by Cristy C. Road. Reprinted by permission of Counterpoint Press. All rights reserved) (see C•3 for larger image).

Bad Habits is not so much a disquisition on the vagaries of love, rather, its awkward and self-conscious cool relies on a shrewd manipulation of the non-conformist language articulated through punk. It is reflective of the very "imperfect people living imperfect lives" that Cristy goes on to describe as "outrageous hordes of freaks, queers, sluts, and delinquents."[44] Its vulgarity is like a wobbly homage to Ginsberg's *Howl* or Billy Childish's "Kissing the arse of the goddess," "they talk of love," or "2 hands, 2 biscuits." To borrow a phrase from Jodie Taylor, *Bad Habits* is a "spewing" of unmitigated rage.[45] In a recent interview, Road revealed that her book is also about "healing from an abusive relationship" and "reconnecting to [her] vagina," which places her work in an overtly feminist context.[46] This must be a powerful and necessary revelation for the author, particularly given her experiences with publishers who found her method of healing through images and words to be unmarketable. Instead, *Bad Habits*, Road has said, "was promoted as a book about drugs and partying."[47] Yet careful readers will appreciate that even the most obvious narrative thread, followed along to what may at first appear to be a foregone conclusion, is never as simple as it seems.

Bad Habits was written in the same year that Fidel Castro stepped down as president of Cuba. It was also the year when Barack Obama became the first African American nominated by a major political party to run for president of the United States. And California had also become the second state after Massachusetts to legalize same-sex marriage. Milestones to be certain, yet queer women of color were still faced with contradictory realities that at once kept us invisible, yet at the same time empowered us to speak through our collective invisibility by strategizing the terms of our own self-representation. Thus, the work of graphic narratives lends itself to "speakability" and alternative forms of representation. It layers, scaffolds, foregrounds, and redraws historical omissions, and it functions as a tool for the recuperation of muted voices from the Latin, Caribbean, and African diasporas. It allows readers to conjure what we are told is not there by bringing the voiceless (through alternative discourse) and the invisible (through the process of inking) back into existence. This is what images do, and these are the words and the lives that rise off the pages of *Bad Habits*.

Queer(ed) Exile

As a graphic narrative, *Bad Habits* allows for the very subversions of the expectations the author experiences as a Cuban woman whose cultural affiliations straddle two worlds. "The more distant I felt from Miami," Road's character muses, "the less of a person I felt, no matter how accepted I was by another American city."[48] José Quiroga's "Queer Desires in Lydia Cabrera" repositions and reframes this temporal dissociation in a way that simultaneously pulls together and pushes apart the central tenets of belonging. Quiroga considers the intriguing dualisms in *El monte*, Lydia Cabrera's 1954 book that explores Afro Cuban religiosity—specifically *Santería*—and exile. In a passage that speaks to what is often the irreconcilability of identity and place, Quiroga simultaneously *locates* the physical reprinting of Cabrera's book "at the site— Miami—where a new Cuban diaspora had been forming since 1959"[49] while at the same time implicating the very political conundrums that Road writes (and draws) about as a queer punk activist. Road expresses disdain for the embargo and also for "Fidel" or "any government that at any point has criminalized human nature or repressed its people sexually or ethnically."[50] Quiroga's interrogation of Lydia Cabrera's influential work usefully contextualizes this disaffection in *Bad Habits*.

Echoing what Quiroga asserts is *El monte*'s provision of "a link with origins (Cuba) for those who had left […] but […] also an act of political defiance" that was "directed at the geographical Cuban space itself,"[51] Road's work demonstrates that the link between the past and present is undeniable. Reaching out across generations, cultural norms, literary genres, and physical locations, these links become constitutive of new paradigms through which parochial attitudes can be effectively challenged and subverted.

When Road's character alludes to an incompatibility between her cultural roots and the subversive DIY punk paradigms that also define her, she makes one of the few direct connections between two ideologically discordant positions. The first is when she declares, "self-pity developed when my ethnic group affirmed my grotesqueness based on how many dicks I'd sucked and the fact that all genders aroused me."[52] The second, and perhaps the most salient to my argument, is when Road states that this very same "self-pity inhabited my skull when even members of my supposed progressive and alternative scene assumed the same."[53] What she describes is a construct that somehow works to reinforce precisely the anti-anthemic, countercultural, and improvisational stylings that have come to define various DIY cultures as irreverent, angry, loud, vulgar, uncompromising, anarchic, and even camp. It is at this complex intersection that "queer and feminist punk analytics" are used to unravel and interrogate punk and its signature forms of resistance.[54] Red Chidgey's "Riot Grrrl Writing," for example, illustrates these kinds of critical schisms:

> Despite the rote list of oppressions riot grrrl manifestos and zines claim to protest against, including racism and classism, systems and structures of oppressions were rarely tackled in zines beyond the occasional grrrl admitting that she was white and privileged and working on it.[55]

Chidgey's observations are not new to black feminist critiques of hierarchical models that exclude the realities of lesbians of color. Chidgey notes that the task of challenging these kinds of privileges "often fell to non-white people" acting as "confronters and educators within their communities," a problem she goes on to state that has "a long history within feminist movements, which are white-dominated."[56] Yet what should not be too hastily dismissed is that the Riot Grrrl movement captured the attention of the mainstream, but more importantly, the imagination of young girls in the United States, Canada, and many parts of Europe. Their commitment was to create "a radical philosophy centred around encouraging girls and women across the country to subvert the stagnant male-dominated underground by creating their own music, art, writing and scenes."[57] In many respects this has also been the goal of black lesbian punks, although it must be said that black lesbian punks have the added challenge of navigating through complex and oblique layers of white privilege.

As a Cuban-American woman whose history is all about assimilating, Road's identity becomes contingent upon her being able to speak and act for herself. She has a constellation of different experiences that compel her to describe her life in terms that are in opposition to those of the men (and women) with whom she has sex, falls in love with, or distances herself from as a way of protecting herself. She attempts to reconcile her anarchist politics with her desire for love, but often finds herself having to do the emotional work that is typically expected of women across a range of social and familial settings.

All "Road(s)" Lead Back to the Beginning

Bad Habits opens with a splash page that sets up the beginning of a journey. In figure 6 we see a man holding the hand of a little girl (Cristy) who is dressed in a bear suit. Both are brown-skinned and have expressions of contentment on their faces. The front of the elderly man's t-shirt has a mixture of words and symbols that one finds in nearly every major metropolitan center across the globe; in this case, he appears to dance a jig against a backdrop of busy city streets, buildings and graffiti. The little girl is positioned forward-facing. Her eyes are closed and her left arm is extended out and away from her side in a natural swinging motion that matches her small stride. What is depicted here is summed up midway through the text on the facing page. "The voices on that strip would seep out of my ears, and out the other, lyrically, in my grandfather's tongue."[58] And this—the lingua franca of

Figure 6. Panel from p. 8, *Bad Habits: A Love Story* (copyright © 2008 by Cristy C. Road. Reprinted by permission of Counterpoint Press. All rights reserved. The "I heart NY" logo was created by Milton Glaser as part of a city marketing campaign for tourists).

a people whose mother tongue has been decoded, deracinated, and merged into monolithic American narratives—collides with hegemonic paradigms, yet also informs alternative subcultural realities.

In an essay that interrogates these tensions, Daniel S. Traber looks at the L.A. punk scene as indicative of largely one-way "border crossings" into ethno-cultural scenes/lives; that while it "claims to desire dissonance and destabilization" instead "depends on boundaries and regulatory fictions staying in place to define itself as oppositional."[59] In taking up Traber's insightful analysis of the outsider within a construct that certainly informs punk culture, Arnoldas Stramskas considers how the idea of self-marginalization perpetuates the very norms punk rockers try to distance themselves from. He notes that "white Americans looking to escape their dominant identity by literally or symbolically aligning themselves with marginalized others" does not necessarily effect an unequivocal separation for punks from hegemonic systems.[60] These, I argue, are the tensions that *Bad Habits* works to illuminate.

In what could be interpreted as a nod to "Ego Trippin," Nikki Giovanni's famous poem about black affirmation, but more specifically here as it relates to Cuba and exile, Cristy states: "Picking my nose as if gold sat in my temples, I thought of the parts of my blood that were constructed of a gorgeous revolution."[61] Giovanni's poetry has been described as "Sometimes angry, often graphic and detailed," and ones that "have chronicled the struggle for identity and national democracy among blacks, women, and other minority groups."[62] What Road's similarity to Giovanni's famous poem shows is that her love story—recounted through the contemporary aesthetics of graphic punk narratology—cannot be properly told without an acknowledgment of the black diasporic experience.[63]

Although Road does in fact lay claim in her book to her Cuban heritage through activism, writing, and art, blackness still seems an intangible, an abstraction, a magical cloak that never fully reveals the wearer's true nature or origins. I argue that, subjectively, the cloak operates as a signifier of default positions from which everything else flows. Firstly, whiteness is presented as the accepted standard by which beauty, intelligence, and goodness are assessed. Secondly, womanhood represents something that complements masculinity. Finally, female reproduction is seen as securing the future of nations. These encoded messages are not accidental. They have been, and are, constructed from oppositional frameworks through which subjects on either side of its configuration understand their places, their functions, and their worth. Granted, there are crossings and exchanges of information and resources, but the benefits are often unequal. I argue that the lives of subaltern groups are mined (and *mimed*) in furtherance of white counterculture agendas. Black, Latino, and Asian punks (just to name a few) have their own unique narrative and should not be indiscriminately grouped under the one-for-all and all-for-one banner of DIY punk subculture. To this end, it could be said that *Bad Habits* points to how "punk's most powerful affects were employed in unknotting the body from its psychic link to the social."[64] This "unknotting" of the body—undertaken at once with a delicate hand to minimize psychic rupture, but also with an unsympathetic excision of a diseased racist legacy—is significant precisely because it demands an act of faith, a recognition that the "Other" within us all is a positive force for change and that change is inevitable.

When Cristy reflects upon her place in the world, on the in-between time when "alternative teenagers become alternative adults, their wayward upbringing either supports them through identity transitions or kills their self-assurance," she muses that she had begun to "realize that punk rock wasn't always female, let alone gay."[65] There is an image of her kissing someone whose gender presentation is difficult to determine, as both are partially cut off by the elongated and narrowed width of the frame. On the facing page she is held aloft by many hands, in a mosh pit, where the juxtaposition of "a disco ball duct-taped to the ceiling" is not at odds with the sounds of "Nirvana […] inside of me, streaming through my blood like an electric pulse of shock rehabilitation."[66] Cristy's identity, and the intensity with which she lives her punk life, is expressed through music and her romantic relationships. When she meets the first of two men for whom she develops strong feelings, she believes it is her fate to find her "soul mates during punk rock shows and natural disasters."[67] She propositions Broc Smith, impressed that he has a "comfort with women who fart in public."[68] Embarking on an unconventional sexual relationship that includes establishing whether or not Broc has ever "gotten it up the ass,"[69] they snort lines of cocaine together, further cementing the connection they have established. Her enhanced state of sexual attraction to Broc makes her feel "a tender and submissive adoration" for him, yet she is ultimately "diverted" by his maleness.[70] Thus, while simultaneously taking on a passive feminine role, Cristy also affirms her right to set out the terms of her own sexual pleasure.

Cristy announces to Broc that she feels "very balanced when I fuck dudes in the butt,"[71] thereby making it clear that she is accustomed to taking control and that her decision to also be submissive is part of her sex play. She delights in Broc's willingness to try anal sex, explaining to him that "fucking people's holes is a substantial part of my bisexual identity[…]."[72] She subverts traditional constructions of women by introducing destabilizing sexual paradigms when she casts Broc as the receiving, penetrated partner. When she eventually begins a sexual relationship with Ashby, a punk rocker she first meets when he shows up one day to repair her computer, she thinks to herself how much she enjoys "orgasms, erections, and jerking off."[73] She also recognizes that her enjoyment of "overt sexuality was always deemed a treacherous route to womanhood."[74] It may be that *Bad Habits* often reads more like an endless soliloquy of pain and frequently overreaches the author's punk war cry against the very conventions it parodies, but it could also be argued that it takes a circuitous route towards challenging pathologizing white-centric scripts. Nevertheless, the book's hyperbole works to underscore tensions that exist between socially, politically, sexually, and ethnically peripheral groups.

The narrative arc of Road's work gestures toward an inclusivity that has been historically lacking in DIY punk subcultures. The imagery she uses to communicate what words alone cannot serves as a visual mapping of the alternate routes she takes to unearthing difficult truths that have been subsumed into larger stories. Writing as a queer woman whose cultural roots extend across landscapes denuded and razed by invading armies, Road in her work sets out critical markers upon which new ideas about race, gender, and sexual expression can be formulated. There are, however, points along the way where *Bad Habits* stumbles. In these places its self-confessional style overshadows other truths that must be told more fully. In these places, too, opportunities for closer critiques of how race, ethnicity, gender, class, and sexual orientation intersect to form whole realities from misaligned narratives are missed. Here, that which can be reimagined can (and should) be drawn into the light. To this end, my analysis interjects the largely unacknowledged voices (and faces) of lesbian punks of color into the white hetero and homonormative DIY punk aesthetic.[75]

Critically (Black) Punk

The contribution to DIY punk by lesbians of color whose artistic expressions are influenced by "larger structures that interpellate" women of color "in a variety of ways"[76] is often eclipsed under the purported umbrella of punk inclusivity. Unlike white middle class male punks whose disaffection with hegemony often has its source in boredom and youthful rebellion, queer punks of color such as NighTraiN and Purity Mkhize represent the multi-issue politics that Road touches on in her work. Road's uneasy recognition of her outsider/insider status—captured in her drawings and situating punk rock (dis)chord at the heart of contentious debates about representation and belonging—marks punk as a signifying practice that lends itself to wider interpretations. Owing to such works as Osa Atoe's collection of queer of color zines, lesbians of color are able to intercede in punk discourse at the juncture where the "productive provocations" that Fiona I.B. Ngô and Elizabeth A. Stinson speak of in "Threads and Omissions" take on new critical meaning.[77] Daniela Caistrano's POC Zine Project, as well as Nyky Gomez's Brown Recluse Zine Distro, also contributes to these critical turns.

Road joins an increasingly long line of women who became part of the punk movement to "find fresh meanings [...]" and to "overturn the pastel shades of post–60s femininity and make an overt statement on a newly emerging, more aggressive understanding of female sexuality."[78] In this regard, although she has subtitled her graphic novel "A Love Story," the essence of her narrative more accurately appears to be about re-inscribing the (black/brown/queer/punk-ti-ficating) self.

Based in part on an almost wholesale rejection of mainstream ideals, as well as punk culture's divergent positions on gender and race that call for wider and deeper interrogations, punk could be "read in part as" an unwelcome and illegitimate "white 'translation' of black 'ethnicity.'"[79] Put another way, the commodification of "Otherness" for the purpose of "authenticating" or elevating the white experience simply perpetuates historical trends of muting (and mutating) the creative black voice. In the abstract this "borrowing" has both been defended and challenged through the acknowledgment of such practices by the very people benefiting from it. Stewart Home, for instance, points out the hypocrisy of these self-serving pronouncements when he argues that the Clash "were able to make a career on the back of pretending to be somehow more 'authentic' than acts such as the Sex Pistols who'd been heavily hyped."[80] White punk bands liberally sampled black music as a way to stand out from the crowd. They wanted to shock and offend not only the establishment—which many saw as symbolic of cultural atrophy and racism—but other white groups whose music may not have replicated the "authentic" black sounds coming out of marginalized communities. What complicates an understanding of these casually constructed affinities is that bands like the Clash use what has effectively become the "spectacle" of difference to distinguish themselves from the pack, while at the same time failing to fully acknowledge that they share "the familiar demographic [...] of mostly white, male, suburban, middle class youths."[81] By co-opting and "translating" the experiences of other cultures, blackness remains the corresponding "negative" to a largely white aesthetic.

Roger Sabin collapses these thorny issues into a short essay that calls into question punk culture's dubious credentials as an all-inclusive tent under which all who subscribe to free expression through the awesomeness of punk are welcome. Sabin takes exception to "the twin ideas that punk somehow transcended the societal forces that gave birth to it, and that it can be judged as being ideologically commensurate with the 'politically correct' standards of the 1980s and '90s."[82] The issue, he argues, is not whether punk has abandoned its anarchist leanings and gone completely mainstream and commercialized, though there is certainly that, but rather that (British) punk has never quite shaken off its far right sympathies or, conversely, the far right's appropriation of punk symbolism and its recruitment of disaffected youth to its causes.[83] This uncomfortable tension is exemplified in Road's character. She is portrayed as a rebellious punk who must negotiate multiple identities through multiply distorted nationalist frameworks, but the difference is that she is under no illusions about how far her challenges to authority will get her.

Road is aware that "[...] existing in America with an alternative lifestyle hardly means immunity from injustice."[84] She is a bisexual Cuban woman whose affinities to DIY punk do not necessarily align with the "non-normative" identity constructs depicted in her drawings, yet she is insistent on contesting self-negating representations. This is not unlike the tensions that Heike Bauer describes in her analysis of what she calls the "graphic lesbian continuum."[85] In the autobiographical and politically inspired drawings of Ilana Zeffren, a Tel Aviv–based lesbian graphic artist, Bauer defines the graphic lesbian continuum as a "visual language of lesbianism that gives centrality to female same-sex life."[86] Speaking in terms that problematize tropes orienting the lesbian body towards a normative into which it/we simply do not fit, Bauer inverts these alienating and enervating postulations by arguing that "the event of becoming is often articulated at least in part through the encounter with verbal, visual and other forms of culture."[87] Looking to Zeffren's drawings to visually explicate the "lesbian landscape" posited by Sara Ahmed in *Queer Phenomenology: Orientations, Objects, Others* (2006), Bauer explores the "lesbian presence" that emerges from the pages of Zeffren's visually graphic continuum.[88] Similar constructions and critically queer excursions appear throughout Road's work.

In figure 7 Cristy is lighting up, drawing on what is presumably a marijuana pipe. The next panel (not shown here) appears to be an image of a politician standing in front of a flag, smiling, with his hand raised in a waving gesture. The flag (which appears to be American) and the politician (who appears to be Hispanic) creates an interesting juxtaposition between the character's ethno-cultural identity as a Cuban and her assimilation into American culture as a rule-breaking, pot-smoking, bisexual punk teenager. On the facing page (figure 8) there are two teenagers—one in an Iron Maiden t-shirt, and the other passing along a marijuana cigarette—sitting on a sofa, facing a table that overflows with "Hot Pockets [...] to make the life of a pothead that much simpler."[89] These are the affirming productions of whiteness.

Firstly, the Hot Pockets symbolize fast food for people with busy lifestyles. Secondly, the American flag is representative of freedoms extended to those who abide by a certain set of rules. Thirdly, there is the politician, who may or may not

Right: **Figure 7. Panel from p. 12,** *Bad Habits: A Love Story* **(copyright © 2008 by Cristy C. Road. Reprinted by permission of Counterpoint Press. All rights reserved).** *Below:* **Figure 8. Panel from p. 13,** *Bad Habits: A Love Story* **(copyright © 2008 by Cristy C. Road. Reprinted by permission of Counterpoint Press. All rights reserved).**

be Hispanic, standing in front of a symbol "with its history and future penetrated both by savvy rebels and conservative maniacs."[90] The irony of anar-
chism co-existing alongside liberal democracy, and the challenges inherent
in reconciling these contradictions in order to define oneself in self-affirming
terms, is where *Bad Habits* proves most engaging. For it is these intersecting
themes, juxtaposed alongside the harsh reality of inequality, racism, violence,
and intolerance, that implicates the American dream. "And while plenty of
independent people with independent minds plaster sidewalks and signposts
with words and images," Cristy says, "in hopes of preserving any culture outside of the white-bread basket of glass condos," heterogeneity melts away,
"and men still rule."[91] Overlaid (often with no hint of irony) onto these narratives is punk subculture and the part it plays in replicating these conflicting
messages.

Experience as Cultural Representation: A Signifying Dialogue

By virtue of her self-identification as an outsider, even within the punk
subculture that she claims as her own, Road's character also deals with the
contradictions that arise in movements and relationships that define their
ethos in oppositional terms. After a night out at a New York strip club fre-
quented by men and women, queers and heterosexuals, punks and suburban
types, Cristy wanders around the dark Manhattan streets. In words and
images she describes the oppositions that make the city tick, but also the
contradictions that prove impenetrable to the uninitiated. She walks the same
streets as others, sometimes seeing what they do, but most often interpreting
life through a prism of refracting light. "With every step through Manhattan,"
she insists, "I could smell the gamble, where the dice could land on preservation or destruction."[92] Just like everyone else, she wants love but does not
know how to recognize it. She wants to belong, but is wary of the cost. "*We
aren't going anywhere,* I think to myself [...] *What are you gonna do, man?
Make the people illegal too?*"[93] In figure 9 the image is of an eerily quiet city
street, as if it is already emptied of the immigrants it does not want, a landscape that is stark and sinister in its monochromatic rendering.

The city buildings that silently witness Cristy's meandering rise into the
night sky, their windows dark, peering down onto streets where alien-looking
eruptions with iron rods protruding upwards from their dull metal covers
line the street, as if spaceships have burst through the protective skin of New
York's subterranean underbelly. "Visions of the deportation of anyone not an

upper-crust, card-carrying consumer, rush me, unwelcomed."[94] Cristy has no illusions about belonging, knowing that at any minute she could be rejected (as she had been with the stripper she propositioned at the club and with the men and women who could not give her the love she craved). So she instead "put on blinders to make my insides feel good."[95] She belonged to the city, but it did not belong to her.

Figure 9. Panel from p. 64, *Bad Habits: A Love Story* (copyright © 2008 by Cristy C. Road. Reprinted by permission of Counterpoint Press. All rights reserved).

Revolutionary Contradictions

Road uses her art and her feminist punk ideology to create "a culturally decipherable and politically coherent location from which to speak, write, and desire."[96] Her counter-messages, steeped at once in tradition, yet also in the art of visual subversion, are instructive. Figure 10 shows an image of a table festively set with what appears to be traditional Cuban dishes: plátanos fritos (fried plantains), Cuban seafood paella, an overflowing bowl of avocados cut in halves, and mojitos adorned with fresh mint leaves. There are also paper napkins and bowls adorned with images of the Cuban flag, a necessary marker that reorients those who are adrift from their cultural roots. The image at figure 11 shows a woman's naked torso from the waist down. Her pubic area is shaved and her sex—in all of its connotations—is contained by a specially designed chastity belt. On either side of the belt, written in large dripping letters, is the word HELP! For Cristy, the first image depicts "family reunions" that were a reprieve from an "atypical life" that allowed her to "reinvest plentifully in my culture, without political drama and irresponsible men."[97] Yet the second image refutes what is implied in the first, and that is the idea of safety and loyalty within the traditional family setting.

Figure 10. Panel from p. 130, *Bad Habits: A Love Story* (copyright © 2008 by Cristy C. Road. Reprinted by permission of Counterpoint Press. All rights reserved).

The vagina—safely locked away and inaccessible to real and/or imagined intruders—functions as a symbol of purity and incorruptibility that can only be guaranteed by a symbolic imprisonment. At once the receptacle for the hopes and dreams of a nation, when freed from external controls and expectations, and when reconnected to a whole body/person, the vagina (as resistance and "voice") becomes a powerful symbol of the expression of free will.

The "sexual (mis)alliance" that Katherine Sugg argues flows from questions of "cultural belonging and betrayal" is a central feature of oppressive actions that disproportionately impact queer Chicanas who are perceived as traitors to femininity and heterosexuality.[98] I extend this argument to include queer women of color across the heteronormative spectrum.

Through her art and music, Road intentionally sets up political/cultural/gendered contradictions as a way of stitching back together the forgotten parts of herself into an unassimilated whole. Coming to understand that "a functioning libido was a sign of good health" and that "embracing safe sex, with or without a ball and chain, was healthy," her character states: "And most people want to fuck."[99] Crucially, and when taken together, the author's writing and images coalesce around issues of race, gender, class, and sexual expression, offering a new take on the multiple exclusions and oppressions

Figure 11. Panel from p. 132, *Bad Habits: A Love Story* (copyright © 2008 by Cristy C. Road. Reprinted by permission of Counterpoint Press. All rights reserved).

that she and other queer punks of color struggle to confront. By breaking free of the chains and expectations that entrap her, she instead engages in a recuperative process that celebrates the array of voices and experiences subsumed in the tyranny of hegemony. While her character masturbates to the sound of Iron Maiden, readers are compelled to reach into the gaps/gutters/ spaces that bring more prominently into view the parts of punk subculture that continue to resist appropriation.

"The first voices I began mimicking," Cristy admits, "were those of angry (mostly American) punk rockers, who were perched inside my headphones."[100] References to Iron Maiden and Aerosmith run throughout the pages of *Bad Habits*, suggesting that Cristy's need to learn English at the age of four in order to attend school in America marked her as different from the very beginning. There is no explanation in the book as to how at such a young age Road was exposed to heavy metal, but the revolution of words and ideas flowing into her brain shaped her view of who she at least thought she could be in America, as opposed to the queer she could never really be in Cuba.

Intersecting Refrains: Punk's G-Spot[101]

After several failed romances Cristy comes to the realization that using sex "as a vision quest" would no longer work. She instead begins seeing it "as an activity to get lost [...]" in, a way to "tend to that G-spot [...]."[102] Defining "sexual revival" and "survival" of herself and others "by the caliber of an orgasm," Cristy pins her salvation on the control of her own body.[103] She redefines the tropes that suppress who she truly is, literally taking into her own hands the rewriting of her sexual—and by extension her cultural, racial, familial, spiritual, artistic, and political—history. Stepping outside of the implied privileges of her white Cuban skin, she can create a different history and representation that intersects with other G-spot renegades, thereby disrupting the exclusionary hegemonic and subcultural narratives she has been assimilated into.

Locating her G-spot is a political statement. It is the path Cristy must embark on to reconnect, to decipher the codes that keep the *of color* parts of herself (and her G-spot sisters) separate, out of reach, marginal. Here sexuality "is a complex term with a multifaceted meaning referring to deep emotional feeling as well as to issues of power and vulnerability in gendered relationships."[104] The character's (and the author's) immersion in DIY punk subculture conflicts with the broader politics of belonging, creating unstable "representations [...] that" give "rise to irresolvable tensions and contradictions."[105] Michael Bennett and Vanessa D. Dickerson's observation is specific to the black body/blackness, and I contend that more than any other colonized (sub)culture, blackness continues to signify what Dickerson refers to as the "visibly invisible."[106] What Dickerson is suggesting is that although on a corporeal level the black body is a materialized presence, on the level of citizenship and all of the benefits one derives from this, it is not. Moreover, being forced to live "practically without a reflection in the world,"[107] as Dickerson notes, for example, of Pecola Breedlove, the character in Toni Morrison's *The Bluest Eye* (1970), means that one can only see oneself in the distorted reflection of the racist or sexist gaze. As both white and *of color* feminists have long argued, being located at "the bottom of a cascade of negative identities, left out of even the privileged oppressed authorial categories called 'women' and 'blacks,'" women of color saw (and continue to see) themselves constantly negated through the politics of difference.[108]

Contesting racist and sexist narratives by subverting the essentializing gaze is a crucial feature of Road's work. And while it is important to point out that the author's white skin brings into sharper relief the antipathy directed towards black-skinned lesbians, what is notable—particularly as it relates to how black lesbian punks navigate their way through confusing (and often self-negating) layers of identification—is that as someone who self-identifies as a queer woman *of color* in real life and also represents this in her drawings, Road works hard to subvert these racialized and misogynist schema. Historically, this places her on the end of a trajectory of racism that some claim has (mostly) resolved itself under a twenty-first-century neoliberal, multicultural banner. These calls for sameness, for access to unwelcoming spaces and for acceptance, are what (white) punk culture—through music, protest and art—purports to deconstruct.

In arguing for the right of visibility that is not contingent upon being legitimized through the assimilative framework within and outside of punk culture, Leah Newbold's critique situates these inequities within a black feminist praxis:

> Needless to say, it pissed me off to realize that though punk is powerful, it is like everything else ... a microcosm of society, and all that oppressive shit that happens outside also happens within.[109]

Similarly, Road literally draws these oppositions in her work through imagery that challenges societal norms of beauty, whiteness, heterosexuality, and exclusion. She does not shy away from drawing images of women with armpit and leg hair. She writes about menstrual blood, masturbation, and sex with both women and men, and her work suggests that she is more likely to seek out the company of those on the extreme margins than compromise her punk ethics in order to strive for conditional acceptance in mainstream culture. Yet had she attempted to celebrate her queer identity in Cuba as recently as the early part of the twentieth century, her punk writing and performances would have been deemed antithetical to revolutionary ideals of womanhood and acceptable expressions of sexual preference. If Road were a dark-skinned Cuban lesbian hoping for equality in Havana, she would have been better off as a prostitute as the "revolution was [...] aggressively hostile to homosexuality."[110] Thus, her commitment to punk (which is dominated mostly by white men), and her desire to maintain her Cuban identity (which defines womanhood as heteronormatively constructed), sets up an interesting dialectic between the anarchist and the racially inclusive principles Road espouses.

Resignifying the Phallus

Through a compelling example that challenges postcolonial hegemonic scripts reducing women's anger (and black bodies) to nothing more than "tits and a pussy,"[111] Road's character is drawn as half human and half machine. In figure 12 Cristy is shown fumbling with a mass of wires that are connected to a generator, which represent her "fantasy of revitalizing vaginal orgasms."[112] The wallpaper in the background appears in several other panels in the book, its pattern consisting of hundreds of tiny alien-type skulls. The floor is littered with pieces of machinery that appear to have been used for spare parts in the building of both the physical body and the generator, suggesting perhaps that her sexual pleasure is under her control and can be manufactured, if she can only put together the right combination of bolts and screws.

Refusing to acquiesce to the status quo, when Cristy announces that in her sexual liaisons with women she "carried the phallus,"[113] she pulls the reader into representation of a completely different order. She has overtly masculinized her whiteness *and* her gender, thereby potentially nullifying the rights that might have otherwise been extended to her as a non-black Cuban woman. What some might see as an aberrant masculinization of the white heteronormative archetype, the author/artist/queer likely sees as an opportunity for expanded interpretations of an already "Othered" self. Through the unique structural elements of the graphic narrative, complex paradoxes that require alternative cognitive engagements with race, gender, desire, and subculture come into play. By intentionally disrupting the social coding ascribed to her visibly white status, the artist has introduced intricate (*mis*)*codings* of assumed roles in heteronormative structures. By this I mean

Figure 12. Panel from p. 134, *Bad Habits: A Love Story* (copyright © 2008 by Cristy C. Road. Reprinted by permission of Counterpoint Press. All rights reserved).

that she has drawn on two distinct formulations of a misdirectional strategy. The first is racial coding that has historically fixed blackness and gender as mutually constitutive of difference. Moreover, as blackness has historically been constructed as always in terminal opposition to whiteness and its self-aggrandizing gestures toward racial purity and civilized behavior, its "performance" is almost always fraught with the weight of "Otherness." The second formulation revolves around sexual expressions and performances that are bound up in the same racial and social codes.

Like the cyborgs of science fiction movies, Road's character has rewired and reprogrammed her machine to spring to life with the flick of a switch and the unlimited potential of the human imagination. The phallus she carries (the hand-held battery operated dildo) allows her to reach "a pinnacle so biologically pure and self-ruling, the spoiled debris of hard love and hard drugs dissipated at a manic pace."[114] She is outside of the pale here, not only in masculinizing whiteness and the act of sex for her own private pleasure, but for coaxing into the light the cyborgian drama that Donna Haraway asserts is "outside salvation history," perhaps even outside the limits of reason.[115]

It can be said that by masculinizing her whiteness and her gender, by setting up oppositional frameworks through images and words, Road's character is "resignifying the phallus and sexual meanings and practices; and the virtuality of a material body in digital space interpenetrated by informational patterns and protruding machinery[...]."[116] Fighting the arbitrary rules and values that promote heterosexuality as the starting and ending points of normality, Road (as author) sets the terms of an ever shifting contract with the world. In order to indulge in "otherworldly desires" her character assimilates and the process "burn[s] a little hole the size of a cranberry in whatever Cuban matter was left in my soul."[117] Yet she recognizes that her outsider status, her punk aesthetic, and her rage are all part of an "American assimilation" based on "perversion and promiscuity, as opposed to prudish conservatism."[118] By redefining the terms of engagement through the symbolism of the cyborg, Cristy has interrupted the commands wired into the alien cyborg brain. By taking control of the mechanical phallus, she queers the norm and deconstructs its most powerful and enduring signifiers: whiteness and reproduction. Demonstrating that women can be the revising, radicalizing impulse in punk discourse, Cristy locates her own punk visage in the shifting space of a queered aesthetic.

Adapting the cyborg as a signifier of punk's own cultural ambivalence is useful here, primarily because of its long association to the already and always "alien" (and appropriated) "Other." I read Road's visual representation of the cyborg, the polymorph and the hybrid as a species discursively constructed from androcentric and racist agendas that subsume "marginal" realities. Intentionally designed as an abstraction, a representational model of superior human functioning, the cyborg is programmed according to the specifications of its creator. The machine's "thinking" flows from a databank that contains information typically based on the values and morals of its creator. The cyborg most often also represents a futuristic race of droids whose distinguishing attributes derive mainly from its mechanistic parts and inhuman strength. The artificiality of its construction actually works as an illuminating contrast to the humanness and ethno-cultural history that have been coded out of its wired memory. Haraway underscores this when she refers to the "fractured identities" of feminism and the myth of unity between all women under that banner.[119]

Haraway's vision of a cyborg myth is one of resistance and transgression, where the reclamation of self and identity from unitary modes of governance begins with shifts in perspective that "might better enable us to contest for meanings, as well as for other forms of power and pleasure in technologically mediated societies."[120] Yet because the cyborg is half human, there is always the opportunity for the machine to learn how to circumvent its master script. Indeed, this is what Cristy so cleverly achieves with her cyborg creation. By "sourcing" parts of herself as a way to (re)build and *remember*, the machine bypasses the master hegemonic blueprint, thereby disrupting the postcolonial objectives of a genderless, raceless, sexless, and unthinking army of droids.

Images of cyborgs often feature hybrid beings with ocular implants and visors that reconstruct, diminish, obscure, or make secondary to the machinery its racial phenotype. Cristy's cyborg is half human from the waist up. She retains her human (and Cuban) features in what Mimi Nguyen suggests is a disruption of the heterosexual "taxonomy of sex/gender/desire, with profound consequences for representation of race and the cyborg subject."[121] Indeed, *Bad Habits* (as does Michael A. Chaney) reminds us that

> [...] cyborg anthropology foregrounds ruptures in the boundaries of the subject as a socio-political manifestation of counter-hegemonic subversion [thus] we may describe the cyborg as the latest in a series of boundary transgressions that began with the category disputations over the black body[...][122]

Road's drawing demonstrates that in theory the cyborg functions as the template upon which what has been previously inscribed can be reprogrammed to operate outside of restrictive gendered and cultural boundaries. Her character uses the energy produced and cycled through the cyborg's mechanical "guts" to power her mechanical phallus, thereby rendering as unnecessary the presence of a man through whom her identity as a woman of color can be reflected back to her through conventional social and sexual intercourse.

But Cristy's growing disillusionment with having sex with two different men she is drawn to for their initial sensitivity to gender equality is borne out by the first when he proclaims her "internal juices" as "gross" and criticizes her "organs" as "too small, too dirty, too dry, or too mysteriously trapped beneath a miniature hood of flesh he didn't even want to deal with."[123] Thus by carrying her own phallus as an act of empowerment, Road's character simultaneously exposes the rifts in subcultural movements and, through the cyborg, fabricates an oppositional reality that repositions her outside of normative gender, sexual, and racial paradigms.

In this chapter I turned to *Bad Habits* to facilitate a deeper understanding of how queer women of color negotiate notions of race, sexual orientation, and gender in male-dominated DIY punk subculture. As a bisexual Cuban punk rocker whose artwork, writing, and music subverts narratives that situate diasporic realities on the margins of normative society, Road employs misdirection in her graphic novel to reclaim the queer(ed) appropriated body. She does so by using visual language to expand the limits of the queer woman of color representational self and to *un-script* sexist and racist narratives. She also simultaneously fills in, and reclaims, the unarticulated shadows and gaps that have been—to borrow Stuart Hall's phrasing—"structured in dominance."[124] By affirming the calls and responses, the struggles and triumphs, the complex journeys across hostile landscapes and, indeed, the queer black body itself, Road's work offers an alternative platform from which queer punks of color might create subcultural realities that are truly inclusive of difference. In redefining herself in terms that resonate for her as a bisexual Cuban punk rocker, and by choosing to express her cultural critique via the medium of comics, Road has literally redrawn the boundaries of debate, forcing a (re)articulation of punk that is inclusive of broader cultural meanings and applications. To this end, her work supports a radical rethinking of queer women of color subjectivity and representation.

Chapter 4

Narrating the Margins
Queer Words and Sexual Trauma
in the "Gutter"—Gloria Naylor's
The Women of Brewster Place *(1982)*

> ... race-d queer discourses often queer queerness itself in
> ways that are, as yet, un- or underarticulated.[1]
>
> Queer times require even queerer modalities of thought, analy-
> sis, creativity, and expression in order to elaborate upon nation-
> alist, patriotic, and terrorist formations and their imbricated
> forms of racialized perverse sexualities and gender dysphorias.[2]

The previous chapters began the work of unraveling what representation
means across multiple contexts by applying misdirection as a methodology
to expose the underlying oppressions that have historically fixed color of representation in terms of what it is not. This chapter takes up Gloria Naylor's
novel to explore the queer(ed) dissonance created through the unique structure and language of sequential art and how representation in literary fiction
can be "read" and defined in more creative and inclusive ways.

The Women of Brewster Place is written as a pastiche of pain, as framed
moments of shattered lives reassembling at the center of a small community
which is itself a traumatized version of a larger social pathology. It begins
with Mattie Michael's horrific beating at the hands of her God-fearing father
who is enraged that she has become pregnant out of wedlock, and she is the
first of seven women whose personal traumas knit together the hardscrabble
lives in this novel. They are women who, for various reasons, have traveled
from near and far in search of acceptance and belonging. They have brought
with them stories that seep into the bricks and mortar, the cracks and crevices,
the gaps and spaces, and indeed into the very fabric of their new community.

My use of the hybrid structure of graphic narratives as an analytical tool

105

for extending the close reading of the rape scene in Naylor's novel is supported by the notion of misdirection that problematizes difficult truths about *of color* relationships, as well as historical complicity in the "profound misreadings" and resulting trauma to the queer(ed) black body.[3] The rape of Lorraine takes place in an alley, the physical structure analogous to the intericonic or "gutter" spaces in graphic narratives. The walls of the alley represent dominant hegemonic paradigms that preconfigure the frameworks through which broader ethnocultural and gender issues are defined. By extending this particular metaphor beyond its ideological applications, I apply the semiotics of misdirection to expand the reader's imagination beyond its comfort zone and to set out paradigm shifts where "Other" realities emerge to alternately challenge and misdirect the oppressive hegemonic gaze.

Ferdinand de Saussure and Charles S. Peirce are most frequently credited with developing contemporary approaches to semiotics, although the study of signs is said to date back to the time of Augustine of Hippo who is credited by some to have been the originator of semiotics.[4] And while contemporary scholars choose a variety of approaches to using one or the other model in their research, my decision (as I noted in Chapter 1) to underpin some of the arguments in this book with the social semiotics advanced by Theo van Leeuwen and Gunther R. Kress indicates at once how complex yet fluid the study of semiotics can be. For my purposes here I am interested in explaining more fully the physical structure of the alley as a sign and some of the attendant rules and meanings attached to it.

In the first chapter I explained that Peirce's triadic model is comprised of a representamen (sign or sign vehicle), an interpretant (the sense that we make of the sign), and an object (something to which the sign refers). In relation to the sign and its constituent parts, we also have to consider Peirce's theory of Firstness (icon), Secondness (index), and Thirdness (symbol). There are many other "Thirdness relationships"[5] that come under the First, Second, and Third categories. For example, the sign itself (firstness), the object (secondness), and the interpretant (thirdness). There is also chaos (firstness), order (secondness), and structure (thirdness).[6] Earlier on I also explained how the concept of misdirection—which if we follow Bergman's reasoning that "two different interpretants can derive different meanings from the same representation, and a given object may be represented by different tokens"[7]— functions as a signifying strategy that is defined by the contexts through which it seeks to effect perceptual shifts. The context in this case is male space (the alley), and the experiences that each individual brings with them in their interpretation of the traumatic (and dramatic), life-changing events that take place in the alley.

When I visualize the alley in Naylor's novel, I see a poorly lit, narrow passageway comprised of equally narrow twists and turns that signify unseen danger. The sense of trepidation in navigating this claustrophobic space is especially heightened at night, when the only signs of life might be rats scurrying through looking for food or a mugger hoping for an easy mark. The alley itself is the form that the sign takes (the representamen), the dimly lit and narrow passageway stands for danger (the object or that which the object represents), and Lorraine and C.C. Baker and his friends are the interpretents (the ones who make sense of the sign relevant to their understanding of the object represented through an icon, index, or symbol). Therefore, although Lorraine experiences some hesitation in using the alley as a shortcut to her apartment, knowing on some level that this structure represents predominantly male space, she ignores her intuition and continues on her way. C.C. Baker and his friends, having more real world knowledge of subterfuge and misdirection, take cover in the shadows of the alley because they interpret this space as a tactical advantage over their innocent prey.

In every conceivable way Naylor's novel is about trauma, its meaning, and the signs that cohere through and around it. It is a work of fiction that exposes uncomfortable truths about inexpressibly painful moments in the lives of women whose skin color, sexual orientation, and independence from men constitutes the "fraught belonging" that Sharon Patricia Holland reminds us is never very far outside of the discursive frame.[8] Although Holland was speaking of the conditional belonging of African Americans within the borders of a nationalist frame, and how readily self-appointed guardians prevaricate on the matter of who does or does not belong, her overall critique specifically shines a light on the eroticism of racism and the violence visited upon black bodies. In this regard, I extend Holland's analysis to argue that when the unique structure of comics is applied to our reading of the gang rape of Lorraine, the physical structure of the alleyway where the rape takes place is analogous to this hybrid comic form. Furthermore, this multi-level/multimodal approach to understanding sexual trauma compels readers to rethink how space can support subterfuge (in the case of the rape of Lorraine), but also how even violated space can be reclaimed (which happens at the end of Naylor's novel) and ultimately transformed.

Trauma that is expressed through the visual lens of graphic narratives and, in this chapter, trauma that is violently enacted between the walls and masculinized space of an alleyway, at once hurtles us toward the imagery of sexual violation, but also away from its destructive force. Ariela Freedman addresses this tension when she writes:

Pain frustrates and isolates in part because of its resistance to communicability; it cannot be adequately explained or displayed, and it resists absolute containment through
either word or image. But because comics employ both word *and* image, they can try
to bridge the internal and external representation of pain; they can tell pain and show
it.[9]

Freedman's observation sits squarely in the field of graphic medicine where
trauma wends its way through displacement, truth, anger, and the spaces and
gaps in our individual and collective memories. I discuss graphic medicine
more specifically in a later chapter, but would note here the growing number
of books that are being published in the field. Some of the more recognizable
titles are Jennifer Hayden's *The Story of My Tits* (2015), Sarah Leavitt's *Tangles:
Alzheimer's, My Mother, and Me* (2012), Bobby Baker's *Diary Drawings: Mental
Illness and Me* (2010), and Katie Green's *Lighter Than My Shadow* (2013).
Where words alone fall short in describing pain, illness, and trauma, graphic
medicine serves as a more expansive and expressive medium.

Where the Margins Are: Naylor's Walled City

Garnering the American Book Award for Best First Novel, *The Women
of Brewster Place* is Naylor's fictional account of a community of poor, mostly
non-white people living on a dead-end, walled-off street in an unnamed city.
At just under two hundred pages, the spare prose is used to powerful effect
in describing the complexities of human suffering. It could be said that Naylor's novel calls forth uncomfortable truths that are sometimes indistinguishable from the lies that hold those very truths at bay. In considering this sleight
of hand, one must take a leap of faith that what is not immediately revealed
will eventually come to light, for there are always two sides (and in-between
places) to every story.

In the opening pages of the novel, Brewster Place is described as the
"bastard child of several clandestine meetings between the alderman of the
sixth district and the managing director of" the fictitious "Unico Realty Company."[10] The wall separating the disenfranchised from the heartbeat of the
city becomes a symbol of the desperation, last chances, and sometimes the
new lives that people living in or moving to Brewster Place experience.
Although their community signifies nothing more than a forgotten strip of
land to the Unico Realty Company, each of their stories—and especially those
of Lorraine and Theresa, the lesbian couple whose relationship was the source
of endless speculation, gossip and even hatred—makes Brewster Place unique
in its own way.

After the gruesome gang-rape of Lorraine by C.C. Baker and his pot-smoking, misogynist sycophants, the women in the community set aside pettiness that often comes from close living. They rally around the couple once referred to as "them," "lezzies," "dykes," or, simply, "The Two" because Lorraine and Theresa come to symbolize the struggles that all of the women living in Brewster Place finally find the courage to address head-on. Focusing on the lives of seven women whose desire for love and acceptance lead them down different paths, the fictitious Brewster Place symbolizes renewed hope and second chances.

The characters Naylor portrays are worn down to nubs, their measurement of themselves always contingent on someone else being worse off than they are. They are the prototypical outsiders, the marginal people whose customs and beliefs—often within their own communities—set them apart from the rest of society, leaving them at the mercy of oppressive institutions that mark them as different. It is this difference that is at once a type of freedom from the oppression of sameness, but which also works as a key vulnerability. By not following the rules, fitting in, or possessing the right lineage, the dispossessed are often seen to be complicit in their own misfortune. To varying degrees, they all traverse similar historical ground and their individual and collective actions are "conditioned by years of instinctual response" to the needs of men.[11] But the memories that reside deep within their psyches and their bodies will lead them not astray, but rather to a place between the shadows where meaning is remade in their image.

Where Naylor's work becomes particularly useful for my critique of how queer women of color are represented in literature (specifically in fiction and graphic narratives), is in the inclusion of a black lesbian couple whose struggle for acceptance in their small insular community is over-representative of the particular hardships experienced by marginalized groups. As the ultimate outsiders, queer women of color do not necessarily benefit from the legal and/or social protections afforded firstly to white men, secondly to white women, thirdly to black men, and lastly to black heterosexual women. Queers of color are the ultimate aberration at the end of a hetero and Eurocentric continuum that defines what is or is not acceptable and the limits of protection certain minority groups should be afforded.

Sexual trauma has a disproportionate impact on socially and politically marginalized classes—transgender folk, lesbians of color, victims of FGM, child brides and other sexual, ethnic minority, religious or political groups—and is often treated differently from trauma experienced and expressed by whites. As Angela P. Harris asserts, "For black women, rape is a far more complex experience, and an experience as deeply rooted in color as" it is "in gender."[12] Harris's words, as this section explores, still hold critical currency. If we also consider Vickroy's reminder that trauma "can be a powerful indicator of oppressive cultural institutions and practices,"[13] we can more fully appreciate the degree to which sexual trauma has become normalized across numerous social and political contexts. Indeed, rape and its resulting trauma is immeasurable, difficult to comprehend, and leaves deep psychological scars on survivors.

The themes of violence in Naylor's novel, as well as the novel's structural and perceptual shifts, present opportunities to think creatively about ways to subvert and rearticulate paradigms that normalize the sexual exploitation of girls and women. It is also an opportunity to consider broader questions about sexual trauma that goes unheard, underreported, and largely unremarked. My critique looks at how stories that impact the lives of queer women of color can be retold through the semiotics of misdirection and how they can be more meaningfully and strategically positioned in larger critical narratives.

Shifting the Frame

Vickroy asserts that trauma is a "tyranny of the past" and that it "interferes with the ability to pay attention to both new and familiar situations."[14] I use the terms sexual trauma, rape, and sexual terrorism to make explicit the devastating impact these acts have upon the bodies and psyches of queer women of color. How these acts of extreme violence are depicted in both fiction and the graphic narrative, and how queer women of color are often represented in the national (white) imaginary as sexually insatiable and perverse, bears examination via alternative frames of reference. These frames of reference disrupt the us/them binary that, Annecka Marshall argues, sets up and reinforces blackness as pathology. Marshall explains that "the development and maintenance of imagery of Black female sexuality has been a primarily 'white' male and, to a lesser extent, 'white' female and Black male means of exerting authority over us."[15] This imbalance of power traces its genealogy to institutions of oppression (slavery, prisons, marriage, religion) that were (and continue to be) set up by the few to control the many. The ultimate systems of control exercised over women's bodies is interlinked with networks that produce fear and ultimately acquiescence to "higher" authorities: church, family, society. This truth is chillingly played out in the story of Mattie Michael. She is the first of seven women whose life unfolds through the crevices and gaps of Brewster Place.

Having gone against the strict rules of appropriate social behavior laid down by her father, a religious man who abided by God's law as if faith alone could eradicate all evil from the world, Mattie drew his wrath by laying down in sin with Butch Fuller, a man of little worth to God-fearing people. Discovering that his virtuous daughter had succumbed to temptation and fallen pregnant, Mattie's father turns his rage on his daughter by nearly beating her to death.[16] The sanctity of Mattie's body, belonging first to God and then to her father, was never hers to willingly and knowingly share with anyone, least of all Butch Fuller. When she was old enough to date, she was expected to keep company with a church-going man who would be chosen by her father. Instead, she was seduced by Butch Fuller's sweet-talking and abandoned by him once he had gotten what he wanted. All through her lifelong days, Mattie only knew a conditional acceptance contingent upon her acquiescence to the needs, demands, and yearnings of men. Falling afoul of this dictum by giving away the only thing that assured her passage into heaven (or, at the least, into a good marriage) made her a woman marked for the violence of a male dominated world.

The significance that I ascribe throughout this chapter to sexual trauma and its destructive and often invisible path is central to debates put forth by scholars who characterize the "gutter" (also known as intericonic space, interframes, or between images) as devoid of meaning or function other than as a relatively unimportant feature signifying a pause or gap in action between panels. Neil Cohn has stated that "the gutter does not provide any meaning—the content of the panels and their union does."[17] I also remain unconvinced by the assertion of Thierry Groensteen that the "gutter, insignificant in itself, is invested with an arthrologic function that can only be deciphered in light of the singular images that it separates and unites."[18] This stance (of empty space in and of itself being insignificant) sets up in real terms the rules of engagement between what Paul Gilroy calls the "heterocultural citizenry" and queers of color who are on the other side of culturally (en)gendered binarisms.[19] As Ann Cvetkovich has made clear, "forms of violence that are forgotten or covered over by the amnesiac powers of national culture, which is adept at using one trauma story to suppress another," is indicative of a society that has lost its moral compass, and one in which far too often, truth is consigned to the gutter.[20]

Cvetkovich's investigation of the narrow terms of nationalist debates regarding the elevation of one form of trauma (nations) over another (the individual), as well as her exploration of what she refers to as "lesbian sites of trauma" which are located outside (or in the "gutter") of the "public culture" argument she names as the locus of her larger critique, sets the stage for broader debates that work to disrupt dominant inscriptions that impact disproportionately on the lives (and bodies) of queer women of color.[21] I unpack here how inscriptions of sexual trauma, based on the "ideological legacy" that Patricia Hill Collins asserts "constructs Black male heterosexuality through images of wild beasts, criminals and rapists," extends to racist literary and cultural productions that at once ignore black women, yet at the same time justify multiple forms of racial and sexual oppression.[22] Following on Groensteen's insistence that the gutter does not "merit fetishization,"[23] a statement which I cannot completely disagree with, what it does deserve is recognition as a site of inferred meaning or, ironically, as Groensteen suggests, as the symbolic site of absence.[24] Absence here, I suggest, is symbolic of queer black erasure, which in turn infers that something (or someone) was once there.

My entry point into this engagement with Naylor's novel begins with a brief summary of the critical frameworks underpinning my approach. I do this to support my overall argument regarding the idea of "lack." As a definitional premise in the construction of meaning, particularly where such meaning either reinforces racial stereotypes or works to "bracket race," lack is historically rooted in oppressive political and cultural systems.[25] These frameworks are necessarily grounded in critical race feminism and queer theory—critical race feminism because our multiple identities (wives, mothers, sisters, daughters "of color") require "that more precise terms are needed to examine racial consciousness, institutional bias, inequality, patterns of segregation, and the distribution of power"[26]and queer theory because this allows for an articulation of lesbian truths that have been historically suppressed in service to the larger cultural norm.

Crossroads

Refusing to retreat from difficult truths, Naylor's writing is grounded firmly in her upbringing as a black woman born just four years before *Brown v. Board of Education* came into full effect. This historical ruling made segregation in public schools unconstitutional, yet it took seventeen more years before *Loving v. Virginia* resulted in the United States Supreme Court striking down anti-miscegenation laws. Thus, while black children were finally afforded access to the same educational resources and schools as white children, marriage—the most inviolable of relationships before the law and God—continued to be the barometer against which all other racial (in)equalities were measured. The decriminalization of sex and sexual orientation was not far behind, with Illinois becoming the first state in 1962 to decriminalize sodomy. This was followed forty-one years later by the United States Supreme Court ruling in *Lawrence v. Texas*, which invalidated anti-sodomy laws in the remaining thirteen states where the criminalization of private same-sex relations was still on the books.

While these events ushered in legal changes that had significant implications for people of color and sexual minorities in America, none went far enough to dislodge or remedy centuries of racial, gender, and sexual oppression. Naylor's characters are similarly situated at a historical crossroads. Confronted with the harsh reality of living in a world where sanctuary is never assured and inequality is almost always guaranteed, the women who live in Brewster Place could be said to disproportionately represent and embody the trauma of a nation. Interwoven with the trappings of freedom for some, for others the unexpected reality of discrimination with a northern face awaited them at the end of their journey.[27]

The experiences that Naylor braids throughout the tangled tresses of trauma's historical path, the women whose experiences she considers as she would her own, are, she has said, "[...] filtered through me and everything I do, everything I ate that morning—that whole thing."[28] Naylor's channeling of truths that others may not so readily own moves us forward through what Vickroy contends is "an experiential approach to memory and history, both elucidating and confronting us with the interconnections between traumatic historical events, memory and the body, as well as how we can ascribe meaning to the past."[29] Queer women of color who epitomize the trope of the "constitutive outsider" relevant to what is "understood, celebrated and remembered about Blackness"[30] are uniquely positioned to rewrite historical misrepresentations that work to perpetuate and justify individual and collective erasure. This palimpsest of words, traced over and over again with the etchings of "fine lines and loops, commas and periods"[31] that women like Mattie Michael and the others in Brewster Place's small community try to make sense of, is encoded with the trauma of centuries of sexual and racial terror.

Trapped behind the walls separating their community of "Others" from the city center, the residents of Brewster Place are compelled to follow the rules of engagement laid down by centuries of cultural and social conditioning. This is the contract. It is an agreement imposed by the powerful and reluctantly entered into by the dispossessed. It is both a racial and sexual contract pressed upon those whose legacies were shaped under its oppressive boot and a contract taken for granted by those who benefited from its colonialist imprimatur.[32] What emerges from this intra-psychic stratification is a condition Sara Ahmed examines in *Queer Phenomenology: Orientations, Objects, Others.*

Taking as her starting point a speculative account put forth by Franz Fanon, who suggests that the political, spatial, cultural and social limits of the racialized body imbues even the most innocent act of reaching for a cigarette as conditioned upon one's orientation to one's surroundings, Ahmed (and Fanon) argue that this *reaching* orients the body towards the familiar, but also away from that which is unknown or unwelcoming of its difference. It is "a performance," Ahmed states, that orients one "toward the future, insofar as the action is also the expression of a wish or intention."[33] But this intention, connected as it is to one's ability to freely reach toward something, is predicated upon familiarity of things outside of the hostile white gaze. Ahmed points out that "racism ensures that the black gaze returns to the black body, which is not a loving return but rather follows the line of the hostile white gaze,"[34] a white gaze that assures itself, through the negation of others, that it is righteous and pure.

This line of gender or sexual or racial hostility, which results in a kind of intentional self-erasure, is captured in the scene below with Lorraine and her neighbors. After an accusation about Lorraine and her lover is made by the neighborhood gossip, the reaction of the other women in the room is telling. They dare not speak out against Sophie's pronouncement for fear that they too will be viewed with suspicion. Lorraine, wanting nothing more than to disappear, stands still "like a fading spirit before the ebony statue that Sophie pointed at her like a crucifix."[35] Here, then, the fear of difference is plain and cannot be ignored.

The immediate and unequivocal rejection of that which Lorraine's union with her lover represents (debauchery, unnaturalness, perversity) has the potential to taint all who dare to challenge Sophie's accusation. By invoking God (the pointed finger that stands in for the crucifix), and passing judgment, Sophie relished the power she wielded at that moment. Her sardonic pronouncement that Lorraine and Theresa have brought a kind of perversion to Brewster Place that is wholly unwelcome finds a receptive and God-fearing audience.[36] To paraphrase Ahmed once more, this unloving return of the hostile white gaze transmitted through the socially conditioned black consciousness weakens and destroys coalitions that might otherwise be formed in the dismantling of racially and sexually charged legacies. And there is a harsh reality in the statement that "women, subordinate classes, and non-whites may be oppressed in common, but it is not a common oppression."[37] This is particularly so in some black communities where the collective response to sexual "Otherness" is seen as both indefensible and incomprehensible. The demonization of sex and Otherness, the "race-ing" of morality and virtue, the elevation of Christian over non-believer, the conflation of heterosexuality and man/womanhood, and the power of the accuser over the accused, work to reinforce the hostile heterosexual gaze along the transgressive and self-negating queer(ed) body.

Naylor's novel serves as a reminder of the lifelong peregrinations of a borderless and traumatized people. We are made to understand this when "the young black woman and the old yellow woman [of Brewster Place] sat in the kitchen for hours, blending their lives so that what lay behind one and ahead of the other became indistinguishable."[38] What Mattie Michael and Miss Eva share in words can, "through the frame—which we may understand as boxes of time—present a narrative, but that narrative is threaded through with absence, with the rich white spaces of what is called the gutter."[39] Stitching together time as it comes to them—in fractured seconds, ruptured minutes, and borrowed hours—their separate memories of life lived on the edge of time forms a temporal bridge that allows them to traverse and join together narratives from one traumatic frame to the next.

Graphic Imagery

Graphic narratives work to contextualize trauma in many unique ways. As a literary art form its interstitial make-up can be expanded to take into account other literary genres that are not quite "in the frame." Graphic narratives also work to slow down and, to some degree, disrupt the process of *how* we read. But it is Leigh Gilmore's observations that provide what I call the linguistic "struts" for the discursive links I work to establish between the trauma depicted in the complex patterns that Gloria Naylor weaves for us on her spiny literary loom and the "pictorial language" that distinguishes graphic narratives from other forms of trauma reportage.[40]

This artistic propinquity, the unrecognized kinship here, could be construed as speaking to the "genealogy of the feminist interpretive strategy" that Gilmore calls "*autobiographics* [italics belong to Gilmore] and its relation to technologies of autobiography."[41] The essential idea behind Gilmore's argument is that rather than basing our understanding of women's self-representation on the traditional ideas and structure of conventional autobiographical work, new strategies must be used to (re)trace a literary genealogy that has been "largely unmapped, indeed unrecognizable, given traditional maps of genre and periodization."[42] Ostensibly, this shift in approach takes us closer to what Gilmore asserts to be "elements of self-representation" that are "concerned with interruptions and eruptions," and "with resistance and contradiction [...]."[43] This, then, is the work of the women who push against the margins while also trying to be a part of the inward-facing community that is Brewster Place.

We must consider how trauma is "framed," how it is laid out on a page, jammed into grids, written in ink and pencil and sometimes even in blood.[44] And we must understand that these "framings" straddle what Mikhail Bakhtin described as the synchronous occurrence of, and tension between, the "authority of discourse and its internal persuasiveness [that] may be united in a single word—one that is *simultaneously* [italics belong to Bakhtin] authoritative and internally persuasive—despite the profound differences between these two categories of alien discourse."[45] It is precisely this kind of "otherness" that ultimately works to subvert the very monolithic scripts that would see queer women of color silenced. Indeed, Bakhtin's incisive descriptions of an attenuated philology—where unquestioning allegiance to a "prior discourse"[46] works to narrow the scope of language, thereby cutting off access to wider linguistic tributaries—is all the more compelling for the synergistic tension it ultimately creates in the intericonic spaces that I critique throughout this book.

By subsuming queer women of color realities into broader nationalist frames of war, genocide, and terrorism, my return to a decades-old novel that refocuses the nationalist lens on subaltern lives that remain just out of the frame attempts to address some of the critical gaps in contemporary works specific to the experiences of lesbians of color. A similar dynamic is persuasively argued by Judith Butler, who considers the implications of war and its centrality in the framing of lives that are valued and those that are not. She writes that the "frame comments and editorializes" on what we see, how we are framed, and how the act of framing effectively frames us.[47] Moreover, "the frame tends to function, even in a minimalist form, as an editorial embellishment of the image, if not a self-commentary on the history of the frame itself."[48] The persons outside of the frame become, as Butler goes on to note, the problem that must be managed but one that "normativity" continually replicates.[49] In other words the frame—government, law enforcement, the prison-industrial-complex—creates the very monster that it then seeks to control or destroy.

In the insular community of Brewster Place, men control women through emotional, physical, and sexual violence. They control the framing of the encounter so that the one who is "framed" is in fact trapped on multiple and complex levels. They set into motion Eve Sedgwick's assertion that the "entire machinery by which 'rape' is signified in this culture"[50] fits into a ready narrative of blackness/otherness as a corollary to whiteness that is perpetually under siege. We see this in how the alley in the novel's rape scene at once historicizes and frames the confrontation between what Lorraine as a lesbian of color represents to C.C. Baker and his friends (the corrupting influence of white culture) and what they represent to her (men with no power, save the very instrument of violence that signifies their own debasement under a historical narrative of alterity).

While contemporary scholarship takes up these issues of trauma, it primarily traces the profound impact this has had on white women, gay men of color, heterosexual men and women of color, and, to a lesser degree, white gay men. Lesbians of color are not specifically identified in these frames, no matter that under the narrow category of "black women," rape and murder are woven so tightly into its fabric. Relatedly, Fionnuala Ní Aoláin asserts that often during negotiations for transitions from war to peace, "the experiences and needs of women are markedly absent or silenced by the general discourse of accounting for the past," be that through mechanisms such as war trials or truth commissions.[51]

In far too many communities of color, lesbians are at risk on multiple levels. Firstly, they are not "real" women because they do not cater to the sexual needs of black men. Secondly, they are blasphemous because they ignore God's law that marriage should only be between a man and a woman. And finally, they bring shame to their race because of their deviant proclivities. Yet what is at stake in narratives that elide the particular trauma of queer women of color is related to Aoláin's assertion that violence against women is "not [a] discontinuous [reality]."[52] Rather, it is all part of a continuum.

During times of violent unrest and the eventual—though certainly not always inevitable—transition to non-aggression, there remain "complimentary patriarchies" that continue to valorize the rule of men and deny or erode the rights of women.[53] I extend Aoláin's observation here, applying it to small insular communities such as Naylor's fictional Brewster Place to demonstrate how discontinuous realities of women and the complementary patriarchies between men has a disproportionately negative impact on the lives of lesbians of color.

Prelude to a Rape

Not unlike that of others who drifted to Brewster Place in search of escape, safety, and new beginnings, Lorraine and Theresa's arrival had been preceded by hardships they could only ever confront in a backward-facing way. They had to first take flight before they could regroup and brace themselves against the tide of disapproval that would see them struck down for their "unnatural" ways. Having been marked early on as women without men, Lorraine and Theresa are viewed with suspicion. The community's frame of reference, itself only a subset of the larger hegemonic discourse that defines who they are and what they are allowed to do, excludes that which sits just a bit off-kilter on the family tree. This excision from the lines and loops and boxes that configure and solidify belonging harkens back to all of the Sophies, in all of the Brewster Places, where people like Lorraine and Theresa who move cautiously in and out of liminal spaces "[…] ain't wanted here!"[54]

There must be, as Chase Gregory argues, an unraveling and reworking of the dualisms that relate to representations of the gutter (or interstitial space) as a site of opposition (implying it has a literal and metaphorical "existence") and also emptiness (suggesting it has no function other than as a separator between panels). His argument that spatiotemporal features in both comics and queer theory arise from similar ideological debates against heteronormative imperatives to reproduce leads him to claim:

> Because "queerness" is placed in opposition to institutions of linear time (family, heterosexual futurism, reproduction, capitalism), its existence disrupts "reproductive temporality" […] and instead posits new temporalities—ones that refuse forward movement through the institutions of generational inheritance and instead fuck with the family tree[…].[55]

Gregory's argument creates an interesting tension between black queer multiplicities and white hetero and homonormative constructs of what family (or belonging) does or does not mean. Yet "fucking with the family tree," as Gregory puts it, further displaces queer women of color in ways that may not have an immediate or similarly deleterious effect on white lesbians or gay men, who also strive for increased visibility in hegemonic systems. Queer women of color must contend with converging systems of oppression, whereby the social construction of race and gender places them outside the prototypical white (and black) family tree. In many respects the "gutter" can be a site of subversion and liberation, a different layer in the "closet," or, as Vickroy suggests in her analysis of history as told through the body politic, an "unmasking [of] how social controls and myths are utilized to abet trauma,"[56] controls that give men like C.C. Baker license to use force as a means of rebuilding an identity that has been systematically destroyed as a consequence of his own dubious birthright.

"C.C. Baker was greatly disturbed by the thought of a Lorraine."[57] The inference in this single sentence, the thought of *a* Lorraine, rather than of *Lorraine*, a person, a human being, is the necessary prelude to the "Othering" that allows for a disconnection between violent actions and responsibility. We see this in socio-political landscapes where war lays the groundwork for unchecked atrocities, where inference is all that is needed to justify the elimination of perceived threats, be those threats to the nation, to the preservation of family, or to the rule of law. Men like C.C. Baker bolster their fragile egos through sexual intimidation of women. Their male genitalia links them to the only form of respect they are able to command from women. These young men, the C.C. Bakers of small insular communities like Brewster Place, wander aimlessly through life looking for some clue as to who they are or if they even exist. Their self-worth is measured in the hardness of their resolve, the cleverness of their scams, the unchallenged control of the dilapidated, rat-infested buildings they call home. Flawed products of the white imaginary that conjured them up from elements of its own monstrous self, they are the savages we have been taught to fear.

Lorraine represents what C.C. Baker cannot control except through force. Even then, the extent of his control is shaped by laws that are only conditionally granted to him because he is—to echo Robert Reid-Pharr's insightful commentary on the conflicted relationship many black men have within and outside of themselves—"eclipsed."[58] The very essence of C.C. Baker's manhood is at once threatened by, yet also contingent upon, the things he desires the most: to be seen, acknowledged, loved. C.C. Baker and his friends want to be loved, yet their idea of love has been shaped by what they have been told they are not: worthy, human, kind, or equal among men. They can only be recognized by someone who fears them and whose life by comparison is irremediably flawed, unfixable, and, in C.C. Baker's mind, "unnatural." Indeed, C.C. Baker understands, perhaps better than even someone like Lorraine, that his miserable life still affords him membership in a network as old as time itself: heterosexuality. He knows that as long as he keeps within those boundaries, his power over women, and his own dead-end life, is assured.

In the ensuing exchange that C.C. and his sycophants have with Kiswana and Lorraine, which is quietly observed by Theresa from the window of her and Lorraine's apartment, C.C. knows how far he is able to push the situation with Kiswana. He is aware that she has a boyfriend and he is at once afraid of the consequences that might arise if he crosses the line with her, but also appreciative of the fact that unlike Lorraine, Kiswana is sexually attracted to men. This affords Kiswana a level of protection that does not extend to Lorraine, whose choice of a woman as her presumed sexual partner leaves her open to attack.

Kiswana makes a joke about C.C. Baker's manhood and his friends cannot help but laugh out of "respect for the girl who had beat him at the

dozens."[59] But when Lorraine "smiled at the absolutely lost look on his face
[...] he curled his lips back into a snarl and tried to regain lost ground by
attacking what instinct told him was the weaker of the two."[60]

Lorraine's passiveness and the threatening response that her smile elicits
from C.C. Baker is observed by her lover, who watches from the window and
presumably hears the exchange. Lorraine is unskilled in the art of signifying.
She has no clue how to play the dozens or engage in misdirection. She does
not know how to deflect attention away from herself or how to participate in
the ritual of talking trash, no matter that she desperately wants to be accepted
into the communal fold.

Incensed that Lorraine has joined in on his public humiliation, C.C.
Baker threatens to "come over there and stick my fist in your cunt-eatin'
mouth!" He follows this up with a threat: "I'm gonna remember this, Butch!"[61]
Lorraine is anything but butch, yet it is the only word C.C. Baker has access
to in his limited understanding of the world. When he and his friends "stood
with their black skin, ninth-grade diplomas, and fifty-word vocabularies in
front of the mirror that the world had erected and saw nothing," it was only
the reflection of one another in their "tinted sunglasses" that anchored them
to the ground.[62] Looking down from the window at the exchange, Theresa
thinks to herself that it is "just like Lorraine to stand there and let someone
else take up for her." She also thinks that perhaps Lorraine has finally "learned
her lesson about these ignorant nothings on Brewster Place."[63] It is worth
noting that the person Theresa feels compelled to defend, if it came to that,
is not her lover but instead the woman who bested C.C. Baker at the dozens.[64]
By choosing to defend Kiswana over her lover, Theresa becomes complicit
in the harsh "lessons" she believes that Lorraine must learn as a matter of
their mutual survival. She has grown quite weary of her lover's timidity, and
when Lorraine complains to her of feeling excluded and their relationship
being the subject of unwarranted gossip, Theresa—exasperated by the para-
noia that precipitated their moves from Detroit, Linden Hills, Park Heights,
and ultimately to Brewster Place—berates her.

"They, they, they!" Theresa shouts. "You know, I'm not starting up with
this again, Lorraine. Who in the hell are they?"[65] she asks, knowing full well
the frustration her lover feels at not being accepted into yet another place,
another community, another "family." It does not help that Theresa, who is
unafraid of innuendo or gossip, and is secure in her sexual expression, is
with a woman who bristles at Theresa's pronouncement that she and Lorraine
are "just a couple of dykes." Lorraine is startled by this, telling Theresa that
it is "a filthy thing to say" and that she (Lorraine) is "not like that."[66] But she
is like *that*. She is *a* Lorraine.

The Alley

Thoughts of the one true friendship she had made with Ben, the lonely handyman of Brewster Place, contributed to Lorraine's fateful decision to take a shortcut through the alley. She had been out for the evening, without Theresa, at a birthday party thrown by two gay friends. Unwilling to give Theresa the satisfaction of knowing that she had not enjoyed herself and had left the party early, Lorraine avoids taking the most direct route back to their apartment. And it was the "claw-edged sweetness of the marijuana" in the air as she made her way into the alley that alerted her to possible danger.[67]

Trying to peer through the shadows, Lorraine pushes down the anxiety rising within her, attributing her nervousness to "senseless fears [that would] multiply until it would be impossible to get through them to the other side."[68] She has been conditioned to ignore her internal voice, choosing instead to admonish herself for being "senseless." The opening of the alley, with its dark secrets contained between imposing walls that muffle its subversive utterances, underscores the conflicted relationship man has with what he has been taught is the pleasure, and also the treacherousness, of a woman's body. Woman is the archetype of Eve the Fallen, of Mary Magdalene, the whore redeemed. It has long been the case that the entrance to a woman's body is dictated by heterosexual discourse that situates her outside of the frame, the panel, or even society.

Lorraine's fear of the unknown (and the unseen) is not entirely without basis. An example often cited by scholars of the sequential arts when the matter of the "gutter" arises is the immediately recognizable *EEYAA!!* in Scott McCloud's book *Understanding Comics* (1993). McCloud draws the reader's attention to several panels that appear to be, but are not necessarily predictive of, an assured outcome. The action and words in the first panel set the reader up to expect that the character being chased by an axe-wielding maniac who is screaming "Now you die" will in fact meet with a certain death. Thus, in the next panel when we "hear" the utterance *EEYAA!!*, we assume the worst; we are misdirected. Yet as McCloud points out, although he "may have drawn an axe being raised," it is the reader whose imagination, experience, or assumptions allow it to drop and decide "how hard the blow [...], who screamed, [and] why."[69] I draw attention to McCloud's example to illustrate the point that the action unfolding page by page in Naylor's novel seems to confirm the reader's assumption that, based upon the chain of events leading up to Lorraine's decision to cut through the alley, something terrible is about to happen. If we visualize Lorraine's progress as being laid out sequentially, from panel to panel, the gaps and interstitial spaces that connect those panels eventually resolve in a terrible fade to Lorraine's own *EEYAA!!* moment.

When Lorraine hears "the first pair of soft thuds behind her" she begins to panic, her instincts kick in, and she starts walking faster. The subsequent thuds "started her running[...]."[70] Here the reader is presented with a dreadful choice. We can either draw upon a range of possibilities to explain away the soft thuds as something Lorraine imagines she hears, for we have already been led to believe that she is an alarmist, or we must accept what our experience tells us is true. But if we premise our conclusion upon a series of inferences that are stitched together from prior experiences of violence or the threat of violence, we can only conclude that the next frame/panel/page/gap will confirm our worst fears about what might happen next. We use our past experiences, our imaginations, and our knowledge about the trauma of others to *visualize* what will happen to Lorraine. We know that the axe will fall.

And we know (or can assume) that the four soft thuds belong to four bodies and that Lorraine—who earlier on in the novel had been described as the "lighter, skinny one" with a "timid mincing walk and the slightly protruding teeth [...]"—will be no match for them.[71] When one of those bodies "that had been pressed against the shadowy building swung into her path so suddenly she couldn't stop in time,"[72] we know that what is about to happen, there, in the "gutter," is shaped by rules that come from the privileged hegemonic frame. Using the pretext of Lorraine having purposely bumped into him, C.C. Baker sets into motion the cruel punishment he had promised to unleash were she ever to cross his path again. By putting himself in Lorraine's path, yet casting her as the initiator of a physical affront to him, he leaves her with no way out. "Can't you say excuse me, dyke?"[73] His query re-establishes a hierarchy of power that was temporarily disrupted when Kiswana stood as his equal on the street and bested him at his own game. Her ability to cast off his authority is not extended to Lorraine because she has stepped outside the protection of the heteronormative circle.

It is not enough that Lorraine has been pathologized by racist, as well as by sexist, agendas, because for men like C.C. Baker, her lesbianism also casts her existence in terms of a deadly pathogen that must be neutralized or eradicated. This pathologizing model that exists among "multiple subordinate groups with intersecting identities" for whom "intersectional invisibility" is the norm results in levels of "self-othering" that unintentionally feed into dangerous and exclusionary narratives.[74] The last sound Lorraine hears before her bladder loosens and her throat constricts, and before she is set upon by her rapists and torn to shreds, are sneakers that "hit the cement with a dead thump."[75] These men used the vantage point they enjoyed from atop one of the walls, "watching her come up that back street."[76] The walls signify containment and are controlled—much like the privileged frame—by the language of men. In the novel they function as the narrative that C.C. Baker and his friends create and re-enact from a poisonous historical script. Women are simply props that help drive the plot toward its inevitable outcome. They have no speaking parts.

The Rape

"Ain't you got no manners? Stepping on my foot and not saying you sorry?"[77] As the director, producer, and main actor in this deadly play, Lorraine's interrogator knows what comes next. He sets the pacing, arranges the scene, and considers the severity of the punishment he will impose. The "gutter" becomes a compressed space, every inch taken up by "the four bodies that now linked themselves across the alley […]," blocking Lorraine's escape.[78] As the scene unfolds, C.C. Baker's inflated sense of himself emerges in stark contrast to Lorraine's internalized sense of worthlessness. He has convinced himself that Lorraine must be punished for breaching the rules of normative sexual engagement, but he must also grapple with his own invisibility in a world where neither he nor any of his friends matter. They spend their days roaming the streets of Brewster Place, "awaiting [a] transformation" that would change their lives, that would someday "propel them into the heaven populated by their gods—Shaft and Superfly."[79] And as they waited for their transformation, they "continually surnamed each other Man and clutched at their crotches, readying the equipment they deemed necessary to be summoned at any moment into Superfly heaven."[80] C.C. Baker and his maladroit band of boys are deadly precisely because they are invisible and have nothing to lose. Lorraine, frightened out of her wits, had also convinced herself that because "she hadn't really seen them […] they weren't there," no matter that one of them had spoken to her.[81] Their invisibility is the only way she is able to convince herself that what is about to happen is a terrible fiction playing out in her mind.

"A hand shot itself around her mouth, and her neck was jerked back while a hoarse voice whispered in her ear," insisting, "You ain't got nothing to say now, huh?" That hoarse voice said, "Thought you were real funny laughing at me in the streets today?"[82] And that same hoarse and threatening voice wondered if Lorraine would see the humor in what he and his friends intended to do to her. There was no easy convergence for Lorraine between the life she had taken up with Theresa and the life she had left behind in the cities and towns where her un-naming fooled no one. And here was C.C. Baker giving her back the name she had refused to accept from her lover, a name that branded her as different, and coming from the lips of C.C. Baker, may as well have been an executioner's call.

Lorraine had stumbled into enemy territory, into the "thin strip of earth that they claimed as their own."[83] These men, knowing they would never amount to anything much, "reigned in that unlit alley like dwarfed warrior-kings [...] and Lorraine found herself on her knees, surrounded by the most dangerous species in existence—human males with an erection to validate in a world that was only six feet wide."[84] This allusion to the psychological emasculation of black men casts Lorraine/queer women of color in the role of what Reid-Pharr argues as scapegoats, as the figure who "reproduces this undifferentiation, this chaos, this boundarylessness."[85] Thus the "violence directed against the goat," Reid-Pharr goes on to note, "would mitigate against the prior violence, the erosion of borders that has beset the entire community."[86] By sacrificing the goat/lamb/outsider, it can be reasoned that C.C. Baker and his friends believe they are restoring balance to their community, upholding an equilibrium that "white men are obliged to recognize."[87] Ironically, it is their own lack of self-recognition that further reinforces their invisibility.

The shared history of oppression that both Lorraine and C.C. Baker are linked into does not equate to them having the same experience of that oppression. This is where the danger lies because, while each person on earth is tied to a history, time moves on and identity is reconfigured by the new history we make along the way. Men like C.C. Baker are frozen in time, uncertain of who they are, where they are heading, or how to get to a different place. In writing about the complex issues that inform debates around identity and difference, Jeffrey Weeks queries, "to what extent should one particular definition of the good and the just prevail over others?"[88] To what degree is violence justified by men like C.C. Baker when it is used to force compliance to an ideal that is itself based upon false principles of equality and fairness? What Lorraine represents to C.C. Baker is a conundrum in want of a resolution. And he sets that resolution out step by step, blow by crushing blow.

"I'm gonna show you somethin' I bet you never seen before,"[89] C.C. tells Lorraine, repeating the words that countless men throughout history have said to countless women and countless girls, many of whom are forced by custom and by law to accept without question. As he rubs Lorraine's face into the crotch of his jeans, his friends laugh, knowing they are protected by the same rules of entitlement that once saw their foremothers enslaved and raped at will. C.C. Baker is resolving a conundrum, taking on what bell hooks has argued is the "privilege of all men," the right to "oppress and brutalize women[...]."[90] Stepping into what he sees as his rightful role, C.C. Baker is able to reinscribe male space through an act of sexual violence.

It is no accident, bell hooks argues, that "at the same time white men were expressing doubts and anxieties about their masculine role, black men chose to publicly proclaim that they had subjugated black women."[91] C.C. Baker predicts that after he and his friends finish with Lorraine, she "ain't never gonna wanna kiss no more pussy."[92] What he is really saying is that his fragile self-worth is inextricably linked to his own objectification as a savage black stud. He and his friends are unable to redirect the hostile white gaze that informs their own self-negating perception of their black bodies, so they set out to destroy what they can control, and that is the queer line of vision that dares to mount a challenge to their manhood. Yet C.C. Baker is as much an "Other" as Lorraine and Theresa, and the tragedy of this is that he knows it to be true.

C.C. Baker springs into action by slamming "his kneecap into her spine," causing Lorraine's body to arch and "his nails to cut into the side of her mouth to stifle her cry."[93] Here, we must again consider the terrorism of rape, what it accomplishes, the people it harms, and the collective responsibility we have to eradicate it from the world. No single approach to unraveling its illegitimate provenance will suffice, for its tentacles reach deep into a history that has been shaped by the violent subjugation of those least able to speak out. For queer women of color the terms of racial and sexual contracts are ever changing, and it may not necessarily be helped by postmodernist theorizing that purportedly moves us on from essentialist debates around gender, race, and sexual orientation. Viewed with skepticism by some on the left and also the conservative right, Patricia Huntington has commented about the fragmentation of subject positions and its implications for alternative race(d) and gender(ed) realities. Drawing on the work of bell hooks, Shane Phelan, and others, Huntington notes that what is significant for bell hooks, is that

> in spite of its potential to break with homogenous concepts of personal and group identity, the feminist turn to French postmodern theory has functioned to recenter and to perpetuate "white authorial presence."[94]

The context for the above analysis derives from what Huntington describes as hooks' aversion to "how the postmodern embrace of heterogeneity, when posed in abstraction from material conditions of racial oppression and economic exploitation, glosses over, if not wholly obfuscates these very real social concerns" of those who are not white and who then, by extension, are also "Othered."[95] It is those very real concerns, intersecting through and across what is arguably recognized as the shared yoke of oppression, that in theory should allow for a common desire among the marginalized to live and let live. Yet in Brewster Place, where flouting the rules is perceived as undermining the efforts of an oppressed people to rise above their circumstances, a different kind of re-centering occurs. The black male presence, threatened on a conceptual level with psychic and psychological extinction, over-corrects and asserts itself by taking on the role of oppressor.

Two of "the boys" pin Lorraine's arms down, while another two "wrenched open her legs," allowing C.C. Baker to kneel down between her legs, push up her dress and tear "at the top of her pantyhose."[96] The use of the word "boys" could be a device meant to misdirect the reader, reframe our perception of the violence that is occurring. But I suggest that it instead heightens the grotesqueness of the rape, underscoring the simultaneous horror of "boys" engaging in unspeakable sexual violence, and the men they are to become gestating in the "formless thuds" Lorraine first heard as her tormentors jumped down from the wall.

Mistaking Lorraine's convulsing body as a sign of resistance, and perhaps even the mocking defiance C.C. Baker had convinced himself that she had directed his way on the street, he drives his "fist down into her stomach," warning her that she had better acquiesce by being still "or I'll rip open your guts."[97] C.C. Baker is unconcerned with Lorraine's fear and her perceived resistance. His lack of concern is bound up in statistics that once indicated a higher rate of executions in the United States of black men accused of rape when the victims were white women, whereas "no man was ever executed in the United States for the rape of a Black woman."[98] While statistics are created to at once control and also to demonize certain groups, many women (either out of fear or shame) do not report their attackers. And Lorraine, cast adrift by her lover and also spurned by the women in the community, has no one to save her or report her attack to, if she in fact survives it.

C.C. Baker has decided to show Lorraine the consequences of being a "cunt," "freak," "dyke," all of which adds up to his own fear and loathing of the female body. He knows Lorraine does not count, that no one will come to her rescue, that she is even more marginalized than he is, and that she will not be believed. He knows this because in this moment he controls the margins, the gaps, and the gutters. His words, and those of his friends, are supported by the wall that frames their utterances, the privileged frame that the reader has (in this instance) been led to believe is controlled by their own interpretive powers. Yet here, the alley has become a staging ground for misdirection, a site where the darkest trickery and the most skillful deception traps innocents like Lorraine in a swirling vortex of confusion.

Lorraine has unthinkingly walked into the middle of a deadly signifying act that she failed to recognize as a challenge, a threat, and a promise in need of fulfillment. If she had understood the game earlier on, she could have predicted the outcome of the trickster's loss of face, read his hate, known his intention. What she does not understand is that C.C. Baker and his boys are staging their rematch with her in the alley, in a space they control, in a recuperation of their pride, and this time they have an opponent whose ignorance of the game assures them of an easy victory. The alley and the rapists have effectively become signifiers, troping murderously on the frightened and outmaneuvered signified. Lorraine's own attempt at misdirection (by taking a shortcut through the alley to fool her lover into thinking she is independent) has become her undoing.[99]

I want to briefly revisit here the seminal work of Henry Louis Gates, Jr., on signifying and how this translates into an ever-shifting representational strategy in African American literature, music, and social interaction. C.C. Baker and his friends are the signifiers in a sexual drama that is forced upon girls and women with cunning and horrifying precision. They are the tricksters, the signifying band of men who roam the streets in search of validation and legitimacy, even if this comes at someone else's expense. They signify against what Gates argues on a semiotic level as "two parallel discursive universes: the black American linguistic circle and the white."[100] Yet one can also argue that in C.C. Baker's case, his black masculinity, and what he perceives to be an unvoiced, yet no less emasculating signifying homosexuality, is more than he can bear. Lorraine is triply signified by her race, gender, and sexual orientation. This makes her the perfect target for C.C. Baker's rage. So in order to redeem his wounded pride he has to signify his ability to assert his power over Lorraine. Thus, in following Gates's theorizing, we come to see that the complex entanglements between the signifier and the signified, and the discursive systems and rules upon which they turn, have trapped Lorraine in a loop of violence that goes beyond the relatively harmless "modes of figuration"[101] that Gates references and to a deeper language of misogyny where words have deadly consequences.

Eschewing any direct comparison to Saussure's dyadic, or two-part model of the sign, yet acknowledging its purpose as what I interpret as a type of linguistic foil for African American vernacular discourse, Gates points out that "black people vacated" the conventional signifier and "then—incredibly—substituted as its concept a signified that stands for the system of rhetorical strategies peculiar to their own vernacular tradition."[102] In other words, black people "undertook this act of self-definition, implicit in a (re)naming ritual, within the process of signification that the English language had inscribed for itself."[103] Yet if, as Gates suggests, to signify is to "engage in certain rhetorical games,"[104] then the rhetoric that led C.C. Baker to visit unspeakable violence against Lorraine's triply signified body is a dangerous game indeed, one in which there are no rules and certainly no fair play.

There was only one word that Lorraine needed to say out loud. Yet even when she used all of her remaining strength, willing the word to rise up and spill from her lips, saving her perhaps with its inference of defeat, acquiescence, penitence, in the end it was too effete a thing in the face of the rage that struck it down. "Please."[105] "The sixth boy took a dirty paper bag lying on the ground and stuffed it into her mouth. She felt a weight drop on her spread body."[106] There is still no sound, even when Lorraine opens her eyes, perhaps believing that if she confronts the evil that is trying to consume her, she can defeat it, make it go away. But she is traumatized, frozen in place. The horror of what she is experiencing is complex and otherworldly.

Ann Cvetkovich acknowledges these complexities when she makes a distinction between episodic trauma (or that which occurs as a discreet event) and that which she states is "insidious or everyday forms of trauma."[107] Rape is a declaration of war on women's bodies and, by extension, on the choices that are made regarding freedom of movement. When Lorraine tries to scream, she is calling forth the screams of all those whose silence is conditioned upon being accepted, not making waves, acquiescing to heteronormative ideals of love and belonging. Just like the screams that are visualized for the reader in comics, the screams coming from the white spaces in between the privileged hegemonic frame, Lorraine's can only be imagined to the extent of the reader's experience.

Yet when the stories that we read or hear about are juxtaposed with images, and human depravity is on display via endless news feeds and social networking sites, the scale of these atrocities (sexual and otherwise) is difficult to ignore. In this regard, and in building an argument for the deployment of different interpretive strategies in the act of reading, Marianne Hirsch's analysis of Art Spiegelman's *In the Shadow of No Towers* (2004) is compelling. Indeed, as Hirsch invites us to consider, Spiegelman's detailed renderings of the fear and surprise etched upon the faces of those who survived 9/11 adeptly "[...] performs an aesthetics of trauma: it is fragmentary, composed of small boxes that cannot contain the material, which exceeds their frames and the structure of the page."[108] Spiegelman's book can be interpreted as a threnody for 9/11, a lament for the dead, a radical schema of lines and odd shapes angling for purchase in a river of grief. His drawings crowd the page and frenetic parabola spills over panel borders that are "[...] assumed to be inviolate in a comic page [adding] to the sense of unleashed action."[109] So, too, is the image of Lorraine, rigid with fear, yet frantic to be heard.

But her eyes screamed. They "screamed and screamed into the face above hers—the face that was pushing this tearing pain inside of her body."[110] What is striking in this passage is the ability of the eyes to scream. This allegorical device requires several things of the reader: the use of one's mind's eye to see the spectacle of terror confronting Lorraine; proximity to her terror through a sympathetic and resolute reading of the passages; and the willingness to give voice to her screams by acknowledging the legitimacy of her queer black existence.

Yet as bell hooks points out, with the advent of the pill and other contraception that afford women more control and freedom over their bodies, men now have "unlimited access" to sex and their attitude towards women often result in "increased exploitation of women as sex objects to sell products and [...] their wholehearted support of pornography and rape."[111] These then are the phenomena that Nicola Gavey addresses in her book *Just Sex? The Cultural Scaffolding of Rape* (2005). These dangerous truths—and all of the gradations in between—concerning sexual relations between men and women create what Gavey goes on to note is "too much ambiguity over distinctions between what is rape and what is *just sex* [emphasis belongs to Gavey]."[112] In other words, when marital or casual sex becomes inseparable from rape, and women are made responsible for the blurring of those lines, this "normative form of heterosexuality [works] as a cultural scaffolding for rape."[113] What this normalization of rape as "just sex" creates is an opt-out clause for men who rely on these misogynistic scripts to side-step responsibility for their actions.

Lorraine's "screams tried to break through her corneas out into the air, but the tough rubbery flesh sent them vibrating back into her brain, first shaking lifeless the cells that nurtured her memory."[114] Then it was "the cells that contained her powers of taste and smell. The last that were screamed to death were those that supplied her with the ability to love—or hate."[115] And the blessing for Lorraine, I argue, must be at the point when she ceased to feel anything at all, when the depravity and the brutality of a single act surpasses her worst nightmare and it becomes impossible to "tell when they changed places and the second weight, then the third and fourth, dropped on her—it was one continuous hacksawing of torment that kept her eyes screaming the only word she was fated to utter again and again for the rest of her life. Please."[116]

In this chapter I looked to the unique structure of graphic narratives to contextualize difficult truths about violence against women of color in small, insular communities. I also further developed the idea of misdirection to argue for different interpretive strategies that would, as Derek Parker Royal suggests, "revisualize [...] 'gutter' spaces that lie outside of our more privileged cultural frames."[117] I demonstrated that the physical structure of the alley where the brutal rape of Lorraine is staged is analogous to the "gutter" space in graphic narratives, in that the juxtaposition of interstitial spaces in fiction, and the spatiotemporal properties of graphic narratives, draws readers into the experiences of the characters in more immediate ways. Royal touches on this when he explains that because comics "utilize picture texts to guide our understanding of narrative, comics can have a more direct effect than that dictated by prose, eliciting a reaction that takes relatively little time to process."[118]

Taking up for a moment Royal's seeming demarcation between text that marries up with images in comics to further and quicken our understanding of a story, and the exclusively text-bound process in prose having less of an immediate effect on our understanding of a story, overlooks the potential of prose fiction and comics to communicate through a common structure, thereby eliciting immediate and visceral effects on what readers take in. The rape scene that was set between the walls of a dark alley where public space has historically been claimed and controlled by men compels readers to think of traditionally text-bound narratives as more than a passive route to taking in information. By setting out an understanding of how the structural relationship between comics and literary fiction can help stitch together the dissociative states experienced by many of the women of Brewster Place, readers are able to fill in the gaps and interstitial spaces of those lives made inexpressible by the indecency of sexual violation. Furthermore, as a tactic deployed most purposefully by the men in Naylor's novel, misdirection was used to control (and to keep in their place) women who aspired to a better life. In this way, misdirection as a signifying strategy in relations between men and women flowed directly from the physical walls and spaces of the alley where Lorraine was raped and through to the powerful sphere of maleness that ensures dominance over women.

Illustration by Kat Williams, UK-based artist.

Illustration by Rahana Daria, UK-based artist.

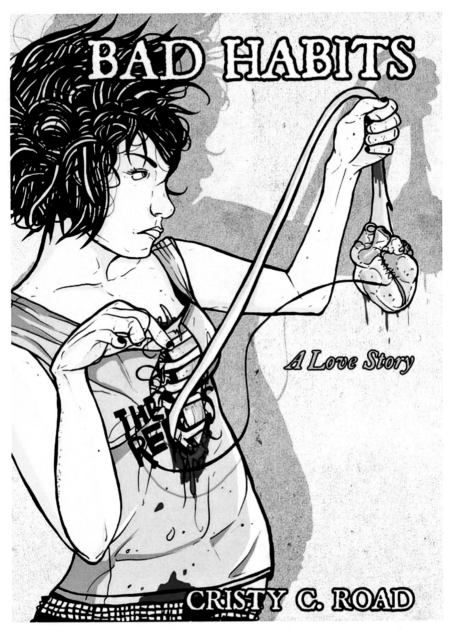

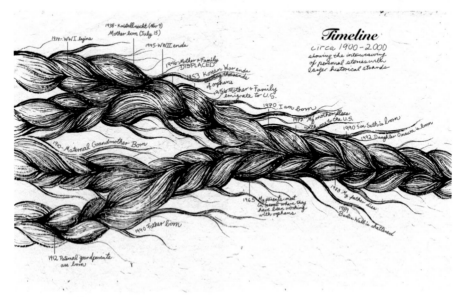

Image from draft in progress, *The Baroness of Have-Nothing and Other Haunting Tales*, by Maureen Burdock (copyright © 2017 by Maureen Burdock).

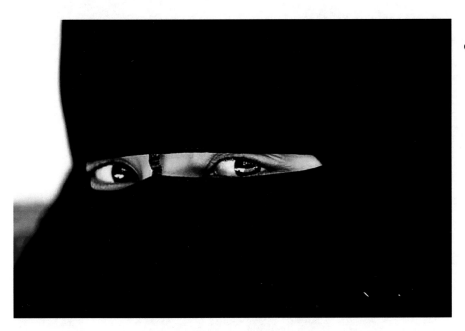

Photograph by Fred Dufour of woman in niqab, from the website *Chatelaine* (reprinted by permission of Fred Dufour. All rights reserved).

Illustration by Carlos Latuff (copyright © 2017 Reprinted by permission of Carlos Latuff. All rights reserved).

Illustration by Johnathan Payne (reprinted by permission of Johnathan Payne).

My Lesbian Experience with Loneliness

(True) Story & Art by
Nagata Kabi

Cover art from *My Lesbian Experience with Loneliness* (copyright© 2016 by Kabi Nagata. Reprinted by permission of Seven Seas Entertainment Press).

C•8

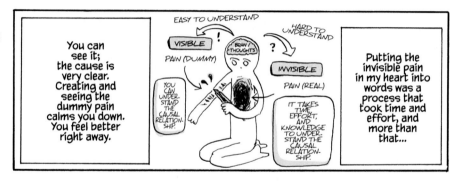

Illustration from p. 13, *My Lesbian Experience with Loneliness* (copyright © 2016 by Kabi Nagata. Reprinted by permission of Seven Seas Entertainment Press).

Illustration from p. 15, *My Lesbian Experience with Loneliness* (copyright © 2016 by Kabi Nagata. Reprinted by permission of Seven Seas Entertainment Press).

Illustration from p. 75, *My Lesbian Experience with Loneliness* (copyright © 2016 by Kabi Nagata. Reprinted by permission of Seven Seas Entertainment Press).

Chapter 5

Critical Meditations on Love and Madness
Emma Pérez's Gulf Dreams *(1996)*

> ... there are different kinds of madness. Some madness doesn't act mad to begin with, sometimes it will knock politely at the door, and when you let it in, it'll simply sit in the corner without a fuss—and grow.[1]

> Insanity—The condition of being insane; unsoundness of mind as a consequence of brain-disease; madness, lunacy...[2]

Previous chapters examined texts that framed queer women of color representation as it has historically been constructed through white Eurocentric paradigms. They featured elements of misdirection and the unique language and spatiotemporal properties of graphic narratives. In this way the texts lent themselves to critical intervention at the sites where oppressive systems intersect to impose "normative" rules of behavior on the queer(ed) subaltern body. This chapter now shifts the discursive lens to focus more closely on the underlying psychopathology of dominant systems that punish individuals who deviate too far from the heteronormative center.

Gulf Dreams is a first-person narrative told by a nameless Chicana lesbian whose love for a married woman is bound up in madness and the limits and contingencies of female sexual expression in male dominated cultures. "I don't know when I realized I was crazy, that I was as diseased as the world [...] but my hallucinations loomed as if real."[3] These are the words of the protagonist in Emma Pérez's *Gulf Dreams*. Written as an intricate dream sequence, Pérez's novel is at once a meditation on madness and obsession and a complex interplay of words and "interstitial gaps," as well as a queer postcolonialist exegesis of hegemonic narratives that obscure the truth of queer Chicana lives.

As Pérez put it three years later in *The Decolonial Imaginary: Writing Chicanas into History* (1999), the gaps that she investigates work to "interrupt the linear [read: patriarchal and colonialist] model[s] of time."[4] By looking backwards in order to understand the present, the future must be understood to exist along the same continuum. Pérez does not "believe in a beginning, a middle [or] an end of history."[5] Nor does she "ascribe to a linear temporality as the only means for speaking and writing history."[6] In *Gulf Dreams*, the protagonist (who is also the narrator) repeats this circular reasoning when she insists, "I don't believe in endings […] I believe in the imagination, its pleasure indelible, transgressive, a dream."[7] Her imagination becomes the only way that she can escape a life that is largely absent of nuance, "non-normative" sexual expression, or the freedom to celebrate difference without apology.

Gulf Dreams is a hypnotic tale that draws the reader into the mind of a Chicana lesbian whose truth is seen through a prism of madness that distorts her reality in a world that does not recognize her humanity or her right to love. She eschews the reality that erases her, existing in an in-between place of dreams and fantastical imaginings. Pulling back the curtain on madness, the novel works as a series of interdependent (and interconnected) events that call for critical meditations on the pathologization of lesbianism and desire. It is a coming-of-age story about madness and passion articulated through interstitial, "decolonized" frameworks.[8]

In this chapter I premise some of my arguments on the historically negative impact of psychiatry relevant to the female psyche, which in this case is represented through the dissociative states experienced by the lesbian Chicana protagonist in *Gulf Dreams*. I also consider the persistent connections that psychiatry has drawn between race, cultural beliefs, "aberrant" sexualities, gender presentation and the resultant construction of pathologies. Reading Pérez's novel through an oppositional gaze, the astute reader comes to see that the protagonist refuses to be represented in terms that construct her as sexually deviant because she is insane or insane because she is sexually "deviant," even though she almost instinctively embraces the very terms that her imagination and dreams work to contest. Furthermore, I argue that *Gulf Dreams* is a novel structured around rhetorical devices that sets the narrative itself as a misdirecting gesture designed to not only "trouble" the flaws inherent in rigid social norms, but to also divert attention away from the protagonist's own fretful subjectivity. I take up this particular theme again in the final chapter where the construct of gender is (re)enacted through an array of misdirecting performances.

Women, Psychiatry and Madness

In a space-time configuration that engages readers on multiple levels, imagination is crucial to *unfixing* "the internal psychic construction of women's identity" as it is defined "in patriarchal culture."[9] This construction that Diane Hamer problematizes through a feminist lens suggests the possibility for a less contentious or ideologically stratified dialogue between psychoanalysis and lesbianism. Yet for lesbians of color, psychoanalysis is not without its inherent dangers. Indeed, for marginalized groups whose psyches have been shaped by persistent discriminatory practices, there is a deep and long-standing mistrust that must first be overcome if therapeutic interventions are to be seen as legitimate. Nowhere is this more evident than in psychiatric case records from the late eighteenth and into the mid to late twentieth centuries that reflect the differential treatment of the mentally ill person of color in state institutions to that of white women and men.[10]

As a disease, madness is interpellated through social conventions and resonates even more profoundly when interwoven with the law. In this regard, I turn briefly to Michele Cammers Goodwin's critique of *Jane Eyre* and her exploration of intersections of "madness, law, gender, and race during the Victorian era."[11] My application of this critical turn towards the racialized and gendered boundaries of *Jane Eyre* and other novels of the era becomes all the more relevant when read through the contemporary lens of *Gulf Dreams*, a lens that at once re-evaluates the construction of the subaltern body as deviant and unworthy of notice, but also takes up the critical gaps in scholarship that have historically failed to engage in any sustained or meaningful way with this very type of narrative.

In drawing attention to feminist scholarship and its surprising inability to *see* or meaningfully engage with madness as it is scripted onto the racialized female body (in this case, Bertha Mason Rochester), Goodwin draws parallels between the historical invisibility of women of color (and the forces that "drive" them insane and ultimately unworthy of serious consideration) and cultural practices that are often deliberately misinterpreted as deviancy or dangerous behavior.[12] My choice of Pérez's novel as a gateway into a critical meditation on queer women of color and madness in literature takes up the scholarly gap that Goodwin argues is absent in such literary works as *Jane Eyre*. Moreover, by extending Goodwin's metaphor of *Jane Eyre*'s black woman in the attic, it could be said that "the attic" exists in any discursive space that renders women silent and relegates them to the social, political, racial, or cultural periphery. This critical turn, taken up by postcolonial scholars who address the gaps in such representational narratives as *Jane Eyre*, signals a necessary shift in how the racialized boundaries of the literary canon are read.[13]

For Jane, Bertha's story is already written and resolved. It is only in want of a context, a box within which to store it away along with the inconvenience of Bertha's assumed madness that prevents Jane from dispatching Rochester's black wife to complete and unalterable irrelevance. Referring to Bertha as a "'corpulent,' 'clothed hyena,' 'the maniac,' 'the lunatic' who is 'purple' and having a 'quantity of dark, grizzled hair, wild as a mane,'" *Jane Eyre* confirms that in the white imaginary of the nineteenth century, the notion of primitivism loomed large.[14] Primitivism was, as Andrew M. Fearnley notes in his incisive review of Celia Brickman and James Waldram's separate studies on mental illness and race,

> [...] a marker in an evolutionist framework [that] remains a fundamental component of psychoanalysis; for neurological descriptions of the brain; and in many contemporary descriptions of particular disorders, most notably accounts of the deterioration process of schizophrenia.[15]

We know from early studies in the field of psychiatry that certain behaviors expressed by women were more likely to be diagnosed as a mental illness, particularly if their outward presentation and object choices fell too far outside the acceptable parameters of societal norms. Such diagnoses (advanced predominantly by "male" psychiatry) could have been due in large part to women being more open to expressing emotional distress, whereas men were more likely to report physical symptoms rather than ones associated with emotions or feelings.[16] Furthermore, the prevalence of such terms as "irrational," "histrionic," "depressed," "difficult," "perverse," "neurotic" or "anxious" was enough to set up a continuum of illness upon which other perceived mental disorders might likely follow, resulting in systems of classification that may very well have inhibited accurate reporting of psychological disturbances. Stereotypes of mental or emotional instability appear throughout *Gulf Dreams*, almost as if madness stains the page with a pathos that can never be fully resolved.

In this novel of misdirection, the protagonist rides pathos to its enabling extremes, disentangling herself from its fleshy embrace only long enough to acknowledge that she (and others like her) are disoriented, lost. She considers those who disentangle their minds from the unyielding and often violent reality of "Otherness" to be the fortunate ones.[17] It is here, through the fractured and misleading lens of reality, that bodies of color become distorted (and diseased) versions of the standard-bearing white heterosexual norm.

Men like Freud, Nancy Tome asserts, held a "masculinist bias" that characterized women as inherently unstable opposites of men.[18] As enforcers of women's morality, male dominated societies use medicine, religion, social control and the law to alternately protect and destroy those who break with convention or who experience psychic breaks *because* of those conventions. Pathologically constructed women are typically the ones who pose the greatest threat to white-centric paradigms. Judged for what they purportedly are not—sane, normal, pure, heterosexual, wives, mothers, daughters—they are judged, and through judgment they are controlled.

In *Gulf Dreams* Ermila is one of those women who experience the daily horror of psychic violence.[19] She pushes against convention, questions the impossible contradictions of a woman's life, and brazenly embraces her "Otherness." Yet like the nameless protagonist in the story, Ermila fails to step into a prescribed role of female acquiescence, so when the men who took turns raping her insisted that they just wanted to "have some fun, fuck her, slap her once or twice [because] some women liked a little roughness,"[20] they used rape as a punishment, as a warning to women arrogant enough to forget their duty to men. Yet by conflating rape with sex, be it consensual "rough" sex or otherwise, is to ignore the fact that rape is about exerting power and control. It is as remotely related to sex as slaughtering wild game with automatic rifles or sports fishing with harpoons is to contributing food to the dinner table.

Later on in the courtroom where the index of patriarchal control that operates on virtually every level of society, we come to understand that it is Ermila and the "Otherness" she represents that is on trial, not the men who raped her. But the nameless protagonist knows the truth of patriarchy. She understands how it works, how it can be turned against women who do not bend to its will. When she follows the trial of the five men who are accused of raping Ermila, she recognizes a kindred spirit's vulnerability, yet also "[admires] her resilience."[21] Nevertheless, she finds herself "morbidly" questioning Ermila "like so many others" had done before.[22] Perhaps sensing a similar kind of "madness" that resides in every woman who is forced into submission by male entitlement, the nameless protagonist "wanted to hear through her quiet rage," wanted to be a witness to the daily horrors of being a woman daring to chart her own course.[23] Thus, placed on a continuum of either madness or alterity, disrupting these narratives turns on the ability of women to use interstitial spaces to effect strategic incursions into toxic, heteronormatively-inflected frameworks.

There is a place, Emma Pérez argues in *The Decolonial Imaginary*, where "oppositional, subaltern histories [...]" are located.[24] That place—as I discuss here in my own critical enquiries into madness—comprised of the intericonic spaces, the "gutters," the gaps, margins, and borders in *Gulf Dreams*. This is the place where women plan insurrections, where wounded bodies and psyches are resurrected to battle yet another day for legitimacy. It is where both memories and ancestors reside. While different words and/or phrases are used to describe power imbalances and the sites of resistance formed in response, what Pérez and other postcolonial scholars/historians explore are how transgressive acts or certain emotional states become operationalized as deviancy outside of liminal spaces. They also explore how the work that interstitial sites do to creatively confront, reinterpret, *decolonize* and ultimately re-inscribe the historical record is essential to the deconstruction of tropes that reinforce discriminatory practices.

Theorizing Space

In reading *Gulf Dreams* through the critical lens of *The Decolonial Imaginary* and other postcolonialist texts, fiction and theory necessarily come together to construct the "lesbian counter memory."[25] I build on Pérez's assertion that "historians must use literary theory in order to make sense of their work"[26] and engage in a critical dialogue between creative and scholarly works by arguing for discursive practices that intervene at the site where entrenched racist, sexist and homophobic narratives are operationalized. This plays out in several ways, one of which is put forth by Ellie Hernández in "Chronotope of Desire: Emma Pérez's *Gulf Dreams*."

Through a process of reclamation, Hernández contends that Pérez has been able to evoke "a discussion of the deeper unconscious aspects of language in the construction of historical subjects."[27] In keeping with Hernández's view, I suggest that through the process of *calling forth* alternative epistemological truths (and approaches) in the (re)making/(re)mapping of the colonized subject/body/mind, the extended altered states experienced by the protagonist in *Gulf Dreams* effectively collapses the historically imposed distance between the colonized and disconnected body and (de)colonized, *of color*, queer acts of subversion. It is evident in *Gulf Dreams* that the protagonist is forged from (yet rails against) the reductionist scripts that forcefully orient her gaze towards the hegemonic and psycho-normative center, leaving her to wander along the edges of borderlands, unanchored and separated from the familiar markers of Chicana/o belonging.

Tracing the lives of men and women who on varying levels appear to be looking towards the next horizon for salvation that never comes, *Gulf Dreams* is not so much a redemptive narrative of the kind that Catrióna Rueda Esquibel describes in her essay "Sor Juana and the Search for (Queer) Cultural

Heroes,"[28] but neither is it completely without reclamations of faith that serve as beacons along the dark corridors of the protagonist's hallucinations. Whether this is enough to keep madness at bay, be that the madness of the world or one's own troubling thoughts, for the protagonist, loving is still an affirmative act.

The protagonist negotiates the spaces between "change as it is formed discursively in the past, by the present."[29] She "unfixes" binarisms that are historically left uncontested in the name of fitting in and maintaining cultural pride, choosing instead to re-*lingualize* the spaces that form her hybrid self. She does so when she confesses to the "young woman"[30] that the way she loves her "remains an act of language," a *mestiza* language that she reaches for to describe the complexities of passion.[31] When the protagonist shares with the "young woman" the myriad ways she has loved her, she is speaking about a constellation of words and thoughts that push back against the limitations of her waking life.[32] When she blames herself for loving the "young woman" in ways "that can only be expressed on paper,"[33] she reminds us of the power of writing, of our ability to create realities that might otherwise remain unseen.

Conditioned to believe that her lesbianism is an illness that must be suppressed so that no one is touched by its contagion, the protagonist symbolizes the challenges facing queer women of color when one's fundamental right to exist is perpetually called into question. Though the protagonist restricts her "nightmares to the privacy of [her own] bedroom" where they are interwoven with her true desires, the "young woman" for whom she pines is not subject to the similar "censure."[34] The "young woman's" sexual and emotional allegiance to men protects her from the kind of suspicion and self-doubt that forces the protagonist down a different path.

I do not mean to suggest that madness, when it is articulated through alternative states of consciousness, is an implicit revolutionary act that ameliorates legitimate psychiatric disorders, for there are indeed mental illnesses that require therapeutic interventions. Shoshana Felman argued this very point in her review of Phyllis Chesler's groundbreaking work on women and madness. She wrote: "quite the opposite of rebellion, madness is the impasse confronting those whom cultural conditioning has deprived of the very means of protest or self-affirmation."[35] Yet for women writers the very linguistic tools that have locked out their reactionary voices are the same tools that have been reclaimed as a means of protest. In this regard, *Gulf Dreams* encourages consideration of how the entwining of such binarisms as women and madness, lesbian desire and perversion, race and otherness, and belonging and displacement can be disrupted and reconfigured. By speaking and writing through discursive spaces that are not dependent upon the white heteronor-mative gaze mirroring back an acknowledgment (or legitimacy) of one's sanity or existence, the language of madness that women are said to speak can instead be transformed into a language of recognition.

Pérez's literary fiction and her critical works follow similar historical arcs, in that both focus on the recuperation and expansiveness of Chicano/a identities. She recognizes that "consciousness is born out of one's intimate awareness of one's oppression"[36] and that work produced by women of color "emerge[s] from *un sito y una lengua* (a space and language) that rejects colo-nial ideology" in all its permutations.[37] Both critical explorations intervene in the historical record, not by attempting to overlay one truth for another, but rather by utilizing a process of defamiliarization to disrupt our customary ways of seeing the world.

As the words and ideas in *Gulf Dreams* revolve around madness and les-bian desire as pivotal junctures from which the subaltern self seeks its recu-peration and departure from heteronormative dogma, consideration must be given to what literature written by women (rather than texts published by men in the medical field) has to say and *how* it is being said. Chicanas have written their own stories about riding the margins, turning emotional trauma back on itself, knowing that there could very well be "something on the other side of crazy [...] across [the] line" where there exists "a certain understand-ing, a special knowledge,"[38] indeed, a new way of envisioning the so-called "mad" self.

Not so far removed from the oppressive morality that Gema Pérez-Sánchez critiques in relation to Ana María Moix's *Julia* (1968), a novel pub-lished under the "close scrutiny of Francoist censorship,"[39] *Gulf Dreams* (and fiction as a whole) works to illuminate and give voice to those who have been left out. Noting that the "sociopolitical context in which Moix published her novel forced her to resemanticize silence as the only possible tool with which to write about lesbianism," Pérez-Sánchez goes on to note that Moix's "word-less process [...] needs the aid of the reader who can recognize the blanks between lines and appropriately read into them, supplying the subversive, missing information."[40] Thus, in borrowing from Moix, my contention is that the reframing of discursive practices that have constructed women's nature as axiomatic of madness is for the protagonist a recuperation of the various parts of her that have been misplaced.

In a field too long dominated by psychoanalytic and psychodynamic mod-els that in many respects seemed to infer that womanhood itself could be a diagnosable disease, the counter-response from women writers must be one that "strategically [occupies] the space of existing literary, medical, and popular models of madness [...]."[41] Marta Caminero-Santangelo sets out to "[inter-rogate] the value of madness itself as a metaphor for resistance."[42] Caminero-Santangelo draws on Teresa de Lauretis's formulation of a space that would more meaningfully ascribe agency to women whose perceived irrational behaviors have been routinely defined against a heteronormatively inscribed psychodynamic model. She notes that when madness is reframed as a "language of non-reason" meant to disrupt "oppressive patriarchal thinking," thereby setting up an "enactment of a peculiarly feminine power," it effectively mimics the very language of the psychopathology that it seeks to subvert.[43]

While simultaneously cautioning against a wholesale acceptance of the cover of madness as a practical tool for resistance and identifying a more effective response relevant to the "use of madness as a metaphor for the liberatory potentials of language," Caminero-Santangelo asserts that "feminist critics must utterly unmoor [madness] from its associations with mental illness as understood and constructed by discourses and practices both medical and popular."[44] For the protagonist, madness mimics the messages inscribed upon her female body, messages that must be purged from her wounded psyche if she is ever to unearth the truth of who she is meant to be. Made reticent by childhood fears, the protagonist wages battle against the arrogance of false paradigms that diminish her, that equate her experiences to the incoherent jeremiads of someone who has lost touch with reality.

Where Madness Begins: Threading the Narrative

Undone by madness, or at least by what she is forced to accept as such, the protagonist has the most vivid moments of self-recognition in the interstitial folds of her dream states. She understands that there are no acceptable words for the sexual attraction she feels for the "young woman" although there is some suggestion that the "young woman," while very likely a figment of the protagonist's imagination (or at least their relationship might be imaginary), represents the internal conflict the protagonist feels in regards to her own lesbianism and Chicana culture. She has, as Pérez perceptively argues in the *Decolonial Imaginary*, been "held linguistically captive for centuries."[45] Through her dreams she becomes what she cannot be in real life. In her dreams she can resist censure, legitimate her love for women, integrate the various parts of herself into a whole, and at last speak the words that will bring her back into existence. Yet what the protagonist is forced to accept is that she must live in exile in order to know, and to become, her true self.

Forever the foreigner who is never good enough, to the oppressor she represents dark and uncontrollable forces (madness, deviancy, femaleness, race) that have no place in the light. But she knows that "to recognize truth is not easy [and] to speak truth is even harder [but] far away from home, I am," she says, "aware of myself."[46] The necessity of distancing oneself from the familiar in order to understand one's unique place in the world is a negotiation as old as time itself. The difference for the oppressed, of course, is the multiple layers of *undoing* that must first be achieved before—as Pérez advocates—a decolonized self can emerge.

In what Pérez terms the "rupturing space" of the decolonial imaginary, for Chicana/o history, there is, she insists, a "time lag between the colonial and postcolonial." This time lag represents the "interstitial space where differential politics and social dilemmas are negotiated."[47] It is in this way that the structure of the novel encourages the reader to suspend judgment in order to get to the truth of madness. By entering the interstices of insanity itself, the reader temporarily dons the cloak of "Otherness" that reveals numerous paths leading to a broad range of oppositional responses.

The protagonist's internalized struggles can be read in any number of ways. From the point of view of psychiatry, for instance, she may be assessed as exhibiting signs of a dissociative identity disorder (formerly known as multiple personality disorder).[48] However, if read from a perspective that sees oppression, racism, sexism, or homophobia as indicators of *societal disorders*, then, as Nadine J. Quehl has noted, the argument becomes one of agency and the ability (or lack thereof) "to appropriate the terms by which they [the mentally ill] have been abused, as they are often positioned outside the domain of 'speakability.'"[49] Quehl explains this by citing an oft-quoted observation made by Nathaniel Lee, the seventeenth-century English playwright. Locked away against his will, Lee was said to have commented: "They called me mad, and I called them mad, and damn them, they outvoted me."[50] What is particularly noteworthy about Lee's comment is that it effectively underscores the power of the medical and psychiatric communities where the poor, the socially non-compliant, and the non-conformists are disproportionately targeted. They are, as Nathaniel Lee and many others before and since have discovered, judged to be emotionally and mentally unstable, a condition not unfamiliar to the protagonist whose struggle to be recognized, to be *seen*, is waged against a legacy of oppression.

Whether or not women's illnesses are rooted in actual misogynistic practices or simply a case of "cynical feminist[s]" zeroing in on "patriarchal structures"[51] as likely culprits of these types of labels is almost beside the point. Rather, it is the negative connotations associated with the labeling itself that is problematic. In other words, it is more about *who* is invested with the authority to diagnose women as especially prone to madness, rather than the misogynistic discourse itself that presents distorted views of what may otherwise be legitimate symptomology arising from long-term stressors such as racism, oppression and violence.

"Remedies don't exist," the protagonist laments. "They haven't been invented. Only behaviors can be changed through habitual prayer," she insists.[52] The thing that the protagonist is getting at is the centrality of madness interwoven with the gratification of pain, of not being able to reconcile one's obsessions or mitigate the impulse toward learned self-negation except through prayer.[53] And so it is that madness and lesbian desire co-exist in an uneasy alliance.

The protagonist demonstrates over and over again that passion is no kin to reason, and that what it dislodges is just as perilous as what it leaves undisturbed. She is undone with the deep emotional work of unrequited longing, taking what crumbs were offered to her from the "young woman," crumbs that were "doled out like flawed jewels [...], the words, like abuse."[54] The archetype of the mad woman is taken to the extreme in Pérez's novel. Women—interpellated through the brown/black/queer body—come to represent wildness/madness that must be controlled, either through medicine and psychiatry or through the language of rationality.

By changing our perception of what actually constitutes madness, we recognize that deviancy—to borrow from Adria E. Schwartz's counterresponse to rigid conceptual formulations of gender role identities, for example—becomes a purposeful (and powerful) misnomer for what is legitimately "our multiply gendered representations and the myriad part and whole and object relations on which they are based."[55] Thus by reading *Gulf Dreams* from a perspective that defines madness along a continuum of psychological sequelae such as post-traumatic stress disorder (PTSD) that results from personal experiences of trauma (be that child sexual abuse, war, or community violence), we might be more sympathetically inclined towards alternative explanations for what might initially be diagnosed as "mad" behaviors. Ultimately, it is when the protagonist forgets to "[listen] to the seam between dusk and dark"[56] that she becomes increasingly unmoored, accepting that neither the certainty of death nor the cravings that would deliver her into death's embrace can cure her.

Through the protagonist's eyes we become privy to her earliest memory where she "track[s] a thin, cinnamon cockroach slithering against a wall [finding] a crack and [slipping] through an opening that [is] invisible, nonexistent."[57] She is two or three years old. Her mother has brought her along on a visit to *la costurera*, the seamstress, because they are too poor to buy their own clothes.[58] *La costurera's* sons take advantage of the two women's inattention, taking the baby's hand and leading her to a bedroom where an older brother stands guard while another rubs his erect penis against her.[59] The cockroach that she tracks with innocent eyes is symbolic of all the things she will be denied by others, yet it also signifies the instinct for survival against all odds. It is ancient and indestructible, a creature that

> lives in our dark spaces [and] constantly reminds us that other worlds exist at the margins of our lives, worlds that obey drastically different orders from the one we know. Roaches construct a whole other reality, which they weave into our own.[60]

It could be said that Schweid's engaging description of an insect that has survived on earth for millions of years is intimately bound up in the psychic disruption and pain experienced by every person of color whose very existence is contingent upon remaining in the shadows, the margins, the "gutters." We are the nightmare that dares present itself in the light of day, the persistent itch from which there is no relief, the "darkness" that never goes away. So, too, does the protagonist, who from that day forward experiences a feeling of numbness and a disconnection from a reality far too harsh for the tender minds of babies and young girls.

The protagonist has internalized her difference, not only from her family where her green eyes set her apart from the rest, but also from herself. She is a child who is so sad that at the age of five she takes hold of a butcher knife and calmly contemplates slicing into her own skin.[61] She comes of age in a town where her passion for women is as much a part of her as the skin she once thought of cutting away. And not so unlike the cockroach that survives millennia of extermination attempts, her thoughts skitter into invisible places that are untouched and unreachable. Yet ironically, it is from these hidden spaces that she gathers her strength, emerging each time with a renewed will to survive, even when the threat of perishing is by her own hand.

Beginnings

Having met through their older sisters when they were fifteen and sixteen, respectively, the protagonist and the "young woman" embark upon what would forever be an uncertain dance of yearning and exploration. At their first meeting they walked to a park and "stood under a tree for hours exchanging glances that bordered on awkward embarrassment."[62] Eventually their eyes settled on one another, communicating a tenderness that, for the protagonist, at least, touched a part of her that she had never before had any awareness of.[63] Uncertain if she had fallen in love at that first meeting, she begins the long and tortuous journey into the madness of longing. The terrible irony of her situation is that it is her love for another woman that is perceived by society to be mad, not the fact that she loves someone else to the point of madness. The kind of love to which sonnets have long borne witness to is denied to those whose identities are co-constructed in racist, misogynist, and homophobic discourse.

Older, and attending college, the "young woman" got into the habit of sharing with the protagonist details of her sexual adventures, deriving and giving pleasure through "seductive words" that through their specificity left the protagonist "wanting [even] more particulars" so that she and the "young woman" could be bonded together in intimacy.[64] "Intimacies of the flesh [were] achieved through words," the protagonist tells us. In her "mad" emotional state, those words constituted their "affair [and] years later" the protagonist "rediscovered [her] compulsion to consummate intimacy through dialogue—to make love with a tongue that spewed desire, that pleaded for more words, acid droplets on [her] skin."[65] We know that language is powerful, that it can effect change, induce fear, heighten desire, or create alternative realities. Yet in her lucid states, the protagonist knows that hers is an imaginary that can only exist in ways that are indecipherable to those who would reject her for defying tradition, for loving a woman who belongs to a man.

Understanding that the object of her desire is married to a man who "owned her" and who depleted the very essence of her in order to create an inflated image of himself, the protagonist adapts by learning how to achieve sexual intimacy without physical touching. The protagonist craves intimacy and the "erotic dialogue" she had become addicted to, and protagonist's delusions become her reality, for delusions are the only means by which she can be with the "young woman" in ways that fulfill her deepest desires.[66] She chases the dragon of obsession and sexual fantasy, uncertain of where it will take her and of how she will respond should it ever become real.[67] Unable to express herself within the limits of the inarticulate androcentric tongue, the protagonist despairs that she will never be able to explain to anyone the emotional connection she shared with the "young woman."[68] There is innocence in the protagonist's fantasies, a way of turning madness back upon itself, misdirecting those whose impression of her is too narrowly defined. She replays her delusions until she achieves a different outcome, one that does not continually pull her outside of truth, as she has come to know it.

The protagonist inverts madness by turning inward for protection from the trickery and emotionally bruising effects of heterosexist scripts. In this regard, the double-consciousness of being Chicana and lesbian, but also Chicana-American, is at work in multiple ways and impacts how misdirection is deployed protectively, but also in a radically subversive manner. As I use the term here, misdirection works to "disguise the method [or the person's authentic self] and thus prevent the audience from detecting it whilst still experiencing the effect."[69] For lesbians of color who wish to navigate through multiple worlds without an authentic self being revealed, the work of performing to societal expectations unfolds along a continuum of "passing." The trickery or deception is in convincing society that queer women of color are "normal" and do not pose a threat to the "natural" order.

Intentionally or not, Pérez has given us a protagonist whose adroit negotiation of reality and fantasy actually challenges society's invalidation of the queer subaltern psychic (and psychological) experiences. The protagonist's journey parallels the many difficult roads trod by other lesbians whose very survival depended upon the deployment of an array of misdirecting practices. Indeed, by "producing a politically radical subtext in the narrative form itself,"[70] Pérez has created a lesbian trickster who at once misdirects attention away from the medical model that labels assertive women as mentally unstable, while at the same time negotiating queer identities across racial and cultural borders. In this regard, Ricki Stefanie Tannen's take on the trickster is illuminating:

> If it is true that the traditional Trickster constellates in a culture in order to combat the adversity and hostility of that culture to certain archetypal energies, then the fictive female sleuth [for example] as constellated in the late twentieth century in North American culture is a postmodern Trickster appearing to have come not to combat but to make a new relationship with the historical adversity and hostility found in western consciousness toward females manifesting autonomy, agency, and authenticity as single, fulfilled, physically strong, and psychologically whole individuals. This is a revolution not a revolt.[71]

Yet this new relationship that Tannen describes as non-combative, as a revolution and not a revolt, does not take mental illness—that is almost always racialized, criminalized, sexualized and/or gendered—into account. The "mad" lesbian tricksters who pass for "sane," "normal," or "feminine" trod similar ground as light-skinned women of color who (as we saw in the introduction and second chapter of this book) sometimes "pass" for white. Both must become adept at operating on multiple levels and across varying and shifting contexts. As tricksters, lesbians must be vigilant and ready to respond to the trickery of others by mastering the game, the guise *and* the performance. Furthermore, lesbians of color must navigate terrain that is markedly different from that of white lesbians. Thus while Tannen's interpretation of the trickster could very well be read as a form of revolution, for queer women of color, the revolution brings with it far greater risks.

Both the protagonist and the "young woman" are deeply scarred by the intrusive hands that have shaped their earliest and most enduring nightmares. They are not the revolutionaries or lesbian tricksters here, at least not yet, because as young girls they still come under the control of a different kind of trickery, one wholly informed by the privilege of men. When the protagonist is older and understands the ways in which the "young woman's" husband "shatters" her dreams, she is speaking of his intrusions into her fantasies of his wife, the woman she cannot imagine her life without. "He stalks through the door like a rupture. Impetuous, he accuses me—the intruder—with glaring eyes."[72] The protagonist's frequent delusions pull her out of linear time, but they also give her the strength to resist censure.

The protagonist is unafraid of her love for the "young woman" and even takes comfort in Pelón's mistrust. "Snubbing me, he sensed I didn't worship him, [he] condemned me, always spurning who I was, what I did, and what I meant to her."[73] The protagonist outmaneuvers Pelón, throwing him off balance and reveling in his fear of her madness. "I enjoyed how I threatened him," she says.[74] By changing the terms of male/female engagement and asserting her right to compete for the attentions of a woman they both desire, the protagonist complicates the implied rules of the game. Her boldness is so unexpected that the only responses Pelón can muster are fear and suspicion. But whether she is aware of it or not, his fear of her madness trumps her success in temporarily throwing him off balance, for he at least is in no danger of being judged for whom he loves.

Divisions

The protagonist understands all too well that the way one speaks, hesitates, pauses or makes sense of things is what places that person in context for those who listen to what he/she says and *how* he/she says it. She learned this early on, and in numerous ways, first with her mother's experience with the white receptionist in the white waiting room at the white doctor's office, where her mother's inability to read or sign her own name deepened the social and racial divide between brown and white worlds. "Pronunciation divided worlds," the protagonist tells us. "In a school where students' names ranged from Hodges and Hutchins to a sprinkling of Garza and González, teachers rejected Spanish sounds."[75] And in the end, they rejected her, the protagonist, and in turn, her utterances were differently paced, heard only as imprecise mumblings of a crazed or inferior mind. She understood she would have to learn their language or perish, so she retreats to interstitial spaces where "Hodges" and "Hutchins" may have once been a Horvitz or a Herschel and (like Jews re-integrating into France after the Second World War) they were also pressured to change in order to fit in.[76] The obvious difference, of course, for a Sánchez or a Torres becoming a Roberts or a Smith is that their brown skin will always mark them as different in a divided world.

Women's survival, and that of their families, depended upon acceptance of roles they were required to play in hierarchical systems that defined them almost exclusively by their gender. The protagonist's mother, sisters, aunts, and cousins learned to trade on their gender with the landowners in order to get work for their brown-skinned men. In El Pueblo itinerant Mexican workers make their living picking cotton on vast swathes of land owned by whites, harkening back to a time when blood wrought from the backbreaking work of the underclass leached into soil that readily absorbed their pain but gave little comfort in return.[77]

But the divisions at home, in their own *pueblitos*, was clear, and it was accepted. "My mother's house rested behind my father's workshop." His "hammering was our financial security."[78] In his upholstery shop behind the family home, her father's work was deemed essential for their security. Women's work (in the fields, inside the home, as currency that opened up the way for their brown-skinned men to gain a foothold on land that once belonged to them) was secondary as befitting their role as caregivers. These were the agreements, spoken or not, that bound men and women together. It was an agreement that implied acquiescence to systems that kept women under the control of men, yet also ensured the survival of the family unit.

The protagonist is descended from a long line of people who journeyed "through land expansive with blood-red horizons, until they stopped and looked around and settled into what was already in their blood."[79] Her real and imagined worlds blend together, making it impossible to discern truth from fantasy. Consumed with desire for a woman she can never possess, she descends deeper and deeper into the liminal divide, taking comfort in the interstitial folds of madness, subversion, and sexual "Otherness." The blood roaring through her woman-loving veins marks her as an outcast whose language of desire is foreign not just to the colonizer's tongue but also to the people from whom she is descended.

Although the protagonist is of the "mestizos/as [who] master the conqueror's language as the language of survival," this language "never belongs to the conquered completely."[80] Furthermore, "for people whose language has been swindled twice, first the Native tongue, then the appropriated tongue, we are forced to stumble over colonizer language."[81] Yet as a survivor who must negotiate multiple realities in order to understand and better articulate the intricate webs that form her own mestiza consciousness, the protagonist (like her ancestors before her), I contend, is in fact fluent in the language of the oppressor.[82] She must be if she is to locate an oppositional framework from which to subvert the tyranny of colonialism.

When the protagonist first meets the woman who will quickly become the object of her fantasies, they are both living with their respective families in El Pueblo, a border town where "humidity bred hostility."[83] Yet it was also a place where the lightness of the protagonist's hair, skin and eyes allowed her passage "through doors that shut out [her darker skinned] sisters and brother."[84] Like other Chicanas/os existing on the periphery of communities that were at best indifferent to their presence and at worst hostile to their demands for survival, she never really fit in. Even a rare visit to the doctor's office for unexplained stomach aches became an embarrassment, a perceived imposition, a dividing line separating those who belonged from those who never would.

> My mother took me to the doctor we couldn't afford. We trudged down a common road, pebbles crackling under our feet, accenting our silence. She held my child's hand in hers. The office was decorated white; white antiseptic walls, a white, dull nurse.[85]

The repetition of *whiteness* seems purposeful here. Representing the ultimate separation between brown-skinned Chicanas/os and those who "tolerate" their presence, for the protagonist and her mother, whiteness becomes associated with wellness, goodness, cleanliness, and intelligence. The receptionist likely intuits that the protagonist's mother is unable to read or write, therefore, by instructing her to fill in forms requiring the most basic information, the receptionist affirms her whiteness through the power she has over the brown-skinned woman. She is humiliated in front of her young child and forced to ask the receptionist to write down the information for her, and her self-effacing posture communicates defeat to her impressionable young child.[86]

Whiteness constructs difference as a barrier, an impermeable border between races. Symbolically, it communicates a power differential mitigated only through corresponding levels of power. As "a social construction [it has] real effects that [have] become a powerful organizing principle around the world."[87] Yet on a community level, where day-to-day survival is often contingent upon fair and affordable access to goods and services, the protagonist and her mother recognize power in a more immediate sense. Their needs— made unnecessarily complex and unattainable—remain largely unmet due to the intersecting levels of micro and macro oppressions that conspire to keep them disadvantaged.

On a micro level, the protagonist understands the power differential between her mother and the receptionist. She knows that something as basic as a fresh cotton dress unsoiled by the heat of the sun beating down on tired and sweaty backs picking cotton for landowners can tell a story without a word ever being uttered.[88] And although she attends schools denied to her mother, whose strong back was more prized for picking cotton than her mind was for charting her own destiny, she too experiences the sting of rejection from her white classmates whose parents "told them to keep away from Mexicans with *piojos*; lice that hatched from eggs exploded like little bombs in hair, bearers," they were warned, "of filth and disgust."[89] She quickly learns that she is their nightmare, a brown, unsanitary menace.

I am not suggesting that people of color are a monolithic group who respond in precisely the same way to white privilege or that poor whites are immune to similar disadvantages or class exclusions. However, what is difficult to contest in a novel such as *Gulf Dreams* is that *representative* whiteness becomes a signifier of dominance. What I mean by "representative" whiteness is that the power that inheres in whiteness can also inhere in those (no matter their race or ethnicity) who have the means to dislodge, or temporarily shift it, from its central position. The protagonist learns this lesson later on in life after the "young woman" she so passionately desires has effectively rejected her advances and instead married Pelón, a man she met in college. She is forced to accept that the "young woman" desires a different life, one that is representative of the heterosexual norm, a life that, relative to her own confused existence, is safer and less controversial. With a husband, the "young woman" becomes representative of whiteness or, at the very least, normality. She is complicit in helping to build her own internal prison, eschewing bodily and emotional freedom for the numbing routine of sameness, for the badge of heterosexuality that at least gives her the right to claim representation on a larger stage.

Madness, Mestiza, Memory

"In that rural Texas town, repression conceived my wishes. To understand what you are doing while you're doing it is powerful[...]."[90] Yet the protagonist is constantly reminded that love is not a right afforded to her kind. She recognizes that she lives "in a place that ruptures and negates this practice," but "even when I'm told," she says, "to hide from public, to meet only in unlit rooms where you can't see us, I'm defiant."[91] It is this intransigence that brands the protagonist as *insane*. She hides from public view only to meet in dark places where her "affliction" cannot be seen or passed on to others, yet she remains defiant. Her "malady" of the mind, as Elaine Showalter has argued in her scholarship on women and mental illness, results from psychiatry's insistence that "women were [...] more vulnerable to insanity than men."[92] They were thought to "experience it in specifically feminine ways, and to be differently affected by it in the conduct of their lives."[93] In other words, it was in a woman's nature to be overcome by a weak and unstable mind.

Reductionist thinking in the nineteenth and twentieth centuries defined women as being slaves to their emotions, while men's thinking was perceived to be based on a more developed and reasoned process. For poor women (and men), as well as ethnic minorities, acting outside of socially prescribed roles could easily be interpreted as non-conforming behavior rooted in psychosis. However, there seemed to be a different set of rules for the better off, whose "bizarre behavior would be described as nervousness or eccentricity until the patient became unmanageable, suicidal, or violent."[94] These are the pernicious notions that literary fiction seeks to expose. In *Gulf Dreams*, the text signifies alterity that pushes against the grain, refusing to be defined or reinvented absent the memory of its past. The protagonist uses words to invent the "young woman" as she needs her to be, understanding that naming the "young woman" would change the dynamic, shackle her from that which she embodies.[95]

There is an unsettling, almost surreal quality to the protagonist's thoughts. The reader must decide if it is a mad soliloquy that has no point except to skitter about the edges of the page or if it is the text itself that brings the madness into existence, naming it and therefore giving it a form, an outlet. Yet where the author/writer advocates for an imaginary that crosses literary, geographical and psychic boundaries, Rafael Pérez-Torres, for example, views *Gulf Dreams* as a novel that examines "the ways bodies are coerced into acting out proscribed sexualized gender roles."[96] He argues that *Gulf Dreams* provides "a vision of queer mestizaje that struggles both to gain recognition within the worlds represented in [Emma Pérez's] fiction and to gain voice through the narratives."[97] And while his focus on how race and sexuality are joined together in the *illegitimate*, at the same time transgressive *narration* of queer brown bodies is important to understanding Emma Pérez's work in the context of queer Chicano/a realities. Nevertheless, Pérez-Torres's reading of *Gulf Dreams* largely ignores the issue of madness and its disproportionately negative diagnostic outcomes for women.

It is remarkable that the descriptors "crazy" and "insane" appear repeatedly in *Gulf Dreams* as a central feature of how the protagonist frames her inner and outer worlds, yet receives only a passing mention in Pérez-Torres's consideration of the intersecting oppressions he interrogates in his critique of the novel. The closest he comes to acknowledging the protagonist's self-perceived madness as a legitimate response to multiple and unrelenting oppressions is when he describes the protagonist's experiences as "emotional turmoil,"[98] a term that is as imprecise as it is devoid of any meaningful acknowledgment that, historically, women's subjugation has been directly tied to patriarchy's impulse to exercise control over us by feminizing madness.[99]

Although Pérez-Torres briefly invokes Julia Kristeva's argument that "language is a point of explosion between the subject and her ideological limits," and that "the body's desires are expressed through a formal linguistic shattering that constitutes changes in the status of the subject,"[100] he fails to take this provocative statement beyond his own assertion that "poetic language is a disruptive language opening up the possibilities of new, potentially ecstatic expression[s]."[101] My approach to *Gulf Dreams* is to "read" madness through a broader constellation of oppressive practices that intersect and result in the invalidation of queer women of color experiences. *Gulf Dreams* does what Kristeva contends that literature should do, and that is to "decenter the closed set and elaborate the dialectic of a process within plural and heterogeneous universes."[102] These closed sets are further decentered when we see the "text [as] a practice that could be compared to political revolution: the one brings about in the subject what the other introduces into society."[103] In other words, the text compels thinking beyond the limits of both its structure and the cultural borders it represents.

As the protagonist grows older, her rejection of the terms that would imprison her (heterosexual, wife, mother) marks her more starkly by other terms that reinforce her difference (queer, Mexican, lazy, ignorant, promiscuous, independent, violent, *extranjero*). These signifiers of difference—with their historically prejudicial connotations—cast women in terms that are unresolvable: hysteric and female; temptress and virgin; aggressive and passive; cunning and innocent. Ultimately, the impossibility of being both a lesbian and a *tejana* woman from a culture that defers to the heterosexual norm compels the protagonist to seek solace in her dreams.

But the uncertainty of the protagonist's life, the internal battles she struggles to overcome, eventually intersects with events that see her childhood molester brought to trial for the rape of another woman. And the "young woman" whom she desires to the point of madness is married to a man who has always been wary of their friendship, jealous of what he suspects they do when they are together. He is the one who defends the rapist and the others at trial, the lawyer who justifies their actions, his arrogance convincing him that they are simply "young boys [who] just need help, some guidance."[104] And because the protagonist is also a woman whose value is unequal to men, she thinks of Ermila, the victim, and wonders: "Who would take the nightmare, have it for her every night so she could rest."[105] She eventually resolves this question herself when she kills "the loud rapist" who himself was victim to an uncle who "covered the length of his back and legs,' throwing him 'to the ground,' a 'right arm wrapped around his throat, choking him [...] a left hand [covering] his mouth, a body [invading] his."[106] The young brown boy, who dances with his own mad demons.

Naming as Witness

In fiction, as in her critical work, Pérez does not retreat from strategies that put at risk the conditional freedoms *allowed* Chicanas in postcolonial America. She asserts that while "women's politics [and voices, I might add] may have been subordinated under a nationalist paradigm [she cites the Mexican Revolution], women as agents have always constructed their own spaces interstitially, within nationalisms, nationalisms that often miss women's subtle interventions."[107] It is of note that *naming* comes so late in the novel, particularly as it is a dominant characteristic of binary systems that intentionally establish and reinforce hierarchies of difference. Yet naming—as a form of bearing witness and as a reclaiming of the self—also allows for different experiences and truths to be articulated (and heard) alongside historical misrepresentations (and *mis-namings*) of those written out of existence.

With the exception of Chencho (one of the rapists), Ermila (the woman who is raped), Juan (the one-time lover of the protagonist), Pelón (the husband of the woman the protagonist is in love with), and Mr. Green (the Anglo landowner), no one else in the novel has a name. The significance of this is unclear, although naming features prominently in the work of gender, critical race theorists and borderland writers who thread together the gaps in historical narratives to aid in the reconstruction of identities and cultures lost to imperialist agendas. We see a type of self-naming in the introduction to *Chicana Feminisms: A Critical Reader* (2003), when the editors reimagine Gloria Anzaldúa's "notion of Chicanas" bodies as *bocacalles* for its more "provocative translation as mouth/street" because it "evokes images of women shouting in the streets or the assertion of Chicana feminisms as public discourse demanding to be heard" as in, one might argue, a collective naming.[108]

Naming works as an affirmation of one's existence, an incontrovertible statement that confers upon humans the ability to recognize their own kind, to assert their right to be called by their given name or to rename themselves as their group configurations or individual fortunes change. This can be interpreted as a gesture toward what seems to be implied in Anzaldúa's work. Anzaldúa suggests that those who go through life as strangers in their own skin do so either because they have been rejected by their community and family for not being "normal" enough or because they have internalized such a level of ambivalence about their own identity and worth that they come to see themselves in the very terms pressed upon them by others. They must find ways to read the signs of self-erasure and despair, while at the same time knowing how not to be afraid of their inner serpents/demons/names; their *Coatlicue.* "She has this fear," Anzaldúa writes, "that she has no names, that she has many names, that she doesn't know her names."[109] Her fear, as I have argued throughout, is not without basis for she has witnessed what becomes of those whose naming is at odds with what society has deemed to be appropriate.

A woman is named "daughter," "wife," "mother," and, later in life, "grandmother" or "wise woman." These titles and labels afford her protection because she has accepted the roles (and rules) implied in these names. A man is called "son," then "husband," then "father" and "grandfather." But he is also called by other names, ones that grant him power over his children, his wife, his sisters. He is the "master" of his home, the provider for his family, the decision-maker, the "protector." His wife and daughters take his name and are known collectively through him, because they have no matrilineal ties to which they are *legally* bound. Forced to forsake one another in order to belong to men, the protagonist in *Gulf Dreams* chooses to name herself as "mad," but this is the language of the Anglos, not Chicanas who—as Anzaldúa has argued—have many borderland names, none of which necessarily denotes madness, but instead acknowledges the cultural importance of ritual, divination, spirits and spirituality.

Enacted through a series of rituals and social conventions, the protagonist's naming (as female, unstable, secretive, incomplete) is also her *unnaming.* She does not fully exist in her own right therefore she can only be completed by a pre-determined narrative that guides her unwaveringly to the altar of heterosexuality. We know from the work of gender/queer/postmodern theorists such as Michel Foucault, Eve Sedgwick, Judith Butler and Julia Kristeva that one of the most recognizable forms of naming are the joyous words "It's a girl" or "It's a boy," announced by parents the world over to fix gender and social expectations through the process of interpellation.[110] It is, as Barbara McKay suggests, the "power of first utterance" that positions us (at least initially) in a certain context.[111] The ability to eventually change our position is not always within our gift, but we can attempt to use misdirection to destabilize and subvert the process of our un-naming, our erasure.

In "Critically Queer," Butler distinguishes between the *act* of naming which in itself holds no authority and the conventions (inscribed into law) that surround the naming that ultimately legitimizes (and brings into effect) the name/identity/fact of a given thing.[112] Using her example of a judge who "authorizes and installs the situation he names [...] [and who] invariably *cites* the law [italics belong to Butler] that he applies, [...]," we know that "it is the power of this citation that gives the performative its binding or conferring power."[113] Thus it is the case that the protagonist is defined and ultimately shaped by legal, social, and mental health citations that compare her to a white hetero-centric norm to which she never quite measures up. She is discursively constructed through a white-centric, heteronormative lens, and her un-naming prevents her from ever fully calling herself back into existence.

"I'm trapped," the protagonist tells us, "between visions and that which I intuit, never sure what's real, but always conscious of how I'm scorned, hated, rejected for who and what I am."[114] She describes how others have named her—"Mexican, dumb, stupid, hateful, ugly [...]"—and how she is a woman who "must learn a world that craves tanned brown, not real brown, not birth brown, just gringo-tanned-at-the-beach, golden brown, not Mexican brown."[115] Yet she must also learn that her displacement is partially achieved through her consent, be it implied or explicit, and also most certainly through force. Her consent because she sometimes chooses sexual intercourse with men who treat her kindly but who are nothing more than bland substitutes for the passion she craves with the "young woman." And sometimes through force because her life has been presented to her as a lie, as an un-naming that leads her to "rooms where men sat fat or lean behind desks smoking cigars [moving] you to the couch in their office, squat down, unzip their pants and shove your head."[116] And the lies she is forced to play out become traps and it is too late for resistance when "you gag [and] your eyes look up, checking the door or a window, a passage to flee [or resist]." And "you become ugly. For money."[117] You become someone else. You become the name they gave you. You *become* mad.

Resistance Madly Writ

The intimacies that the protagonist builds for herself as a way to reach a queer(ed) *mestiza* consciousness is illustrated throughout *Gulf Dreams* in ways that must be read through multiple points of view in order to fully understand that her longing is real, even though the consummation of her sexual desire with the "young woman" may not be. When she says, "I invent you daily, hungering, awakened from sleep to hold you lying on me,"[118] she is also reinventing herself and her language in ways that outsiders do not understand or that she has long forgotten. Ultimately, she can only ever be herself (or so she believes) by riding the edges of her dreams, hoping that visions of the "young woman" will "free [her] from insanity."[119] But is this freedom she craves recuperative, generative, a wild thrash of desires unhindered by the pressing needs of the madness put upon her, or is the source of her pain an invention of an already unstable mind?

We know from the protagonist that whenever she predicts that her "life will shift," that it "will finally reverse itself [...]," she "will [once again] begin to desire [the "young woman"] and desire will fuel more delusions. And when delusions are streamed through prisms of intolerance and rejection, desire becomes "[a] nightmare that won't end," unless it is, the protagonist threatens, through suicide.[120] The protagonist is haunted by the "young woman," believing that she has been deceived by "language I've never heard before, language I've yearned for. You speak cleverly, you're so clever."[121] Oddly, the protagonist seems to comprehend the impossibility of her desires, while at the same time pursuing them. "We stand at the entrance, door open, not inside, not outside, only at its entrance. We stand. Exiled."[122] The place the protagonist describes, that simultaneous gesture she makes towards the past and the present, the real and the unreal, the gaps and the frame, is tied to the language of wanting, the language of indeterminacy and madness. One might say that her longing is lyrical, indeed Sapphic, if madness can at all be likened to the poetics of love. But can she slake her thirst with dreams? Can she coax forth the forbidden desire that presses for release from what can only be described as the parsimonious grip of historical rectitude? Is her madness to an undoing or a salvation?

Mistaking the "young woman's" kindness "for a wish," the protagonist admits that she has come "face to face with lunacy," causing her to doubt "what others ordained to be normal as if their lives were something to entreat."[123] For the protagonist, "normal" (read: heterosexual, white, moralistic, unchangeable) may as well have been death.

The tension between gender identity and sexual orientation (and the myriad ways this plays out in social and private arenas) warrants consideration of how lesbianism comes to be interpreted as madness. Adria E. Schwartz suggests that our "core gender identity, traditionally thought to be a bedrock of essential mental health [...] is actually more about understanding categories and attaining mastery of the linguistic ordering of culture."[124] I might add that insofar as some humans may claim no specific gender identity, history shows that psychoanalysis has been quick to step into the breach. It does so by suggesting that the refusal to be one thing or another is a sign of "psychosis and other serious personality disturbances."[125] Although this particular tension is not made explicit in *Gulf Dreams*, the protagonist's madness, I argue, is mirrored back to her by a society unable to reconcile the troubling manifestations of its own lunacy.

The protagonist is trapped in the debilitating role of pathologized "Other." She believes there is no cure for "people like us."[126] With no positive cultural reflections of her lesbian identity, she begins to define herself in non-negotiable terms. Disconnected from the internal compass that for untold centuries has set itself aright by the orientation of the stars, the land that she and her ancestors once knew has fallen off its axis. She is caught up in an endless loop of self-negation and, unable to find the way back to her true center, she spins out of control.

Borderlands

The word "borderland," like the people it has come to represent, is a complex term holding multiple meanings. It at once describes geographical areas where Chicano/as have been locked out from that which once belonged to them, where fences erected against brown Chicano/a bodies that are not made to mingle in the rarified circles of white culture are meant to reinforce differences. Yet borders can also represent that which is held separate (Chicana, lesbian, lover) from that which is promoted as "real" or "reasonable" or even "sane." The protagonist reads borders like she reads the "young woman's" hesitations. Moving between realities is her strength, her protection. Borders also signify places where, as Gloria Anzaldúa puts it, Chicanas, lesbians, lovers "listen [...] to the seam between dusk and dark."[127] In what Anzaldúa further describes as *La Coatlicue* state, or the cluster of psychic elements comprised of *Coatlicue, Cihuacoatl,* and *Tlazolteotl,* the subconscious comes to represent the "consuming internal whirlwind, the symbol of the underground aspects of the psyche."[128] We are made to understand that *Coatlicue* "depicts the contradictory,"[129] just as the language between imperialists and the oppressed sets up uneasy contradictions and tensions between the belief in mysticism (which features prominently in *of color* histories and literature) and "reason," which features just as prominently in colonialist narratives. Both Pérez and Anzaldúa speak from interstitial cultural spaces that rework these narratives, ultimately allowing borderland writers to lay claim to (and re-imagine) the unspeakable that is within and without.

Culture informs who we are and what we become. And while the "young woman" derides *la Virgen de Guadalupe* that the protagonist wears around her neck, proudly declaring herself to be an unbeliever,[130] the "young woman" simply fails to comprehend that she has replaced one symbol of faith for another. Tied to holy matrimony that is blessed by the church and the government, she is no less shaped by her culture than the protagonist whose religious beliefs she mocks. The protagonist knows this, reminding the "young woman" that she had once been "a good Catholic girl [who recited] the 'Act of Contrition' without a mistake, avowing its magic."[131] The protagonist ridicules the "young woman's" beliefs, wondering if her husband's influence "could dissolve what twenty years of kneeling at an alter [sic] to pray Hail Mary's had drilled into her."[132] The protagonist is convinced that Pelón's wife had turned her back on the rituals of religion.[133] But has she? Or is it the case that she has simply chosen to express her devotion to God's law through the safety of heterosexuality, a law that unequivocally repudiates the protagonist's lesbian existence?

"You were a symptom," the protagonist reflects when thinking of her desire for the "young woman." A symptom, she claims, "of [an] irrevocable illness."[134] An illness, one might say, that is rooted in a psychopathology premised upon the erroneous assumption that men speak the language of rationality whereas the inverse holds that women do not. "You think I'm crazy. I am. Crazy to think someone else will do for me what I must do for myself."[135] Implicit in this statement is an acknowledgment by the protagonist that she has the capacity to differentiate between "legitimate" mental disorders and the unreasonable expectations of others that could be (mis)interpreted as being "crazy." When she admits to being "tortured daily," stating, "I create torture," more uncertainty is introduced into the story, illustrating how elusive and misunderstood a thing madness can be. The protagonist accepts that she will never resolve the enigma of who she is through the eyes (or reality) of someone else.

The unresolvable tension the protagonist experiences works to ensnare her in a web of confusion. While she refuses to be consigned to a life of invisibility, she continues to accept that she and the "young woman" are "trapped in social circumstances," ultimately giving in to a "propriety that kept [them] apart."[136] Her love for the "young woman" has no "natural" outlet, thus her addiction to the idea of lesbian love with the "young woman" becomes so powerful that something as innocent as "a kiss on the cheek" inflames her for hours.[137] As we might intuit from the protagonist's constant musings about the "young woman," she conceives of their relationship as a romantic one and she speaks and acts accordingly. The smell of honeysuckle riding in on a breeze reminds the protagonist of the "young woman," triggering memories she tries to forget.[138] Yet when she lingers long enough in the borderland spaces from whence her dreams come, she acknowledges how easily she becomes enamored of women. And while she takes care to warn the "young woman" about her "dishonesty," her "carelessness,"[139] in the end, when her dreams remain unfulfilled, she says: "There is no cure for my illness, the insanity I rehearse. Nothing will change me, not even you, my beautiful symptom, the one who will not judge me harshly."[140] Here the protagonist turns her illness into a metaphor that is at once conceptually dynamic (in that it requires an acknowledgment of her multiple subjective realities) while also suggesting that her ability to change is immutable, fixed, static.

Gulf Dreams problematizes issues that continue to shape contemporary discourse regarding culture, race, sexual orientation, ethnicity, and belonging. Its non-linear narratological structure compels a rethinking of how readers process, and ultimately make sense of, that which falls outside of heteronormative parameters. Misdirection "decolonizes" the way literature is written and read. It opens up much needed alternative spaces through which new truths can emerge and it serves as evidence that "mad women" who have been demonized and locked away in physical and metaphorical "attics" can use literature to change the terms by which they are defined. By extricating the queer psyche from the tangled web of mental illness, *Gulf Dreams* shines a light on (and interrogates) the oppressive conditions from which madness often originates. The idea of madness, particularly in how it is often described in terms that are similar to those used to further marginalize ethnic and sexual minorities, is complex, often subjective, and almost always treated in terms of how this "condition" responds to therapeutic, psychopharmacological, or even religious interventions.

Throughout this chapter I argued that oppositional strategies created in response to dominant cultural and political narratives that have historically made little to no room for dissenting opinions serve several purposes. Firstly, they act as a type of *witnessing* relevant to oppressive practices that to this day continue to devalue or suppress minority voices. Secondly, they represent a call for women to take up arms (in a manner of speaking) and write the disappeared (queer, black, brown, other-gendered) body back into existence.

Thirdly, they reorient the heteronormative gaze by creating alternative paradigms through which *knowing* (in all its forms) can be shared and valued on multiple levels and in a variety of ways. And finally, these oppositional strategies de-pathologize queer women of color desire by challenging tropes that equate sexual expression with deviancy, primitivism, or mental illness.

Chapter 6

Body Crossings

Gender, Signifying and Misdirection
in Jaime Cortez's Sexile/Sexilio (2004)[1]

> Capturing the partiality and relationality of identities as they
> are lived and narrated demands that we capture "being" as a
> movement without end, as an enabling transivity.[2]

> I wanted to challenge the correlation of maleness with mas-
> culinity and running the fuck; the correlation of femaleness
> with femininity and getting run over in bed.[3]

Relying on misdirection and the hybrid form of graphic narratives to
articulate new and more positive ways of reading "queer assemblages," the
previous chapters have gone some way in establishing a dialogic bridge that
connects and pieces together the myriad ways in which queer women of color
representation complicates easy assumptions about identity. Jaspir K. Puar's
application of the term "queer assemblages" is useful here in that it more
accurately describes the "queering" (and reclamation of) liminal spaces and
transgressive bodies. Although Puar's focus is on the war on terror and its
skewed and racist narrative, the over-arching discourse she presents touches
on queer assemblages that gesture toward "spatial, temporal, and corporeal
convergences, implosions, and rearrangements."[4] Indeed, this is an apt
description of misdirection and its queer(ed) performances throughout history. Resisting imperatives that fix the queer body within categories that
approximate an unattainable, and indeed an undesirable norm, in this chapter
misdirection works to deconstruct hetero and homonormative imperatives
regarding transgender identity.

Adela Vázquez's biography, written in graphic narrative form, follows
her journey from Cuba to the shores of the United States of America via the
Mariel Boatlift. Adela is portrayed as a flamboyant character whose identity
as a transgender woman brackets her life experiences on both shores, and

her decision to defy cultural expectations and norms by loudly and insistently proclaiming her right to exist forms much of *Sexile's* narrative arc. Adela is brash, unapologetic, opinionated, and, unbeknownst to her, arriving in America shortly after the Centers for Disease Control and Prevention (CDC) published a report that described symptoms in five gay men in California who were exhibiting a "rare lung infection, Pneumocystis carinii pneumonia (PCP)," as well as other infections.[5] These symptoms were the precursor to the AIDS epidemic. Thus Adela's identity, and how she came to be perceived and treated by the dominant heteronormative culture, was additionally shaped by this unknown illness. Her story is compelling on many levels, not the least of which is her courage in embracing her transgender identity and making no apologies for who she is.

While a chapter that takes as its focus MTF transgender identity may seem out of place in a book that has largely concerned itself with deconstructing stereotypes that situate cisgender lesbians of color on the periphery of "normative" identity constructs, my over-arching intention has been to shake up these constructions by inverting narratives that elevate one type of reality/identity/gender expression over another. As the visual and written narratives in Jaime Coretz's mesmerizing graphic novel unfold, readers come to understand how misdirection—inherent, I argue, in the polysemic capacity of the graphic narrative form—loosens the grip of hetero and homonormativity's stranglehold on the collective psyche by opening up constricted psycho-sexual-cultural pathways that lead to multiple truths. In this regard Susan Stryker's incisive observation sounds an important beginning chord here.

Stryker asserts that transgenderism is about "claiming the transformative power of a return from abjection."[6] Her critique of the historical divide between non-trans and transgender activists is important to my own framing of what it means to be *out of place*, how this return from abjection comes to the fore in *Sexile*, and the part that *trans*-ing plays in misdirection by adding to, and complicating, notions of gender and sexual expression under an increasingly normative "queered" umbrella.

In the introduction to *Sexile* the reader is confronted with what is described as a traditional transgender nursery rhyme, although there is no reference to its origin. The first line establishes what is at stake for the transgender person whose identity is bound up in a cultural hegemony that sets her claim up as already illegitimate and unobtainable. "The woman that I'm going to be"[7] is a transitive phrase that requires the reader to understand the notion of becoming, of *trans*-ing, of accepting the premise that there is fluidity within and between genders, a premise that sets out its stall in the very first pages of Cortez's graphic novel to assert the presence of "difference" as an uncontestable right. The woman that Vazquez is *going* to be/become relies heavily upon misdirection as a strategy in her *becoming*.

Here I want to place into context my own understanding of what transgender means. The prefix *trans* is an antonym for the prefix "cis." As an antonym "trans" means across, beyond, through, on the other side of, to go beyond.[8] Thus my understanding of *trans*gender is in the ability of the prefix *trans* to link with various nouns and adjectives in order to change the angle of vision through which we understand ourselves as well as the world around us. For example, *trans* (lingual), *trans* (cultural), *trans* (national), translation, transfigure, transfix and transcending are descriptors that indicate movement, renewal, multiplicity and juxtaposition. I use the term *trans*-ing here to better describe the fluidity of gender performance, how these performances "translate" over time and through different contexts, and the altered states and realities it triggers by way of its signifying repetition.

What is at stake is the building of new frameworks that support alternative conceptualizations of gender identity and performance. *Trans*-ing liberates the transgender body from the limbo between visibility and erasure, legitimacy and criminality, desirability and repulsion. Therefore if the act of *trans*-ing radically opens the way for a return from abjection, then misdirection points the way home.

I want to briefly mention here the importance of pronouns in self-representational transgender narratives. While it is not practical in this chapter to switch between male and female pronouns in my engagement with Adela Vázquez's story, or to use gender-neutral terms ("hir," "ze," "per," "sie," "ey," "zir," "em," "eirs") that sometimes add more confusion than clarity for those unfamiliar with these pronouns, where possible I have used Adela's surname or the pronouns that she uses at different stages in her life to mark her evolving awareness of her preferred gender identity. In most cases this is the feminine pronoun, although in approximately the first third of the book it is the masculine pronoun. Indeed, this *trans*-itioning between masculine and feminine pronouns speaks to a rejection of discourse that continues to define gender in rigid binary terms.

My focus on transgender lives as part of a larger project on queer women of color representation links misdirection with the growing transgender scholarship and cultural production of gender and sexual orientation. The purpose is to underscore how gender identity and expression are fluid and at times illusory and how misdirection becomes inextricably tied to transgender "performance" and the gendered "legitimacy" of this marginalized group. In this chapter then I focus on Cortez's graphic narrative about the life of Cuban *(s)exile* Adela Vázquez to argue that misdirection in the visual/textual form of graphic narratives, as well as in literary fiction, compels a rethinking of how gender is both constructed and deconstructed. By describing gender in non-binary ways and reinterpreting the *of color* trans body as a site where hegemonic paradigms can be contested, misdirection redraws the boundaries by effectively closing the distance between what is real and what is imagined. Successfully negotiating the indeterminate performative spaces between the heterosexual and the homo/trans erotic, misdirection becomes a signifying practice expressed in multiple ways.

Critical (Trans)Nationalisms

Existing scholarship regarding transgender marginalization, sex work, and the prevalence of HIV and AIDS in transgender communities is well established. Therefore my contribution takes a slightly different turn here, in that it looks through the frame of graphic narratives to reach beyond the limits of the male/female, gender/sex dyad, particularly as these categories relate to the experiences of transgender women of color.[9] I apply misdirection to dislodge and re-evaluate critical debates that have sometimes collapsed transgender concerns into (predominantly white) gay/lesbian issues, thereby ignoring the multiple oppressions suffered by this group.[10] In arguing for the importance of acknowledging the lives of transgender women of color in any balanced examination of the violence and oppressions that impacts them, we must, as Viviane Namaste rightly suggests, advocate for a "detailed, contextual analysis of the different ways social relations of race, labor, and gender intersect" in a manner that helps us to "adequately understand" the complexities underpinning these issues.[11]

The lack of a living wage, proper healthcare, social networks, or safe spaces drive many trans women to the sex trade. They are then vilified as being immoral and sub-human because their choices do not reflect the impossible expectations of an intolerant society.[12] Put another way, positioned as we are at the bottom of the scale of attributes that delineates the human race from animals, people of color as a whole have been historically characterized as the antithesis of all that is considered pure. Thus to reject the privileges (however small) that in even the poorest countries in the world are afforded to men, transgender women of color are seen to have crossed the very last bastion of morality. As a result, society has repeatedly shown that these transgressions must not go unremarked or unpunished.

In what some trans scholars have recognized as a "hetero-gendered"[13] system that essentially fails to acknowledge the "Otherness" in itself, Susan Stryker's emerging political consciousness as a newly "out" transgender person was first tested publicly in 1995 at a conference sponsored by the Center for Lesbian and Gay Studies in New York. Jim Fouratt, a founding member of the Gay Liberation Front and a veteran of the Stonewall Riots, was said by Stryker to have referred to trans people as "profoundly psychopathological individuals who mutilated their bodies [...], believed in oppressive gender stereotypes [...], held reactionary political views, and [...] had been trying for years to infiltrate the gay and lesbian movement" in a bid to bring about its demise.[14]

The negativity between transgender and non-trans people is problematic for at least two reasons that come to mind. Firstly, Fouratt's comments derive from the same exclusionary language and practices that continue to negatively impact the lives of gender non-conforming people across the globe. While activists such as Fouratt may achieve some legitimacy in upholding the tenets of heteronormativity, this is only a temporary reprieve from other battles still being waged for equal representation under the law. Ultimately, Fouratt engages in a double negation (of himself and his "queered" transgender kin) that effectively "contains" queer politics within primarily queer arenas. Secondly, to be seen as *out of place*, as not fitting in, even under the presumed inclusiveness of the queer tent, further troubles the notion of identity by fixing it in a place that is itself inherently unstable.

We have seen similar anti-transgender proselytizing from the likes of Janice Raymond, who once asserted that "all transsexuals rape women's bodies by reducing the real female form to an artefact, appropriating this body for themselves."[15] For Hilary McCollum there is an inescapable (and worrying) fragmentation of the self that occurs in transitioning from one gender identity to another, be it through surgical means or through signification across multiple contexts. McCollum maintains that "a male-to-female will always be a man whether he's had his penis cut off and breasts put there or not," going on to argue that because men are "brought up with much more status than women," they have not experienced "the same oppressions as women."[16] However, it is my view that when cis people define gender identity and expression based solely upon an already dubious either/or premise, we run the risk of becoming suspect in our quest for the very relevancy and equal treatment that we all seek.

By stepping too far outside of socially acceptable roles and boundaries, transgender people are often blamed for inviting ridicule and violence into their lives. This is especially the case in prisons where outward signifiers that do not match perceived or legally assigned gender roles often result in rape, mutilation, "protective" confinement, or death. Society takes little responsibility for its own unwillingness to vigorously address these violations, instead engaging in what Gabriel Arkles has cited as a "deliberate indifference" that places certain individuals at increased risk of harm.[17] Aimee Wodda and Vanessa R. Panfil note that in the legal arena those who have committed deadly violence against transgender people sometimes draw on a "trans panic" defense to justify their actions.[18] The trans panic defense is framed by "cultural values regarding masculinity and heteronormativity" where the emphasis is on a "binary system of gender and an aversion to anything outside the boundaries of heterosexual (cisgender male and cisgender female) sexual activity."[19] Although in recent years transgender people have begun to accrue more legal rights, there remains an underlying narrative that places the onus on victims to avert the very violence they are accused of inviting. This then absolves— if not legally, then psychologically—those who commit violent acts against gender non-conforming people of responsibility for their actions.

Ultimately, my use of the phrase *out of place* in the opening to this chapter might be interpreted as an unconscious slip that reinforces the very polarities that I seek to disentangle. However, what I mean by this phrasing is that the act of being *out of place*, of deploying misdirection as a strategy for recognition and survival, becomes the framework through which "graphic narratives" can more effectively "work as creative catalysts and as political interventions[…]."[20] Graphic narratives therefore can, as Theresa M. Tensuan notes, "refigure" the "visual iconographies that shape our understanding and imagination of gendered bodies, national identities, and the work of culture."[21] In this way, then, the terms "queer," "out of place," and "misdirection" are meaningful exactly because of their contribution to a vernacular of dissent.

Theorizing the (Trans)National Ga(y)ze

My arguments in this chapter are framed by queer and transgender theory, as well as a transnational praxis that takes up issues of sexual and political exile, racism, gender performance, and *of color* self-representation. I argue that by using misdirection to blur the lines between what we imagine we see and what our minds signal to us as being objectively true, identity is reinforced as the *performance* it has always been. In this regard Judith Butler's oft-cited deliberations on gender performativity are particularly apt.

> The very criterion by which we judge a person to be a gendered being, a criterion that posits coherent gender as a presupposition of humanness, is not only one that informs the ways we do or do not recognize ourselves, at the level of feeling, desire, and the

body, in the moments before the mirror, in the moments before the window, in the times that one turns to psychologists, to psychiatrists, to medical and legal professionals to negotiate what may feel like the unrecognizability of one's gender and, hence, of one's personhood.[22]

What *Sexile* compels us to think about when issues of gender and sexual expression (as well as the concomitant regulations that are often triggered in response to non-normative gender performances) arise is that even when one person is having sex with another, particularly in the case of one partner being trans identified, sexual expression can play out in any number of ways. Ultimately, it is how each person self-identifies that must be the starting point to framing debates and engaging with the ideas that flow from them. Having a basic understanding of terminology that broadly describes gender non-conforming people works to demystify harmful stereotypes and expose the regulatory practices of what Talia Mae Bettcher describes as "identity enforcement" or those beliefs and laws imposed upon gender non-conforming bodies through violence or threats of violence.[23]

Definitions of gender identity and expression are often encumbered by ideological positions that can become increasingly rigid in direct proportion to perceived levels of threat to the hetero or homosexual norm. As a state of being that straddles the gender divide, transgenderism is complex and contentious. Scholars on many sides of the debate struggle with where to situate transgenderism in queer coalitional politics. Given that *Sexile* is a story about self-representation, the *exiled* trans body, and the politics that underpin how such bodies are inscribed in racially, sexually, and politically charged ways, I argue that an understanding of the terminology underpinning these schisms is essential to the development of broader and more inclusive narratives.

Turning briefly to Katrina C. Rose's useful, though medically framed definitions of transgender and transsexual, we are made to understand the disjunction experienced by transsexuals "whose internal sense of being male or female is at variance with his or her physical appearance and desires to correct the variance via hormone and/or surgery."[24] The salient point here, repeated in various other descriptions of the term, is that transsexuals believe there is something about their physical bodies that requires "correcting." Their internal and external narratives do not align, ultimately causing psychic dissonance.

On the other hand, Rose's definition of "transgender" describes a category rather than disruptions in psychic states. She notes that "as it is widely used today, [transgender] is an umbrella term" which is inclusive of "other categories of gender-variant people[...]."[25] Used by both transgender and queer activists, the term "gender-variant" works as a contestation of binarisms that situate gender within restrictive psychosexual paradigms. It conveys the multiple ways in which queer(ed) black bodies that are always already constructed as non-normative push back in creative ways against heteronormative scripts that tie gender to race and race to a continuum of deviance and criminality.

Where scholars have largely accepted that transgender has become an umbrella term that is inclusive of a seemingly inexhaustible array of gender expressions and presentations, Paisley Currah highlights some potential pitfalls in lumping together so many other-gendered expressions and identities in one politicized space.[26] She questions if "the use of the label—even one coined to include a myriad of practices and identities—inadvertently create[s] the impression that 'transgender' can be domesticated, contained in a relatively fixed social location, and thus risk reproducing the exclusions created by a politics of identity?"[27] Going on to ask what the consequences might be "of *not* invoking this relatively recent identity politics category in advocacy for those who trouble gender norms," Currah concedes that the lubricious nature, or slipperiness of the term, makes it difficult to undertake a meaningful analysis without serious consideration of a myriad of issues impinging upon the very resolution its advocates appear to seek.[28]

Judith (Jack) Halberstam certainly does not disagree with the term's invocation, but does suggest that the "inclusivity of its appeal has made it quite unclear as to what the term might mean and for whom."[29] These seem to be precisely the cultural shifts required to dislodge the hegemony of gender from its privileged perch. By acknowledging the discursive limits of identity and gender or sexual expression, we must accede to the proposition that gender is fluid and can therefore only be defined by the individual.

Cristin Williams's research into the etymology of the term "transgender" and its evolving meanings over the years is instructive. Noting that the expansiveness of the term's more contemporary usage underscores the complexities of gender identity and expression, Williams points out one of its most important meanings, and that is to "group together different kinds of people who might otherwise have virtually no social contact with one another."[30] On the face of it, this comes across as opposite to the very inclusiveness transgender activists struggle to achieve. But Williams goes on to explain that such groupings "across fine gradations of trans experience and identity can facilitate communication and hence build the experienced reality of a shared community with overlapping and intersectional social needs and political goals."[31] Nevertheless, this *trans*-ing of cultural and even gender barriers seems to have its limits, particularly in regards to sexual desire and what it signifies in a society that still contextualizes sexual expression against a normative of whiteness and a default heterosexual orientation. My attempts to untangle this discursive knot through an analysis of *Sexile* is accomplished primarily through the discursive loop of misdirection and re-signification.[32]

Marielitos

Sexile tells the story of Adela Vázquez (formerly known as Jorge Antonio Vázquez), a Cuban exile who arrived in South Florida on May 13, 1980, on a shrimp boat called the *Lynn Marie*. Eager for the opportunity to optimize her life chances in a country where gender non-conforming identity was marginally less threatening to American masculinity than it was to the restrictive, hyper-machismo sexual and gender expressions in post-revolutionary Cuba, Vázquez—along with criminals and the "insane" who had been released from Cuba's prisons and mental asylums—braved the approximately 198 nautical miles from Cuba to Florida.[33] Written as a Spanish and also English version, *Sexile/Sexilio* was published as an HIV prevention publication. Jaime Cortez (self-admittedly lacking in "abilities as an illustrator, writer, researcher and theorist") produced an unvarnished account that took 800 hours to complete.[34] His art, he has written, reflects the "transnational, transgendered, transformative and fully transfixing" life of Jorge Antonio Vázquez's journey to womanhood in the time of HIV/AIDS.[35]

Stating that his father raised him "to be a verb," to "be about my actions and the things I was able to complete or accomplish [because] just being myself was not validated," Cortez learned how to reach within himself to locate the "internal drive" that helped him to embrace art as his true calling.[36] He in turn used the graphic narrative form to interject the unspeakable into *la lengua*, or a language that reinvents itself through the individual and varied experiences of its readers. His production of a dual language text, translated into English from the Spanish, and vice versa, underscores the power of *trans-ing*.

Forced to choose freedom of expression over repressive geopolitical posturing, "Marielitos" rode the waves of change that were set in motion on the first day of April 1980 by five men who drove a bus through the gates of the Peruvian embassy in Cuba. They sought and were granted asylum.[37] Although the Mariel Boatlift, as the subsequent exodus came to be known, itself only lasted for a period of approximately seven months (from April to October 1980) in the region of 125,000 Cubans crossed the Strait of Florida in 1,600 vessels.[38] They chose voluntary exile in a country ideologically opposed to the revolution that had shaped their lives, as well as the lives of their parents and grandparents, effectively leaving behind parts of their culture that they would try (with varying degrees of success) to replicate in America.[39]

Set during the very beginning of a decade that would bear witness to the personal devastation of the AIDS crisis, and only eleven years after the Stonewall Riots, *Sexile* touches on the anxieties emerging from the nationalist agendas of two nations locked in an ideological war.[40] The cover of the book is of a naked man swimming away from, and towards, something as yet unknown. The expression on his face is one of great sadness. He appears to be swimming underwater, as numerous air bubbles float upwards in the surrounding space, giving the impression of movement. The image at figure 13 is repeated near the end of the book, accompanied by a moving lamentation on the loneliness and uncertainty of exile.[41]

Arriving in a country that was—as Patrick "Pato" Hebert writes in the forward to *Sexile*—"at best, ambivalent about their presence," Vázquez and "other queer Cubanos struggled to reimagine themselves [...]"[42] in the midst of gay men in New York and Los Angeles, falling desperately ill from a mysterious disease.[43] In the early eighties HIV/AIDS was still a relatively unknown disease. However, from the first diagnosis in 1981 to the year 2000, it had claimed in the region of 448,060 lives. In 2011, the number of deaths stood at 13,834, a significant reduction from the height of the epidemic. While the early days of the crisis saw mostly whites diagnosed with the disease, by 1996, African American men had higher representational numbers than any other ethnic or racial group.[44] African American men accounted for "an estimated 44% of new HIV infections in 2010, even though they represented only 12% of the U.S. population."[45] Statistics also revealed that while "Hispanics/Latinos represented 16% of the population," they "accounted for 21% of

Figure 13. Cover art, *Sexile/Sexilio* (copyright © 2004 by Jaime Cortez. Reprinted by permission of AIDS Project Los Angeles, and the Institute for Gay Men's Health. All rights reserved (see C•4 for larger image).

new HIV infections."⁴⁶ In San Francisco alone, African Americans and Latino transgender people who injected drugs accounted for 46 percent, with 69 percent of those "40 years and older at the end of 2013."⁴⁷ In this way, graphic narratives like *Sexile* have been uniquely placed to reach audiences who may not typically look for information about HIV/AIDS via mainstream media sources. Furthermore, due to the personalization of Vázquez's story in the form of visual and textual biography, the universality of the message makes difficult subjects (transgenderism, HIV/AIDS, cancer, and so on) potentially less threatening to those who may not have direct experience of these issues.

The ability of comics to break down cultural and/or personal barriers to having difficult conversations with medical professionals or loved ones about life threatening illnesses or the resulting psychological trauma has been successfully applied in the field of graphic medicine, a term coined in 2007 by Ian C. M. Williams. Graphic medicine describes how comics can "capture the emotional intensity of medical narratives" and "critically comment on the delivery and impact of health care" in ways that "amplify the voice of the patient in the clinical" and serve as a "powerful way to tell stories about the medical profession and those who come into contact with it."⁴⁸

There are a number of contemporary works in the field of graphic medicine or "auto/pathography," as discussed by Pramod K. Nayar in "Communicable Diseases: Graphic Medicine and the Extreme."⁴⁹ Joyce Brabner and Harvey Pekar's *Our Cancer Year* (1994) takes a humorous yet poignant look at the challenges a married couple faces when one of them is diagnosed with lymphoma. Sarah Leavitt's *Tangles: A Story About Alzheimer's, My Mother, and Me* (2012) addresses the range of emotions the author and her family go through in dealing with her mother's Alzheimer's diagnosis. What Nayar points out is that these works "appropriate the endless potential in the medium of comics to 'communicate' disease," notably underscoring the discursive interplay between the idea of disease becoming more "communicable," as in "representable in the medium of the auto/pathography."⁵⁰ Trauma narratives, whether they address issues of physical or mental illness, recovered memories of incest, or the devastating effects of war crimes, fall along the continuum of graphic representations that promote deeper understandings of who we are in relation to our bodies (as well as the trauma that we hold inside our bodies) and the palimpsest of forgotten memories pushing insistently to the surface.

In what she refers to as "familial and historical entanglements," Maureen Burdock uses a "braided timeline that telegraphs the idea of radical interwovenness" to explain how memory that is received in new and ever-shifting contexts "creates a new texture and feeling around those memories."[51] Burdock offers an illustration of this braided timeline (see figure 14), and asks the question

> Does memory begin with threads of longing? Those threads of thinking-feeling—motion and emotion—pull us back, they compel the return trips, the back-and-forth of the shuttle, that eventually create the woven texture that is memory. The thin line of text, the Aboriginal song line, the braided chord, the neural pathway, the lifeline, the crimson capillary, the trace, the trail, the ghost path, the shadow site. Where such lines can be found, there is the possibility of movement through time-space in multiple directions.[52]

The braid is but a metaphor for birth, displacement, illness, death, and renewal. Its radical interwovenness with memory and history serve as a mapping of significant events in a life, as a conceptual timeline where, "like readers of comics, readers of maps must negotiate visual and written elements to produce meaning."[53] Jaime Cortez's rendering of

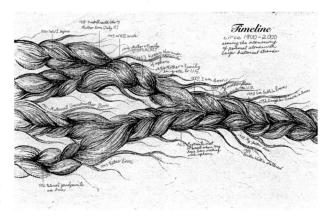

Figure 14. Image from draft in progress, *The Baroness of Have-Nothing and Other Haunting Tales,* by Maureen Burdock (copyright © 2017 by Maureen Burdock (See C•4 for larger image).

Adela Vázquez's life through sequential art also produces its own kind of mapping and meaning and is but one strand among many in the radical interwovenness leading up to the HIV/AIDS epidemic.

Sexile picks up on the themes of trauma that previous chapters in this book have explored. Whether trauma is "performed" through the semiotics of misdirection that come to life through the gaps and gutters of graphic narratives and literary fiction where multiple iterations of invisibility and erasure push up against the hegemonic center is not necessarily the focus in this chapter, although it certainly touches on these things. Rather, it is *how* trauma and identity are performed and what these performances come to mean in self-representational narratives of the transgender experience.

The Grand Entrance

Sexile is an epic story befitting the "bawdy humor and pathos" Jaime Cortez reports experiencing when he first interviewed Adela Vázquez for a piece he was doing for a website. His decision a year later to tell Adela's story turned on the "idea that [Adela's] life is extraordinarily rich in lessons on being resilient and negotiating risk."[54] The first chapter, *La Infanta Caliente*, opens with an image of Fidel Castro riding in an open-top vehicle, waving to admirers. The caption, which could apply either to Castro himself or to the infant boy on the following page, reads: "Not to brag, but my birth was revolutionary."[55] Vázquez was born on November 8, 1958, and his reference likely referred to Castro and his rebel fighters pushing their way across Cuba and eventually entering Havana on January 8, 1959, approximately nine days after Fulgencio Batista fled the country. Unlike Batista, Castro had no interest in being controlled by the United States, and with Batiste out of the way, Castro was able to form a government free from American influence.[56]

The splash page that signals the beginning of the narrative is mono-chromatic, as are all the pages except the cover, which is an arresting sky blue. Stylistically plain in contrast to the old stately buildings in the background where people gather on balconies to catch a glimpse of Castro and witness an important moment in Cuba's history, Vázquez was born on a night when Castro and "the rebels [...] were fighting their way across Cuba."[57] And in the manner of a drag performer looking out over an adoring audience, figure 15 shows Vázquez's "grand entrance" into the world.[58] The images foretell a life that would reach beyond the borders of nation and gender, eventually depositing Vázquez on American soil. But the journey across the ocean to her new home comes at a personal cost, just as it had for the thousands of others who left behind family, lovers, and friends. Seeding the imagination with the imagery and radicalizing insolence of queer(y)ing transnationalist tongues, *Sexile* takes the reader on a journey through a post-revolutionary Cuba that had little tolerance for anti–Cuban rhetoric and even less for its effeminate homosexual and transgendered compatriots.

As recounted to Jaime Cortez by Adela Vázquez, and echoed through the voices of other Marielitos, there was little tolerance in Cuba for men who dressed or acted like women.[59] Vázquez recalls meeting other gender non-conforming people whose aversion to heterosexual norms and expectations often saw them sentenced to labor camps in the mistaken belief that this would "fix" them.[60] Vázquez's wry observation that "fundamentalists do the same shit everywhere"[61] is echoed by Pat Califia in her equally wry description of transphobic feminists.[62] What Califia apparently finds most disturbing

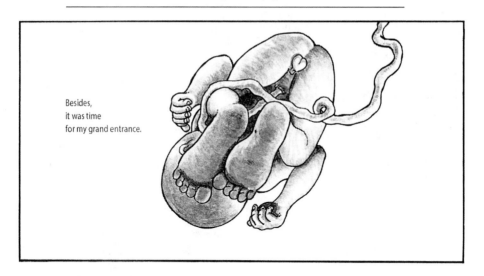

Besides,
it was time
for my grand entrance.

Figure 15. Illustration from p. 4, *Sexile/Sexilio* (copyright © 2004 by Jaime Cortez. Reprinted by permission of MPact Global Action for Gay Men's Health and Rights, Jaime Cortez, the Institute for Gay Men's Health, and APLA. All rights reserved).

about "feminist fundamentalism" is that, along with the Christian Right, it "share[s] an obsession with issues of sexual conduct and representation."[63] This obsession, Califia points out, is historically premised upon "deep-seated, sincere, but irrational moral beliefs"[64]—the same beliefs, I submit, that legitimize violence against anyone deemed to be non-conforming.

Being gay "'represented the worst things that can happen to anyone in Cuba.'"[65] The respondent—who is making this statement in Silvia Pedraza's essay "*Los Marielitos* of 1980: Race, Class, Gender, and Sexuality"—goes on to note that he was "not a communist, [he did not] like the government, [and he was] a homosexual."[66] The respondent's anti-revolutionary sentiments effectively mark him as a non-conformist whose implicit refusal to embrace the revolution's machismo ideology places him at odds with the cultural, political and sexual norms of his countrymen. He takes on all of the invectives—"Puto," "Pajaro," "Pervertido," "Pato," "Maricon"—illustrated so graphically in *Sexile*.[67]

Insomuch as these crude expressions are meant to signify fundamental differences in object choice, behavior, sexual identity, and even loyalty to the privileges that inhere in masculinity, for Vázquez they did not so much cause shame as they opened his eyes to an inner part of himself that he had yet to fully recognize and embrace. To the extent that he could name himself as "a baby queer [who] didn't even understand what I was yet," even though others apparently knew or suspected, simply meant that his identity and eventual self-acceptance would come to be defined in ways that held meaning for him.[68]

The Male (Latin) Gaze

In considering the cultural mores that govern sexual behavior and gender expression in Latin American countries and communities—be they located in Cuba, Brazil, Argentina, Costa Rica, Puerto Rico, Chile, Miami, Los Angeles or New York—one must resist equating gender presentation as a like-for-like correlation of sexual preference. I am careful to avoid this kind of essentialist approach, aiming instead for a broader examination of epistemologies that function interstitially in ways that disrupt the linking of sexual orientation, gender, and race to rigid binarisms that operationalize difference as the basis for exclusion rather than as a continuous shaping of sexual and human expression. Along this continuum there are heterosexual men who engage in penetrative sex with gay men, yet retain their status as "real" men because they resist taking on the feminine, historically sexually subservient role. Susana Peña, following Tomás Almaguer, underscores these boundary (and body) crossings when she discusses how object choice and sexual expression between men in the United States and Latin America differ.

> [...] whereas sexual object choice is the primary determinant of one's sexual identity in the United States (a man who chooses to have sex with another man is "gay" or homosexual while a man who desires to have sex with a woman is "straight"), in Latin America sexual aim (the desire to penetrate or be penetrated) forms the primary determinant of identity. According to this system, the penetrated partner—referred to by terms such as *pasivo, maricón, mariposa*, or *loca*—is much more stigmatized than the active/penetrating man.[69]

In his field study of sexual relations between Nicaraguan men and the almost inevitable comparisons of the construction and practice of homosexuality in the United States, Roger N. Lancaster warns that like-for-like correlations of gay sex are inaccurate. While he acknowledges that there "is clearly stigma in Nicaraguan homosexual practice," he is careful to point out that "it is not a stigma of the sort that clings equally to both partners."[70] Instead, "it is only the anal-passive cochón that is stigmatized. His partner, the active hombre-hombre, is not stigmatized at all and, moreover, no clear category exists in the popular language to classify him."[71] The essential point here is that as the hombre-hombre continues upholding popular notions of masculinity, his sexual relations with men are nothing more than an extension of his power over the feminine and the effeminate.

Lancaster goes to some lengths to explain that, essentially, the *active* partner who penetrates the *passive* partner is "just a normal Nicaraguan male."[72] Expressing it another way, he clarifies that "one is either a cochón [faggot/recipient of anal sex] or one is not."[73] This type of sexual posturing seems borne out early on in *Sexile* when Vázquez insists that he does not want to be called gay, proclaiming that even when he penetrates men in what he asserts is not "gay sex," the roles of who is the woman and who is the man are clear.[74] He (Vázquez) is always the woman. And therein lies the conundrum, the ideological tension, the misdirection underpinning the heteronormative and queerly performative divide. As R.W. Connell cogently argues in "A Very Straight Gay: Masculinity, Homosexual Experience, and the Dynamics of Gender," the "dynamics of hegemony in contemporary Western masculinity, the relation between heterosexual and homosexual men is central, carrying a heavy symbolic freight."[75] So, too, I hasten to add, is this "freight" at the crux of antipathies that exist between transgender people and their "authentically" queer kinfolk.

Transitions

When Jorge Antonio Vázquez voices a desire to have his penis fall off (*mi pinga se me caería*) when he turns ten and have it magically regrow into a vagina,[76] he is making a declaration it would seem that "expose[s] and contest[s] the normalizing process of identity's construction."[77] For Vázquez, becoming a "complete girl" can only happen in the most literal sense.[78] At the tender age of nine, Vázquez believes that he must be surgically altered in order to become fully congruent with his true self. He has no specific name for himself, but he alternates between the words he has internalized and the desire to re-appropriate those very same words for self-empowerment (see figure 16).

At such a young age, Vázquez does not yet have the language to fully express his feelings of being at odds with his assigned gender, but he intuits that if a psychic and physical congruence is to occur he must not only *act* the part of a girl, but *be* one as well. At fifteen he enters a drag pageant, intuitively understanding the blurring of lines between farce and his authentic self.[79] In figure 17 we see that Vázquez affirms his right to exist on his own terms when in the first frame he boasts: "When I stepped on stage, all of my classmates got real quiet. My shit was too real for them."[80] In the second frame he is seen mid-stride, walking in the exaggerated way that many women have been conditioned to move, crossing one foot in front of the other and turning

Figure 16. Illustration from p. 6, *Sexile/Sexilio* (copyright © 2004 by Jaime Cortez. Reprinted by permission of MPact Global Action for Gay Men's Health and Rights, Jaime Cortez, the Institute for Gay Men's Health, and APLA. All rights reserved).

his upper body to and fro to match the rhythm of his steps and the swaying of his hips. In that same frame, he boasts: "Hair. Body. Face. Mama let them HAVE IT."[81]

What the audience "had," it could be said, was permission to affirmatively collude/participate in what Bettcher describes as a "rhetoric of deception."[82] Bettcher's explanation of this type of rhetoric as underpinning the defense's case in the 2002 murder of Gwen Araujo for allegedly camouflaging her "true" gender during a sexual liaison with three heterosexual men sees its opposite in the full drag performance that Vázquez puts on for an audience who has full knowledge of what they are witnessing. Unlike the three non-trans men (two of whom had previously had sex with Araujo in full knowledge of her anatomy) who claimed to have been victims of rape through Araujo's deception, Vázquez uses the rhetoric of misdirection to enlighten and entertain.

Although Vázquez did not win the pageant, the experience left him feeling empowered.[83] Yet in order to make sense of what is seen and how the brain processes this information, audiences must achieve "closure," the process that helps us to use our experiences to stitch together fragments of information in order to make meaning or sense of things.[84] McCloud rightly notes that "in an incomplete world we must depend on closure for our very survival."[85] For some trans people, achieving congruency (or "closure") between gender identity and expression has historically hinged on how medical science and the legal system have interpreted these fundamental questions. In this regard, the Gender Recognition Act 2004, for example, could be seen as a bridge of sorts, linking one fragmented experience (or "self") to another. As Karen Kopelson has convincingly argued,

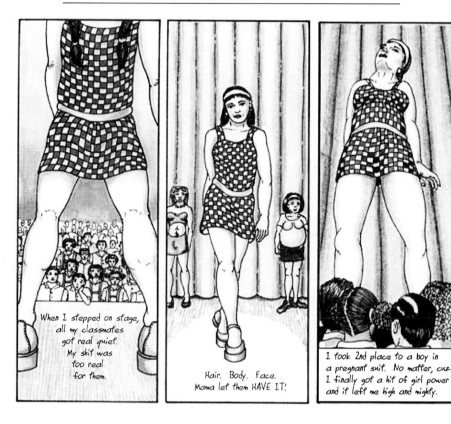

Figure 17. Illustration from p. 10, *Sexile/Sexilio* (copyright © 2004 by Jaime Cortez. Reprinted by permission of MPact Global Action for Gay Men's Health and Rights, Jaime Cortez, the Institute for Gay Men's Health, and APLA. All rights reserved).

when gender and sexuality are understood as expressions of repeated expressions, rather than as expressions of an authentic self, conveniently bounded identity categories tend to dissolve and a productive confusion takes their place.[86]

This "productive confusion," or the opportunity for "resignification,"[87] is where the queer graphic narrative and misdirection work so well together to disrupt our enduring notions of what constitutes gender. As cultural analysis, graphic narratives reflect not only the uncertainties of an ever-changing world, but also the possibilities that flow from ideas that diverse groups bring to the table. Moreover, the work of queer theory "challenges us to move beyond rather than into the governing structures of available, and oppositional, designations for sexuality."[88] But in the 1980s, at the time of the Mariel Boatlift, there was no consensus in theory or in activist movements regarding the rightful *place* of transgender people in society. Therefore it would have been difficult for gender non-conforming *(s)exiles* like Vázquez to negotiate a reality outside of the prevailing gender-binary system against which queer activists sought to define themselves. An example can be seen in figure 18, when Vázquez receives official notification from the *Ministerio de Fuerzas Armadas Revolucionarias* that he has been conscripted into the army.

Vázquez's reaction to the draft notice is one of disbelief, but also humor. He decides to parlay this distressing news into an opportunity to subvert one of hegemony's most recognizable and cherished symbols: military aggression. The irony of receiving a draft notice when he so firmly sees himself as a woman is not lost on him. Cortez draws our eye to an image of a pensive-

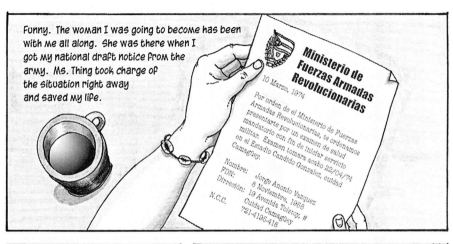

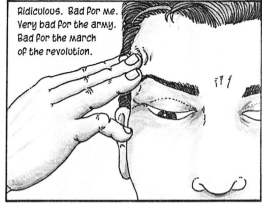

Figure 18. Panels from p. 11, *Sexile/Sexilio* **(copyright © 2004 by Jaime Cortez. Reprinted by permission of MPact Global Action for Gay Men's Health and Rights, Jaime Cortez, the Institute for Gay Men's Health, and APLA. All rights reserved).**

looking young man dressed in male clothing, with the remaining words in the caption reflecting his most private inner thoughts. He speaks of himself in the third person, the text reading: "Ms. Thing took charge of the situation right away and saved my life."[89] We can only infer that by "saving his life," he means he has figured out a way to avoid military service.

As Vázquez continues to express disbelief at receiving such depressing news, the last panel on the page is blacked out on either side, with the middle section framing an image in figure 19 of Vázquez sliding open the panel as one would a set of doors. The caption reads, "I'll have to go [...] deep into the closet,"[90] with text on the following page revealing the double meaning when he says, "and find the perfect military ensemble."[91]

Figure 19—Panel from p. 11, *Sexile/Sexilio* (copyright © 2004 by Jaime Cortez. Reprinted by permission of MPact Global Action for Gay Men's Health and Rights, Jaime Cortez, the Institute for Gay Men's Health, and APLA. All rights reserved).

The reader may well experience a bit of cognitive dissonance between the text and images on the preceding page, which show a glum-looking young man, followed by an image of Vázquez suddenly dressed in a woman's halter top, sunglasses perched on his head, wearing flip flops and striking a coquettish pose. On this same page, and in the remaining panels, our knowledge and experience of hyper-masculine institutions and their stance on homosexuality is confirmed when we see Vázquez using these homophobic attitudes to his advantage. As we move towards closure from one frame to the next, even without first seeing the next several images, our experience tells us that Vázquez's over-the-top mincing will likely be successful in helping him to avoid the draft.[92]

After being unceremoniously turned away from military duty, Vázquez applies himself to obtaining a teaching degree. He eventually takes up a teaching post, and in the same flippant manner he exhibited when receiving the draft notice, he recalls showing up for classes each day with "a little foundation and some tasteful rouge."[93] Yet in spite of glowing reviews, he was asked to resign, a request that came as no surprise to him. Unwilling to don the mask of heterosexuality as a way to fit in, he promises himself that no one is ever going to prevent him from expressing his true self. He draws on the strength of the women in his family, of which he counts himself as one, refusing to settle for being defined by other people.[94] From an early age Vázquez had begun thinking of himself as female. He includes himself in the collective "we are" when describing the tenacity of the women in his family. He believes his gender identity and expression to be congruent, at least insofar as he can reconcile this with laws and social customs that tell him he is different, that he is *out of place*. And it is this self-acceptance and resilience that would come to serve him well in his eventual transition to America.

Transformations

Vázquez's desire to live life on his own terms was clearly at odds with social expectations in 1980s Cuba. Yet in taking up new work in a factory where he supervised prisoners on a labor crew who, one might argue, excelled at misdirection and who were also marginalized by society, Vázquez eventually learns about Camagüey. It was through this network that he was able to more fully explore and express who he was, find kindred spirits to drink and socialize with, and to put on pretend fashion shows for one another.[95] What is notable about Camagüey, a popular cruising area for gay men, or more specifically its website that advertises to gay men, are certain Cuban words translated into English idioms. The website offers gay men a public space in which to "practice" cruising. The operative word, of course, is "practice."

In effect, by imitating the mannerisms and performances of drag queens, it could be argued that Vázquez was practicing misdirection, practicing to become a woman. Yet this begs the question "What is a woman?" If we briefly consider Toril Moi's detailed critique of *The Second Sex* (1949), the overriding message that emerges is that there is no definitive answer to what a woman is, except perhaps Moi's warning that "anyone who tries to read" de Beauvoir's work "through the lens of the sex/gender distinction is bound to misunderstand" her. Arguing that de Beauvoir's book "shows us that what it means to be called a woman, or to call oneself a woman, is a question that cannot be settled once and for all," Moi's position moves my own that much closer to self-representation as a valid approach to defining one's gender identity.[96]

Exile

The breach at the Peruvian embassy changed everything for those who would come to be known as Marielitos. Setting in motion a *trans*ition that Vázquez had been preparing for his entire life, the actions of Hector Sanyustiz and his comrades reverberated throughout Cuba and beyond. In recounting the events leading up to his departure from his homeland, Vázquez's wry critique of relations between Cuba and the United States reflected the deep mistrust each country harbored towards the other. This mistrust had been scripted upon the bodies of each Marielito making the crossing to Florida. In effect, it was Castro's masterpiece of misdirection. Having agreed to accept refugees who were unable to settle in other countries, then-president Jimmy Carter's decision to open U.S. borders was allegedly seen by Cuba as an opportunity to rid itself of its undesirables.

Leaving Cuba was Vázquez's chance to finally exercise freedoms that had been expressly forbidden in the country of his birth. Spurred on by his mother, who understood that Cuba was no place for gender variant people, Vázquez began the necessary arrangements for his new life.[97] Casually informing immigration officials that he was "a fag and wanted to emigrate," he was met with derision but ultimately issued a passport.[98] Arriving at the entrance to the military base where those who wanted to leave Cuba were required to go, supporters of Castro's regime were on hand to express their contempt of Vázquez and others whom they believed to be traitors to the revolution.

Figure 20 shows a mob of angry men surrounding Vázquez's taxi. They hurl invectives, make rude gestures, and do all they can to show their contempt.[99] It takes a hefty tip for Vázquez to convince the driver to deliver him inside the gates of the army base, although once there he waits all day for a bus that never arrives. Attentive readers will also notice in figure 20 the "Chevrolet" emblem on the car's dashboard, an iconic symbol of America's economic dominance over Cuba. The pre-embargo agreement between Cuba and the United States allowed for shipments of Buicks, Oldsmobiles, Studebakers, Plymouths and Fords to the island.[100] It seems the height of irony that an American car delivering Vázquez on the first leg of his trip to the land where he might live more openly as a woman would play such a central role in his exile from Cuba.

Vázquez, stranded and begging for help from a soldier who eventually agrees to sneak him out of the base in the back of an army truck, quickly realizes that he has been tricked. He has been delivered back into the midst of the angry pro–Castro mob, and his presence at the entrance to the military base is seen as disloyal to the Castro regime, yet because he is perceived to

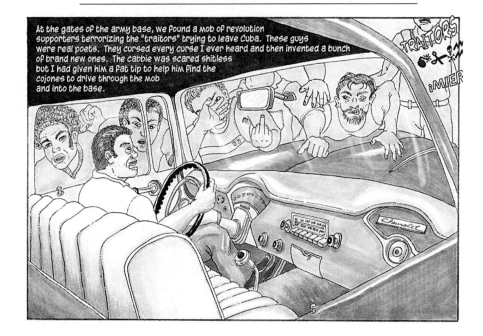

Figure 20. Illustration from p. 23, *Sexile/Sexilio* (copyright © 2004 by Jaime Cortez. Reprinted by permission of MPact Global Action for Gay Men's Health and Rights, Jaime Cortez, the Institute for Gay Men's Health, and APLA. All rights reserved).

be a man because he is dressed like one, it could be said that Vázquez's misdirecting performance saved his life. Insofar as Vázquez's attackers fail to recognize that heterosexuality is an illusion that reinforces rigidly held beliefs of what being a man means, he has manipulated their sensitivities by tapping into the only form of gender expression they understand. Arriving the next day back inside the gates of the military base, and once he is safely on the bus that finally arrives, Vázquez takes the pesos given to him by his mother and tosses them out the window. It is his final gesture of expatriation from a homeland that does not understand or recognize him. It would be another eight days of waiting out a tropical storm at Mariel Harbor before boarding the *Lynn Marie*.

In the series of frames/panels depicting the anxieties and fears of the Marielitos, Jaime Cortez uses five frames, four of which are similar in size, with the fifth drawn in a long rectangular shape, to suggest that the length of time in the scene is longer than the duration in the smaller frames. As one of the men speaking to Vázquez expresses fear that Castro allowed them to leave only to see them perish at sea, the image of a man falling into the water is dramatically rendered.[101] The speech balloons in the four smaller frames tell of the hopes and fears of the others, but in the first frame we see only Vázquez's face captured from his forehead to the area just above his nose. His swollen and heavily bruised left eye dominates the frame and he is telling the man who expressed fear of being thrown overboard that it no longer matters.

In the second frame Vázquez is asked if he has family in Florida. He responds in the negative, yet expounds on his answer with reassurances that he is going to meet an American woman who is anticipating his arrival.[102] From what we have learned thus far about Vázquez's life, we can infer from his statement that he is speaking of coming home to him/herself. The last frame shows the heavily bearded chin of a man with an appreciative grin, surmising that the woman waiting for Vázquez must be beautiful. Again, one hardly needs to turn the page to know Vázquez's private thoughts about the future, a future where he will have a new name and the chance to embark upon a new life. His bruised and unshaven face is at peace and he contemplates what beauty means, telling himself that he is "gonna be beautiful [...] like the revolution in the flesh. Like hope."[103] He has scarcely come out of his reverie when he hears someone shout, "It's America!"[104] It is here that the transformative power of queer performance operating alongside the trickery of misdirection finally align. It is also from this point forward where Vázquez starts to consistently refer to himself as a woman, or as a man becoming a woman, so to the greatest extent possible the remainder of this chapter will reflect this.

Signifying Practices and Misdirection

As I have discussed throughout this book, on a conceptual level misdirection works to divert, mislead, or draw attention away from one thing in order to appear as another—as in magical tricks, shell games, scavenger hunts, warfare, politics, detective novels, or drag performances. Queer, on the other hand, more broadly "unmasks the social practices that construct 'normality' and leads [...] to question[s] [regarding] the values embedded in such constructions."[105] But is the effect of the two words joined together, *queer misdirection*, deployed as a strategy for survival or is it, at its most fundamental level, a function of irreconcilable parts seeking a coherent whole? As performance, misdirection has a storied past. Queers excel at it, and the most captivating performances by heterosexuals on the stage and screen have drawn on queer culture's dramatic flourishes.

Upon reaching America, Vázquez embarks on a transformative journey of misdirection that takes him all the way from the military training camp at Fort Chaffee, Arkansas, to his eventual resettlement in California. The theme of America as the land of plenty for people who "aren't supposed to want special shit if it's only for themselves" continues in the next series of panels.[106] Welcomed to the shores of a new country by "tall [...] beefy" soldiers and what he called "fancy Cuban womens" handing out rosaries, American soda, flags, Bibles and Wrigley's chewing gum, Vázquez was both scared and excited.[107]

Vázquez experiences a range of emotions that bear little relation to the life of hardship he had left behind in Cuba. Believing he has arrived in a country where his sexual expression, race, and gender would not preclude him from enjoying what he imagined to be America's endless bounty, it would not take very long for the reality of a similar form of disenfranchisement to what he had left behind in Cuba to reveal itself.

Overwhelmed by his new life, but determined to carve out his own niche, Vázquez soon meets another queer exile from Havana who had been at Fort Chaffee for a month and had earned privileges because of his ability to speak some English. On American soil for less than two days, he is offered friendship and a place to stay, no matter that the offer is based on an understanding that sex is the expected payment.[108] Coming to understand that some things never change, no matter what country one is from or the language one speaks, Vázquez is comfortable with seduction and the benefits it brings. "It's beauty and sex and getting me what I need." It was, he thought, a "different country [but the] same exchange—pussy power, baby, pussy power."[109] The transformation from ugly (male) duckling into a female beauty is repeated several times in *Sexile*. As Vázquez negotiates the sexual transaction with his new friend, his external presentation merges into an internal sense of himself as a fully actualized woman. The task of the reader, then, is to make these performative and cognitive leaps along with Adela Vázquez.

In the events that follow, and if we have learned anything thus far about the complex lives of transgender people and how many are impacted by poverty and driven into the sex trade, the only practice Adela has had in becoming what she perceives a woman to be has been as someone whose value begins and ends in sexualized encounters. "All of the rules we lived with in Cuba were gone. Freedom was like a drug we didn't know how to take, and there was a lot of drama."[110] Adela recalls that families drifted apart, some women started businesses as prostitutes, and her own sex life "really blew up."[111] When she eventually leaves Fort Chaffee and is relocated to California, she takes up residence with Rolando Victoria, her sponsor.

The splash page at figure 21 depicting a larger-than-life, saintly-looking,

Figure 21. Panel from p. 45, *Sexile/Sexilio* (copyright © 2004 by Jaime Cortez. Reprinted by permission of MPact Global Action for Gay Men's Health and Rights, Jaime Cortez, the Institute for Gay Men's Health, and APLA. All rights reserved).

eyeglass-wearing Rolando Victoria holding a miniature Adela is instructive on many levels. It not only visually illustrates the "unfinished" gender non-conforming body, it also merges together the political, legal, and social lessons transgender women must learn in order to survive in unfamiliar and possibly hostile environments. And either through guile, subterfuge, distraction or misdirection, their survival is dependent upon learning these lessons well. For Adela, Rolando was not just her sponsor: "He was the most bitchy, hilarious, faggoty faggot ever. I adored her."[112] The mixing of masculine and feminine pronouns is no mistake here. Rolando is a gay man, but like Adela, he represents a complex subjectivity that resists narrow categorizations. In this regard, Hortense J. Spillers's contestation of racist and sexualized tropes that work to symbolically and legally erase the black patrilineal line, for example, is useful in understanding how the ambiguously gendered *of color* trans body is just as displaced and reviled.

> [...] the names by which I am called in the public place render an example of signifying property plus. In order for me to speak a truer word concerning myself, I must strip down through layers of attenuated meanings, made an excess in time, over time, assigned by a particular historical order, and there await whatever marvels of my own inventiveness. The personal pronouns are offered in the service of a collective function.[113]

What is intriguing about Spillers's comments is that they echo similar tensions taken up by *of color* gender and sexual studies scholars. Where her dispute with historical narratives focuses on the misnaming (or un-naming, as I have discussed elsewhere) of black women as not belonging to or associated with a father-figure who in white culture is integral to *naming* for the sake of legitimizing the patrilineal line, queer and trans people of color have also been denied a name that ties them to a "legitimate" identity. I argue that the graphic narrative allows the subjugated body to re-emerge in challenging, critically engaging, and meaningful ways.

Misdirection's Lessons

In the last two chapters of *Sexile*, Adela learns important lessons that help her to survive in America. Rolando Victoria defines them as the "six commandments of living in the U.S.A." He ticks them off for Adela's benefit, with perhaps the most salient one being "You are forever crowned by the pain of exile [so] get used to it, girl."[114] Rolando's pearls of wisdom would serve Adela in good stead as she attempts to make sense of who she is in relation to a new country where the guarantee of free expression is steeped in contradiction. Through the art of signifying and misdirection, *Sexile* reconstructs Adela's story as a form of visual excess that is at once disturbing yet also seductively radical in its refusal to disavow stereotypes that reinforce negative perceptions of the transgendered body.

As a mode of representation, it can be said that signifying is misdirection's semiotic kin. One (the signifier) often speaks or acts through the representational system familiar to the other (the signified) to communicate "levels of meaning and expression" that Henry Louis Gates, Jr., insists "might otherwise remain mediated or buried beneath the surface."[115] But because uncensored communication is not a freedom extended to everyone, signifying (or misdirection) becomes "an ideal way to confound a Eurocentric [or other nationalistic] bias."[116] It works, I argue, as a portal through which resistance and alternative realities are creatively expressed. Therefore, what becomes useful in the framing of *Sexile* as a tale of signifying misdirection is James V. Morrison's assertion that misdirection is "Homer's means of testing the limits of his tradition [as an oral poet] by exploring possibilities outside the standard myth,"[117] although he does go on to clarify that beyond the Homeric context, misdirection is a "tactic more closely attuned or aligned with performance itself."[118] This alignment, however, must be convincingly delivered if audiences are to open themselves up to the unfolding story.

If we pay close attention to the same series of panels that I made reference to earlier on, we will be better able to understand the idea of misdirection as a tactic that relies on a certain degree of audience collusion. In order for the performance (or the trick) to work, on some unconscious level we must want it to work. Performance, whether we engage with this through film or the stage, is an extension of the performances we all re-enact in our day-to-day lives. The relevance of the performance is contingent upon its context.

Returning momentarily to the scene where Vázquez's interlocutor asks about his ties in America, Vázquez had claimed that although he has no family in America, "there's a woman—an American woman. She's waiting for me," to which the man comments that she must be very beautiful and wonders if she has a sister.[119] Vázquez deflects this question by stating, "No, mi amigo. There is only one like her."[120] But we see in the last frame that Vázquez is thinking to himself the *truth* of what he chooses not to say out loud: *Mi negro, todavía no puedo decrite su nombre po'que ni yo lo sé* ("I can't tell you her name yet, mi negro, cuz I don't even know it myself").[121] We know from the images, but also from the process of stitching together random pieces of information based on our own experiences, that Vázquez is *trans*-ing his new life in Florida as an American woman. She, this new arrival to U.S. shores, is the one who is waiting for him to fully integrate his life into hers and emerge anew. Vázquez did what scores of others whose truth does not align with the "normative" center have done. In order to survive the trip on the boat, he allowed certain assumptions to go unchallenged, thereby using misdirection to do the work of outright denial.

As previously noted, it could be said that Vázquez's utterance of an untruth has prepared the interlocutor/audience for later events, because the "goal [of misdirection] [is to make] foreshadowing [...] consistent with the subsequent narrative."[122] Filtered through cultural, racial, sexual, political, religious, and gender paradigms, foreshadowing and its ultimate resolution follows in a long tradition of counter-response that deploys visual and verbal sleight of hand to reveal history's ambivalent relationship with its flamboyantly performative self. In this regard *Sexile* astutely problematizes "the contradictory space between the narratives that pop culture and institutions construct, and the unseemly reality these narratives obscure."[123]

Like Vázquez, the people on the *Lynn Marie* possess only limited knowledge of America. Some may have known people who had left Cuba long before, settling in Florida and other American cities, and bringing back with them during brief visits stories of opportunity and freedom. Others, motivated to leave their homeland for political or even artistic reasons, found the actual reality of their new lives to be somewhere in between truth and fiction. However, for people like Vázquez, fiction is often a necessary tool for surviving reality. In a sense, America represented a massive stage upon which "ambivalent transaction[s] of fatal contradictions" could be performed.[124] My contention here is that these *trans*actions eventually lead Vázquez to take up sex work as a strategy of survival in the land of equal opportunity. The issue of gender ambiguity (and the freedom and risks associated with it) relies in large part on fantasies that heterosexuals expect to have fulfilled in sexually titillating, yet psychologically congruent ways.

Underlying the "anxious labor" that Eithne Luibhéid insists is required to sustain the "unstable" heterosexual norm, misdirection's unintended effect problematizes both hetero and homo-nationalist and normative scripts.[125] In this vein, Sandy Stone advocates for a decisive move away from subjectivities that operate within "the traditional gender frame," cautioning that those who occupy these spaces "become complicit in the discourse which one wishes to deconstruct."[126] Tracing and illuminating the seemingly irresolvable conundrums of sexual orientation across contexts, Heike Bauer makes explicit in her argument regarding language and the etymology of sexual vocabularies that "literary and philosophical works can lay claim to having inspired the terms and concepts in which we think about modern sexuality" and that sexuality itself "is a contingent concept, dependent in its meanings on context and interpretation."[127] Bauer's analysis also underscores the importance of the *visual* literariness of sexuality—the shifting paradigms and evolving interpretations/performances of what we see and how we make sense of it, not solely in Western terms, but also transnationally.

In figure 22 we are made to understand in the most fundamental of ways the indeterminacy of sex and gender when the image and text on the splash page sets up a cognitive dissonance between what we see and what we have been conditioned to accept as "normal" representations of gender. Under the heading "Womanizing," which is clearly a play on *becoming* a woman as well as being objectified by sexist rhetoric as one, Cortez has drawn an image of a naked person with breasts, a penis, and long, femininely styled hair. This "intermediate" body, as Gayle Rubin puts it in "Of Catamites and Kings: Reflections on Butch, Gender, and Boundaries," is posed square to the frame and facing forward.[128] The body itself is surrounded by words that bring it *into* and *out of place*. The effect of the image, its indeterminacy, illustrates how misdirection might function to help readers/audiences make sense of (or link together) the snippets of seemingly unconnected or incongruent realities. I discuss some of the text in relation to the body around which it is inscribed.

> My feet began insisting on more and more cute strappy shoes. This is one of the most major mysteries of gender.
> At first, the cock pain was horrible. I felt like my cock, the root of manhood, was resisting the hormones. Now my cock has become one emotional bitch. It only gets hard for guys I really like.[129]

Notwithstanding the unfortunate sexist overtones of the above statements, what appears to be at stake is Adela's desire for a successful metamorphosis into everything female. When she comments upon the mysteries of gender, she taps into the essence of theoretical arguments that become increasingly complex with each discursive foray into the irresolvable conundrum of human existence itself. And when she proclaims at one point that "'cock' is the only word as beautiful as 'sista,'" yet goes on to describe the penis as "one emotional bitch,"[130] she further complicates an ambivalence that alternately seeks its resolution in self-acceptance, or worse still, a descent into self-debasement.

If Adela is unable to convince herself that she is female because the term itself is imprecise, her success thus depends upon distraction/misdirection to convince those who come into the sphere of her physical and emotional space that she is, for all intents and purposes, not just *a* woman, but instead the ultimate woman. In convincing others, she reinforces this fact (or fiction) for herself. Thus when we are misdirected from that which we have been socialized into believing is "real" (penises, vaginas, biology), to a convincing

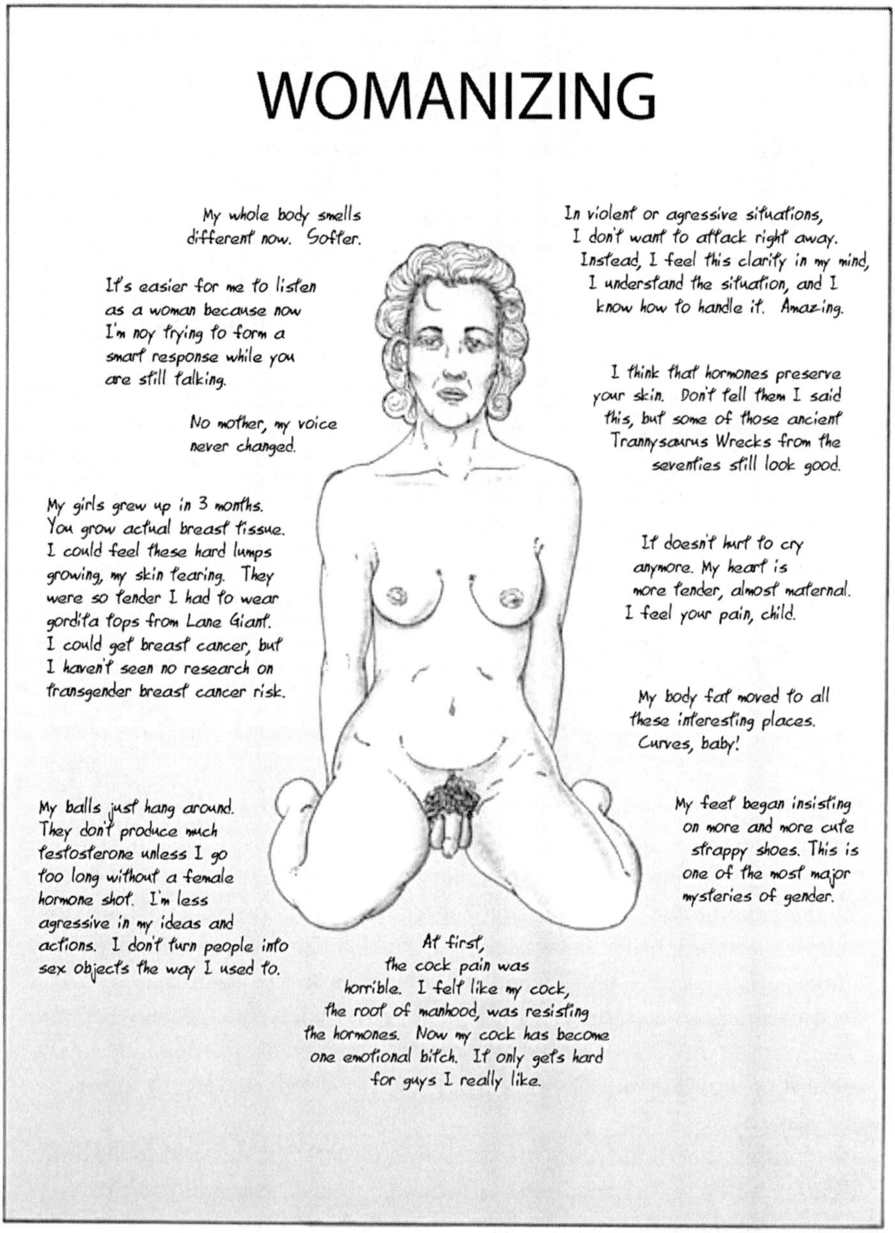

WOMANIZING

My whole body smells different now. Softer.

It's easier for me to listen as a woman because now I'm noy trying to form a smart response while you are still talking.

No mother, my voice never changed.

My girls grew up in 3 months. You grow actual breast tissue. I could feel these hard lumps growing, my skin tearing. They were so tender I had to wear gordita tops from Lane Giant. I could get breast cancer, but I haven't seen no research on transgender breast cancer risk.

My balls just hang around. They don't produce much testosterone unless I go too long without a female hormone shot. I'm less agressive in my ideas and actions. I don't turn people into sex objects the way I used to.

At first, the cock pain was horrible. I felt like my cock, the root of manhood, was resisting the hormones. Now my cock has become one emotional bitch. It only gets hard for guys I really like.

In violent or agressive situations, I don't want to attack right away. Instead, I feel this clarity in my mind, I understand the situation, and I know how to handle it. Amazing.

I think that hormones preserve your skin. Don't tell them I said this, but some of those ancient Trannysaurus Wrecks from the seventies still look good.

It doesn't hurt to cry anymore. My heart is more tender, almost maternal. I feel your pain, child.

My body fat moved to all these interesting places. Curves, baby!

My feet began insisting on more and more cute strappy shoes. This is one of the most major mysteries of gender.

Figure 22. Panel from p. 60, *Sexile/Sexilio* (copyright © 2004 by Jaime Cortez. Reprinted by permission of MPact Global Action for Gay Men's Health and Rights, Jaime Cortez, the Institute for Gay Men's Health, and APLA. All rights reserved).

approximation of the real (signifying performances of femininity and masculinity), it is the work of graphic narratives to offer up alternative ways of seeing, and engaging with, these shifts. Learning how to become a woman, negotiating body-crossings that run counter to "normative" ideals of gender identity and expression, and balancing the reality of having both a penis and breasts is the daily reality for untold numbers of transgender people who elect not to have gender reassignment surgery and who cannot easily "pass."

"Passing" Performances

When Adela begins to seriously explore what it means to be a woman, she goes at it with a single-minded (and, I daresay, unfortunately narrow) focus. Having convinced herself that the woman she strives to be is all about fashion and sexual attractiveness, Adela must also acknowledge that she has no idea about the other side of women's reality.[131] She knows little about the public harassment of women by men who grab their crotches or make sexist comments when women walk by, signaling to them what their intentions are if only they (women) would recognize their special status of being singled out for male attention, no matter how crude or hostile.[132] It finally occurs to Adela that living as a woman means leaving behind male privilege and the attendant feelings of relative safety.[133] More than any other, the visual and textual combination in these panels lend added layers of meaning to this statement, precisely because it inverts the hyper-sexualized narratives that permeate nearly every aspect of women's lives.

There is a more explicit connection between the aggressive male posturing women are often subject to and its grounding in historically sexist and racist narratives. In "Passing for White, Passing for Man: Johnson's *The Autobiography of an Ex-Colored Man*," for example, C. Riley Snorton sets out the terms that underpin a troubled narrative of alterity for the protagonist in James Weldon Johnson's book. Citing Kimberly Benston, who writes of a simultaneous self-affirming and self-negating black gaze, C. Riley Snorton suggests that "such scenes [the protagonist's prolonged self-appraisal in the mirror] present a simultaneous enactment and theorization of consciousness taking place at key textual moments." In this regard, "African American identity looks on an image of being at once external and internal to itself, an echo or reflection that must revise in order to better to see itself."[134] Similar ambiguities are evident throughout *Sexile*, particularly towards the end of the book when Adela takes her first illegal dose of hormones.[135] The reaction of her friends is telling.

In the first panel (not shown here), one man says: "Girl. As your friend,
I gotta tell you, you don't look pretty, you don't look real and you'll never
pass."[136] The second panel sees another friend exclaiming that one cannot
simply stop being a man, explaining to Adela that being a man was how God
had made her.[137] Even Adela's mother, who championed her departure from
Cuba because she knew of the particular hardships she faced, questioned
how she would ever "become a woman with that deep voice of yours."[138] In
the final frame, we are made to understand that for Adela, the long and treacherous journey to womanhood was not simply a passing notion, but instead
a deeply felt desire to align her gender identity with her outward forms of
expression.

> I'm not going to lie. It hurt. Maybe it was karma, because even though I had always
> been attracted to being like a woman, I had deep fears about changing my gender, so
> instead I would join in when my gay friends were talking shit about trannies.[139]

Falling short, some might suggest, in successfully misdirecting the
"authentic" queer gaze of her friends, Adela was undeterred. Taking on extra
work as "Adela [the] She-Male"[140] exotic Cuban dancer as a means of support,
Adela understood better than her gay male friends that gender was, as C.
Riley Snorton put it in regards to race and identity, something of a "sliding
signifier."[141] Using this concept as my referent to progressing final arguments
regarding the transphobic hetero and homonormative gaze, and the impact
this has on the gender non-conforming body, I turn to a brief discussion of
one of the most iconic sliding signifiers of all, and that is blackface. While
this may seem as *out of place* as the inclusion of transgender women in my
overall arguments regarding queer women of color representation, what it
speaks to are the extremes the subjugated body will sometimes go to in order
to be seen not only in a more realistic light, but to be seen at all. That the
blackface, *trans*-ing, gender-bending performances of misdirection have the
ability to subvert (and sometimes forcefully refocus) the normative gaze is
evidenced through the spatiotemporal shifts in graphic narratives.

Karen Cronacher reads this notion of subverting the normative gaze
through the performance of blackface, as productive in its ability to not especially reveal anything about African Americans, for example, but rather to
"reveal something about that dark continent of the white male phobias and
desires, and 'the horror, the horror' of the white male's experience of gender
and racial difference."[142] In the old minstrel shows (which have been re-
appropriated as a form of drag, but also by black artists disrupting and ultimately dismantling what Cronacher calls "the colonial frame of representation"), audiences often missed the underlying "social critique."[143] Similarly,

Jaime Cortez's rendering of Adela's life could be interpreted as an intentional parody that relies on outrageous mockery of rigid binarisms as a way to compel audiences to "*face* the mask and unmask the *face* [italics belong to Cronacher] underneath" it.[144]

The social critique throughout *Sexile* intersects at sites that trouble conventional notions of gender identity, particularly the very specific issues that transgender women face in striving for economic independence, healthy lifestyles, and acceptance from within and outside of their communities. But all too often transgender women are forced into the sex trade, as was ultimately the case with Adela. "I was a good fuck but a lousy ho. I hated it when they wanted to have dinner first [...] so awkward. As a prostitute, I had no sexual freedom. I was a product, a service, an idea, but never a real human being."[145] Adela's distress turns on her status as an exile, the transience of community, and the uncertainty of her future.

"Some days I felt like the pain was going to swallow me up. I had this pain," she says, "of being an exile, a transgender and a sex worker."[146] She believes that had she not taken drugs to relieve the pain, she "would have been lost or maybe dead," acknowledging that the reality of her life was "not pretty, but [was] the real deal."[147] In the last few pages of *Sexile*, there is a bookend image to the cover page, this one slightly altered and showing Vázquez once again swimming towards and also away from something. It is a fuller drawing than the cover page of her naked body, this one showing her physical transformation to womanhood. In what Will Eisner has described as the "flat, eye-level view," we see that the nails on Adela's left hand are long and painted with nail polish. This visual perspective "informs the reader of details," in this case, Adela's hand pushing towards the front of the frame, reaching perhaps for a new life.[148] Her breasts are full and firm, the result of the hormones she injected to achieve "closure" or gender coherence. The penis remains; it is a part of her that reminds the audience/reader that misdirection takes Adela (and us) to "all the in-between places [that Adela calls] home."[149] She lifts the mask, telling us that "this beautiful freak body is home" and telling us "every day I love it."[150]

This chapter developed arguments based in large part on the irresolvable question of gender identity and the right to self-determination in how gender is individually expressed. Drawing upon misdirection to unpack these difficult questions and (re)imagining alternative ways of negotiating the often hostile terrain that gender-variant people experience in still largely heterocentric spaces, this chapter served as the "creative catalyst" that Theresa M. Tensuan has described as a way to dislodge the cultural hegemony that sustains multiple and intersecting oppressions. Moreover, this chapter framed

Adela's story from a perspective that reworks, *misdirects*, redefines, and *transgresses* "normative" realities that typically exclude transgender lives. By including people who are deemed to be *out of place* because of their race, sex, gender identity and expression, religion, or culture, this chapter has attempted to broaden the stage upon which *performance* (in virtually every aspect of life) signifies a deeper and more complex level of gender expression. In the book's introduction, Adela Vázquez implores us to wait for the woman she is going to be, the one that "waits for me across the sea … if you see her, tell her please … wait my lady, wait for me."[151] This chapter has shown that Adela's wait to become the woman she longs to be is limited only by our unwillingness to shift the terms of the debate and engage in an honest accounting of how, when all is said and done, we are all to varying degrees *out of place*.

Chapter 7

A Long Journey
to Her Own Queer Self

Beldan Sezen's Snapshots
of a Girl *(2015)*[1]

When your mother denied you, I took and wove you to my
skin [Birhan Keskin].

Beldan Sezen was born in Germany to Turkish immigrant parents. Although the belief systems that shaped the experiences of her parents go largely unremarked in her book, the conversations she attempts to have with her mother in a three-part coming out story opens the way for a broader exploration of the subtexts through which Turkish identity engenders a more nuanced articulation of what it means to be a queer daughter from a traditional Turkish culture.

Sezen's graphic narrative offers a largely non-linear, though engaging, visual and textual exegis on her coming out process. Graduating in 2002 from the Amsterdam Cartoon School, she quotes Scott McCloud to explain her interest in comics: "'Comics are sequential art that offer range and versatility with all the potential imagery of film and painting plus the intimacy of the written word.'"[2] Throughout *Snapshots of a Girl*, these creative mediums are expertly woven together into a mesmerizing semiotic fugue. In this chapter I consider how expressions of queer identity formed through culture-bound contexts complicate and very often derail the coming out process. I focus my analysis primarily on the three parts of the author's coming out, as each attempt at being heard (and accepted) by her mother plays a central role in how the author ultimately writes and illustrates her own truth. I also show that the ongoing process of coming out is a type of misdirection that is determined (as I explained elsewhere) by the contexts through which it seeks to effect perceptual shifts. Put another way, misdirection takes on many guises that in turn take their cues from whatever setting or situation necessitates a move toward reorientation, deflection, or contestation.

Identities and Labels

For those who spend their lives navigating systems where individual and collective identity has been predetermined by laws and social customs that make the centrality of race, gender, class and religion the primary determinants of one's worth, coming out adds an additional layer of complexity to a deck that is already stacked. In *Snapshots of a Girl*, misdirection positions the author's story in a more synergistic alignment with her lesbian identification, thereby making it less deterministically inscribed by traditional social customs. The perceptual shifts that the author draws on to "name" herself in more affirmative language is enhanced by her drawings and the changing contexts through which misdirection helps to move the story forward.

Turkish tradition and culture limits how much women are able to express their needs and desires. Had the author come of age when the 1926 Penal Code and "numerous Constitutional articles constructed women's sexuality as a potential threat to public order and morality and therefore in need of regulation," she would have had no voice at all.[3] Although she was born in a more contemporary time when feminists had successfully advocated for legislation that secured important rights for Turkish women, there were nevertheless contexts through which perceptions of women's roles had not shifted very much at all. In fact, while the Penal Code had seen several sweeping amendments through the years, culminating in its full reform in 2004, "with the exception of two revisions, none of the amendments concerned women's rights or women's right to bodily autonomy."[4] Rights to a safe and secure existence extended to the family, not the individual.[5] And since women were not seen as individuals outside of or within the family, the rights of the family were by default the rights of men.

Reading Pictures in Hyper-Mediated Spaces

Beldan Sezen uses the semiotics of the graphic narrative form to offer up a visual and textual collage of events and experiences that shaped her queer life. Laying down thick black lines that she liberally uses as borders, she offers a visual rendering of how diversionary reframing (explained earlier in this book) accrues to encode her body and her mind as unequivocally oriented toward a heterosexual norm. Unable to see beyond the traditions that influence her romantic choices, she enters into unsatisfying sexual relationships with men, at least one of whom seems to intuit that she is queer long before her own consciousness opens her up to this truth. Ironically, her gradual awakening to the possibility of being with a woman happens after she goes for a walk and comes across a cinema showing of *Desert Hearts*, a film described by Jackie Stacey as one that allowed lesbians to feel "uplifted by the romance between two women that does not end in disaster or punishment."[6] What *Desert Hearts* managed to do was to challenge tropes that routinely portrayed lesbian desire as sexually immature imitations of "real" sex with men. Reviews of the film written at the time of its release almost universally praised the sex scene between Cay Rivvers and Vivian Bell as the most convincing and imaginative part of the film.

Subsequent to the narrator's viewing of *Desert Hearts*, there is an unmistakable internal shift that occurs. She is markedly happier, a fact noticed and commented on later by her boyfriend. In a pivotal scene when she and her boyfriend are in bed, she attempts to arouse him in the way that she likely saw in the film. "Baby," he says, as she presses her lips against his nipples, "you know no matter how hard you try I just don't have any breasts."[7] Failing to make the connection between the lesbian desire triggered within her by the film, and her continued involvement in unsatisfactory heterosexual relationships, she becomes involved with two more men before finally understanding (and embracing) the truth of her feelings for women.

Lesbian films have often served as critical turning points in the lives of women whose sexual orientation has been heavily regulated through hegemonic formations of normativity. As cultural critique, films have historically presented subject matter that is reflective of the times in which we live, although this often meant that queer women of color were completely excised from the arc of the story or portrayed as hyper-masculine sexual aggressors.

When *The Birth of a Nation* opened in cinemas in 1915 it accomplished two important things: it established film as a medium through which a particular and exceedingly xenophobic view of the world could be delivered uncensored to mainstream audiences and it exposed America's disturbing propensity for racially motivated violence against people of color. I am not suggesting that *Desert Hearts* and *The Birth of a Nation* derive from similar creative or ideological impulses, but rather that both films were ahead of their time in how highly controversial topics were visually consumed by audiences and the impact this had on shaping perceptions about the sexual and racialized "Other." And while *Desert Hearts* was panned by a number of film critics for its stilted dialogue and lackluster acting, it was nonetheless recognized by feminists as an important moment in the positive portrayal of sexual intimacy between women. To this end, Jackie Stacey describes the vastness and magical space of the desert in Deitche's film, particularly in how representationally this particular metaphor works to capture the confusion of coming out, but also how it opens up the potential for emotional libera-tion.

> The desert functions as a transformative space, a place where the miles and miles of wide-open landscape can absorb the past and new possibilities can be found. Mythi-cally, it is the place of adventure and self-determination. This is Cay's territory.[8]

The author's depiction of scenes from *Desert Hearts* turns a two-dimensional representation of her sexual awakening as a lesbian into the sug-gestion of a three-dimensional space where readers can be engaged on a more visceral level. And while comics use speed lines and zip ribbons to give the appearance of motion, as well as sequential layouts of frames and panels to indicate the passing of narrative time, they are still just a static representation of the world around us. Films, on the other hand, provide the opportunity for a more dynamic visual and emotional engagement by virtue of their mov-ing images and frame-to-frame action. Nevertheless, one could argue that similar cognitive processes are engaged in making sense of what we compre-hend on a visual level via sequential art, where we piece together meaning through sound effects (WHAAM, PING, BOOM, BIFF! BAM! POW!). Sezen demonstrates this in the panel where she offers readers a glimpse into her internal thoughts on *Desert Hearts*.

In the first frame we see free-spirited Cay Rivvers leaning through a car window to kiss the emotionally reserved Vivian Bell. The second frame shows an image of a perplexed young woman (the narrator) looking out at herself from the viewpoint of a character in the film and also as an audience member shrouded in shadow with just the back of her head visible, taking in the action on the screen. She is effectively a part of the film while also being an observer of the dueling emotions within her psyche. In the third frame the author uti-lizes the technique of the "fourth wall" to show Vivian reaching out to the narrator, effectively breaching the imaginary border between the audience and the character she plays in the film.[9] When she extends her hand outside of the celluloid frame and toward the young woman who is watching the action unfold, the subliminal message in this gesture ties in with Vivian's own sex-ual awakening with the narrator's growing awareness of her feelings for women. This particular reading is supported to some degree by film theory or, rather, by feminist critiques of film theory that work to deconstruct the binarisms of heteronormative visual regimes. Tamsin Wilton opines that to sit in the dark with a number of strangers releases one for a while from the unremitting pressure of presenting the self—and retaining control of that presentation as "correctly" gendered, sexed and desiring—under the surveillance of the public arena. This unique social experience, unexplored by theorists of the cinema, certainly shapes the different pleasures which women, men, queers and non-queers extract from film spectatorship, variously oppressed/privileged as they may be by the relentless policing of dress, gesture and behaviour.[10]

Because she frames her own spectatorship by replicating the inside of a movie theater with a heavily blacked-out panel, images of the characters on the movie screen provide the only source of light in the author's drawing. The intimacy of darkness allows the narrator to explore feelings long suppressed by cultural expectations and emotional uncertainty, a technique that is used again in parts 1 and 2 of the narrator's coming out to her mother. Here Sezen depicts Vivian Bell and Cay Rivvers emerging from the hypermediated spaces of their celluloid enclosure to connect with the narrator as spectator, and perhaps others like her who might also be in the audience. Anne Friedberg asserts: "for the film spectator, the darkness that surrounds the frame both minimizes its borders and calls us to play upon its boundaries."[11] In this way the author pushes the limits of time and reality by showing the movie character stepping outside the boundaries of her celluloid life to reach out and connect with the one person in the audience whose imagination is ripe for a different kind of truth.

Revealing more than we are able to take in at once, film has the ability to create "a historically specific shared temporality, setting limits on how long the spectator can dwell on any one object or experience any one story, and thus socializing (or we might say, binding) the gaze."[12] To unpack the notion of spectatorship further, Freeman offers a useful interpretation of a type of de-heterosexualization of the filmic gaze, which from a methodological standpoint could be argued as being analogous to how queer graphic narratives and comics subvert and decenter heterobinarisms. Sabine Hake's review of Francesco Casetti's book *Eye of the Century: Film, Experience, Modernity* offers an alternative critical perspective on the relationship between film theory and spectatorship. A particularly salient point made by Hake, which on its face seems to both contradict and also uphold arguments regarding the importance of film in facilitating individual spectatorship as activism, follows:

In the same way that [Casetti's] reconstruction of the cinema as the eye of the century leaves out the power of cinema as a public sphere, it also brackets entire aspects of visuality, most problematically its relation to gender and sexuality, in favor of a phenomenological model that reinstates the human being at the center of the apparatus. Consequently, even the technology (in the narrow sense of cameras and projectors) and the apparatus (in the broader sense of institutions and discourses) take a back seat to the intricacies of individual spectatorship.[13]

In *Snapshots*, as is the case in sequential art generally, readers play the role of spectators and cultural critics. Sezen uses the apparatus of drawing (pens, pencils, ink, paper, kneaded erasers, fixative) to help readers visualize the "sounds" of silence. She also uses these tools to literally draw the confusion and anxiety of coming out and the process her character goes through in trying to get her mother to "hear" her truth. By pulling the reader into the "polite agreement of a shared silence,"[14] Sezen expertly conveys the reticence of a good Turkish daughter going out of her way to acquiesce to a sacrosanct cultural imperative. Having been brought up in a culture of "invisibility, guilt, and shame,"[15] the concept of *ayip*, the Turkish word for "shame," places Sezen's comments and imagery in a particular cultural, and often specifically gendered, context. Indeed, the intransigent grip of patriarchy dictates the degree to which queers in many countries around the world push back against the debilitating effects of hiding their sexual orientation. In citing an unattributed Arabic saying that "'a man's honor lies between a woman's legs,'" Jewel Daney identifies a chilling corollary between the policing of women's bodies and the fragile egos of men who would rather murder those who bring shame on the family than accept the rights of every human being to choose their own path in life.[16]

Visualizing the Sound of Silence

Helping readers to visualize sound in graphic narratives and comics, and therefore to *hear* sound, is in many ways dependent upon the skill of the illustrator in how they draw readers into the narrative arc of a story. An excellent example of this can be seen at figure 23 where, rather than using words to represent death, the illustrator draws a skull to suggest sound, to convey that the figure lying prone on the ground is expelling a death groan.[17] Because comics are a "'mute' medium in which a series of symbolic signs have been developed to depict sound,"[18] our imagination fills in to help us "hear" the character's death rattle.

Moreover, that which is missing from figure 24 finds its corollary in Feyza Burak Adli's use of the term "veiled periphery," which is particularly apt when considering the almost endless historical examples of multiple erasures and silences experienced by women.[19] Where the veil symbolizes modesty and what Eve Kosofsky Sedgwick described as a symbol "suffused with sexuality," there is another, "apparently opposite set of meanings it hides."[20]

Figure 23. Illustration by Stan Sakai, from *The Shrouded Moon Part 2*. First published August 1, 2001, by Dark Horse Comics (reprinted by permission of the artist. All rights reserved).

In other words, the veil (and the periphery where modesty, heterosexuality, and religious edicts are observed and enforced) that "conceals and inhibits sexuality comes by the same gesture to represent it" as a "metonym of the thing covered and as a meta-phor for the system of prohibi-tion[...] by which sexual desire is enhanced and specified."[21] Thus the act of coming out from behind the veil of secrecy and shame forces a re-examination of the very thing that is being withheld from view or left unsaid. I examine this vexing problem more closely when I discuss Sezen's use of darkness as metaphor for both the veiling and unveiling of queerness.

Figure 24. Photograph by Fred Dufour of woman in niqab, from the website *Chatelaine* (reprinted by permission of Fred Dufour. All rights reserved) (see C•5 for larger image).

Acculturation and Its Queer Limits

Snapshots of a Girl exposes the difficult truths that are oftentimes awk-wardly expressed through familial love. In ways similar to Cristy C. Road's radical punk stylization of a beating heart drawn on the front cover of *Bad Habits*, the very first page Sezen offers up in her book is a rough approxima-tion of a human heart. The ascending aorta is there, as well as the right and left ventricular arteries drawn with thick stems tapering off into smaller, branch-like tributaries. Sezen cleverly uses this tributary of words to form the outline of the heart itself, and the words that she chooses serve as a refu-tation of the polite silence that she, and others like her, are expected to honor.[22]

Using Alice Walker's words (and thus setting out a black feminist/wom-anist/radical queer framework), the swirling text in *Snapshots* reads: "No per-son is your friend (or kin) who demands your silence, or denies your right to grow and be perceived as fully blossomed as you were intended."[23] The power of Walker's statement stands in stark contrast to an image soon after in *Snapshots* where the confused and stunned-looking narrator in figure 25 is surrounded by repeating loops of the word "What."[24] My reading of these two very different images—the heart shown in the prologue to the book and

Figure 25. Illustration from p. 27, *Snapshots of a Girl* (copyright © 2013 by Beldan Sezen. Reprinted by permission of Arsenal Pulp Press. All rights reserved).

setting out a black womanist statement one might expect to see as resolution to a confused life, and the image of the narrator surrounded by swirls of doubt—turns on competing ideological positions the author sets out to reconcile. But we would do well to bear in mind Sara Ahmed's trenchant observation that it is ultimately the "'straight line' [that] *shapes the very tendency to go astray*" (italics belongs to Ahmed) and that "what is astray does not lead us back to the straight line, but [rather] shows us what is lost by following that line."[25] For my purposes in this chapter, it is the story in between these two images (or lines) that must be repeatedly told in order to contest the "diversionary reframing"[26] of heteropatriarchy. Stories that are fractured, mislaid,

confused, and sometimes irresolvable must ultimately be given over to a signifying misdirection that reaches between the spaces of our erasure to disrupt
the hostile heteronormative gaze.[27]

From Whence Came the "I"

If it is the case that Turkish migrants to Germany have been interpolated
into race-inflected, xenophobic narratives of the "Other," a narrative that is
itself intrinsically tied to the limits of the hegemonic imagination, where then
does this position the Turkish lesbian whose sexual orientation already places
her outside the boundaries of culturally acceptable behavior? The wider significance of this question is entangled in the politics of a secularism that sits
too comfortably alongside religious conservatism. Although Turkey had
existed "for nearly a century [as] a model of a modern secular Islamic
nation,"[28] when the Justice and Development Party (AKP) rose to power in
2002, the desire for membership in the G-20 eventually overshadowed (and
eroded) political and social gains for women. Although Turkey's candidacy
to the EU in 1999 saw efforts to address women's status and speed up changes
"with a view to eliminating discrimination against women,"[29] the backdrop
to this feel-good story was the increasing precarity of women's rights in Turkish society.

It is important in understanding the wider context in which conservative
agendas under the AKP fundamentally changed the national narrative from
one of the advancement of rights for women to one that under the leadership
of Recep Tayyip Erdoğan largely assigned responsibility for upholding morality and family values to women. While pursuing a conservative-liberal syn-
thesis that would bring Turkey into closer alignment with Western democratic
policies, the AKP nevertheless held fast to the "centrality of the family institution" that essentially glorified "traditional gender roles."[30] Therefore, when
we interrogate the intersections in Turkish politics, religion, and culture,
where power coheres to establish de facto male entitlement over women's
basic rights, we can better understand the importance of hybrid works like
Snapshots that push back against the rising tide of cultural essentialism.

I want to very briefly revisit here Freudenburg and Alario's discussion
of "diversionary reframing," which they identify as the hallmark of political
tricksters.[31] I do so to illustrate the oppositional position taken up by Sezen,
whereby she uses well-placed symbolia to articulate the tension between feminism and the cultural messages of obedience and allegiance that she absorbed
as a child. Writing the names of feminist authors, critics, lesbian and gay

activists on the spines of books; spelling out ideological positions on the sides of buildings; and using t-shirts to announce activist beliefs introduces a countervailing misdirection to "normativity" and signals a turn toward the extradiegetic level of storytelling. In this regard, such symbolia is most effective when readers come to understand that the sub-text is the real story, and the central story is most often the diversion. Political cartoonists have played an important role in exposing this diversionary reframing through strategic reframings of their own, as seen in figures 26 and 27.

The same interstices, gaps and gutters through which political cartoonists reach for inspiration are the techniques that advance Sezen's coming out story. In looking back on a childhood where even at an early age she was subconsciously experimenting with gender fluidity, Sezen was the "girly tomboy" who played games of dare with her friends.[32] She had fantasies of being the hero, of unproblematically morphing into the leading man in Hollywood movies so that she would be the one in romantic pursuit of the leading ladies.

On the most fundamental level of early cognition, a child's world is

Top: Figure 26. Illustration by Carlos Latuff (copyright © 2017 Reprinted by permission of Carlos Latuff. All rights reserved) (see C•5 for larger image). *Bottom:* Figure 27. Illustration by Joep Bertram (reprinted by permission of Joep Bertram. All rights reserved) (see C•6 for larger image).

shaped by implicit and explicit messages of heteronormativity. Children are socialized into, and oriented toward, paradigms of whiteness and heterosexuality from which all else is measured. There is an expectation that girls will grow out of being tomboys and that boys will leave behind their sissy ways. For many queers, however, the larger and more insistent message is that in order to be with a woman, one must be a man. Sezen challenges these outmoded notions in the introduction to her book. She links together two childhood memories that would become significant in how she later conceptualizes "difference" in the context of her queer identity.

Picking up on the theme of daring described early in the introduction to *Snapshots*, Sezen's character is shown as a little girl with pigtails, wearing a dress with a belted waist, grinning and holding a pocketknife in her right hand. In the next image we see the iconic Victorinox emblem of a cross and shield drawn on the handle that marks it as a Swiss Army knife. The next image shows a child's small hand, with fingers spread wide, thrusting the point of the knife with increasing speed "into the space between [her] fingers." The text reads: "Who dares?"[33] Two pages later, this childhood game of dare is linked to an equally dangerous one of falling (like her idol Kristy McNichol, the narrator tells us) "for the same sex."[34] These complex and intersecting challenges are communicated through two hybrid forms: that of the queer woman of color subject and the medium (in this case, graphic narratives) through which the queer subject misdirects in an effort to subvert or reorient the hegemonic gaze. An example of how the hybrid body and misdirection work together to anticipate and ultimately contest narratives that code the queer subject as irreconcilable with normative constructions of identity is depicted in figure 28.

The author draws a segmented body that is being pulled in a number of different directions. On an emotional and intellectual level, she recognizes that the notion of home and what it represents is conditioned upon acquiescence to an agreed set of values. In order to become whole, to reconnect to a system that refuses to fully recognize or accept her individuality, means she must suppress her desires in deference to a larger heteronormative agenda. However, in the calculated placement of visual "hooks," Sezen's drawing (figure 28) sets out a conceptual puzzle that she leaves to readers to resolve for themselves.

What I am suggesting here is that one of the central turns queer of color feminism took in the twentieth century, especially in regard to locating individual and collective subjectivities at the intersection of literary discourse and cultural critique, was in the creative application of visual and literary "hooks." What I mean by this is that language and imagery used together

Figure 28. Panel from p. 72, *Snapshots of a Girl* (copyright © 2013 by Beldan Sezen. Reprinted by permission of Arsenal Pulp Press. All rights reserved).

have the ability to "queer" and destabilize the hyper-mediated spaces of the literary canon. Deconstructing these coded spaces through comics, music, art, poetry, literature, or film is an act of "witnessing" that uses misdirection to set up a more relevant critical framing. This is exemplified in the conceptual art of Johnathan Payne, shown at figure 29.

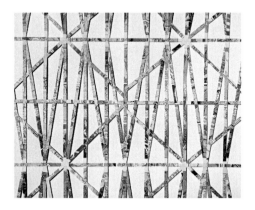

Using the interstices of space as (in my opinion) a form of misdirection that compels acts of witnessing, Payne (whose work is influenced by Ray Yoshida's comic abstraction art forms) notes that making comic lattices to create space for "femme, brown, queer, and black mythologies" is to "create another possibility for looking."[35] Although I am not fully convinced that Payne's art supports this particular narrative, his conceptual work does require audiences to see the world beyond their own cultural and ethnic borders. As we know from the work of Nella Larsen and others who have written about the signifying act of "passing" through racial as well as heteronormative borders, how we are seen is dependent upon how we have come to see ourselves. In other words, rather than operating from a position of passing *out* of our true (queer, black, gendered) selves by seeking a false and ultimately tenuous equivalency with white heteronormativity, we must instead pass *into* and openly occupy the spaces in which our existence has historically been denied. In this way, creators of hybrid storytelling show that the greatest contribution of literature and art to humanity is in its ability to open up multiple windows into the world of others.

Figure 29. Illustration by Johnathan Payne (reprinted by permission of Johnathan Payne) (see C•6 for larger image).

Coming Out to Mother: The Injunctions of Silence—Part 1

The first time the question of the narrator's sexual orientation comes up with her mother is in 1991, during a family visit in Duisburg, Germany. After a meal with her mother and sister that is filled with laughter and conversation, the narrator and her sister clear the table and return a few minutes later to resume their visit. But the mood has abruptly changed, as they find their mother sitting on the sofa with her arms crossed and a deep frown on her face. They quickly intuit that something has gone wrong, whereupon they begin asking their mother for an explanation, all the while expressing increasing bewilderment at her stubborn silence and failure to meet their gaze. Playing a game of twenty questions, ranging from "Are you sad?" to "Is it something we said?" to "Are you in pain [or] sane?" they eventually give up and wait her out.[36] Their mother eventually unfolds her arms and reaches for the bag that now sits completely outside of the frame, as if the bag itself is toxic and has caused a terrible injury. She then reaches into the bag that had been on loan to her from her daughter, bringing out a tiny sketch of two naked women kissing. What follows is a classic scene played out innumerable times between parents and their LGBT children.

The narrator's sister is positioned in the foreground of the next series of frames, demanding an answer from their mother as to why the sketch, and what it implies, should matter. Sezen has drawn her character as a silent spectator in this exchange, with an expression that is troubled and shows her reflecting on a memory of herself as a small child in the middle of conflict. Her sister is admonishing their mother, saying: "That's what all the fuss is about? I may fall in love with a woman, too. She's still your daughter. There's nothing wrong with being with a woman!"[37] Their mother finally responds by saying she simply does not wish to discuss the matter. The next image shows the narrator lying in bed next to her mother, who is fast asleep. It is worth noting that her arms are crossed in exactly the same manner as her mother's had been earlier in their exchange. As she stares into the darkness, her face is streaked with tears and she thinks to herself that she has never before felt so cold while lying next to the woman who brought her into the world, the inference being that a parent's love should be unconditional.[38]

The expectations that we set for ourselves are intertwined with the risks we take in coming out to our families. What is at stake by coming out is the possibility of alienating family members at a time when their support is essential to reconciling the paradox of being both *someone* and *no one* at all.[39] In societies where rigid adherence to cultural norms present myriad problems for queer women of color, many of whom are saddled with the added expectation of upholding community norms, behavior that is seen as inimical to the family structure complicates the already difficult decision to come out. The trade-off is to either continue compartmentalizing our lives, thereby ensuring acceptance by our families of origin, or to create alternative families where who we are is based on our own perceptions rather than on the unloving return often reflected back to us by society.

The hyper-mediated discourse of "honor" and family loyalty that is once again on the rise in socially conservative societies ensures that coming out as queer will be perceived as a threat to morality and the sanctity of the family. Moreover, when women who demand control of their own bodies and reproductive choices are perceived by conservatives (in this case Recep Tayyip Erdoğan, who infamously claimed that abortion was "a sneaky plan to wipe the country off the world stage")[40] as being hostile to the preservation of a nation, the demonization of lesbians is never far behind. For Habib Burcu Baba, the ideological distance in Turkey between queer identity and heteronormativity is vast. In citing a comment made in 2010 by Aliye Kavaf, Turkey's state minister for the affairs of women and families, Baba noted that Kavaf's belief that gay people are sick tied in with the eventual abolishment of the Ministry of Women.[41]

On their faces, Baba notes, claims that homosexuality is an illness, threats to shut down the Ministry of Women, and the prime minister's call for women to "make children" are the "seemingly unrelated consequences of the same sexual ideology [used] to regulate and control individuals through the institution of heteropatriarchal family"[42]—an ideology with far-reaching implications for those least able to mount direct challenges to a heteronormativity that is dressed up to mimic progress, but which in reality is nothing more than the trickster's glad-handing in a hall of mirrors. The Turkish government's recent indefinite ban on all LGBT events in Ankara has been justified as concern over public safety and morality, but I suggest that its real purpose is twofold. The first is not unlike Maupassant's literary technique of trapping his characters in an "authorial strategy of sameness which robs them of individuality or originality."[43] The second, and certainly equally damaging goal of the Turkish government, is to rigorously police public and private behavior in the LGBT community,[44] thereby chilling dissent and warning of potentially harsh consequences for deviation from an imposed political and cultural norm.

Research on LGBT coming out experiences has shown that even in the most socially progressive families and communities, disclosing one's sexual orientation can be difficult, anxiety producing, and often unplanned.[45] While for some being accidentally "outed" might be a fortuitous event, a way to begin a conversation that might not otherwise be had, for those living in socially conservative families and communities, being "outed" often brings with it severe consequences.[46] While Sezen's accidental coming out happened within a relatively safe space, and she seemed in no danger of being imprisoned, raped, or tortured, she did stand to lose the respect and love of her mother. Furthermore, the potential damage to the emotional and physical well-being of LGBT youth as a result of parental disapproval or rejection cannot be underestimated.

There have been a number of studies linking victimization to increased suicide rates among LGBT youth. One such study conducted by Richard T. Liu and Brian Mustanski found that "after suicide attempt history, LGBT victimization was the strongest predictor of self-harm, being associated with a 2.5-fold increased risk."[47] The victimization that Liu and Mustanski make reference to is situated along a continuum of behaviors that run the gamut from name-calling to physical and sexual assault to social exclusion and to murder. Although the narrator's first attempt to come out to her mother resulted only in silent tears and a sleepless night, the deeper implications—parental disapproval and, by extension, the disapproval of her wider family—played out in a variety of fairly predictable ways relative to her choices going forward. She became politically active, first while still dating men, and later with a group of women living in a squat house in Oberhausen, in West Germany's Ruhr Valley. She quickly became involved with other activist organizations, and from there it was a logical transition to emotional and sexual relationships with women.[48]

Coming Out to Mother: Who Should Be Ashamed?—Part 2

There is a recurring question in *Snapshots*; one part is accusatory and the other turns on inference. The two parts of the question intersect to highlight the contradictions, falsehoods, secrets, and threats that are crucial to controlling individual behavior and setting the terms of private and public exchange. The question attempts to distinguish between the object of shame and the person responsible for bringing the shame. Yet this one question cannot be answered without an acknowledgment of wrong-doing, which would deepen the shame on the part of the doer, or by contesting the deed that was done, which might resolve the damage done to the person compelled to bear the shame. Who controls the narrative, the misdirection, the forces that use shame as a shield against discovery and a guarantee of silence? "Who brings shame?"[49] Using the visual language of graphic narratives to delve into subjects that are far too painful to express in words alone, the author confronts the power of shaming by calling it out and deconstructing it through a queer feminist framework.

Having fully embraced her new life as an out loud and proud lesbian, Sezen and a friend publish an anthology focusing on the lives of queer women of color who live in, or hail from, Germany.[50] We see a young Sezen on stage, performing what is presumably a poem from the anthology. The image sensitively captures the anxiety, yet also the determination, of a young dyke trying to reconcile her old life of secrecy and denial with her new queer feminist awareness. Her poem unflinchingly calls out the "who" and the "what" of shame, forcing it from the shadows and into the light of a powerful reckoning. "Who should be ashamed? All the uncles shouting 'faggots' in the daytime and fucking their sons at night ... who should be ashamed? All the fathers calling their daughters 'whores' and beating them up? Who should be ashamed?"[51] Proud of having published her first book, but apparently giving little thought to how it would be received, she sends a copy of it to her mother.

The narrator's second attempt at coming out to her mother, both as a young woman striking out on a different ideological path than women of her mother's generation and also as a lesbian and feminist, receives a predictably non-committal response. Speaking with her mother by phone, the narrator asks if her mother had received the anthology. Her mother responds with a terse "Yes, thank you," which dissuades the narrator from further probing. Determined to have a conversation with her mother about the book, as well as the uncomfortable issues it raises about silence and shame, the narrator revisits the issue during a family visit to Turkey.

Unable to break through the injunctions of silence, the narrator once again uses the cover of night to examine difficult truths. Pressing her mother for acknowledgment, love, and ultimately for acceptance, she uses darkness as a portal through which both she and her mother might find common ground. Using a pitch-black background with white lettering and various Emanata[52] to show their respective emotions and physical locations (because no actual people can be seen), Sezen's character initiates a conversation with her mother about the anthology. She begins by asking a question she already knows the answer to, but it is a relatively neutral one that at least gets the conversation started. "So, did you get my book?"[53] The response from her mother is once again a terse "Yes."

Implicit in the question the narrator puts to her mother is a plea for recognition. Her mother's response—as it had been before—is an attempt at foreclosure regarding a subject she does not wish to revisit. But the darkness emboldens the daughter, enabling her to push past her mother's resistance, and by completely removing gradations of light from the panel, the author metaphorically casts aside the tyranny of silence to take up what Martha J. Cutter describes as an "unruly tongue" that "becomes a symbol for an unruly identity that challenges [...] stereotypes of femininity but [also] the theoretical structure of patriarchal authority in the world she inhabits."[54] The darkness misdirects the intent behind the unruly tongue, giving it a relatively safe haven in which to express words that are inexpressible in the light of day.

It needs to be said here that the darkness in *Snapshots* is not the kind, for example, described by Joseph Conrad in *Heart of Darkness* (1999). Conrad's title infers duplicity in the hearts of men and impenetrable darkness at the very heart of the Congo. Nor is it the strict either-or of religious teachings where demonic forces are said to lurk in the darkness while angels bring the light that opens us up to divine love. Rather, the darkness portrayed in *Snapshots* is meant to misdirect attention away from what we have been socially conditioned to see and thereby understand, and instead to a place where we draw on different cognitive strategies to help us delve below the surface and unpack what we have also been conditioned not to see.

That which we can or cannot see or perceive, either on a cognitive level relevant to spatial distinctions or on an emotional level based on differing belief systems, is a recurring theme in *Snapshots*. Extending the metaphor of the closet as darkness/secrecy/shame and even liberation, the cognitive dissonance created by the pitch-black page forces the reader/audience to take cognitive (and ideological) leaps that they would not otherwise attempt. Perhaps the darkness in *Snapshots* is precisely the opening that both the mother and the narrator need to speak difficult truths.

As the conversation between the narrator and her mother progresses, with her mother's resistance to answering her daughter's increasingly probing questions being gradually worn down, the reader and narrator simultaneously experience a moment of clarity. Located at the bottom right edge of the pitch-black panel is one word, "Snap," illuminated by a small table lamp that is turned on immediately after the following exchange: "You know *that's* just what I am." "It's not that," comes the mother's reply. "W ... what?" is the stunned response from the narrator. And finally, "I don't care if you are *that* or not," says the mother and the light of understanding is represented by the "snap" of a lamp being turned on.[55]

The daughter's long-awaited desire for acknowledgment and acceptance from her mother is momentous. The panel on the following page reflects this as it is fully illuminated and shows the narrator and her mother positioned at a physical distance from one another, yet surrounded by words that will ultimately bring them together. "What really upsets me is the language you use!" "I didn't raise you to use such words! To be so rude!" "I raised you with beautiful words so you would hear and use beautiful words; not this! That's what really upsets me and makes me sad."[56] The panel resolves with the image of the narrator looking perplexed and even a bit shame-faced. Having assumed that her mother's resistance to engaging in important conversations with her equated to an aversion to her queer identity, in reality her mother's discomfort was actually centered on what she perceived to be her daughter's ill-mannered approach to broaching private issues. Yet what remains unsaid is the negative connotation in the self description of the narrator as "that," when she asserts, "You know *that's* just what I am,"[57] as though the word that *that* refers to is diseased or too dangerous to utter out loud, even in the darkness of the metaphorical closet they are both speaking through.

Ironically, when the narrator comes out to her father two years later, his reaction is in marked contrast to an earlier exchange whereby he falls back on tradition and takes her to task for her poor manners. Having come of age in a different era than that of her parents, and adopting a more casual approach to social interactions, during a family visit the narrator invites her boyfriend to help himself to whatever he can find in the refrigerator. Her father becomes so incensed by her lack of manners that he declares, "You're not my daughter!"[58] Yet when she comes out to him as a lesbian during another family visit, he is completely unperturbed by her disclosure. He tells her about the disparaging names the men he goes to the local pub with use to refer to the mayor of Berlin, explaining to her that his own view is that the mayor's politics is what counts, not what he does in his bedroom.[59] He then asks her if everything else is okay, offers her a stick of chewing gum, and advises her not to share the news with her mother, as he does not think she would understand.[60] What her father has offered his daughter is an acceptance that is conditioned upon silence. His request that she remain silent diminishes the importance of her disclosure, effectively relegating her back to the closet, albeit one that she can at least come out of in his presence.

Coming Out to Mother: Kadinlari Severim—Part 3

There is ambiguity in the language of coming out, complex layers of meaning in the lines, dashes, dots and pauses through which we attempt to untie our (queer) (y) ing tongues. And where performance masquerading as one thing points toward the truth of something else, it is because we have learned to use subversion and misdirection to express the inexpressible. Yet when there is no context, no point of reference, no positive representations of our queer of color selves, and no ability to effectively contest the tropes that vilify who we are, we take out pen and pencil and ink and paint to draw ourselves (and our stories) anew in a spatio-temporal heterotopia where counter-spaces support a simultaneous mirroring and a contestation of the private/public spaces in which we live, or, alternatively, those from which we are excluded. In this way it could be said that Michiel Dehaene and Lieven De Cauter's critical engagement with Foucault's heterotopia gestures toward the unique hybridity of sequential art to support similar mirroring and contestations of space.

In the context of how public/private spaces are negotiated in a "postcivil society" (a term Dehaene and Cauter borrow from Frederic Jameson to describe as a type of dirge for a once civil culture),[61] the authors note that Foucault was gesturing specifically toward "various institutions and places that interrupt the apparent continuity and normality of ordinary everyday space."[62] They go on to note that because these institutions (such as military schools, museums, psychiatric institutions, and so on) "inject alterity into the sameness, the commonplace, the topicality of everyday society," these places were referred to as "'hetero-topias,'" literally meaning "other places."[63] The relevance of heterotopias or, more to the point, our engagement with and location inside or outside of various institutional laws and frameworks, positions graphic narratives as an excellent platform through which critical spectatorship is so creatively expressed.

Whether it is via graphic narratives that have made it to mainstream audiences, such as Amruta Patil's *Kari* (2008), Melanie Gillman's *As the Crow Flies* (2017), Elisha Lim's *100 Crushes* (2014), and Tee Franklin's *Bingo Love* (2018), or web comics by Yao Xiao, Blue Delliquanti, Molly Alice Hoy, and Taneka Stotts, affirmative representations of queerness in the hybrid semiotics of sequential art offer ways to transcend and challenge public and private erasure. Therefore when we say—as the narrator boldly proclaims in *Snapshots of a Girl*—"Kadinlari severim," "I love women," it is a clear and unambiguous declaration of identity. And when the narrator goes on to bracket these words alongside "Ayip eden kim?" "Who is rude?" and "Bana böyle bakmayin," "Don't look at me like that,"[64] she reclaims the parts of herself that have been pulled in multiple directions. Taken together, these oppositions ("I love women" and "Don't look at me like that") set up a dialectic that paves the way for a unification of opposites. Even as the narrator rails against the culture and customs that refuse to acknowledge her existence, she still seeks legitimacy, even if it is within the spaces that she is compelled to create for herself.

Cristina Delgado-Garcia's insights are particularly apt here. In her essay on *Palestine*, Joe Sacco's widely acclaimed graphic narrative on the Israeli-Palestinian conflict, she examines the meaning of space in its political and ideological context. Relying in part on Henri Lefebvre's notion of "'representations

of space'" and "'representational spaces,'"[65] Delgado-Garcia draws parallels
between Sacco's images of destroyed Palestinian homelands, alongside visual
representations of Palestinians being "temporally [expelled]" from the page.
These visual representations work to enhance the horror of displacement of
a people whose private and public spaces are under constant assault from a
legal and ideological system that supports the rights of one group to the material and psychological detriment of another. Graphic narratives are capable
of bringing to the fore these inequalities. By opening up spaces where readers
can bear witness to the hyper-policing that causes incalculable loss and grief
in Palestinian communities, graphic narratives shake up the way we see the
world. The images in *Snapshots* mount a compelling argument for these tensions. Sezen sets out radical counter-spaces where marginalized groups no
longer accept being defined solely in opposition to expected norms, but
instead to turn normativity into the unexpected.

Home

In the fall of 2001, the narrator phones her mother with important news
about a serious romantic relationship she has entered into with another
woman. Her mother, perhaps weary of having her daughter's lifestyle pressed
upon her, or simply uninterested in pursuing an issue she believes has been
resolved, terminates the call. The narrator is shown with a surprised look on
her face, saying, "Mom?"[66] into the telephone receiver. Their communication
falls off dramatically that year, and when they do speak at all the mother's
tone is "polite but brusque."[67] Sezen's account of a coming out that happens
in fits and starts is not an uncommon occurrence, nor are the mixed messages
she receives from her mother. Coming out is an evolving process.

The journey that the narrator embarks upon in firstly coming out to
herself and then to others would not be so dissimilar to the journey parents
and loved ones embark upon to understand the importance of the disclosure.
The paradox here lies in the act of disclosure, which is itself anxiety-producing.
In the case of the narrator, the act of speaking openly with a traditional Turkish mother about sex implies no contradiction between the disclosure and
the continuum of sexual desire upon which the disclosure is located. Therefore the newly un-closeted queer anticipates that once the disclosure is made,
the mixed signals or contradictory actions from family and friends that would
then undermine the disclosure should have been resolved with the initial
disclosure.

The paradox of being *out* while also being asked to respect the sensibilities of others is explored by Kevin Barnhurst in his article "Visibility as Paradox: Representation and Simultaneous Contrast." Barnhurst gives the example of MTV Networks, a division of Viacom, which launched a television program in 2005 that aimed to represent LGBT people in a positive light within the entertainment industry.[68] While referring to their programming as a "'sponsor-friendly cable channel,'" implying that the company understood its obligation to its financial supporters, they "bleep[ed] out expletives and expurgate[ed] scenes to avoid giving offense to non-queer viewers, despite the channel declaring itself not just gay friendly but one with the LGBT communities."[69] The company's stance was nothing less than a conditional acceptance, based largely on protecting its revenue stream with sponsors. Its implicit agreement to censor images deemed to fall outside of the boundaries of "polite" society effectively re-marginalized the very community it was "outing" to heterosexual television viewers.

In December of 2002 the narrator and her mother have another telephone conversation. This time her mother informs the narrator that her sister and her sister's boyfriend will be visiting for Christmas. The following conversation ensues: "Yes, Mom, I know." "So, what about you?" "What do you mean, 'what about me?'" "Well, are you also coming?" "What about my girlfriend?" "What about her?" "Well, I'm not coming without her!!" "Of course she can come." "It's about time you accepted tha..." "Who said she can't come?" "So, are you coming?" "Yes, yes."[70] The narrator and her mother exist at different ends of the ideological spectrum. On the one hand there is an implicit agreement that although the tradition of polite silence in Turkish culture has been breached by the daughter's persistence in getting her mother to acknowledge her queerness, there is also an expectation that family connotes an expansiveness into which everyone fits, either through marriage or other informal configurations. The narrator, it could be said, has an expectation that because she is part of her mother's family, then this *belonging* should logically extend to her lover.

Part 3 of the narrator's coming out shows her being welcomed by her mother to the holiday celebration. While both maintain a polite distance from each other, the narrator's girlfriend and other guests chat amongst themselves, with the narrator recognizing feelings of being overwhelmed. Noticing her mother go into the bedroom, open the closet door, remove a jewelry box and rummage through it, the narrator then observes her handing her lover a small bag, saying: "That is the tradition in our culture."[71] And as the narrator continues to look on, she sees a smile appear on her lover's face as she pulls out a small gold pendant from the bag.[72] Her mother then explains to the narrator's lover: "That's what you give the daughter-in-law when welcoming her into the family."[73] This statement, delivered without fanfare or an expectation of anything in return, is remarkable for its directness and honesty, two things the narrator had heretofore been unable to get from her mother.

When coming out is conditional upon putting someone else at ease, either by coming out only in certain situations or reorienting our queer selves to such a degree that we are indistinguishable from the heterosexual norm, is it truly a coming out or just another form of compartmentalizing our lives, making the idea of us/the "Other" more palatable to mainstream sensibilities? Sezen's visual mélange speaks to the disconnect innumerable LGBT people have felt in trying to reconcile their true identities with the unloving return reflected back to them in the eyes (and laws) of intolerant cultures, traditions, families, social networks, and educational and legal systems. Her refusal to accede to a traditional cultural narrative that would have her collude in her own marginalization is visually rendered in a hodgepodge illustration style that mimics the fits and starts of her coming out process. There are no straight lines connecting her back to herself, no easy answers that will transport her to a state of a blissful, uncomplicated life. And even though she understands (like so many before her) that she is a queer woman of color tangled up in a long history of "Otherness," she also knows that she finally has the power to draw (and write) herself into a new beginning.

Chapter 8

A Delicate Dance with Demons

Kabi Nagata's My Lesbian Experience with Loneliness *(2016)*

Two important writers (both known to varying degrees for their existential views of the world and our place in it) extended the subject of loneliness from the realm of its much-maligned position as a condition of desperate people no one really cares about to an intellectual premise lending itself to weighty philosophical discussions about the higher virtues of solitude. Paul Tillich, the German existentialist philosopher, held the view that "our language has wisely sensed the two sides of being alone. It has created the word 'loneliness' to express the pain of being alone, and the word 'solitude' to express the glory of being alone."[1] In *Reborn: Journals and Notebooks, 1947–1963*, Susan Sontag wrote: "I want to be alone, to find it nourishing—not just a waiting."[2] Sontag, of course, knew Tillich. She made passing reference to him in her journals, although not in relation to his scholarly work, but instead making note of his appointment (which succeeded Hans Cornelius) as a professor of philosophy at Frankfurt.[3] Tillich was also an important mentor to Sontag when she matriculated as a student at Harvard.[4]

My reference to Tillich's erudition on the philosophy of loneliness and solitude, and Sontag's poignant expression of matters that weighed heavily upon her mind long before her death in 2004, is meant to set out the basis for a more in-depth exploration of hermeneutical phenomenology in relation to Kabi Nagata's manga memoir *My Lesbian Experience with Loneliness*. To this end I turn to the work of Paul Ricoeur, or rather to a matrix (see Table 1) developed by Noelle Leslie Dela Cruz based on a specific strand of his work. What is useful about Dela Cruz's model is that it builds toward a hermeneutical phenomenology of comics.[5] While other research such as Carlos Kong's

217

"SuperQueeros—Our LGBTI Comic Book Heroes and Heroines," Donald E. Hall's *Reading Sexualities: Hermeneutic Theory and the Future of Queer Studies* (2009), and Karin Kukkonen's *Contemporary Comics Storytelling* (2013)[6] also apply phenomenological hermeneutics as an interpretive device to further critical analysis of alterity in sequential art, Dela Cruz's matrix explicitly links the formal elements of comics to a hermeneutics and visual rhetoric/aesthetic that can be applied as broadly as originally intended by Ricoeur. My argument here is that the hybridity we come to expect in sequential art interacts in a complementary way with Ricoeur's interest in "time and narrative, memory, intersubjectivity, justice, political philosophy, and ethics."[7] These elements that come together in life to make a story, albeit not always in a linear way, form the basis of Ricoeur's theorizing regarding emplotment as discordant concordance, an argument in which the hybrid language, symbolism, and structure of sequential art stands in agreement.

Nagata's *shōjo yuri* manga revolves around "discordances [that are] part of the story and disturb the order, in the end [becoming] part of the story [...] taken up and represented in the plot."[8] In other words, the way stories unfold in manga is largely through the discordance and concordance of Japanese Visual Language, which I come to shortly. But briefly, where in Western comics the story is structured through a concordance of panels, frames, and captions, manga goes further by incorporating culturally specific signs and symbols upon which the emotional thrust of a story relies. Nosebleeds are perhaps the most recognizable symbols in manga, representing various states of arousal or perverseness, depending upon the amount of blood flowing from the character's nose. For Nagata, recurring signs of her lability manifest in wide-eyed stares, cruciform popping veins, vertical lines that drape the top half of her blushing and/or tear-stained face, and is a recurring morpheme in her book.[9]

Relying on five formal elements identified by Will Eisner as features distinguishing comics from non-pictorial writing, Dela Cruz's matrix is based less on Eisner's turn toward the technical aspects of these elements in sequential art and more on the use of "Imagery," "Timing," "Framing," "Expressive Anatomy," and "Writing" to explore issues of intersubjectivity and the historical and cultural factors contributing to individual character formation. For the sake of brevity, I have shown in Table 1 only one of the five elements that comprise Dela Cruz's matrix, but my analysis of Nagata's book is drawn almost exclusively from "Expressive Anatomy" and "Writing."[10] It is also worth noting that Dela Cruz's paper explores hermeneutics through *shonen*, which is manga that is typically aimed at a young male demographic, whereas my analysis is based largely on *shōjo*, which is geared toward girls. However, I am particularly interested in a sub-genre of *shōjo* known as *yuri*, which focuses on emotionally and sexually intimate relationships between girls. The distinction here is that whereas some *shōjo* turns on tropes of romantic schoolgirl crushes, *My Lesbian Experience with Loneliness* instead delves headlong into a visually and heart-rending story of a chronically depressed woman's journey to self-recognition and lesbian desire.

At its most basic, hermeneutics is concerned with the interpretation of texts, most notably religious texts, although over time this changed to include many other language-based (and visual/artistic) productions. In "The Task of Hermeneutics" Ricoeur offered a working definition of the term as the "theory of the operation of understanding in its relations to the interpretation of texts."[11] Valérie Angenot provides a slightly different interpretation of the term when she states that in discourse theory, hermeneutics focuses on the "interpretation and the analysis of underlying layers of meaning that exceed the literal or obvious signification of textual and visual motifs."[12]

Formal elements of comics	Axis of popular culture and history	Axis of intersubjectivity
Expressive anatomy	What messages about race, gender, class, sexual orientation, age, religion, nationality, ethnicity, and other aspects of identity are conveyed by the portrayal of the body? What ideological assumptions, if any, are conveyed or critiqued through the depiction of facial expressions, gestures, body postures, and body shapes? Are there any cultural stereotypes that are reinforced or debunked?	How do the characters' facial expressions, gestures, and body postures reveal how they feel about themselves and others? Do the characters' physical appearances vary based on point of view? How are the physical attributes of characters depicted in remembrance, introspection, fantasy, or imagination? Are the characters shown to communicate through body, in addition to verbal, language? If so, what does this body language say about the nature of their relationships?

Table 1 (Dela Cruz)

I do not intend to expound on the merits of hermeneutics or on the various schools of thought that have arisen around it, as this has been thoroughly (and no doubt more expertly) covered by hermeneutic scholars. My interest in hermeneutics is primarily as an interpretive framework through which a particular philosophical (and psychological) understanding of Nagata's manga memoir can be presented. From a methodological standpoint, hermeneutics is broadly considered here in its most creative form, described by Ingrida Vaňková as a "model of unification that accounts for the creativity involved in making sense of the various aspects of a person's life." Vaňková further explains that this model of unification is

> a picture of an entity whose constitution is entirely mediated by the signs, symbols, texts, traditions, practices, and other significant elements which together make up the various cultures in which people live.[13]

The physical and imagined worlds we create to facilitate humans gaining a better understanding of who we are goes some way in capturing the many forms of language we use to express what Ricoeur has suggested is a "temporal unfolding of life" that is analogous to the "unfolding of a narrative."[14] According to Ricoeur, our self-awareness and knowledge of ourselves expands and matures through reflection. By putting forth our own narrative, he suggests that we learn how to "narrate [ourselves] in other ways."[15] Thus the unification which Vaňková considers becomes one where the application of expressive anatomy and the technique of framing in sequential art can be used to set up a mediation between the hermeneutics of loneliness and the transformative space from which healing begins. Put another way, what does the body tell us about language? What is the relationship between language and its queer(y)ing subjects? There are myriad things that language can do when it is released from the limitations of structural conventions that impede its discursive potential.

There is a great deal of concordance in the "sequential unfolding" of events in the texts which Vaňková considers in her discussion on "narrative configuration" and the comics' form.[16] Although Vaňková makes no explicit connection to the spatiotemporal structure of comics, there is a corollary that she, unwittingly perhaps, establishes between the visual-textual elements in sequential art and the model of the text upon which Ricoeur's hermeneutic methodology is based. Indeed, the application of a Ricoeurian hermeneutics across multiple discursive platforms sees the alignment of what Scott McCloud famously described as "closure" and what Vaňková describes as Ricoeur's "time of configuration."[17] Noting that this configuration is an "ideal time which is characterized by the integration, culmination, and ultimate closure of the events that make up a story,"[18] Vaňková suggests that insofar as it is ruled by the need for agreement in the way of closure, narrative configuration is structurally ideal as it combines "a variety of disparate elements forming a temporal totality."[19] What Vaňková is getting at, and the connection that I believe is crucial to a hermeneutical approach to Nagata's book, is that in any text in which our individual stories unfold, we "encounter a configuration that can lead us to re-understand, to reconfigure, our prior under-standing of who we are."[20] Such an understanding, expressed through the bold framing of *My Lesbian Experience with Loneliness*, also finds its poten-tiality in the visual aesthetics of a signifying *kaishakugaku*.[21]

Nicholas Davey's arguments in this area contribute to progressing my own position regarding the usefulness of phenomenological hermeneutics in Nagata's work. While Davey's focus on the aesthetics of hermeneutics in understanding and appreciating visual art/paintings initially appears to be at the opposite end of the spectrum from sequential arts, the relationship is really quite similar.

> Contemporary philosophical hermeneutics embraces the conviction that the ability of the said to point to and reveal the unsaid makes linguistic understanding a paradigm case for grasping the nature of artistic understanding.[22]

Davey goes on to suggest that "far from subordinating image to word, hermeneutical aesthetics is concerned with the sensitive use of words to bring forth what is held in an image."[23] Nagata's manga memoir uses indelicate, painful, challenging, and often impolite words to emphasize the uncomfort-able witnessing of mental illness. If we go on to consider Davey's analysis that the "articulateness of careful verbal utterance resides not in what is declared but in how the declared silently resonates in the mind of the listener [...]," it brings us to his further point that the "density of either depends upon an ability to invoke, to make luminous or audible their respective visual or sound-worlds."[24] The issue here, as Davey further clarifies, and which Scott McCloud and other comics scholars have long asserted, is that although the "totality of what is held within a painting can never be seen in a single glance, it is the word that directs us to what has yet to be seen."[25] It is also, I argue, what things stand for and what they gesture toward, the visual and textual combined to represent alternative realities, hopes, and dreams. Sontag once made the observation that if we are to discern completeness, we must be in possession of an "acute sense of the emptiness which marks it off," going on to argue that in order to "perceive emptiness, one must apprehend other zones of the world as full."[26]

Neither Sontag nor Davey were speaking to the "art" of comics and how the presentation of words through speech bubbles, captions and the like shape what we see and how the images those words gesture toward create meaning. Yet their respective opinions on the ability of a painting to exceed its visual boundaries when it is facilitated by written language is a funda-mental principle in sequential art. Insofar as any particular form of art ges-tures toward a "unity of what can and cannot be said (or represented) ... at

the same time it may make a tacit proposal for upsetting previously conse-
crated rulings on what can be said (or represented) ... [and it therefore] issues
its own set of limits."[27] Through her choice of words and JVL, Nagata ignores
the aesthetics of silence that in classical art aims to regulate and hold fast to
the notion of beauty (or even tragedy) as being inexpressible and perhaps
even diminished by the inadequacy of words. She instead uses the page as a
canvas upon which she creates a dizzying account in images and words of
her descent into the abyss of mental illness.

Misdirection and the Fetishizing Western Gaze

The drawing style in manga, or what Neil Cohn refers to as "Japanese
Visual Language," relates to a mode of "pictorial communication [...] that
stereotypically appears in manga of the world [...] while 'manga' is a socio-
cultural artefact that may or may not be actually written in JVL."[28] However,
a point to be made here about JVL productions that are directed at international consumers is the absence of obvious racial markers. Monica Chiu, for
example, discusses this trend of producing "culturally odorless"[29] manga that
does away with "Japaneseness both in facial features as well as in references
to Japanese culture," although at the same time she notes that manga turns
on very "culturally-specific (Japanese) visual language."[30] There is tension
among manga scholars as to the usefulness, and indeed the critical depth, of
Koichi Iwacuchi's explanation of the "culturally odorless." I make no attempt
in this chapter to wade into this particular debate, but I do find Iwacuchi's
proposition worthwhile in reading *My Lesbian Experience with Loneliness*
through a queer feminist, postcolonial lens. As I come to momentarily, this
choice of reading also falls afoul of arguments put forth, for example, by Terry
Kawashima, who challenges what she considers to be a generally superficial
understanding of manga and its particular interpellation of race and ethnicity.
    One example of the (mis)coding of race that has been put forth by
Kawashima is in relation to the *Sailor Moon* series which is targeted at a
young female demographic. The series follows the adventures of Usagi
Tsukino, a schoolgirl with magical powers. To Westerners, the Sailor Moon
character looks white, an assessment that Kawashima, following Frederik
Schodt, refutes. When asked by students why Sailor Moon looks white,
Kawashima responds by explaining that the character "looks just as 'Japanese'
as she looks 'white,'" going on to note that it is the viewer's interpretation of

race, which is shaped by cultural conditioning, that gives rise to such mis-perceptions.[31] Kawashima further notes that reading "visual images in specific racialized ways" establishes a type of racial hierarchy where we "privilege certain cues at the expense of others," which in turn "lead to an over-determined conclusion."[32] Her observation is borne out in multiple ways, not the least of which are those we are currently seeing expressed in the United States of America, where the mere presence of black men and women in largely white spaces triggers white anxiety. The coding of people of color—be it based on clothing, hairstyles, music, or just being black—is especially problematic when sexual orientation and gender is added to the mix. In this way, the "culturally odorless" representation of self in Japanese manga is, almost by default, filtered through the privileged lens of whiteness against which the inherent worthiness and value of people of color are measured.

In figure 30 the large, imploring eyes, oversized head, and melodramatic expressions of emotion typically found in manga also speak (albeit indirectly) to the exaggerated representations of "Otherness" that continue to circulate in popular culture. While some may argue that Asian lesbians represent a markedly different social and cultural reality than that of queer women of color in other parts of the world, the fact remains that they too are subject to "whitening" practices that neutralize "Otherness," making it more palatable (and relatable) to Western tastes. In this regard, Japanese manga passes the metaphorical "smell" test by downplaying or "neutralizing" racial markers. Yet by not drawing attention to differences in our life stories, and failing to celebrate the things that make us unique, these omissions simply become more pronounced. In this way, Nagata's relative silence around issues of race and culture introduces a paradigm shift that puts the "culturally odorless" "model minority" into the very racialized spotlight that contemporary manga appears to work hard to avoid. And while "character designs which are visually abstract from specific race are not characteristic of all manga," which is evidenced in "*seinen* manga (young adult manga)" and the "*gekiga* genre,"[33] that which is produced for international audiences seem to make whiteness the default model upon which identity is based.

Although the narrator painstakingly addresses issues of social isolation, eating disorders, anxiety, poor self-esteem, self-cutting, and trichotillomania, and she does so by using JVL throughout, her cultural identity only comes through via such iconic Japanese markers as the Love Hotel, her interest in manga, using the traditional form of greeting (bowing) when she first meets the lesbian escort, and prominently displaying a package of ramen noodles, which is said to have originated in China but made its way to Japan via Chinese tradesmen in the nineteenth century.[34]

In thinking through the notion of race and culture alongside misdirection, particularly with relevance to queer women of color whose invisibility "travels" across the very transcultural borders that introduced manga to worldwide audiences, the discursive work remains one of excavating voices and identities from the ruins of civilizations remade in the image of European conquerors. The racist tropes that manga could be said to challenge through its uniquely expressive visual language and "odorlessness" come into play when readers of color fail to see themselves reflected back in affirmative ways from its pages. And while Mio Bryce et al. argue that in spite of the "growing global popularity of *manga*, considerable and complex intercultural misconceptions often become obstacles for the appreciation of the medium,"[35] I submit that one can appreciate manga, its storyline and its unique visual language while also having an expectation that their own cultural and racial background does not accede uncritically to its homogenizing influence.

Figure 30. Cover Art from *My Lesbian Experience with Loneliness* (copyright© 2016 by Kabi Nagata. Reprinted by permission of Seven Seas Entertainment Press) (see C•7 for larger image).

Taking up Trinh T. Minh-Ha's formulations on the critical importance of artistic work to demonstrate "on the one hand, a political commitment and an ideological lucidity, and […] on the other hand [work that is] interrogative by nature, instead of being merely prescriptive," makes way for transcultural exchange that is not already bracketed by an established and unyielding hegemony.[36] Globalization, whether it is in the guise of "cultural exchange" or promoted as a more efficient and fair system of trade, or a recognition that the world's resources are finite and technological advances must be shared if the planet is to survive, also serves as an important reminder that transcultural productions "cannot travel without being passed among people, a process that also results in it being changed by the needs, desires and fears of those who take it up."[37]

Therefore while manga's seemingly "odorless" ethnographic inflection is thought by some scholars to be misunderstood as an uncritical acquiescence to Eurocentric ideals of beauty (whiteness) and the universality of man (the West), the shifting contexts through which misdirection operate uniquely positions manga as a tool that perpetuates negative readings of the "Other." John Russell's critique on this very subject further illuminates how "race" travels within and across cultural and national borders to replicate these "perduring stereotypes of the black Other," which he goes on to point out have, to a great extent, been

> reinforced by the centrality of American discourse on the nonwhite Other in Japan, which, with the cultural authority and the distributive currency of American mass media and popular culture, has resulted in Japan's uncritical acceptance and indigenization of the racial hierarchies they project.[38]

The caveat, however, is that the "Other" must consciously resist the default paradigm of "blissfully multicultural group[s] where people of all origins are (supposedly) united in equality"[39] that has been such a successful formula in the production of manga for global consumption. For the culturally and historically aware reader, there is a particular type of aesthetics that is instantly recognizable as inauthentic and polarizing to people of color who are often on the periphery of the very fan clubs that Sandra Annett believes allow them to "'contest and sometimes even subvert the imagined worlds of the official mind and the entrepreneurial mentality that surround them.'"[40] People of color must resist being diverted (or misdirected) from what is *not* there, and instead interrogate creative productions that do not reflect positive images (or any images at all) of who we are. Conversely, and in the relatively nascent industry of rap music in Japan, some performers darken their skin and wear dreadlocks as a misguided homage to African American rappers, failing to understand the irony of "un-disappearing" blackness by making it visible in its most ludicrous and stereotypical forms.

These emulations of a particular, and certainly not widely representational, style of African American fashion and music add multiple layers of complexity to discussions regarding the appropriation (or the purported subversion) of racial stereotypes as expressions of respect or a performative "shout out" to people of color. Nina Cornyetz reframed this debate as one where the "blackening of the bodily self has become a desired index in Japan" that "upsets conventional twentieth-century inferential symbolic homilies on black skin."[41] Yet it is difficult to reconcile images of Japanese youth with artificially darkened skin as signifying admiration for, and solidarity with, black youth, when alongside this mimicry are characterizations in contemporary manga that embody many of the racist tropes that continue to circulate in popular culture. Moreover, by equating the absence of difference with a politics of racial blindness, or the "whitening" of manga as a new and radical cultural aesthetics, issues that are especially specific to queer women of color who already exist at the periphery of competing ideological movements are pushed that much closer to the margins of what is increasingly becoming an uncritical homogenizing discourse. And when mental illness is factored in (or out, as the case might be), queer women of color suffer from a visual mis-alignment and misrecognition deterministically inscribed by the interpella-tion of new, and supposedly "raceless," subjectivities that travel largely unexamined across transcultural borders.

I argue that by its very "odorlessness" manga is in fact "raced" because it brackets cultural homogeneity on one side of a historical script about who Asians are expected to be within their own geographical borders, while the other part of the narrative that travels outside of those borders relies on uncritical examinations of *self* on the part of audiences at the receiving end of the visual "whitewash." Put another way, when manga travels transcultur-ally, it does not automatically take along with it consideration of how it will be consumed and interpreted. In the relative echo chamber of culturally homogeneous groupings, what is sometimes produced in manga are approx-imations of the self, packaged primarily for (white) Western consumption. Therefore, identity, as Trinh T. Minh-Ha suggests, is largely unquestioned when it is not caught up in the added complexities of displacement. She writes:

> Perhaps vindicating and interrogating identity takes on a peculiarly active significance with displacement and migration. It becomes inevitable with the questioning of estab-lished power relations, or with the daily meddling with the ruling culture. For those who feel settled at home in their land (or other lands) where racial issues are not an everyday challenge, perhaps self-retrieval and self-apprehension are achieved without yielding to the urge to assimilate, to reject, or to fight for a space where identity is fear-lessly constructed across difference.[42]

As an Asian lesbian whose experiences of self-harming and depression constitute much of her memoir, Nagata, in her frank visual and textual recounting of her life story, stands as witness to the complex levels of psychic pain that often go unremarked in communities of color. Perhaps uninten-tionally, the misdirection inherent in figurative as well as literal representa-tions of the "model minority," the strong black woman, the tough and unflappable Latina, or the indomitable will of two-spirit people links Nagata's memoir to a (queer/black/Other) hermeneutics that compels a different type of response whereby the contexts through which pain is either ameliorated in unhealthy ways—as it is with the narrator's self-cutting—or channeled into a more positive and creative activity—such as the narrator's eventual immersion in manga to free herself from an internal dialogue that had for years trapped her in a vortex of shame and uncertainty—becomes the lens through which illness (and its words) are reconsidered.

Nagata's ability to pull the reader into her pain through the "Expressive Anatomy" that makes the graphic narrative form the perfect tool for communicating the most private thoughts in multiple ways speaks volumes about her artistic abilities. As Will Eisner explains, it is "patently clear that when a skillfully limned image is presented it can trigger a recall that evokes recognition and the collateral effects on the emotion."[43] As can be seen from multiple images in the book, the oversized eyes and intense unwavering stare of the narrator looking out at the reader is unnerving, but indicative of an art form that is limited only by imagination and skill. Where Nagata's inattention to race and ethnicity actually brings these issues into sharper focus, her conceptualization and visual rendering of mental illness sets up a compelling tension at the intersection where the pathologization of mental illness in communities of color in the West is mediated through the very mechanisms of manga that allow for what Annett, in citing Anna Lowenhaupt Tsing, refers to as "collaborative friction," or mediating across and through ideological and/or cultural differences.[44]

Although the visual tropes in manga, or what Robin E. Brenner refers to as "visual character traits," are not purely about a preferred drawing style,[45] "in a world where a character's emotional life is key, their nature is made manifest in their appearance."[46] In *shonen* manga, male characters are often represented as confident and arrogant, although they can also be emotionally damaged.[47] Their spiky hair, thick eyebrows, wide eyes and easy smile marks them as heroes in *shonen* manga.[48] In *shōjo* manga, female characters are often depicted as caricatures of femininity, drawn in garish and hypersexualized ways, as popularized in such works as Naoko Takeuchi's *Sailor Moon* or Miyagi Riko's *Love Monster*. Some of the book covers in these series depict blond-haired, wide-eyed, white-skinned adolescent Japanese girls in tight-fitting and revealing clothing. These tropes, described by Emily Jane Wakeling as a complex negation of hegemonic gender stereotypes, in her opinion contribute to new discursive engagements in feminist art.[49] Acknowledging that *shōjo* is either dismissed or heavily probed in contemporary Japanese society as immature and unedifying productions, Wakeling also confirms that it is "only in the closed world of *shōjo* culture that girls negate these wide-held stereotypes."[50] Thus, based on feminist discourse that aims to contextualize *shōjo* manga as a subversive response to the moralistic views of traditional Japanese society, as I have already pointed out, Kabi Nagata's manga memoir at once complicates, and illuminates, important critical debates that must be more deeply explored.

Rather than adhering to the visual tropes of mainstream *shōjo* manga, Nagata's unflinching focus on depression in a society with at best ambivalent attitudes toward mental illness has turned her into a minor celebrity. Manga enthusiasts such as Nana Iro recognize Nagata's courage in "outing" mental illness in such a direct and unapologetic way. She notes that in spite of the "western sphere's uphill struggle with validating mental health issues, contemporary Japanese society continues to eschew the notion, perceiving mental ministrations as something to be kept shut tightly behind closed doors and contained deep within the confines of the individual's mind."[51] Nagata's resistance to romanticizing mental illness as a way to diminish its threat (or, rather, her threat) to the social order does not mean she underestimates its power. In fact, her personal account of loneliness underscores a wider psychological malaise, referred to in Japanese youth culture as *hikikomori*.[52] But rather than completely succumbing to the extreme social isolation that is *hikikomori* or taking her own life, as so many young people do when faced with the unrealistic expectation of perfect achievement in virtually every aspect of their lives, the narrator has an epiphany. She renews her interest in manga, and by putting her story out to the world, she de-stigmatizes the very conditions that in Western culture attach to a spectrum of "Othering" that persistently equates race/ethnicity/difference with psychopathology.

Addressing my central interest in the hermeneutics of loneliness in Nagata's book, particularly in relation to an array of other symptoms that might be suggestive of deeper psychological issues for the narrator, what must also be considered is the short distance between mental illness and stigma, and the chilling effect this can have on seeking help.

The way mental illness is perceived by certain cultures can often have a direct impact on how individuals eventually come to see themselves. Citing studies on the connection between mental illness and self-esteem, Patrick Corrigan notes that people living in cultures that are "steeped in stigmatizing images, persons with mental illness may accept these notions and suffer diminished self-esteem, self-efficacy, and confidence in one's future."[53] In a study where schizophrenia was the primary focus, researchers compared social attitudes about mental illness in Australia to those in Japan. They found that Japanese respondents "were more likely to attribute personality of a person, such as nervousness or weakness, as the causes of schizophrenia and depression compared with Australians."[54] The narrator's own attitude is reflective of larger societal opinions that blame mental illness on weakness of character rather than on biological determinants. "When other people couldn't see that I was trying, it felt like no matter how hard I tried, it wouldn't really be trying at all."[55] This self-negating thinking effectively isolates the narrator even more, and in turn contributes to a worsening of her depressive symptoms. She is hesitant to reach out to friends because she believes they will hate her if she bothers them with her problems, and because she wants to avoid the complications that might arise if she turns to extended family for support, she decides not to consider them as a possible resource. In effect, she has talked herself out of the very intervention and support she needs.[56]

A Not So Private Report

Sabishisugite Rezu Fūzoku Ikimashita Repo, or the work that would eventually come together as *My Lesbian Experience with Loneliness*, started out on the Japanese art board *Pixiv*.[57] The Japanese language version of the book was published in 2016 as a single print volume, with Seven Seas Entertainment republishing it a year later in English. Seven Seas acquired the rights to publish *My Solo Exchange Diary Volume 1*, Nagata's much-anticipated sequel. It continues the story of Nagata's struggle with mental illness, as well as her increasingly difficult relationship with her parents.

The relatively inoffensive, pink-washed two-tone pages of *My Lesbian Experience with Loneliness* stand in stark contrast to the explicit despair communicated to the reader through the rich and disturbing symbolism in Nagata's drawings. Forming a deeply personal account of the narrator's struggles with depression, *My Lesbian Experience with Loneliness* is a narrative limned with a type of emotional despondency that perfectly matches the exaggerated stylistic iconography and dramatic storylines of Japanese manga. Several of the elements that make manga distinctive from Western comics—how a character dresses, the style of their hair, their smile, the fullness or thinness of their lips, the jewelry they wear—is all part of character design that forms individual personalities.

In Nagata's book, the narrator's very plain clothing, as well as her general lack of adornment—which is the very antithesis of the various manga styles—amplifies the internal violence of her psychic breakdown. Her exaggerated facial expressions and body language add to a disconcerting landscape awash in the images and symbols of her emotional unraveling. Nagata uses many of the visual symbols that are the stock in trade of manga artists: drops of sweat which represent nervousness; copious tears to express intense distress; popping veins appearing either on the forehead or the hands to signal increasing irritation or anger; and a great deal of blushing to imply embarrassment.[58]

And while her lesbianism is almost incidental to her psychic distress, as a twenty-eight-year-old virgin who has never been kissed, never held meaningful long-term employment, has an eating disorder, and is so desperate for physical touch that she turns to a lesbian escort agency for companionship, her sexual orientation still plays an important part in how she eventually comes to see herself through a wider emotional spectrum. Thankfully, for those who may also be in psychic distress and in need of support, Nagata's *Sabishisugite Rezu Fūzoku Ikimashita Repo* turns out to be not so private after all. Not unlike Jaime Cortez's graphic rendering of the AIDS crisis and transgender identity in *Sexile*, using images to discuss difficult topics can be liberating and removes some of the stigma.

The Beginning

Nagata begins her story with an admission that at the age of twenty-eight she has never dated anyone, held a real job, or had sex.[59] The narrative does not actually start at the beginning but instead at the end, with an image of the narrator's naked and semi-reclining body on a diagonally drawn candy-striped bedcover. We learn fairly quickly that she is in a Japanese Love Hotel, an establishment where rooms can be rented on an hourly basis, although unlike the ubiquitous run-down and unhygienic by-the-hour motels in America, some Love Hotels are "just as luxurious as a five-star hotel room, yet they cost a fraction of the price for an overnight stay[...]."[60] Single people and married couples living in multigenerational households in Japan lack privacy. This in turn contributes to the popularity of the Love Hotel industry.

According to a report published in 2017 by the National Institute of Population and Social Security Research, more than 40 percent of men and women ranging in age from 18 to 34 have never had sex.[61] While the research around this particular report only accounted for heterosexual sex, it nevertheless points to long-term virginity as concerning, but not necessarily out of the ordinary in Japan. But coupled with depression, low self-esteem, self-harming, lack of motivation, and virtually no social life, virginity and loneliness make Nagata's story immediately relatable to the unflatteringly named "freeters" and "parasite singles" who often remain in the family home well into their thirties and forties.[62] And therein lies the crux of the narrator's problems. She is directionless, has moved back home with her parents, is unable to hold down long-term employment, and is helpless to stop herself from spiraling out of control.

In the very first image in *My Lesbian Experience with Loneliness*, the foreground takes up much of the frame. There is a side view of a naked woman whose gaze is directed squarely on the narrator's frozen and somewhat alarmed face. The narrator's body is leached of all color; it is, in fact, bone white. Whether or not this is an intentional signifier of the "culturally odorless" style of Japanese manga or a deeper psychological reflex signifying the narrator's overall inability to recognize or engage normally with social cues, we do learn from the narrator that "when it comes to anything sexual," she is "about as experienced as a newborn … or something like that."[63] The caption informs the reader that it is the middle of the day in June 2015 and that the woman whose face is turned away from the reader is a lesbian escort.[64]

If we return for a moment to Dela Cruz's matrix, it is clear that the narrator's "Expressive Anatomy" communicates distress, bewilderment, anxiety, shyness, and perhaps even an element of fear. This is the intersubjective state through which the narrator lets the lesbian escort know (mostly through non-verbal cues) that she is a sexual novice. While the relationship between the narrator and the lesbian escort is not one of emotional equivalence, and is not based on a classically defined therapeutic relationship, it can be said to be most closely predicated upon the notion of interpersonal intersubjectivity. In the constitution of the subject, interpersonal intersubjectivity considers that

> *gestures* directed towards others—partial acts that the others must receive and to which they must respond (the *gesture* being an incomplete action that others complete and whose meaning is only constructed and defined in the interaction itself)—are at the basis of what comes to be constituted as shared meaning, as mind (consciousness) and as self.[65]

A similar line of thinking posited by Phil Schulte argues that who we think we are as conscious beings will change, based on the context within which we operate. The meaning of our actions, he suggests, "is only to be found within these contexts," as the very idea of ourselves as "discrete, delineated individuals, each living out the private meanings of our lives, begins to look chimerical."[66] He goes on to say that "we are all sway to a shift of context pulling us into quite different ways of being."[67] In many ways, Schulte's description mirrors my own theorizing in this book on how misdirection acts as a signifying strategy defined by the contexts through which it seeks to effect perceptual shifts. The journey the narrator takes to arrive emotionally, psychically, and indeed physically at a place where she is so desperate for human contact that she hires a lesbian escort is shaped by multiple and ever-changing contexts.

"Help" Wanted

After graduating from high school, attending university for just six months before dropping out, and taking up brief stints in low-paying, soul-destroying jobs, the narrator rapidly descends into depression. "Knowing I didn't belong anywhere, that I had nowhere to go every day, made me extremely anxious," the narrator admits.[68] Feeling unmoored, as if the self she once knew had faded away into nothingness, she takes up a part-time job hoping that an emotional connection with her co-workers might restore her to a state of happiness.[69] Unfortunately, her wishful thinking proves to be no match for her depression, and she is once again caught up in the endless loop of negative thinking that pushes her ever closer to the invisibility she is so desperate to escape. In what could be an intentionally ambiguous play on words, the narrator is seen on the telephone, uttering a stock phrase recited by innumerable people around the globe: "Hello? I saw your help wanted ad…"[70] Here, the word "help" at once signifies psychological distress, a cry for attention and safety. But it also communicates the narrator's desire to be part of a workplace environment that would offer her a ready-made, substitute family.[71]

By now it is clear that the narrator's understanding of herself in relation to others (the interpersonal intersubjective) is that her self-worth is inextricably bound up in an ability to earn an income and become self-sufficient. But as she soon discovers, the thrill of eventually finding a job is quickly offset by her untreated depression. She starts calling in sick to work and rapidly cycles back into a state of unrelenting despair, recognizing that the unconditional acceptance she so desperately craves would have to come from within herself rather than from strangers.[72] Her repeated descent into a deeper state of depression is largely facilitated by negative self-talk: "I didn't think I deserved to eat"; "If I bought cake I'd definitely pay for it"; "I didn't deserve to drink alcohol."[73] Yet far from being atypical, the narrator's problems reflect similar features of comorbidity among the wider population of adolescents and young adults. Her depression is comorbid with her cutting, but with her additional issues of binge eating and starvation, it is likely she would fall under a classification of multimorbidity.[74]

The narrator's nonsuicidal self-injuries (NSSI), while common among both male and female adolescents, have been found in clinical studies to have a higher prevalence among girls.[75] The narrator self-harms to achieve release from her psychic pain, and not unlike the release experienced from using drugs, self-harming often results in feelings of calm and a sense of being in control. For our narrator, who is shown in a panel with both of her forearms bandaged, self-cutting is a means to a very specific end: being noticed and rescued. Having once read about a girl who hurt herself, the narrator vividly recalls the words as if they were meant just for her. "'I don't really understand the pain in my heart. It doesn't have any real form. But it's easy to understand the pain when it's my body that's being hurt. It calms me down.'"[76] After reading this, the narrator thinks to herself: "…I totally got it."[77] In their review of the literature on Deliberate Self-Harm (to include its analgesic effects), Donald E. Greydanus and Daniel Shek write:

> Self-cutting may occur in attempts to relieve "a terrible state of mind" in those engaged in such behavior. The self-cutting behavior, though confusing to others, often serves as a way of releasing intense and unbearable pain from suppressed negative feelings driven by underlying depression and anxiety from conflicts with family and/or peers.[78]

Thus, what the narrator understands about herself, what she in fact "got" from what she had read, was a way to put into words the invisible pain of her heartache and loneliness. Furthermore, through the action of self-cutting, she demonstrates that she alone holds the power to release her pain. This is evident in figure 31. The narrator's right arm is extended away from her body and is crisscrossed with scars. She is holding a knife and making new cuts. The center of her chest is a rough-edged black hole that looks as if it were seared into her chest. It is meant to represent the unbearable pain weighing on her heart. The thoughts she has drawn flowing from her brain to the knife in her hand and back through a repeating circuit of self-harm read: "You can see it; the cause is very clear. Creating and seeing the dummy pain calms you down. You feel better right away."[79] Here the narrator's particular kind of subjectivity links back to the interpersonal intersubjective. In her desire to escape the psychic turmoil that threatens to destroy her, she uses self-harming as a *gesture*, as a way to connect to others who might complete her. Her self-representation is of a wounded and out-of-control human being.

Mead, having extended Wilhelm Wundt's work on the relation of language to gesture, notes that whichever classes these gestures come under, they are "already significant in the sense that they are stimuli to performed reactions,

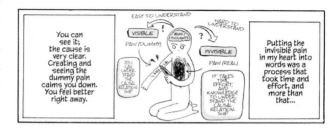

Figure 31. Illustration from p. 13, *My Lesbian Experience with Loneliness* (copyright © 2016 by Kabi Nagata. Reprinted by permission of Seven Seas Entertainment Press) (see C•8 for larger image).

before they come to have significance of conscious meaning."[80] I come back to this shortly, as it is relevant to the narrator's return to the family home and her disappointment in the failure of her parents (and, by extension, society) to recognize cues that point to the pain and longing she is unable to adequately express in words alone. This is in no way an act of intentional misdirection or subterfuge on her part, but rather a plea for help directly expressed through the messages she has literally inscribed upon her body. Her depression is so acute that she is completely immobilized by the sheer weight of it. Surrounded by thought bubbles that speak to her internal panic and unresolved issues with food, anxiety, and depression, the narrator wonders: "What's the best way to just die?"[81]

In one of the more visually disturbing frames, the narrator is in bed with the covers pulled up to her chin. Her eyes are open wide and the typical morphemes are present: the cruciform symbol appears on the knuckles of her left hand to represent popping veins, her face is flushed red, and the jagged edges of her frustration is captured in an oversized expletive, much like all capitalizations in emails denote shouting. Collectively, the three panels on this page point to an agonizing indecisiveness. The first contains the oversized letters and the narrator's wired and wide-eyed expression with the captions: "GODDAMMIT!!" "GRAR!" "IF THIS IS HOW IT IS, I'VE GOT NOTHING TO LOSE!" "I'LL CLAW MY WAY OUT OF BED WITH MY LAST DYING BREATH!"[82] The second panel shows the narrator with her eyes closed, tears on her face, her image receding and being gradually swallowed up in a black cloud. The third panel opens up a visual doorway into the narrator's internal turmoil. She is shown as a small figure being pressed from all sides by verbal rebukes contained within jagged-shaped text bubbles. These types of text bubbles indicate that the character is upset, which is borne out by internal dialogue related to the narrator's binge eating and depression. It is her belief that death would be a far easier solution than grappling with seemingly unresolvable issues.[83]

Nagata uses a variety of narrative techniques to construct interiority. While manga is a traditionally expressive and exaggerated form of sequential art that pulls readers into a visually and textually rich world, it is largely the private and unregulated thoughts of the narrator that draws us almost unwillingly into her agitated emotional states. The narrator's astute self-assessments regarding her loneliness and depression positions her as both witness to her own unraveling and also as the voice of reason anchoring her to familiar points of reference. Moreover, it is likely within the gift of "restorative hermeneutics"[84] that the narrator might draw upon her sporadic moments of lucidness to tackle the uncertainties that keep her perpetually in crisis.

O'Dwyer, following the Ricoeurian line of thought on the self, warns against falling prey to a limited vision of human possibilities and frailties.

> Narrowness of vision can centre on one side of the polarities which Ricoeur sees as framing human existence; polarities of freedom and finitude, of responsibility and fallibility, of good and evil, and of self and other [...] the closed "circle" results in a diminishment of perception, a narrowing of vision, and a closing off of possibility and understanding.[85]

The narrator has enclosed herself in an endless loop of self-diminishment arising from her anxiety and depression. She is unable to see beyond the edges of her illness long enough to sustain a sense of wellness and potential. Instead, her illness has framed her existence, putting her at risk of being seduced by lack, rather than buoyed by possibility. Thus for the narrator, the intersection between solitude and connection has become unnavigable.

An example of her inability to regulate her emotions, to negotiate the tensions that are part and parcel of the human experience, is when she describes the irresistible urge to binge after long periods of starvation. So strong is her compulsion that she consumes raw ramen noodles right out of the pack because she cannot take the time to cook them. Given that raw noodles are quite crunchy and hard, eating them uncooked results in flecks of blood appearing on the jagged remains the narrator is shown holding in her hands at figure 32.

There is rich symbolism in the narrator's gesture. Although very likely unintentional on Nagata's part, the irony of the narrator holding up the compressed square of raw noodles cannot be missed. Read through a Western lens, the gesture is almost a mirror image of the thin unleavened wafer held aloft by priests during the Eucharist, while the flecks of blood on the jagged edges of the noodles could be said to represent the blood of Christ. When worshippers accept the wafer (which symbolizes the body of Christ) they are looking for absolution, relief from their transgressions, forgiveness. Can it not also be said that through the consumption of food, the narrator is also seeking a form of absolution? "[...] I had no choice in the matter. A desire to

Figure 32. Illustration from p. 15, *My Lesbian Experience with Loneliness* (copyright © 2016 by Kabi Nagata. Reprinted by permission of Seven Seas Entertainment Press) (see C•8 for larger image).

eat would suddenly take over my brain, so powerful that it almost drove me mad. I could do nothing in that state of binge eating, which was a serious problem."[86] Although the narrator is somewhat at a remove from her self-destructive actions, part of her also recognizes that she needs help. "Is that," she queries herself as she looks at the blood-flecked noodles in her hands, "how much I wanted to eat?"[87] Perhaps it is a stretch to equate the Western idea of transubstantiation to the ramblings of a depressed and anxiety-ridden binge eater, for the narrator's condition is not a celebration of rebirth, but rather recognition of a self-destructive impulse far beyond her ability to control. Nevertheless, the extremes that are represented here are crucial to an understanding of the emotional devastation people with depression experience.

I want to stay for a moment with the notion of one thing signifying another (the bread and wine representing the body and blood of Christ) and the narrator's external manifestations of her pain (the ramen noodles and *her* blood) representing her internal struggle for renewal and healing so we can better understand how she sees herself—"It's like I have a cup full of water on my head and if I spill even a drop, I'll be out"[88]—and how others see her—"Hmm. There's no cup, you know."[89] The narrator's perceptions of herself diverge from the reality reflected back to her by her parents and others. There is nothing, as her mother innocently points out to her, *on* her head. But there is, the reader knows, definitely something *in* her head.

No "Straight" Path to Acceptance

The crux of the narrator's problems appears to be a yearning for unconditional love and acceptance from her parents. This has colored many of her interactions with people outside of her family system, ultimately setting her on a path to self-destruction. There are no traumatic childhood experiences that she identifies as triggering her depression and anxiety. She does not report ever having become separated from her parents in the street or in shopping malls; there is no physical chastisement that may have damaged her trust in adults; there is no hint of mental illness that could have been passed along to her from her parents or other relatives; and there is no indication of being witness to violence within or outside of the family home. Nevertheless, I want to return to Mead's interpretation of Wundt's theorizing on the relation of language to gesture, as it is useful in helping to unpack several scenes Nagata almost casually draws our attention to, where the issue of attachment (or lack thereof) at the pre-verbal stage might explain the narrator's feelings of helplessness as an adult.

Mead gives the example of a parent-child dynamic whereby the child cries (he calls this the "stimulating cry") and the parent (who is expected to respond to this stimulus by paying attention to the child in order to understand and resolve the reasons for the crying) provides the "answering tone" which results in a "consequent change in the cry of the infant-form."[90] In other words one action triggers another, thereby causing a further action that resolves the original stimuli. We have, Mead explains, an "interplay going on with the gestures serving their functions, calling out the responses of the others [and] these responses becoming themselves stimuli for readjustment, until the final social act itself can be carried out."[91] In our narrator's case, the final act at the pre-verbal stage may never have been played out, or it may have been so inconsistently applied that the source of her anxiety as an adult is on a continual loop of incompletion. Thus the language of loneliness that vexes her could have been imprinted from infancy.

In reflecting back on how she had arrived at such a lonely and miserable place, the narrator takes us through the high (and low) points of her life; from intentionally starving herself to binge eating to physically collapsing in the hallway of her house. Believing that she is completely out of options, she eventually moves back in with her parents. However, her emotions continue to go from one extreme (listlessness) to the other (hyperactivity). Her symptoms seem to mimic bipolar disorder, which can be comorbid with self-cutting, binge eating, substance abuse, and sexual promiscuity. Recent research suggests that bipolar disorder is "highly heritable, with genetic influences explaining 60–85% of risk."[92] Moreover, a "large number of family studies have consistently documented that BPD aggregates in families."[93] Although never named as such, the narrator's bursts of energy and renewed commitment to getting better alternate with her feelings of sadness, low energy, hopelessness, and suicide ideation, thus making a diagnosis of bipolar disorder possible. However, whether or not the narrator suffers from Cyclothymic disorder or Bipolar disorder I or II is neither here nor there for purposes of this chapter. My intention is simply to underscore the usefulness of manga (and, by extension, JVL) to heighten the sense of despair and loneliness communicated to the reader through the narrator's story. This intense engagement with the narrator's illness works well later on, when her first encounter with a lesbian escort (which is an extended scene from the opening pages of the book) partially resolves her need for emotional intimacy.

Unable to adequately explain her return to the family home, other than to repeat a doctor's advice that she takes some time off, her parents are mystified by their daughter's situation. However, as we quickly come to find out, for the narrator, her parents' opinion "was everything."[94] Indeed, she recalls

that their approval was her "sole driving force,"[95] and without it she was rud-
derless, unable to form healthy adult relationships or come to see herself as
worthwhile. Once settled back into the family home, the narrator renews her
efforts to stave off the inevitable disappointment of her parents. She self-
talks herself out of bed, goes on long walks, and once again starts looking for
employment.

Back living with her parents, the narrator realizes that she must put
more effort into having a normal life. She eventually finds a part-time job in
a bakery where she begins to feel a sense of accomplishment. Hoping that
her parents will see her efforts as worthy of their love and attention, she offers
to contribute to the household bills but is discouraged from doing so because
her father does not believe her part-time job rises to the level of a legitimate
"salaried" position. Rather than working through her issues and constructing
her own self-affirming narrative, she gives in to the expectations of her parents
by going on endless job interviews for full-time positions. Rejected by one
employer after another, she eventually comes across one who thinks to ask
her what it is she really wants to do. Another asks her the very same question,
which in turn becomes her "light-bulb" moment. She realizes that what she
wants most is to renew her interest in manga, a field where she had previously
met with moderate success. Thus, with the last employer's encouragement
replaying over and over again in her mind, she embarks on a journey that
brings remarkable but, sadly, only temporary changes.

Delving into the fantasy world of manga proves to be quite therapeutic
for Kabi Nagata. In an interview about the experience of creating *My Lesbian
Experience with Loneliness* and the ideas that shaped her work, Nagata's
response—"I can even see bad things as happier things when drawing"[96]—is
clearly reflected in a panel she draws where her old insecure and needy self
is shown on the floor, red-faced and bawling, clinging desperately to the
shirttails of her emerging, more emotionally determined self. The image also
represents the struggle between self-acceptance—"It was the discomfort of
accepting myself while other people didn't"—and worrying about the expectations of others—"But it was definitely better than what I'd had before."[97]
Finding herself with a level of motivation she had only ever before been able
to sustain for brief periods of time, Nagata's character continues working at
part-time jobs while submitting her stories to various manga contests. She
avoids social contact, quits her part-time job, and quickly descends back into
a depressive state.

This up and down cycle repeats itself over and over again, based in large
part on how the narrator perceives herself and how she wishes to be perceived
by others. As her condition worsens—"it was like everything in my head had

fallen out and I couldn't read text"[98]—she returns to see a doctor and is prescribed medication that evens out her moods. She notices that the first thing to improve is her ability to read and understand text, which in turn makes her determined to identify the source of her pain so that she can address it. In due course she comes across a book on mental illness in pubescent children (even though by this time she is twenty-eight). She recognizes some of her symptomology in the examples she reads, especially in descriptions of clinginess in childhood (hers continued well into sixth grade); physical contact with a parent that triggers sexual arousal (although she attributes her curiosity about her mother's body—her breasts in particular—to the infant stage of development).[99]

What the narrator finally manages to work out is that she wants comfort from a woman but because her longing is also sexual, she would prefer that it come from someone who is not her mother. This amorphous idea that the narrator has of comfort is represented in a drawing of a gigantic soft cushion that she literally falls into to experience an unconditional, enveloping acceptance. Does this mean, she is shown asking herself, "that I was looking for the relationship I had with my mother as a baby?"[100] The image that is positioned next to the caption shows an infant swaddled in a pink blanket, with tiny hearts forming a floating semi-circle around her and the woman (her mother) who is gently cradling her.

Therapeutic Sex in a Love Hotel

Wanting to be seen and affirmed, the narrator initially concludes that her loneliness will abate if she gets massage therapy or if she can find someone on Twitter who might be offering "free hugs."[101] Making explicit that the person's gender is not a factor, the narrator is nevertheless quite clear that sexual intimacy would have to be with a woman, even though she resists being identified as one gender or another. To paraphrase the oft-quoted words of Virginia Woolf, it seems that for the narrator, only women are able to stir her imagination.[102]

Ironically, the skepticism regarding Woolf's sexual attraction to women, that Patricia Morgne Cramer points out is leveled against the writer by contemporary queer scholars, mirrors the ruminations of Nagata's narrator in relation to her obsession for parental approval. Cramer makes note of two claims, one by Mitchel Leaska and the other by Karyn Z. Sproles. Both opined that Woolf's attraction to women (specifically to Vita Sackville-West), while clearly bound up in sexual desire, also spoke to the basic instinct of children to seek "comfort, unconditional love, attention, and security" from a parent.[103] Leaska, Cramer notes, "insists that Virginia's passion for Vita was rooted in an unresolved infantile longing for maternal nurturance."[104] Cramer rightly calls these critiques outdated, particularly because in her view they seem to be based in "Freudian and sexologist stereotypes of lesbian and gay men."[105] The relationship of these critiques to Nagata's own infantilization of her character underscores the fact that the narrator's lesbianism seems to be appended to the story rather than (as the book's title alludes to) being the story itself. This resistance to being defined as one way or another, while similar to the ideological stance taken up by queers in many parts of the world, what sets the performance of non-binary sexual identity in manga apart from what we are accustomed to seeing in Western contexts, is explained by Chris Kincaid as one of cultural differences. Whereas Americans, Kincaid argues, see links between sexuality and identity, he points out that the Japanese do not perceive it in the same way. He goes on to give an example whereby in "traditional Japanese culture men could have homosexual interests," but "this didn't override their duty to have a wife and raise a family."[106] These cultural differences are also seen in manga and anime, where sexual expression or ideas are a "small part of a character's identity."[107]

The central thrust of *My Lesbian Experience with Loneliness* is the narrator's desire to win unconditional approval from her parents, although most notably this is bound up in an even deeper desire to revisit the physical and emotional comfort she derived as a child from her mother. This sets up a confused merging of the narrator's psychological distress and her fear, as she states, being "excessively afraid of being defined as a woman."[108] She follows up this provocative statement with a surprising level of insight when she explains that her fear of being defined as a woman has nothing to do with any desire to be a man, but is instead based on her wish to first be seen as herself.[109] This calls attention to an important shift toward the narrator's growing self-acceptance and a sexual identity long overshadowed by her mistaken belief that her very existence is contingent upon approval from her parents. Her claim to a non-binary, gender-questioning stance comes quite late in the book, once again underscoring the primacy of the narrator's mental illness, which is vividly expressed throughout via the (visual) lens of a hermeneutical phenomenology.

The truths that unfold at the Love Hotel introduce an important paradigm shift in Nagata's story, one that reframes her life in terms of her sexual awakening and the support she needs in exploring it, rather than as a problem that is solely attributable to her mental illness. While in some ways it might be a stretch to compare Nagata's experience of engaging in sex with a lesbian escort in a Love Hotel to the sex surrogate role played, for instance, by Helen Hunt in the 2012 film *The Sessions*, there are interesting similarities. Polio has left Mark O'Brien (played quite convincingly by John Hawkes) paralyzed from the neck down and bedridden. Helen Hunt (as the real-life Cheryl Cohen-Greene) is hired as the sex surrogate who helps O'Brien lose his virginity.

Nagata's character experiences both a psychic and social "paralysis," leaving her unable to form healthy attachments. She has never had a romantic relationship or long-term friendships, yet her fear of losing herself forever to depression and loneliness, of taking the permanent way out of her pain through suicide, slowly loses its hold. It is her reintroduction to drawing manga and journal writing that gives her a purpose and proves to be the catalyst she needs to break through emotional barriers that have kept her from living a full life.[110] She recognizes that she must first learn to understand her own feelings before she can achieve any meaningful level of wellness, so it is through a combination of gathering real-life experiences that would give her "more things to write about,"[111] and using these experiences to determine how best to stay ahead of her cycles of depression, that her breakthrough comes.

"A bridge had sprung up over the course of the night, connecting me to a continent I'd thought was unreachable. It was easier to breathe."[112] The metaphor invoked here is particularly apt. Where mental illness, sexuality, and gender intersect to construct barriers to living a full life, the narrator intuits a different kind of landscape rich in possibilities for psychic healing and sexual pleasure. Here Nagata sets up a productive dialogue between the visual and textual elements of sequential art. Her narrator decides to literally write (and fuck) her way out of illness by using manga to excavate the sharp, glittery pieces of self-doubt swirling in the untended recesses of her mind. By hiring a lesbian escort, she accomplishes a feat she previously thought was beyond her psychological and social abilities. Having come to identify/represent herself solely in terms of her illness, tending to her sexual needs was fraught with an extremely high level of anxiety, outweighed only by a more pressing need to be held and even loved.

Within the traditional field of sex therapy, surrogates are trained to interact with patients who have a wide variety of physical disabilities and/or mental health issues. This is also the case in queer sex work where, just like their more traditional counterparts, queer sex work happens "within a suspended reality where the relationship is restricted to a specific context."[113] Explicit within this context is an understanding on both sides that boundaries must be adhered to and roles clearly defined.[114] Once the narrator worked up the courage to contact the lesbian escort agency, she set about making herself presentable for her first sexual encounter with a woman.

"For the first time in years, I removed the hair on my arms, legs, and armpits. I cleaned up my pubic hair, too."[115] The narrator reflects on this, recalling that she used to be fine tending to her ablutions once every five days but since gaining a new lease on life, she even changes her underwear and clothing every day.[116]

Realizing that taking care of herself emotionally and physically opens her up to possibilities she had never before considered, the narrator is shown surrounded in a semi-circle of tiny bubbles, standing proudly atop giant lettering that spells out "STABILITY."[117] In the next frame her face, with a stunned expression plastered on, is shown in close-up against a splat of pink goo bracketed by two captions that read: "My longing for the sexual contact I'd denied up until then ... it **exploded**, finally freed."[118] Having sublimated her sexual desire onto her obsession for parental approval, the narrator realizes that by directing the same level of energy into her own needs and using her skills in drawing manga, she is able to achieve a more optimistic point of view for longer periods of time.[119] Her last area of resistance in fully accepting herself (and by extension being accepted by the lesbian escort) is the bald spot on her head that she can do nothing about. Her obsession over her patch of baldness threatens to turn into a full-blown emotional meltdown, but she has learned how to manage her anxiety through self-talk. "Don't think about anything! Be empty!"[120] With this gentle self-admonishment she finally manages to make an appointment for her first encounter with a lesbian escort, thinking with relief, and certainly a great deal of naïveté, that she is "going to be saved."[121]

The narrator has convinced herself that being saved by a lesbian escort, whose relationship to clients is often a business transaction and occasionally therapeutic, will solve her problems and put her firmly on the road to recovery. "I'm so ready for someone to comfort me. To melt away my years of loneliness. I want her to hold me, and not just for a few seconds."[122] By placing unrealistic expectations on her encounter with the lesbian escort, the narrator is transferring her past unresolved issues for attention from her parents onto another presumably nurturing figure. The escort's role is to maintain a professional distance and manage the client's sexual expectations, while at the same time being careful not to alienate her.

Riding the edges of her various obsessions, from worrying about what her parents might think if they knew what she was planning, to convincing herself to make the booking with the escort, the narrator reassures herself that the agency must "surely [have had] clients with mental health issues [...]," going on to surmise that a "little bald spot wouldn't bother them."[123] This discursive tactic of having the narrator focus obsessively on a single flaw, when in fact she has failed to adequately resolve the multitude of issues that have beset her from an early age, effectively misdirects the reader, inviting a level of collusion with the narrator in thinking that were it not for her last remaining obsession, her sexual awakening could be just the "treatment" she needs to put her on the path to a better version of herself. Yet the narrator is reminded that no matter how much she attempts to shed her old self for a new version, the thing that lives inside her is never far away from emerging. She imagines this internal version of herself as a dark and looming apparition waiting for her return to her hellish existence.

The apparition representing the part of her mind that is unwell literally steps out of her skin by unzipping it as one might by emerging from the back end of a Panto Horse costume. The pantomime horse show with its prancing and crowd-pleasing antics comes to an abrupt halt the moment the people inside the costume step outside of it. But during the performance, it falls to the person representing the head of the horse to use their eyes so that those bringing up the rear can get through the routine in one piece, as it were. Here, the "costume" being shed by the apparition is the narrator, who is shown slumped over from the waist with her arms and head dangling lifelessly in the casual grip of her subconscious self. The message here suggests that her illness can reappear at any time, reanimating her in the way that a puppeteer or ventriloquist brings an inanimate prop to life.

The apparition reappears several more times in the lead up to the narrator's meeting with the lesbian escort. We see it on the periphery of, and often central to, the frame when the narrator is feeling exposed and vulnerable in relation to her sexual awakening, which is tangled up in her obsession to be valued by her parents. Its first appearance is when it is lying in a passive, resting position, next to the narrator. Its placement here represents an important breakthrough for the narrator. Representing her subconscious, the apparition reminds her of the futility of her efforts to escape an illness that has shaped her very existence. But recognizing exactly what her shadow self is trying to do, she thinks: "In the pursuit of comfort, some people end up

Figure 33. Illustration from p. 75, *My Lesbian Experience with Loneliness* (copyright © 2016 by Kabi Nagata. Reprinted by permission of Seven Seas Entertainment Press) (see C•8 for larger image).

hurting themselves mentally and physically, like clinging to bad sexual relationships."[124] The narrator's clarity of thought here, even when her anxiety
threatens to trigger another emotional meltdown, suggests that she is becoming more invested in discovering what triggers her descent into despair and
how she might manage it. On her way to meet with the lesbian escort, she is
shown on the station platform, waiting for her train to arrive. A thought
comes to her mind unbidden, that in that very moment, alone and not knowing what to expect from her first sexual encounter, she wishes she had a
friend. When she disembarks from the train, early for her meeting at a pre-
arranged location, the lesbian escort happens to see her and queries if she is
Nagata-San, which is the honorific commonly used between the Japanese as
a sign of respect, although the honorific changes depending upon age, social
ranking, kinship, and so on.

Ironically, when the narrator and the lesbian escort set off together for
the Love Hotel, the narrator is so disarmed by the escort's open and upbeat
manner that she feels relieved and excited about the possibility of their
encounter actually turning out to be a positive experience. Nagata shows the
two of them walking down the street, side by side, as if they are just two
friends out for the day. Both have smiles lighting up their faces, and the narrator thinks the escort appears "all friendly and smiling, so it [isn't] weird.
What a relief!"[125] She goes on thinking to herself how easy it seems to talk to
the escort and is emboldened enough to believe that she might actually be
able to manage a few words herself.[126] They eventually decide on a hotel and
choose a room with simple décor and a nearly all-white color scheme.

The narrator is unaccustomed to sharing intimate details with strangers,
yet when the escort casually questions her about any previous sexual experience she has had with men or women, she admits she has never dated anyone or had intimate encounters. Understanding the delicacy of the situation,
the lesbian escort deftly turns around a potentially awkward moment by
telling the narrator what an honor it will be to usher her through her first
sexual experience. From a therapeutic perspective the escort demonstrates a
high level of competence in quickly understanding the situation, while at the
same time encouraging the narrator to ask for what she wants. "Even if I did
have things I wanted her to do," the narrator thinks, "I could never say that!"[127]
The scene quickly shifts and the reader is left to wonder what it is the narrator
cannot bring herself to say. As the escort invites the narrator to join her in
the bath and proceeds to wash her all over, she continues her casual questioning to get a better sense of the narrator's level of tolerance for sexual intimacy. As had been the case in other situations where the narrator felt
vulnerable yet determined to understand her motivations, the escort's ques-

tions trigger important information about herself that she had not previously considered. Admitting to being socially awkward and likely to never go out on a date, the narrator admits that meeting with an escort should be something she experiences at least once in her life. The escort praises her for her courage, reaffirming the narrator's right to ask for anything she wants, telling her: "Today is your secret pleasure."[128]

The details of the sex act between the narrator and lesbian escort are not as important here as the narrator's complete unpreparedness for, and her shock at, the level of emotion necessary to be fully present during sexual intimacy. Her literal and metaphorical nakedness with another human being increases her feelings of insecurity, causing her to feel exposed, clumsy, sexually naïve, and unable to turn off the thoughts racing through her mind. While the escort is trying to give her pleasure, it occurs to the narrator that she had skipped many important steps in relationship building. "I had jumped over a huge swath of things you're supposed to experience in human relationships," going instead directly to the "tournament finals."[129] In the next panel we see the narrator imagining herself on a bicycle, the captions on either side reading: "I'd thought that, somehow, this sex stuff would happen naturally [...] but what if it didn't?"[130] The implication is that once you ride a bicycle you never forget the mechanics of it. However, no matter what the escort does, the narrator is so consumed by anxiety that she is unable to enjoy her first sexual experience. Running out of ideas, the escort encourages the narrator, who is by this time almost completely detached from what is happening, to touch her.

"Even though I'd been sad, thinking I might die without ever touching breasts other than my mother's ... even though I wanted to touch them so much ... my body wouldn't move.... I couldn't put my arms around her ... it was so unreal—like I was watching people on the other side of a screen."[131] The narrator's session with the lesbian escort eventually ends, much to her relief. She is disappointed in herself for not being able to open up her heart and lose herself in the moment, and it is only later that she realizes that positive and fulfilling sexual intimacy is about the ability to communicate. Although her first sexual experience was not what she had anticipated, primarily because she had based her ideas about sex on *bōizu rabu* or *yaoi* manga, it motivated her to locate better resources to learn about her own body and about sex between women.[132]

In the final pages of Nagata's manga memoir, the reader is offered a more optimistic narrative, one that sees the narrator pulling together the many disparate parts of her life into a relatively coherent and satisfying whole. The narrator realizes that writing about, and also drawing characters for the work she is beginning to receive from magazines, no longer reflects her interests or the person she is becoming. It occurs to her that if she wants to read stories that offer a more complex rendering of a person's struggles and aspirations, she would need to base it on her own life. She realizes that by being honest about her own struggles with mental illness and sexual relationships, she would be creating an opportunity for those with similar secrets to engage in open and more affirming dialogue. The response to her work was immediate, positive, overwhelming, liberating, and eventually published in book form as *My Lesbian Experience with Loneliness.*

Kabi Nagata's manga memoir started an important conversation among Japanese youth about mental illness and misconceptions that can exacerbate otherwise treatable conditions. Shining a critical light on the pressures and unrealistic expectations that Japanese youth internalize, Nagata grapples with the myth that hard work and good moral character will lessen, if not completely eradicate, psychological troubles. By telling her story through the expressive anatomy of manga, she effectively draws upon the genre to give voice to the loneliness and despair that had grown to a maddening susurration in the dark recesses of her mind.

Contrary to what the title of Nagata's book implies, there are no direct links made between lesbianism and loneliness. Whether or not this is an unintentional dissonance created through the hermeneutics of manga, it places Nagata's story alongside others where the quest for a connection to something larger than us is a recurring and universal theme. What Nagata's story accomplishes is that it locates queerness on a continuum of sexual awakening that "normalizes" the angst and uncertainty people experience during their first intimate encounter. By effectively making lesbianism secondary to her battle with mental illness, rather than the cause of it, Nagata has succeeded in establishing a hermeneutics that clarifies, at least in part, her dance with the demons of loneliness.

Conclusion

It seems to me that what has been missing in queer scholarship to date is a different type of experimentation with the multimodality of comics and the polyphonic voices in literary fiction. It is why through the semiotics of misdirection I have attempted to bring into closer alignment the missing pieces of a complex discursive puzzle that turns on multiple views and approaches. Therefore, this book has been about representation and how it is expressed across multiple platforms, systems, theories and methodologies.

Having taken a critical look at the role that the hybrid structure of sequential arts plays in supporting an expressive re-articulation and re-inking of queer women of color representation in literary discourse, this book has demonstrated that the semiotics of the dispossessed, which are writ large in an all-pervasive and consuming hegemony, can openly (and also subversively) contest our historical erasure. By showing how misdirection and the signifying semiotics of comics work in tandem to open new pathways into understanding queer women of color representation, this book sets out an initial blueprint for further exploration of the structural affinities between literature and comics and how these structures communicate across boundaries to illuminate that which is relegated to the shadows.

During the time that I spent writing this book, so much has changed in the fields of graphic narratives and comics. Although queer women of color are still under-represented in graphic narratives, what is being published nowadays is far more reflective of our individual and collective experiences and lives, be this in relation to trauma, sexual orientation, identity, race or culture. Melanie Gillman's *As the Crow Flies* (2017), Tee Franklin's *Bingo Love* (2018), Elisha Lim's *100 Crushes* (2014), and of course the artists featured in this book go some way in inking queer black bodies back into the frame. But if we set aside for a moment the distinction between what constitutes a graphic narrative and what is really just a comic book, or if we count webcomics that are not in book-length form but are targeted at queer women of color, the range of titles increases exponentially.

Grace Ellis and Shea Beagle; Olivia Dinnall; Maddie Gonzalez; Micheline Hess; Taneka Stotts; Roxanne Gay; and Sarah Graley are just a handful of the amazing talent creating more representative works for, and about, queer women of color. Even our most iconic superheroes and villains (Batwoman, Apollo, the Green Lantern) have come out of the closet to shake things up and help create alternative paradigms through which complex queer identities can be brought more prominently to the fore. And while this book may seem to have taken quite a circuitous route to advocating for meaningful and generative representations of queer women of color in literary fiction and graphic narratives, when we think about representation and what this actually means, there really is no one way to express the complexities of a life. In this way the arguments raised in this book hinged on gigantic leaps of imagination. Indeed, understanding the structural relationship between literary fiction and graphic narratives required the introduction of new discursive frameworks (or perhaps simply a new way of unpacking the existing ones) to disrupt hegemony's ambivalent framing of the queer(ed) "Other." I hope this book has opened the way for a fuller exploration of misdirection, its signifying semiotics, and the contexts in which it operates.

Chapter Notes

Introduction

1. Neil Cohn, "Un-Defining 'comics': Separating the cultural from the structural in 'comics,'" *International Journal of Comic Art*, 7 (October 2005), 6.

2. Refer to Noah Berlatsky's article, "Racism and Comics: Good Intentions are Not Enough," in *The Atlantic*, December 2, 2013. See also "To Ignore is to Deny: E. W. Kemble's Racial Caricature as Popular Art," in *The Journal of Popular Culture*, 21 July 2007, by Francis Martin, Jr.

3. Refer to the July 21, 2008, issue of the *New Yorker* magazine, with cover illustration by Barry Blitt. https://www.newyorker.com/magazine/2008/07/21

4. Gary Younge, "The Serena cartoon debate: calling out racism is not 'censorship,'" *The Guardian*, 13 September 2018, https://www.theguardian.com/commentisfree/2018/sep/13/serena-williams-cartoon-racism-censorship-mark-knight-herald-sun

5. *Ibid.*

6. Sherene Razack, *Looking White People in the Eye: Gender, Race, and Culture in Courtrooms and Classrooms* (Toronto: University of Toronto Press, 2001), 18.

7. *Ibid.*

8. The idea of developing misdirection as a structural framework upon which my research on queer women of color representation turns was first discussed on October 7, 2014, at a interdisciplinary conference on "Violence in Queer and Trans Lives: A Dialogue Between the Humanities and Health Professions," held at the University of Surrey, England. I was asked to provide a synopsis of my research, which at that point was still quite fluid, which is to say that I was still in the process of figuring it out. As I struggled to find a succinct way of explaining the direction I hoped to take in my research, the idea of misdirection popped into my head as the most logical explanation of how I intended to take an interdisciplinary approach to comics, literary fiction, gender, race, sexual orientation, and culture. Misdirection at once seemed to be the unifying idea I had been searching for, but also the entry point into a deeper exploration into how the hybridity of comics might support a turn toward alternative, and more generative, expressions of "difference" in literature.

9. Ruth Ronen, *Possible Worlds in Literary Theory* (Cambridge: Cambridge University Press, 1994), 229.

10. Jafarai S. Allen, "Black/Queer/Diaspora at the Current Conjuncture," *GLQ*, 18 (2012), 215.

11. *Ibid.*

12. *Ibid.*, 212.

13. See for example Jason Fabok's work in issues 13 and 14 of Detective Comics, 2012; and Richard Ortiz's work in Wonder Woman 77 Special Number 1, for DC Comics, 2015.

14. Richard Harrison: "Seeing and Nothingness: Michael Nicoll Yahgulanaas, Haida Manga, and a Critique of the Gutter," *Canadian Review of Comparative Literature*, 43.1 (March 2016), 52.

15. *Ibid.*, 54.

16. Christopher Green, "Fluid Frames: The Hybrid Art of Michael Nicoll Yahgulanaas," *Art in America*, November 2, 2017, https://www.artinamericamagazine.com/news-features/news/fluid-frames-the-hybrid-art-of-michael-nicoll-yahgulanaas/

17. Paola Bacchetta, Fatima El-Tayeb, and Jin Haritaworn, "Queer of colour formations and translocal spaces in Europe," *Environment and Planning D: Society and Space*, 33.5 (2015), 771.

18. *Ibid.*

19. Will Eisner, *Comics & Sequential Art: Principles and Practices from the Legendary Cartoonist* (London: W.W. Norton, 2008), xi.

20. *Ibid.*, 8.

21. Scott McCloud, *Understanding Comics:*

The Invisible Art (New York: HarperCollins, 1993), 9.

22. Stephen Weiner, *Faster Than a Speeding Bullet: The Rise of the Graphic Novel* (New York: Nantier, Beall, Minoustchine, 2003), xi.

23. *Ibid.*

24. Qiana Whitted, "'And the Negro thinks in hieroglyphics': comics, visual metonymy, and the spectacle of blackness," *Journal of Graphic Novels and Comics*, 5.1 (2014), 79.

25. *Ibid.*, 80.

26. *Ibid.*, 79.

27. Henry Louis Gates, Jr., *The Signifying Monkey: A Theory of African-American Literary Criticism* (New York: Oxford University Press, 1988), 75.

28. *Ibid.*, 76.

29. Whitted, "And the Negro thinks in hieroglyphics," 79.

30. Claudia Mitchell-Kernan, "Signifying, Loud Talking and Marking," in *Signifyin(g), Sanctifyin', and Slam Dunking: A Reader in African American Expressive Culture*, ed. by Gena Dagel Caponi (Amherst: University of Massachusetts Press, 1999), 311.

31. *Ibid.*

32. Frances Gateward and John Jennings, eds, *The Blacker the Ink: Constructions of Black Identity in Comics and Sequential Art* (New Brunswick: Rutgers University Press, 2015), 3.

33. Monica Chiu, ed., *Drawing New Color Lines: Transnational Asian American Graphic Narratives* (Hong Kong: Hong Kong University Press, 2015), 2.

34. Percy B. Shelley, *Shelley: A Defence of Poetry*, ed. by F.B. Pinion and M.A. Cantab (London: James Brodie Ltd., [1821] 1955), 43.

35. bell hooks, *Black Looks: Race and Representation*, New ed. (Oxon: Routledge, 2015), 2.

36. Ben Lander, "Graphic Novels as History: Representing and Reliving the Past," *Left History*, 10.2 (Fall 2005), 113–114.

37. Judith Butler, "Withholding the name: translating gender in Cather's 'On the Gull's Road,'" in *Modernist Sexualities*, ed. by Hugh Stevens and Caroline Howlett (Manchester: Manchester University Press, 2000), 59.

38. Thelma J. Shinn, *Women Shapeshifters: Transforming the Contemporary Novel* (Connecticut: Greenwood Press, 1996), xv.

39. *Ibid.*, xv.

40. Sheena C. Howard, *Black Queer Identity Matrix: Towards An Integrated Queer of Color Framework* (Peter Lang Publishing, 2014), 65.

41. *Ibid.*

42. *Ibid.*, xv.

43. Susy Zepeda, "Mapping Queer of Color Methodology," *GLQ: A Journal of Lesbian and Gay Studies*, 15.4 (2009), 623.

44. Michael Bennett and Vanessa D. Dickerson, "Introduction," in *Recovering the Black Female Body: Self-Representations by African American Women* (New Brunswick: Rutgers University Press, 2001), 2.

45. *Ibid.*, 2.

46. Mikhail M. Bakhtin, *The Dialogic Imagination: Four Essays by M.M. Bakhtin*, ed. by Michael Holquist, trans. by Caryl Emerson and Michael Holquist (Austin: University of Texas Press, 1981), 259.

47. *Ibid.*

48. See "Black Women and Their Fictions in the Twentieth Century," at http://english.columbia.edu/black-women-and-their-fictions-twentieth-century

49. Lori Harrison-Kahan, "Her 'Nig': Returning the Gaze of Nella Larsen's 'Passing,'" *Modern Language Studies*, 32.2 (Autumn 2002), 120.

50. Lorraine Elena Roses and Ruth Elizabeth Randolph, *Harlem Renaissance and Beyond: Literary Biographies of 100 Black Women Writers 1900–1945* (Boston: G.K. Hall & Co., 1990), xxiv.

51. *Ibid.*

52. See in general Lorraine Elena Roses and Ruth Elizabeth Randolph, *Harlem Renaissance and Beyond.*

53. Jessie Redmon Faucet's novel, *Plum Bun*, was published in the same year as Nella Larsen's *Passing*. Like Larsen, Fauset's book also took up the controversial issue of racial passing.

54. Dorothy West's novel focused on the issue of "colorism" in black communities. This was a disparaging term used to describe blacks who were "color struck" or enamored of the white ideal to such a degree, they often spurned other blacks whose skin tone was considered too dark.

55. For a fuller discussion on Afrofuturism, see Charlene Taylor-Stone's article at https://www.theguardian.com/science/political-science/2014/jan/07/afrofuturism-where-space-pyramids-and-politics-collide

56. Martha J. Cutter, "Sliding Significations: Passing as a Narrative and Textual Strategy in Nella Larsen's Fiction," in *Passing and the Fictions of Identity*, ed. by Elaine K. Ginsberg (Durham: Duke University Press, 1996), 86.

57. Harrison-Kahan, "Her 'Nig': Returning the Gaze of Nella Larsen's 'Passing,'" 111.

58. George Hutchinson, "Nella Larsen and the Veil of Race," *American Literary History*, 9.2 (Summer 1997), 344.

59. bell hooks, "Whiteness in the Black Imagination," in *Displacing Whiteness: Essays in*

Social and Cultural Criticism, ed. by Ruth Frankenberg (Durham: Duke University Press, 1997), 168.

60. A. Javier Treviño, Michelle A. Harris and Derron Wallace, "What's so critical about critical race Theory?" *Contemporary Justice Review*, 11.1 (March 2008), 7.

61. *Ibid*.

62. Marc Black, "Fanon and DuBoisian Double Consciousness," *Human Architecture: Journal of the Sociology of Self-Knowledge*, 5.3 (Summer 2007), 394.

63. Treviño, Harris and Wallace, "What's so critical about critical race theory?" 8.

64. Cutter, "Sliding Significations," 84.

65. Treviño, Harris and Wallace, "What's so critical about critical race theory?" 8.

66. Susan Sontag, "Regarding the Torture of Others" http://www.nytimes.com/2004/05/23/magazine/regarding-the-torture-of-others.html?_r=0

67. See for example Paul Hirsch's article, "'This Is Our Enemy': The Writers' War Board and Representations of Race in Comic Books, 1942–1945," *Pacific Historical Review*, 83.3 (2014).

68. See for example Cord A. Scott's book, *Comics and Conflict: Patriotism and Propaganda from WWII through Operation Iraqi Freedom* (Annapolis: Naval Institute Press, 2014).

69. Harrison-Kahan, "Her 'Nig': Returning the Gaze of Nella Larsen's 'Passing,'" 120.

70. Black, "Fanon and DuBoisian Double-Consciousness," 397.

71. Jennifer Terry describes "deviant historiography" as a way of setting out "the complex discursive and textual operations at play in the historical emergence of subjects who come to be called lesbians and gay men." For a fuller discussion, refer to Terry's article, "Theorizing Deviant Historiography," *A Journal of feminist cultural studies*, 3.2 (1991), 284.

72. Benita Roth refers to the "nested contexts" of activism and organizing across multiple-issue platforms in *Separate Roads to Feminism: Black, Chicana, and White Feminist Movements in America's Second Wave* (Cambridge: Cambridge University Press, 2004), 2.

73. McCloud, *Understanding Comics*, 124.

74. Beldan Sezen, *Snapshots of a Girl* (Vancouver: Arsenal Pulp Press, 2015), 85.

75. While *yuri* is a genre of *shōjo* that focuses on lesbian romance and relationships, Nagata's memoir does not strictly follow the conventions of *yuri* as it does in works by Takemiya Jin, Nishi Uko, Morishima Akiko, or Nakamura Kiyo. For an in-depth and expert discussion of *yuri* and works by the authors mentioned here, refer to

Brigid Alverson's interview with Erica Friedman entitled: "Defining Yuri Manga: Q&A with Erica Friedman." https://www.barnesandnoble.com/blog/sci-fi-fantasy/defining-yuri-manga-qa-erica-friedman/

76. Ann Keniston and Jeanne Follansbee Quinn, eds, "Introduction: Representing 9/11: Literature and Resistance," in *Literature after 9/11* (New York: Routledge, 2008), 7.

77. Reiterating the central argument of her earlier work "Can the Subaltern Speak," Spivak noted that "no perspective critical of imperialism can turn the Other into a self, because the project of imperialism has always already historically refracted what might have been the absolutely Other into a domesticated Other that consolidates the imperialist self." See "Three Women's Texts and a Critique of Imperialism," *Critical Inquiry*, 12.1 (Autumn 1985), 253.

Chapter 1

1. In opening remarks given at a 2016 conference on Space, Identity and Memory at Birkbeck, University of London, Esther Leslie spoke at length about politically coded spaces where power breeds injustice that is played out in multiple and often undetectable ways.

2. Susana M. Morris, "More Than Human: Black Feminisms of the Future in Jewelle Gomez's The Gilda Stories," *The Black Scholar*, 46.2 (April 2016), 33.

3. Karin Kukkonen, "Comics as a Test Case for Transmedial Narratology," *SubStance*, 40.1 (Issue 124), 36.

4. *Ibid*.

5. Daniel Chandler, *Semiotics: the basics* (New York: Routledge, 2017), 29.

6. Bronwen Martin and Felizitas Ringham, *Dictionary of Semiotics* (London: Cassell, 2000), 7–8.

7. Martin and Ringham, *Dictionary of Semiotics*, 8–12.

8. Theo van Leeuwen, *Introducing Social Semiotics* (London: Routledge, 2005), 3.

9. *Ibid.*, 4.

10. *Ibid.*, 3.

11. *Ibid*.

12. *Ibid.*, 47–48.

13. Scott Simpkins, "Tricksterism in the Gothic Novel," *The American Journal of Semiotics*, 14 (Winter 1998), 11.

14. See for example *The Racial Contract* by Charles W. Mills, in which he lays out the rules of Engagement between whites and people of color. Mills notes that the "general purpose

of the Contract is always the differential privileging of the whites as a group with respect to
the nonwhites as a group, the exploitation of
their bodies, land, and resources, and the denial
of equal socioeconomic opportunities to them."
(p. 11).

15. William R. Freudenburg and Margarita
Alario, "Weapons of Mass Distraction: Magicianship, Misdirection, and the Dark Side of Legitimation," *Sociological Forum*, 22.2 (June
2007).

16. M. Clay Hooper, "'It Is Good to Be
Shifty': William Wells Brown's Trickster Critique
of Black Autobiography," *Modern Language
Studies*, 38.2 (Winter 2009), 30.

17. Gustav Kuhn and Luis M. Martinez,
"Misdirection—past, present, and the future,"
Frontiers in Human Neuroscience, 5 (January
2012), unpaginated.

18. James V. Morrison, *Homeric Misdirection*
(Ann Arbor: The University of Michigan Press,
1992), 3.

19. *Ibid.*, 8.

20. *Ibid.*, 20.

21. *Ibid.*, 3–4.

22. Kuhn and Martinez, "Misdirection—
past, present, and the future," unpaginated.

23. These terms and their general descriptions are based in part on discussions that took
place on the Comixscholar Listserv in early February 2015, and my subsequent analysis of such
"burst frame" techniques as Winsor McCay's
"Petit Sammy Eternue," and Kieron Gillen and
Jamie McKelvie's "Young Avengers," where Loki
clutches a help wanted advert, extending his
hand outside of the frame and making a direct
appeal to readers for help in steering new
Avengers his way.

24. Karin Kukkonen, "Metalepsis in Popular
Culture: An Introduction," in *Metalepsis in Popular Culture*, ed. by Karin Kukkonen and Sonja
Klimek (Berlin: Walter de Gruyter & Co., 2011),
1.

25. Theo van Leeuwen, "Semiotics and
Iconography," in *Handbook of Visual Analysis*,
ed. by Theo van Leeuwen and Carey Jewitt
(London: Sage Publications, 2001), 94.

26. *Ibid.*

27. Shane Denson, Christina Meyer and
Daniel Stein, "Intersections: Comics and transnationalism—transnationalism and comics," eds.,
in *Transnational Perspectives on Graphic Narratives: Comics at the Crossroads* (London: Bloomsbury, 2013) *Transnational Perspectives on Graphic
Narratives: Comics at the Crossroads* (London:
Bloomsbury, 2013), 1.

28. *Bringing Up Father* was a long-running

comic strip about Jiggs and Maggie, a nouveau
riche Irish-American couple. While Maggie
strives to match her social presentation to their
newfound wealth, Jiggs constantly seeks to subvert it.

29. Laura Doyle, "'These Emotions of the
Body': Intercorporeal Narrative in *To the Lighthouse*," *Twentieth Century Literature*, 40.1 (Spring
1994), 45.

30. Eve K. Sedgwick, *Tendencies* (London:
Routledge, 1998), 3

31. Kukkonen, "Comics as a Test Case for
Transmedial Narratology," 36.

32. Jonathan Kemp, "'Her Lips are Slightly
Parted': The Ineffability of Erotic Sociality in
Muriel Spark's *The Driver's Seat*," *Modern Fiction
Studies*, 54.3 (Fall 2008), 546–547.

33. Sedgwick, *Tendencies*, 3.

34. Gloria T. Randle, "Between the Rock and
the Hard Place: Mediating Spaces in Harriet Jacobs's *Incidents in the Life of a Slave Girl*," *African
American Review*, 33.1 (Spring, 1999), 43.

35. *Ibid.*

36. John Arthos, Jr., "The shaman-trickster's
art of misdirection: The rhetoric of Farrakhan
and the million men," *Quarterly Journal of
Speech*, 87.1 (June 2009), 41.

37. *Ibid.*

38. C.W. Spinks, "Trickster: Cultural Boundaries and Semiosis," *The American Journal of
Semiotics*, 14.1–4 (Winter 1997), 4.

39. Homi K. Bhabha, "Signs Taken for Wonders: Questions of Ambivalence and Authority
under a Tree outside Delhi, May 1817," *Critical
Inquiry*, 12 (Autumn 1985), 154.

40. Pippa Stein, *Multimodal Pedagogies in
Diverse Classrooms: Representation, rights and
resources* (London: Routledge, 2008), 2.

41. Henry Louis Gates, Jr., "The 'Blackness
of Blackness': A Critique of the Sign and the Signifying Monkey," *Critical Inquiry*, 9.4 (June
1983), 688.

42. Henry Louis Gates, Jr., *The Signifying
Monkey: A Theory of African-American Literary
Criticism* (Oxford: Oxford University Press,
1988), 239.

43. At its most basic signifying can be described as innuendo, double-speak, playing the
dozens, talking trash, or cleverly phrased verbal
banter that is rapid-fire and draws on numerous
cultural references. For a general overview, see
Carol D. Lee's *Signifying as a Scaffold for Literary
Interpretation: The Pedagogical Implications of
an African American Discourse Genre* (Urbana,
IL: National Council of Teachers of English,
1993).

44. Gates, *The Signifying Monkey*, 70.

45. *Ibid.*, 71.

46. Marcyliena Morgan, *Language, Discourse and Power in African American Culture* (Cambridge: Cambridge University Press, 2002), 24.

47. Pauline Greenhill, "'The Snow Queen': Queer Coding in Male Directors' Films," *Marvels & Tales*, 29.1 (2015), 112.

48. *Ibid.*

49. I borrow the phrase "circulating currents of contradiction" from Anoop Nayak's essay, "'Pale warriors': skinhead culture and the embodiment of white masculinities," in *Children's Cultural Worlds*, ed. by Mary Jane Kehily and Joan Swann (Chichester: Wiley, 2003), 259.

50. Scott McCloud, *Understanding Comics: The Invisible Art* (New York: HarperCollins, 1993), 62.

51. *Ibid.*, 62–63.

52. Hortense J. Spillers, "The Permanent Obliquity," in *Changing Our Own Words: Essays on Criticism, Theory, and Writing by Black Women*, ed. by Cheryl A. Wall (London: Routledge, 1990), 129.

53. Evelynn Hammonds, "Black (w)holes and the Geometry of Black Female Sexuality," in *The Black Studies Reader*, ed. by Jacqueline Bobo, Cynthia Hudley, and Claudine Michel (New York: Routledge, 2004), 304.

54. Ali Brox, "'Every age has the vampire it needs': Octavia Butler's Vampiric Vision in Fledging," 19.3 (2008), 391.

55. Ashley Manchester, "Teaching Critical Looking: Pedagogical Approaches to Using Comics as Queer Theory," *SANE Journal: Sequential Art Narrative in Education*, 2, no. 2 (April 2017), 3.

56. See Kat William's work at https://www.katwilliamsillustration.com

57. Freudenburg and Alario, "Weapons of Mass Distraction," 153.

58. bell hooks, *Black Looks: Race and Representation*, New edition (Oxon: Routledge, 2015), 120.

59. Quoted from Barbara Smith's essay, "The Truth That Never Hurts: Black Lesbians in Fiction in the 1980s," in *Third World Women and The Politics of Feminism*, ed. by Chandra Talpade Mohanty, Ann Russo, and Lourdes Torres (Bloomington: Indiana University Press, 1991), 110.

60. Penelope Ingram, *The Signifying Body: Toward an Ethics of Sexual and Racial Difference* (Albany: State University of New York Press, 2008), xiii.

61. *Ibid.*

62. *Ibid.*, 26.

63. *Ibid.*

64. Although Freudenburg and Alario's arti- cle was written in 2007, the specific example they gave of protestors demanding the withdrawal of troops from Vietnam, being branded unpatriotic, is of course the very same argument being used today to discredit the actions of black athletes responding to the Trump administration's ideological alignment with white supremacists.

65. Pramod Nayar, "The Rhetoric of Silence/ing: *Hush*," *Margins: A Journal of Literature and Culture*, 3.1 (2013), 34.

66. Richard T. Rodriguez, "Imagine a Brown Queer: Inscribing Sexuality in Chicano/a-Latino/a Literary and Cultural Studies," *American Quarterly*, 59.2 (June 2007), 493–494.

67. Mae Gwendolyn Henderson, "Speaking in Tongues: Dialogics, Dialectics, and the Black Woman Writer's Literary Tradition," in *Changing Our Own Words: Essays on Criticism, Theory, and Writing by Black Women*, ed. by Cheryl A. Wall (London: Routledge, 1989), 20.

68. Hillary Chute and Marianne DeKoven, "Introduction: Graphic Narrative," *Modern Fiction Studies*, 52.4 (Winter 2006), 767.

69. *Ibid.*, 768.

70. AnaLouise Keating, "From Borderlands and New Mestizas to Nepantlas and Nepantleras: Anzaldúan Theories for Social Change," *Human Architecture: Journal of the Sociology of Self-Knowledge*, 4.3 (2006), 6.

71. *Ibid.*

72. *Ibid.*

Chapter 2

1. Trish Salah, "What Memory Wants: Broken Tongue, Stranger Fugue in Fall on Your Knees," *Canadian Review of American Studies*, 35.2 (2005), 2.

2. Gregory O'Dea, "Framing the Frame: Embedded Narratives, Enabling Texts, and *Frankenstein*," *Romanticism on the Net*, 31 (2003), 2.

3. Refer to "The Construction of Space in Comics," in *A Comics Studies Reader*, ed. by Jeet Heer and Kent Worcester (Jackson: University Press of Mississippi, 2009), 157, 160.

4. Robyn Warhol, "The Space Between: A Narrative Approach to Alison Bechdel's 'Fun Home,'" *College Literature*, 38.3 (Summer 2011), 10.

5. Stephanie Cawley, "Postcolonial Feminism and Comics," *The Stockton Postcolonial Studies Project* at https://blogs.stockton.edu/postcolonialstudies/postcolonial-feminism-and-comics/

6. Tabish Khair, *The Gothic, Postcolonialism and Otherness: Ghosts from Elsewhere* (London: Palgrave Macmillan, 2009), 3.

7. Julia Round, *The Gothic in Comics and Graphic Novels: A Critical Approach* (North Carolina: McFarland & Company, Inc., 2014), 5.

8. Thierry Groensteen, *The System of Comics*, trans. by Bart Beaty and Nick Nguyen (Jackson: University Press of Mississippi, 2007), 159.

9. Ann-Marie Macdonald, *Fall on Your Knees* (London: Vintage, 1997), 1.

10. Toni Morrison, *Paradise* (London: Vintage, 1999), 3.

11. Toni Morrison and Nellie McKay, "An Interview with Toni Morrison," *Contemporary Literature*, 24.4 (1983), 414.

12. See the full interview with Toni Morrison, as above.

13. MacDonald, *Fall on Your Knees*, 25.

14. Erwin Feyersinger, "Diegetic Short Circuits: Metalepsis in Animation," *Animation: An Interdisciplinary Journal*, 5.3 (2010), 279.

15. Cedric Gael Bryant, "The Soul Has Bandaged Moments: Reading the African American Gothic in Wright's 'Big Boy Leaves Home,' Morrison's 'Beloved,' and Gomez's 'Gilda,'" *African American Review*, 39.4 (2005), 542.

16. Pascal Lefèvre, "The Construction of Space in Comics," in *A Comics Studies Reader*, ed. by Jeet Heer and Kent Worcester (Jackson: University of Mississippi Press, 2009), 157.

17. Warhol, "The Space Between," 2.

18. Elizabeth Marshall and Leigh Gilmore, "Girlhood in the Gutter: Feminist Graphic Knowledge and the Visualization of Sexual Precarity," *Women's Studies Quarterly*, 43.1&2 (Spring/Summer 2015), 6.

19. *Ibid.*

20. Fans of Charlotte Brontë will of course, recognize Thornfield Hall from *Jane Eyre* (1847). The attic in Brontë's novel was where Bertha Mason, Edward Rochester's "insane" Creole wife, was locked away.

21. Franny Howes, "Imagining a Multiplicity of Visual Rhetorical Traditions: Comics Lessons from Rhetoric Histories," *ImageText: Interdisciplinary Comics Studies*, 5.3 (2010), 10.

22. *Ibid.*, 4.

23. *Ibid.*, 10.

24. Warhol, "The Space Between,'" 8.

25. Groensteen, *The System of Comics*, 43.

26. *Ibid.*

27. Mario Saraceni, *The Language of Comics* (London: Routledge, 2003), 5.

28. Lefèvre, "The Construction of Space in Comics," 157, 160.

29. MacDonald, *Fall On Your Knees*, 12.

30. In the novel, MacDonald clues the reader into the narrator's unreliability when she writes: "But memory plays tricks. Memory is another word for story, and nothing is more unreliable," 270.

31. Eugenia DeLamotte, "White Terror, Black Dreams: Gothic Constructions of Race in the Nineteenth Century," in *The Gothic Other: Racial and Social Constructions in the Literary Imagination*, ed. by Ruth Bienstock Anolik and Douglas L. Howard (North Carolina: McFarland & Company, Inc., 2004), 19.

32. Patricia Hill Collins, *Black Feminist Thought: Knowledge, Consciousness, and the Politics of Empowerment*, 2nd ed. (London: Routledge, 2000), 25.

33. Hilde Staels, "Embracing Difference in Ann-Marie Macdonald's Fall on Your Knees," *Orbis Litterarum*, 64.4 (2009), 324.

34. See for instance Allan Berube's essay, "How Gay Stays White and What Kind of White It Stays," in *The Making and Unmaking of Whiteness* (Durham, NC: Duke University Press, 2001).

35. See for example Hull, Scott, and Barbara Smith's influential book, *All the Women Are White, All the Blacks Are Men, but Some of Us Are Brave* (New York: The Feminist Press, 1982).

36. Eve Kosofsky Sedgwick, *Tendencies* (Durham, NC: Duke University Press, 1993), 8.

37. *Ibid.*

38. Churnjeet Kaur Mahn, "The Queer Limits of Pratibha Parmar's *Nina's Heavenly Delights*," *Journal of Lesbian Studies*, 17.3–4 (2013), 5.

39. *Ibid.*

40. Burkhard Scherer, ed., *Queering Paradigms* (Switzerland: Peter Lang AG, 2010), 1.

41. Karen Tongson, "Queer Fundamentalism," *Social Text 121*, 32.4 (Winter 2014), 120.

42. MacDonald, *Fall On Your Knees*, 118.

43. See <http://www.bu.edu/bhlp/Resources/Islam/health/guidelines.html>

44. Adrienne Rich, "Compulsory Heterosexuality and Lesbian Experience," *Journal of Women's History*, 15.3 (Autumn 2003), 19.

45. *Ibid.*

46. MacDonald, *Fall On Your Knees*, 260.

47. *Ibid.*, 546.

48. For detailed discussions on "second sight" and the "veil," refer to "Ever Feeling One's Twoness: 'Double Ideals' and 'Double Consciousness' in The Souls of Black Folk" by Ernest Allen, Jr., volume 9 of the 1992 special issue of *Contributions in Black Studies*. See also Kathleen Marie Higgins's, "Double Consciousness and Second Sight" in Jacqueline Scott and A. Todd Franklin's, *Critical Affinities: Nietzsche and*

African American Thought (New York: State University of New York Press, 2006). Also refer to W.E.B. DuBois's book, *Darkwater: Voices from Within the Veil* (New York: Dover Publications, 1999).

49. Macdonald, *Fall On Your Knees*, 380.

50. *Ibid.*, 448.

51. *Ibid.*, 60.

52. *Ibid.*, 260.

53. *Ibid.*, 125.

54. *Ibid.*

55. This idea of dress, and what certain styles may signify relevant to different cultural or racial groups, is addressed in quite a clever way in Toni Morrison's short story, "Recitatif." By leaving out the race of the two main female characters, Morrison forces the reader to examine their own preconceived notions about racial signifiers. (Refer, for example, to Carmen Gillespie's *Critical Companion to Toni Morrison: A Literary Reference to Her Life and Work*).

56. Douglas Martin, "A Village Dies, A Park is Born," *New York Times*, January 31, 1997, http://www.nytimes.com/1997/01/31/arts/a-village-dies-a-park-is-born.html.

57. Nancy Duncan, ed., "Renegotiating Gender and Sexuality in Public and Private Spaces," in *Bodyspace: Destabilizing geographies of gender and sexuality*, London (Routledge, 1996), 128.

58. See for example Richard Tewksbury's essay, "Cruising for Sex in Public Places: the structure and language of men's hidden, erotic worlds" in *Deviant Behavior*, 17.1 (January–March 1996); or Robert Aldrich's "Homosexuality and the City: An Historical Overview" in *Urban Studies*, 41.9 (August 2004).

59. For a detailed analysis on this topic, refer to Seth Koven's book, *Slumming: Sexual and Social Politics in Victorian London* (Princeton: Princeton University Press, 2004). He sets forth a convincing case that examines the philanthropic and sociological aspects of the upper classes visiting slums, while also underscoring the prurient aspect driving many of those very same excursions. The combination of the prosaic yet desperate realities of the poor, with the repressed sexuality of wealthy "do-gooders," often resulted in what Koven notes were "sites of personal liberation and self-realization—social, spiritual, and sexual—for several generations of educated men and women." (p. 5)

60. Macdonald, *Fall On Your Knees*, 530.

61. *Ibid.*

62. *Ibid.*

63. *Ibid.*

64. *Ibid.*

65. *Ibid.*

66. *Ibid.*

67. Salah, "What Memory Wants," 2.

68. *Ibid.*, 237.

69. Macdonald, *Fall on Your Knees*, 562.

70. *Ibid.*

71. *Ibid.*, 492.

72. *Ibid.*

73. *Ibid.*, 87, 89.

74. Staels, "Embracing Difference," 326.

75. For a fuller discussion on Derrida's coinage of the term "phallogocentrism," see Carole Dely's article, "Jacques Derrida: the 'perchance' of a coming of the otherwoman: the deconstruction of 'phallogocentrism' from duel to duo," *Sens-Public* (2007), which includes excerpts of a 2000 interview with Derrida in *Le Monde de l'éducation*. In that interview, Derrida commented: "I speak mostly, and have for a long time, about sexual differences, rather than about one difference only—twofold and oppositional—which is indeed, with phallocentrism, with what I also nickname 'phallogocentrism,' a structural feature of philosophical discourse that will have prevailed in the tradition."

76. In *Reading Lacan* (Ithaca: Cornell University Press, 1985), Jane Gallop undertakes a close reading of several key passages in two editions of Lacan's "La Signification du phallus"; the 1966 edition and the 1971 edition, where she focuses on the feminine article "la," which appears in the first edition, and the reversion to the masculine article in the later version. She sees this linguistic anomaly as supportive of Lacan's overall contention that the phallus should be differentiated from the penis, and that it is, according to Lacan "[...] less the organ, penis or clitoris, which it symbolizes" (p. 136). My own take on the centrality of the phallus (or what it represents) in critical debates is meant to shift arguments back to the site where intersecting oppressions conspire to mute the subaltern voice. In order to disrupt or attempt to dismantle these sources of power, I contend that their construction must be understood from less historically traditional points of view.

77. Luce Irigaray, *This Sex Which Is Not One*, trans. by Catherine Porter with Carolyn Burke, 1st ed. (Ithaca: Cornell University Press, 1985), 68.

78. *Ibid.*

79. Macdonald, *Fall On Your Knees*, 549.

80. Duncan, "Renegotiating Gender," 128.

81. Macdonald, *Fall On Your Knees*, 548.

82. *Ibid.*, 235.

83. Metastatic is used here as a literary term, meaning there is a rapid transition from one point to another, suggesting that the topic or

issue at hand is of too little importance to mull over.

84. MacDonald, *Fall On Your Knees*, 58.

85. Hélène Cixous, "The Laugh of the Medusa," in *Feminisms: An Anthology of Literary Theory and Criticism*, rev. by Robyn R. Warhol and Diane P. Herndl (Hampshire, England: Macmillan Press, 1997), 348.

86. MacDonald, *Fall On Your Knees*, 549.

87. *Ibid.*, 550.

88. *Ibid.*, 143.

89. *Ibid.*

90. *Ibid.*

91. *Ibid.*, 69.

92. *Ibid.*, 144.

93. *Ibid.*

94. *Ibid.*

95. *Ibid.*, 68–69.

96. *Ibid.*, 170.

97. *Ibid.*, 437.

98. *Ibid.*, 3.

99. See for example Grace M. Jantzen's compelling book, *Becoming Divine: Towards a Feminist Philosophy of Religion* (Manchester: Manchester University Press, 1998). Jantzen moves the debate about religion from its preoccupation with "violence, sacrifice, and death [that is] built upon mortality not only as a human fact but as a fundamental philosophical category," to one where "[...] new ways of considering religion, human flourishing, identity, and difference, and ecological concern" becomes the focus. (p. 2)

100. In her essay, "Feminism and the Sociology of Religion: From Gender-blindness to Gendered Difference," Linda Woodhead looks at first, second and third wave feminism to "survey [its] impact on the literature of the sociology of religion," suggesting that a "third wave of feminism has coincided with an analogous methodological shift in the sociology of religion in a way that has proved fruitful for the study of religion and gender." Refer to *The Blackwell Companion to Sociology of Religion* (Massachusetts: Blackwell Publishing, 2001), p. 80. See also Pamela S. Anderson and Beverley Clack's *Feminist Philosophy of Religion: Critical Readings* (London: Routledge, 2004).

101. MacDonald, *Fall On Your Knees*, 548.

102. Toni Morrison, *Playing in the Dark: Whiteness and the Literary Imagination* (New York: Vintage, 1993), 8.

103. Gill Valentine, "(RE) Negotiating the 'Heterosexual Street': Lesbian Productions of Space," in *Bodyspace: destabilizing geographies of gender and sexuality*, ed. by Nancy Duncan (London: Routledge, 1996), 148.

104. MacDonald, *Fall On Your Knees*, 288.

105. *Ibid.*, 293.

106. MacDonald, *Fall On Your Knees*, 262.

107. *Ibid.*

108. *Ibid.*

109. This is a musical term that requires notes to be "broken down, crushed." When the notes of a chord are played, they are not exactly simultaneous, but instead are played from the bottom to the top. The term derives from the Italian verb *acciaccare*, meaning "to crush."

110. "Psychomachia" is a Latin poem written by the Christian poet Aurelius Prudontius. It means "Battle for Man's Soul" or the struggle between good and evil.

111. MacDonald, *Fall On Your Knees*, 262–263.

112. *Ibid.*, 263.

113. *Ibid.*

114. *Ibid.*

115. Alison Blunt and Gillian Rose, eds., *Writing, Women and Space: Colonial and Postcolonial Geographies* (New York: Guilford Press, 1994), 3.

116. MacDonald, *Fall On Your Knees*, 290.

117. *Ibid.*, 15.

118. *Ibid.*, 67.

119. *Ibid.*, 63.

120. *Ibid.*, 67.

121. In his essay, "'A Music Seeking Its Words' Double-Timing and Double-Consciousness in Toni Morrison's *Jazz*," Richard Hardack draws on W.E.B. DuBois's idea of "double consciousness" to examine themes of race and music in Toni Morrison's novel. The "dialectic hierarchy" he speaks of relates to DuBois's "two unreconciled strivings; two warring ideals in one dark body." See, *Callaloo*, 18.2 (1995), 451.

122. MacDonald, *Fall On Your Knees*, 97.

123. Noel Ignatiev, *How the Irish Became White* (Oxon: Routledge, 1995), 35.

124. *Ibid.*

125. See for example Eamon O'Flaherty's article, "Ecclesiastical Politics and the Dismantling of the Penal Laws in Ireland, 1774–82," *Irish Historical Studies*, 26.101(May 1998); as well as R. E. Burns's, "The Irish Penal Code and Some of Its Historians," *The Review of Politics*, 21.1 (January 1959).

126. See for instance Bram Stoker's *Dracula* (London: Puffin Books, [1897] 1986); Ann Radcliffe's *The Italian* (London: Oxford University Press, 1968); or Robert Louis Stevenson's *The Strange Case of Dr Jekyll and Mr Hyde* (London: Longmans, Green, and Company, 1901).

127. This idea is taken up by James Smethurst in his essay, "Invented by Horror: The Gothic and African American Literary Ideology in Na-

tive Son," *African American Review*, 35.1 (Spring 2001); and by Cedric Gael Bryant in, "'The Soul Has Bandaged Moments': Reading the African American Gothic in Wright's 'Big Boy Leaves Home,' Morrison's 'Beloved,' and Gomez's 'Gilda,'" *African American Review*, 39.4 (Winter, 2005).

128. In the introduction to *Lesbian Gothic: Transgressive Fictions* (London: Cassell, 1999) Paulina Palmer draws parallels to many of themes in Gothic writing, and the subversive elements of lesbian fiction. She points out that the "stylistic eccentricities' of both genres '[…] portray an eccentric, disruptive subject who exists in marginal relation to mainstream society." (p. 1)

129. MacDonald, *Fall On Your Knees*, 503.
130. *Ibid.*
131. *Ibid.*
132. *Ibid.*, 504.
133. *Ibid.*
134. *Ibid.*, 161.
135. *Ibid.*
136. *Ibid.*, 359.
137. *Ibid.*, 327.
138. *Ibid.*, 30.
139. *Ibid.*, 91.
140. *Ibid.*, 34.
141. *Ibid.*, 360.
142. *Ibid.*, 370.
143. *Ibid.*, 374.
144. *Ibid.*, 388.

Chapter 3

1. Donna J. Haraway, *Simians, Cyborgs, and Women: The Reinvention of Nature* (London: Free Association Books Ltd, 1991), 176.

2. To avoid confusion, throughout this chapter I refer to the character in the book as "Cristy" and the author of the book as "Road."

3. Michael A. Chaney, "Introduction" in *Graphic Subjects: Critical Essays on Autobiography and Graphic Novels* (Madison: The University of Wisconsin Press, 2011), 6.

4. Put simply, sequential art consists of what Scott McCloud describes in *Understanding Comics: The Invisible Art* as "juxtaposed pictorial and other images" laid out in "deliberate sequence" that is "intended to convey information and/or to produce an aesthetic response in the viewer" 9.

5. Symbolia, a term coined by Mort Walker, is a fairly standard technique deployed in comics/graphic narratives. Clio Sady, a Portland-based artist, uses this strategy to great effect in her self-published comic pamphlet, *Nothing to Hide* (2012).

6. Refer to the press release for *Bad Habits* by Softskull Press on their website <http://softskull.com/bad-habits-a-love-story-2/>. See also Heidi Andrea's interview with Road in Autostraddle, at <http://www.autostraddle.com/queer-latina-punk-artist-cristy-c-road-the-interview/>; details from her own web page at <http://www.croadcore.org/bio.htm> ; and her band's webpage at <http://www.the-home wreckers.com/info.htm>

7. Rachel Russell and Melissa Tyler, "Branding and Bricolage: Gender, consumption and transition," *Childhood*, 12.2 (May 2005), 223.

8. Refer to John Gentile's November 5, 2013, interview with Cristy Road in *Punknews.org*, at <http://www.punknews.org/article/53472/interviews-rad-women-who-make-rad-art-5-cristy-road>

9. See Devyn Manibo's August 9, 2012, interview with Cristy at <http://bitchmagazine.org/post/smart-diggin-deep-with-cristy-c-road-art-queer-poc-zines-feminist-magazine-books-music>

10. Cristy C. Road, *Bad Habits* (Berkeley: Soft Skull Press, 2008), 100.
11. *Ibid.*, 23.
12. *Ibid.*
13. Patricia L. Price, "Cohering Culture on *Calle Ocho*: The Pause and Flow of *Latinidad*," *Globalizations*, 4.1 (2007), 85.
14. Road, *Bad Habits*, 28.
15. *Ibid.*
16. Fernando Ortiz, *Cuban Counterpart: Tobacco and Sugar*, trans. by Harriet De Onis (Durham, NC: Duke University Press, 1995), 98.
17. Road, *Bad Habits*, 28.
18. *Ibid.*, 11.
19. *Ibid.*, 27.
20. Refer to Tina Vasquez's July 23, 2013, interview with Cristy C. Roads at <http://www.curvemag.com/Curve-Magazine/Web-Articles-2013/Page-Turner-Christy-C-Road/>
21. Elisa A. Garza, "Chicana Lesbianism and the Multigenre Text," in *Tortilleras: Hispanic and U.S. Latina Expression*, ed. by Lourdes Torres and Inmaculada Pertusa (Philadelphia: Temple University Press, 2003), 201.
22. *Ibid.*
23. Refer again to Tina Vasquez's July 23, 2013, interview with Cristy C. Road at <http://www.curvemag.com/Curve-Magazine/Web-Articles-2013/Page-Turner-Christy-C-Road/>
24. *Ibid.*
25. *Ibid.*
26. Refer again to the January 25, 2013, interview by Heidi Andrea in *Autostraddle*. See also the April 17, 2013, interview, "On Feminism,

Identity & Latinas in Arts and Literature," by Andrea Dulanto in The WIP.

27. Stephen Duncombe and Maxwell Tremblay, *White Riot: Punk Rock and the Politics of Race*, ed. by Stephen Duncombe and Maxwell Tremblay (London: Verso, 2011), 24.

28. Dick Hebdige, "Bleached Roots: Punks and White Ethnicity," in *White Riot: Punk Rock and the Politics of Race*, ed. by Stephen Duncombe and Maxwell Tremblay (London: Verso, 2011), 43.

29. Hebdige, "Bleached Roots: Punks and White Ethnicity," 43.

30. See for example William H. Wisner's article, "The Perilous Self: Loren Eiseley and the Reticence of Autobiography," *The Sewanee Review*, 113.1 (Winter 2005); Francis R. Hart's "Notes for an Anatomy of Modern Autobiography," *New Literary History*, 1.3 (Spring 1970); and Sidonie Smith and Julia Watson's *Reading Autobiography: A Guide for Interpreting Life Narratives*, 2nd ed. (Minnesota: Regents of the University of Minnesota, 2010). And finally, see in general, James E. Breslin's essay, "Gertrude Stein and the Problems of Autobiography," *The Georgia Review*, 33.4 (Winter 1979).

31. Elisabeth El Refaie, *Autobiographical Comics: Life Writing in Pictures* (Mississippi: University Press of Mississippi, 2012), 9.

32. Before Gillian Whitlock's use of "autographics" as a term describing life narrative through the graphic art form, Nelson Goodman argued in 1976 that art is only autographic if the distinction between its original and forged form is significant. See for example, Jerrold Levinson's article, "Autographic and Allographic Art Revisited," *Philosophical Studies*, 38.4 (1980).

33. Gillian Whitlock and Anna Poletti, "Self-Regarding Art," *Biography* (Honolulu), 31.1 (Winter 2008), v.

34. Gillian Whitlock, "Autographics: The Seeing 'I' of the Comics" *Modern Fiction Studies*, 52.4 (Winter 2006), 970.

35. *Ibid.*, 966.

36. Whitock and Poletti, "Self-Regarding Art," vii.

37. *Ibid*.

38. Maxine Baca Zin and Bonnie Thornton Dill, "Theorizing Difference from Multiracial Feminism," *Feminist Studies*, 22.2 (Summer 1996), 321.

39. *Ibid*.

40. Catrióna Rueda Esquibel, *With Her Machete in Her Hand: Reading Chicana Lesbians* (Austin: University of Texas Press, 2006), 148.

41. *Ibid*.

42. Julia Downes, "Riot Grrrl: The Legacy

and Contemporary Landscape of DIY Feminist Cultural Activism," in *Riot Grrrl: Revolution Girl Style Now!* (London: Black Dog Publishing Limited, 2007), 33.

43. Lauraine Leblanc, *Pretty in Punk: Girls' Gender Resistance in a Boys' Subculture* (New Brunswick: Rutgers University Press, 1999), 125.

44. Road, *Bad Habits*, 103.

45. Jodie Louise Taylor, "Spewing Out of the Closet: Musicology on Queer Punk," in *Musical Islands: Exploring Connections Between Music, Place and Research*, ed. by Elizabeth Mackinlay, Brydie-Leigh Bartleet, and Katelyn Barney (Newcastle Upon Tyne: Cambridge Scholars Press, 2009)

46. See Sophia Seawell's "An Interview with Cristy C. Road: On Zines, Publishing, and Capitalism," in *Culture Interviews* at <http://bluestockingsmag.com/2014/03/28/an-interview-with-cristy-c-road-on-zines-publishing-and-capitalism-part-1-of-3/>

47. *Ibid*.

48. Road, *Bad Habits*, 131.

49. Jose Quiroga, *Tropics of Desire: Interventions from Queer Latino America* (New York: New York University Press, 2000), 78.

50. Road, *Bad Habits*, 131.

51. Quiroga, *Tropics of Desire*, 80.

52. Road, *Bad Habits*, 131.

53. *Ibid*.

54. Refer to Fiona I.B. Ngô and Elizabeth A. Stinson's "Introduction: Threads and Omissions" in *Women & Performance: A Journal of Feminist Theory*, 22.2/3 (2012), 166.

55. Red Chidgey, "Riot Grrl Writing," in *Riot Grrrl: Revolution Girl Style Now!* ed. by Nadine Monem (London: Black Dog Publishing Limited, 2007), 128.

56. *Ibid*.

57. Downes, "Riot Grrl: The Legacy and Contemporary Landscape of DIY Feminist Cultural Activism," 23.

58. Road, *Bad Habits*, 9.

59. Daniel S. Traber, "L.A.'s 'White Minority': Punk and the Contradictions of Self-Marginalization," *Cultural Critique*, 48 (Spring 2001), 32.

60. Arnoldas Stramskas, "Making Sense of Punk Subcultures in the Neoliberal United States," *Groups and Environments*, 3 (2013), 116.

61. Road, *Bad Habits*, 129–130.

62. Amy Alexander, *Fifty Black Women Who Changed America* (New York: Birch Lane Press, 1999), 251.

63. As I use it throughout this chapter, the "black experience" is not exclusive to African American history, but rather is inclusive of the

collective histories of black-skinned people from African, Caribbean, and Latin American diasporas.

64. Tavia Nyong'o, "Do You Want Queer Theory (or Do You Want the Truth)? Intersections of Punk and Queer in the 1970s," *Radical History Review*, 100 (2008), 114.

65. Road, *Bad Habits*, 106.

66. *Ibid.*

67. *Ibid.*, 54.

68. *Ibid.*, 55.

69. *Ibid.*, 113.

70. *Ibid.*, 56.

71. *Ibid.*, 113.

72. *Ibid.*

73. *Ibid.*, 168.

74. *Ibid.*

75. Refer to Osa Atoe's collection, *Shotgun Seamstress: a zine by and for black punks* (Tacoma: Mend My Dress Press, 2012). Artists such as Andrea Rhinestone Eagle, Marilyn of Aye Nako, and Kali Boyce of NastyFacts, represent a wide spectrum of sub-alternative punk discourse that continues to be muted by the "white noise" of DIY punk.

76. Esquibel, *With Her Machete in Her Hand*, 148.

77. Ngô and Stinson, "Threads and Omissions," 167.

78. Lucy O'Brien, "The Woman Punk Made Me," in *Punk Rock: So What? The Cultural Legacy of Punk*, ed. by Roger Sabin (London: Routledge, 1999), 188.

79. Dick Hebdige, *Subculture: The Meaning of Style* (New York: Methuen & Co Ltd, 1979), 64.

80. Stewart Home, *Cranked Up Really High: Genre Theory and Punk Rock* (Hove: CodeX, 1995), 32.

81. Otto Nomous, "Race, Anarchy and Punk Rock: The Impact of Cultural Boundaries Within the Anarchist Movement," in *White Riot: Punk Rock and the Politics of Race*, ed. by Stephen Duncombe and Maxwell Tremblay (London: Verso, 2011), 202.

82. Roger Sabin, "I Won't Let That Dago By: Rethinking Punk and Racism," in *White Riot: Punk Rock and the Politics of Race*, ed. by Stephen Duncombe and Maxwell Tremblay (London: Verso, 2011), 58.

83. *Ibid.*, 63.

84. Road, *Bad Habits*, 13.

85. Heike Bauer, "Graphic Lesbian Continuum," in *Graphic Details: Jewish Women's Confessional Comics in Essays and Interviews*, ed. by Sarah Lightman (North Carolina: McFarland, 2014). I also note here that Bauer makes clear that her application of the term "graphic lesbian

continuum" is owing to Adrianne Rich's "lesbian continuum" in its "challenge [to] [...] the 'compulsory heterosexuality' that structures our lives." (See in general Bauer's argument in "Graphic Lesbian Continuum").

86. *Ibid.*, 99.

87. *Ibid.*, 106.

88. *Ibid.*, 98.

89. Road, *Bad Habits*, 13.

90. *Ibid.*, 12.

91. *Ibid.*, 13.

92. *Ibid.*, 65.

93. *Ibid.*

94. *Ibid.*, 65–66.

95. *Ibid.*, 66.

96. Katherine Sugg, "The Ultimate Rebellion: Chicana Narratives of Sexuality and Community," *Meridians: feminism, race, transnationalism*, 3.2 (2003), 158.

97. Road, *Bad Habits*, 130.

98. Sugg, "The Ultimate Rebellion," 140.

99. Road, *Bad Habits*, 131–132.

100. *Ibid.*, 23.

101. As I use it here, "G-Spot" moves beyond locating and fixing women's sexual pleasure within narrow heterosexual parameters. I argue that it is also about "Girl-Spots," where lesbians of color come together below the white male hetero and homonormative radar to make their own music and set out the terms of their own punk engagement.

102. Road, *Bad Habits*, 135.

103. *Ibid.*

104. Mumbi Machera, "Opening a Can of Worms: A Debate on Female Sexuality in the Lecture Theatre," in *Re-thinking Sexualities in Africa*, ed. by Signe Arnfred (Sweden: Almqvist & Wiksell Tryckeri AB, 2005), 157.

105. Michael Bennett and Vanessa D. Dickerson, eds., *Recovering the Black Female Body: Self-Representations by African American Women* (New Brunswick: Rutgers University Press, 2001), xi.

106. Vanessa D. Dickerson, "Summoning Somebody: The Flesh Made Word in Toni Morrison's Fiction," in *Recovering the Black Female Body*, 197.

107. *Ibid.*

108. Haraway, *Simians, Cyborgs, and Women*, 156.

109. Leah Newbold, "On Class, Punk, Organizing and Anti-Affluence Activism," in *Shotgun Seamstress: Zine Collection*, ed. by Osa Atoe (Tacoma: Mend My Dress Press, 2012), 96.

110. Lois M. Smith and Alfred Padula, *Sex and Revolution: Women in Socialist Cuba* (Oxford: Oxford University Press, 1996), 172.

111. Road, *Bad Habits*, 158.
112. *Ibid.*, 135.
113. *Ibid.*, 56.
114. *Ibid.*, 137.
115. Haraway, *Simians, Cyborgs, and Women*, 150.
116. Mimi Nguyen, "Queer Cyborgs and New Mutants: Race, Sexuality, and Prosthetic Sociality in Digital Space," in *American Studies: An Anthology*, ed. by Janice A. Radway, Kevin K. Gaines, Barry Shank and Penny Von Eschen (Chichester: Wiley-Blackwell, 2009), 373.
117. Road, *Bad Habits*, 132.
118. *Ibid.*
119. See in general pp. 155–161 of Haraway's *Simians, Cyborgs, and Women*.
120. *Ibid.*, 154.
121. Nguyen, "Queer Cyborgs and New Mutants," 373.
122. Michael A. Chaney, "Slave Cyborgs and the Black Infovirus: Ishmael Reed's Cybernetic Aesthetics," *Modern Fiction Studies*, 49.2 (2003), 267.
123. Road, *Bad Habits*, 30.
124. Refer to Stuart Hall's "Race, Articulation, and Societies Structured in Dominance," in *Black British Cultural Studies: A Reader*, ed. by Houston A. Baker, Jr., Manthia Diawara, and Ruth H. Lindeborg (Chicago: The University of Chicago Press, 1996).

Chapter 4

1. Layli Phillips and Maria R Stewart, "I Am Just So Glad You Are Alive: New Perspectives on Non-Traditional, Non-Conforming, and Transgressive Expressions of Gender, Sexuality, and Race Among African Americans," *Journal of African American Studies*, 12.4 (2008), 383.
2. Jasbir K Puar, *Terrorist Assemblages: Homonationalism in Queer Times* (Durham, NC: Duke University Press, 2007), 204.
3. Sharon Patricia Holland, *The Erotic Life of Racism* (Durham, NC: Duke University Press, 2012), 2.
4. Daniel Chandler, *Semiotics: The Basics* (London: Routledge, 2017), 2.
5. Refer to Mike Bergman's article, "A Foundational Mindset: Firstness, Secondness, Thirdness," where he uses the term "Thirdness" as shorthand to denote the first, second, and third. http://www.mkbergman.com/1932/a-foundational-mindset-firstness-secondness-thirdness
6. *Ibid.*, 8.
7. *Ibid.*,3.

8. Holland, *The Erotic Life*, 19.
9. Ariela Freedman, "Sorting through My Grief and Putting It into Boxes," in *Knowledge and Pain*, ed. by Esther Cohen, Leona Toker, Manuela Consonni, and Otniel E. Dror (Amsterdam: Rodopi, 2012), 382.
10. Gloria Naylor, *The Women of Brewster Place* (London: Vintage, 1982; repr. 1999), 1.
11. *Ibid.*, 45.
12. Angela P. Harris, "Race and Essentialism in Feminist Legal Theory," in *Critical Race Feminism: A Reader*, ed. by Adrien Katherine Wing (New York: New York University Press, 1997), 15.
13. Laurie Vickroy, *Trauma and Survival in Contemporary Fiction* (Charlottesville: University of Virginia Press, 2002), 4.
14. *Ibid.*, 12.
15. Annecka Marshall, "From sexual denigration to self-respect: resisting images of Black female sexuality," in *Reconstructing Womanhood, Reconstructing Feminism: Writings on Black Women*, ed. by Delia Jarrett-Macauley (London: Routledge, 1996), 10.
16. Naylor, *Brewster Place*, 23.
17. Neil Cohn, "The limits of time and transitions: challenges to theories of sequential image comprehension," *Studies in Comics*, 1 (2010), 136.
18. Thierry Groensteen, *The System of Comics*, trans. by Bart Beaty and Nick Nguyen (Jackson: University Press of Mississippi, 2007), 114.
19. Paul Gilroy, *Against Race: Imagining Political Culture Beyond the Color Line* (Cambridge: Harvard University Press, 2000), 243.
20. Ann Cvetkovich, *An Archive of Feelings: Trauma, Sexuality, and Lesbian Public Cultures* (Durham, NC: Duke University Press, 2003), 16.
21. *Ibid.*, 3.
22. Patricia Hill Collins, *Black Sexual Politics: African Americans, Gender, and the New Racism* (London: Routledge, 2004), 102.
23. Groensteen, *The System of Comics*, 112.
24. *Ibid.*, 113.
25. Similar to arguments put forth by such black feminist scholars as Patricia Hill Collins, Audre Lorde, bell hooks, and Toni Morrison, in her 1990 essay, "Race and Essentialism in Feminist Legal Theory," Angela P. Harris interrogates feminist positions that would see "Woman" (this arguably being a universal signifier of sameness) as "leached of all color" [and that] works to "remove black women [thereby allowing] white women [to] stand as the epitome of Woman." (p. 592)
26. Michael Omi, "(E)racism: Emerging Practices of Antiracist Organizations," in *The Making and Unmaking of Whiteness*, ed. by

Birgit Brander Rasmussen and others (Durham, NC: Duke University Press, 2001), 270.

27. Naylor, *Brewster Place*, 24.

28. Maxine L. Montgomery, *Conversations with Gloria Naylor* (Jackson: University Press of Mississippi, 2004), 125.

29. Vickroy, *Trauma and Survival in Contemporary Fiction*, 167–168.

30. Matt Richardson, *The Queer Limit of Black Memory: Black Lesbian Literature and Irresolution* (Columbus: Ohio State University, 2013), 4.

31. Naylor, *Brewster Place*, 47.

32. Inspired by what Carol Pateman had set out to explicate in *The Sexual Contract* (Oxford: Blackwell Publishers, 1988), Charles W. Mills extended her framing of social contracts through a feminist lens to account for other such contracts whose essential aim was to establish a structure of dominance by those in power over those who would be enlisted to serve their needs. In *The Racial Contract* (Ithaca: Cornell University Press, 1997), Mills focused on systems of domination that structured race along lines of exclusion. Based on a conflation of phenotypes and the underlying fear whites had of other ethnic cultures, it was easy enough for social contracts to morph into contracts that secured white domination. Pateman and Mills co-authored *Contract & Domination* (Cambridge: Polity Press, 2007), a merging of ideas that attempt to deconstruct the multiple entry points of racial and sexual domination.

33. Sara Ahmed, *Queer Phenomenology: Orientations, Objects, Others* (Durham, NC: Duke University Press, 2006), 109.

34. *Ibid.*, 111.

35. Naylor, *Brewster Place*, 145.

36. *Ibid.*

37. Charles W. Mills, *The Racial Contract* (Ithaca: Cornell University Press, 1997), 138.

38. Naylor, *Brewster Place*, 34.

39. Hillary Chute, *Graphic Women: Life Narrative and Contemporary Comics* (New York: Columbia University Press, 2010), 6.

40. For a broader discussion of the "grammar" of comics, refer to Gillian Whitlock's essay, "Autographics: The Seeing 'I' of the Comics." From the perspective of "seeing" and its impact on how we interpret what it is that we see, Whitlock examines both Susan Sontag and Marianne Hirsch's respective articles on the Abu Ghraib atrocities. Drawing on the work of Gunther Kress and Theo van Leeuwen, Mario Saraceni reminds us of their "grammar of visual design" model, whereby the "syntactic and semantic rules" also apply to images. (See "Relatedness:

Aspects of Textual Connectivity in Comics," in *The Graphic Novel* (2001).

41. Leigh Gilmore, *Autobiographics: A Feminist Theory of Women's Self-Representation* (Ithaca: Cornell University Press, 1994), 5.

42. *Ibid.*

43. *Ibid.*, 42.

44. See Volume 1, Issue 1 of the 1977 *A Marvel Super Special: Kiss*. For this issue each member of the band Kiss had vials of blood drawn by a doctor. These vials were later mixed in with the vats of ink used to produce the comic books.

45. Mikhail M. Bakhtin, *Dialogic Imagination* (Austin: University of Texas Press, 1981), 342.

46. *Ibid.*

47. Judith Butler, *Frames of War: When is Life Grievable?* (London: Verso, 2009), 8.

48. *Ibid.*

49. *Ibid.*

50. Eve K. Sedgwick, *Between Men: English Literature and Male Homosocial Desire* (New York: Columbia University Press, 1985), 9.

51. Fionnuala Ní Aoláin, "Women, Security, and the Patriarchy of Internationalized Transitional Justice," *Human Rights Quarterly*, 31.4 (2009), 1056.

52. *Ibid.*, 1064.

53. *Ibid.*, 1057.

54. Naylor, *Brewster Place*, 145.

55. Chase Gregory, "In the Gutter: Comix Theory," *Studies in Comics*, 3.1 (2012), 113.

56. Vickroy, *Trauma and Survival in Contemporary Fiction*, 167

57. Naylor, *Brewster Place*, 161.

58. Robert F. Reid-Pharr, "Tearing the Goat's Flesh: Homosexuality, Abjection and the Production of a Late Twentieth-Century Black Masculinity," *Studies in the Novel*, 28.3 (1996), 373.

59. Naylor, *Brewster Place*, 162.

60. *Ibid.*

61. *Ibid.*

62. *Ibid.*, 161.

63. *Ibid.*, 163.

64. *Ibid.*

65. *Ibid.*, 134.

66. *Ibid.*, 164.

67. *Ibid.*, 168.

68. *Ibid.*

69. Scott McCloud, *Understanding Comics: The Invisible Art* (New York: HarperCollins, 1993), 68.

70. Naylor, *Brewster Place*, 168.

71. *Ibid.*, 129.

72. *Ibid.*, 168–169.

73. *Ibid.*, 169.

74. In their article "Intersectional Invisibility: The Distinctive Advantages and Disadvantages

of Multiple Subordinate-Group Identities," Valerie Purdie-Vaughns and Richard P. Eibach examine the numerous intersecting points that complicate a single identity group membership relevant to cultural, racial, ethnic, and sexual status.

75. Naylor, *Brewster Place*, 169.

76. *Ibid.*

77. Naylor, *Brewster Place*, 169.

78. *Ibid.*

79. *Ibid.*, 161.

80. *Ibid.*

81. *Ibid.*, 169.

82. *Ibid.*

83. *Ibid.*

84. *Ibid.*, 169–170.

85. Reid-Pharr, "Tearing the Goat's Flesh," 373.

86. *Ibid.*

87. *Ibid.*, 374.

88. Jeffrey Weeks, "The Value of Difference," in *Identity: Community, Culture, Difference*, ed. by Jonathan Rutherford (London: Lawrence & Wishart, 1990), 95.

89. Naylor, *Brewster Place*, 170.

90. bell hooks, *Ain't I A Woman: Black Women and Feminism* (London: Pluto Press, 1981), 87.

91. *Ibid.*, 96.

92. Naylor, *Brewster Place*, 170.

93. *Ibid.*

94. Patricia Huntington, "Fragmentation, Race, and Gender," in *Existence in Black: An Anthology of Black Existential Philosophy*, ed. by Lewis R. Gordon (London: Routledge, 1997), 189.

95. *Ibid.*

96. Naylor, *Brewster Place*, 170.

97. *Ibid.*

98. Nicola Gavey, *Just Sex?: The Cultural Scaffolding of Rape* (East Sussex: Routledge, 2005), 27.

99. See in general Henry Louis Gates's discussion of "black rhetorical tropes [that are] subsumed under signifying," in *The Signifying Monkey*, 52.

100. Henry Louise Gates, Jr., *The Signifying Monkey: A Theory of African-American Literary Criticism* (New York: Oxford University Press, 1988), 45.

101. *Ibid.*, 54.

102. *Ibid.*, 47.

103. *Ibid.*

104. *Ibid.*, 48.

105. Naylor, *Brewster Place*, 170.

106. *Ibid.*

107. Cvetkovich, *Archive of Feelings*, 32–33.

108. Marianne Hirsch, "Editor's Column: Collateral Damage," *PMLA*, 119 (2004), 1213.

109. Will Eisner, *Comics and Sequential Art: Principles and Practices from the Legendary Cartoonist* (London: W.W. Norton, 2008), 48.

110. Naylor, *Brewster Place*, 170.

111. hooks, *Ain't I a Woman*, 102.

112. Gavey, *Just Sex?*, 2.

113. *Ibid.*

114. Naylor, *Brewster Place*, 170.

115. *Ibid.*, 171.

116. *Ibid.*

117. Derek P. Royal, "Foreword; Or Reading Within the Gutter," in *Multicultural Comics: From Zap to Blue Beetle*, ed. by Frederick Luis Aldama (Austin: University of Texas Press, 2010), xi.

118. *Ibid.*, x.

Chapter 5

1. Nathan Filler, *The Shock of the Fall* (London: The Borough Press, 2014), 26.

2. Oxford English Dictionary

3. Emma Pérez, *Gulf Dreams*, 2nd ed. (San Francisco: Aunt Lute Books, 1996), 133.

4. Emma Pérez, *The Decolonial Imaginary: Writing Chicanas into History* (Bloomington: Indiana University Press, 1999), 5.

5. *Ibid.*, xix.

6. *Ibid.*

7. Pérez, *Gulf Dreams*, 157.

8. Throughout this chapter I draw on Pérez's argument that much like the differential consciousness posited by Chela Sandoval in "U.S. Third World Feminism: The Theory and Method of Oppositional Consciousness in the Postmodern World," the "decolonial imaginary" in Chicana/o history is a theoretical tool for uncovering the hidden voices of Chicanas." (Refer to *The Decolonial Imaginary*, p. xvi).

9. Diane Hamer, "Significant Others: Lesbianism and Psychoanalytic Theory," *Feminist Review*, 34 (Spring 1990), 135.

10. See for example Mab Segret's article, "Exalted on the Ward 'Mary Roberts,' the Georgia State Sanitarium, and the Psychiatric 'Specialty' of Race," *American Quarterly*, 66 (March 2014). She cites an article in a 1949 issue of *Ebony*, noting that the Milledgeville State Hospital had "been cited ... as the worst in the nation and its Negro wards described as unbelievable 'this side of Dante's inferno'" (p. 72). Refer also to *The Protest Psychosis: How Schizophrenia Became a Black Disease* (2010), Jonathan M. Metzl's in-depth critique of how schizophrenia

evolved from being a condition afflicting whites who were seen to be generally harmless and suffering from "emotional disharmony," to a disease that in changing social times, became a popular diagnosis to assign labels of rage and criminality in black subjects.

11. Michele Cammers Goodwin, "The Black Woman in the Attic: Law, Metaphor and Madness in *Jane Eyre*," *Rutgers Law Journal*, 30.3 (1998–1999), 600.

12. In a play on the title of Sandra M. Gilbert and Susan Gubar's 1979 book on women and madness in Victorian England, Michele Cammers Goodwin deconstructs racist tropes in *Jane Eyre* that work to marginalize and even demonize Bertha Mason Rochester, the black wife of Edward Fairfax Rochester. Locked away in an attic and robbed of her money and dignity, for Goodwin, Bertha Mason Rochester's plight underscores the tendency of "most *Jane Eyre* scholars [to] overlook the intersection of race, gender, and mental illness in the novel," further noting that "their oversight is particularly surprising with regard to the black woman in the attic." (p. 607). Goodwin argues that if readers/scholars "choose[s] to listen," the "victims of this dark [Victorian] age, their muted voices having been long overlooked and disregarded, may be audible in literature" (p. 609).

13. Postcolonial scholars have also critiqued the absence (or the aberration) of the "queer(ed)" black body in other Victorian novels that have been critically praised for their representation of "woman" as synonymous with whiteness, goodness, and purity. See for example Jennifer DeVere Brody's, *Impossible Purities: Blackness, Femininity, and Victorian Culture* (Durham: Duke University Press, 1998).

14. Goodwin, "The Black Woman in the Attic," 624.

15. Andrew M. Fearnley, "Primitive Madness: Re-Writing the History of Mental Illness and Race," *Journal of the History of Medicine and Allied Sciences*, 63.2 (April 2008), 249.

16. Jane M. Ussher, *Women's Madness: Misogyny or Mental Illness?* (Hertfordshire: Harvester Wheatsheaf, 1991), 164.

17. Pérez, *Gulf Dreams*, 139.

18. Nancy Tomes, "Feminist Histories of Psychiatry," in *Discovering the History of Psychiatry*, ed. by Mark S. Micale and Roy Porter (Oxford: Oxford University Press, 1994), 353.

19. Pérez, *Gulf Dreams*, 139.
20. *Ibid.*, 101.
21. *Ibid.*
22. *Ibid.*
23. *Ibid.*

24. Pérez, *The Decolonial Imaginary*, 5.

25. Ellie Hernández, "Chronotope of Desire: Emma Pérez's *Gulf Dreams*," in *Chicana Feminisms: A Critical Reader*, ed. by Gabriela F. Arredondo and others (Durham, NC: Duke University Press, 2003), 157.

26. Emma Pérez, "Staking the Claim: Introducing Applied Chicana/o Cultural Studies," in *The Chicana/o Cultural Studies Forum: Critical and Ethnographic Practices*, ed. by Angie Chabram-Dernersesian (New York: New York University Press, 2007), 121.

27. Hernández, "Chronotope of Desire," 157.

28. Catrióna Esquibel, *With Her Machete in Her Hand: Reading Chicana Lesbians* (Austin: University of Texas Press, 2006), 73.

29. Pérez, *The Decolonial Imaginary*, 32.

30. The "young woman" is never named in the novel except in terms of being a friend, wife, or the object of the protagonist's desires.

31. Pérez, *Gulf Dreams*, 137.
32. *Ibid.*
33. *Ibid.*, 147.
34. *Ibid.*, 61.

35. Shoshana Felman, "Women and Madness: The Critical Phallacy," *Diacritics*, 5.4 (Winter 1975), 2.

36. Emma Pérez, "Sexuality and Discourse: Notes from a Chicana Survivor" in *Chicana Lesbians: The Girls Our Mothers Warned Us About*, ed. by Carla Trujillo (Berkeley: Third Woman Press, 1999), 160.

37. *Ibid.*, 161.

38. Kate Millet, *The Loony Bin Trip* (New York: Simon and Schuster, 1990), 85.

39. Gema Pérez-Sánchez, "Reading, Writing, and the Love That Dares Not Speak Its Name: Eloquent Silences in Ana Maria Moix's *Julia*," in *Hispanic and U.S. Latina Lesbian Expression/Tortilleras*, ed. by Lourdes Torres and Immaculada Pertusa (Philadelphia: Temple University Press, 2003), 91.

40. *Ibid.*, 104.

41. Marta Caminero-Santangelo, *The Madwoman Can't Speak: Or Why Insanity is Not Subversive* (Ithaca: Cornell University Press, 1998), 9.

42. *Ibid.*
43. *Ibid.*, 1.
44. *Ibid.*, 2.
45. Pérez, *The Decolonial Imaginary*, 49.
46. Pérez, *Gulf Dreams*, 49.
47. Pérez, *The Decolonial Imaginary*, 6.

48. As a diagnosis, multiple personality disorder has been highly contested in the psychiatric community. According to LaBruzza and Méndez-Villarubia, some clinicians have questioned its validity as a legitimate diagnosis, par-

ticularly given claims that therapists working with highly suggestible clients have too readily promoted this diagnosis when perhaps it does not quite fit the symptomology. For a fuller explanation, see *Using DSM-IV: A Clinician's Guide to Psychiatric Diagnosis* (New Jersey: Jason Aronson, Inc., 1994), 333.

49. Nadine J. Quehl, "Queering 'Madness': Possibilities of Performativity Theory," *Alternate Routes: A Journal of Critical Social Research*, 20 (2004), 115.

50. This quotation also appears in Roy Porter's *A Social History of Madness: Stories of the Insane* (London: Phoenix Giants, 1987), 3.

51. Ussher, *Women's Madness*, 20.

52. Pérez, *Gulf Dreams*, 150.

53. *Ibid.*

54. *Ibid.*, 62.

55. Adria E. Schwartz, *Sexual Subjects: Lesbians, Gender, and Psychoanalysis* (London: Routledge, 1998), 70.

56. Gloria Anzaldúa, *Borderlands/La Frontera: The New Mestiza*, 3rd ed. (San Francisco: Aunt Lute Books, 2007), 63.

57. Pérez, *Gulf Dreams*, 60.

58. *Ibid.*, 59.

59. *Ibid.*, 60.

60. Richard Schweid, *The Cockroach Papers: A Compendium of History and Lore* (Chicago: University of Chicago Press, 1999), xiv.

61. Pérez, *Gulf Dreams*, 15.

62. *Ibid.*, 11.

63. *Ibid.*

64. *Ibid.*, 52.

65. *Ibid.*

66. *Ibid.*

67. *Ibid.*, 27.

68. *Ibid.*

69. Gustav Kuhn and Luis M. Martinez, "Misdirection—Past, Present, and the Future," *Frontiers in Human Neuroscience*, 5.172 (2011), unpaginated.

70. Jeanne Rosier Smith, *Writing Tricksters: Mythic Gambols in American Ethnic Literature* (Berkeley: University of California Press, 1997), 2.

71. Ricki Stefanie Tannen, *The Female Trickster: the mask that reveals Post-Jungian and Postmodern Psychological Perspectives on Women in Contemporary Culture* (East Sussex: Routledge, 2007), 10.

72. Pérez, *Gulf Dreams*, 51.

73. *Ibid.*, 64–65.

74. *Ibid.*, 65.

75. *Ibid.*, 16.

76. Refer to Henry Samuel's article, "Jews pressured into adopting 'French-sounding' sur-

names fight to change them back," in the *Telegraph* at: http://www.telegraph.co.uk/news/world news/europe/france/7898978/Jews-pressured-into-adopting-French-sounding-surnames-fight-to-change-them-back.html

77. It is of note that sharecropping (undertaken by migrants who did not own land) and tenant farming (where land was rented from owners by tenant farmers, who in turn hired sharecroppers to work in their stead) was itself delineated into hierarchies of power between whites who did not have the financial means to own land outright, but who had the tools and equipment to farm rented plots, and Mexicans and blacks who had nothing to bargain with except the sweat of their brow. This created a situation whereby white tenant farmers became largely absentee 'sub-renters' who deluded themselves into thinking that because they could hire minorities to work for them, they had achieved a higher rung on the socio-economic ladder. [Refer in general to pages 10 and 70 in Neil Foley's *White Scourge: Mexicans, Blacks, and Poor Whites in Texas Cotton Culture* (Berkeley: University of California Press, 1997)].

78. Pérez, *Gulf Dreams*, 18, 19.

79. Emma Pérez, "Queering the Borderlands: The Challenges of Excavating the Invisible and Unheard," *Frontiers: A Journal of Women Studies*, 24.2/3 (2003), 122.

80. Pérez, "Sexuality and Discourse: Notes from a Chicana Survivor," 168.

81. *Ibid.*

82. Adela C. Licona, "'(B)orderlands' Rhetorics and Representations: The Transformative Potential of Feminist Third-Space Scholarship and Zines," *NWSA Journal*, 17.2 (2005). The most basic, yet provocative explanation of *mestizo/a* is offered by Serge Gruzinski when he writes: "The mestizo processes of the modern era normally appear against troubled a background [sic], against a setting of shattered identities [and] although not all mestizo phenomena are necessarily the product of conquest, those stemming from Western expansion into the Americas inevitably arose from the rubble of defeat," 33.

83. Pérez, *Gulf Dreams*, 15.

84. *Ibid.*

85. *Ibid.*, 43.

86. *Ibid.*, 43–44.

87. Birgit Brander Rasmussen, with Eric Klinenberg and others, eds, *The Making and Unmaking of Whiteness* (Durham, NC: Duke University Press, 2001), 8.

88. Pérez, *Gulf Dreams*, 44.

89. *Ibid.*, 22–23.

90. *Ibid.*, 71.

91. *Ibid.*, 73.
92. Elaine Showalter, *The Female Malady: Women, Madness and English Culture, 1830–1980* (London: Virago Press Ltd., 1987), 7.
93. *Ibid.*
94. *Ibid.*, 26.
95. Pérez, *Gulf Dreams*, 139.
96. Rafael Pérez-Torres, *Mestizaje: Critical Uses of Race in Chicano Culture* (Minneapolis: University of Minnesota Press, 2006), xvii.
97. *Ibid.*
98. *Ibid.*, 174.
99. The "feminization of madness," or madness as the "female malady," has been most notably discussed in Elaine Showalter's 1985 publication of, *The Female Malady: Women, Madness, and English Culture, 1830–1980.*
100. Pérez-Torres, *Mestizaje: Critical Uses of Race,* 176.
101. *Ibid.*
102. Julia Kristeva, *Revolution in Poetic Language* (New York: Columbia University Press, 1941; repr. 1984), 14.
103. *Ibid.*, 17.
104. Pérez, *Gulf Dreams*, 118.
105. *Ibid.*, 79.
106. *Ibid.*, 112.
107. Pérez, *The Decolonial Imaginary*, 11.
108. Refer to *Chicana Feminisms: A Critical Reader,* ed. by Gabriela F. Arredondo and others (Durham, NC: Duke University Press, 2003), 2.
109. Anzaldúa, *Borderlands/La Frontera*, 65.
110. Judith Butler famously challenged then narrowly defined constructions in *Gender Trouble: Feminism and the Subversion of Identity* (New York: Routledge,1990), her well-known work on gender performativity, as well as in some of her later works. See also Kristeva, Foucault, and Sedgwick's critiques of the fallacy (or more precisely, what could also be called the "phallocy") of gender construction.
111. Barbara McKay is the Director of the Institute for Family Therapy in London, England. She coined this term in the course of personal communication with her colleagues.
112. Butler of course drew upon the work of J.L. Austin to develop her own theories on utterance and interpellation in relation to gender and queer performativity.
113. Judith Butler, "Critically Queer," *GLQ,* 1.1 (1993), 17.
114. Pérez, *Gulf Dreams*, 115.
115. *Ibid.*, 115–116.
116. *Ibid.*, 114.
117. *Ibid.*, 114–115.
118. *Ibid.*, 147.
119. *Ibid.*, 146.
120. *Ibid.*, 130.
121. *Ibid.*, 131.
122. *Ibid.*
123. *Ibid.*, 131–132.
124. Schwartz, *Sexual Subjects*, 69.
125. *Ibid.*
126. Pérez, *Gulf Dreams*, 150.
127. Anzaldúa, *Borderlands/La Frontera*, 63.
128. *Ibid.*, 68.
129. *Ibid.*, 69.
130. Pérez, *Gulf Dreams*, 49.
131. *Ibid.*
132. *Ibid.*
133. *Ibid.*
134. *Ibid.*, 149.
135. *Ibid.*
136. *Ibid.*, 28.
137. *Ibid.*
138. *Ibid.*, 45.
139. *Ibid.*, 149.
140. *Ibid.*

Chapter 6

1. The title of Jaime Cortez's book is based on an essay written by Pedro Bustos, who gives credit for coining the term to Manolo Guzman, a Puerto Rican academic. Cortez interprets the term as being "full of longing, awareness, invention and displacement," p. vii. My own understanding of the term is based on the physical exile of queerly sexual bodies in transnational contexts. In this chapter, and for the sake of brevity, I use the shortened version of the book's title. (Note: All images in this chapter are used with permission from Jaime Cortez, who generously provided many of the originals).
2. Carlos Ulises Decena, *Tacit Subjects: Belonging and Same-Sex Desire Among Dominican Immigrant Men* (Durham, NC: Duke University Press, 2011), 8.
3. Pat Califia, *Sex Changes: The Politics of Transgenderism* (San Francisco: Cleis Press, 1997), 5.
4. Jasbir K. Puar, "Queer Times, Queer Assemblages," *Social Text,* 23.3/4 (Fall-Winter 2005), 121.
5. Refer to "A Timeline of HIV and Aids," https://www.hiv.gov/hiv-basics/overview/history/hiv-and-aids-timeline
6. Susan Stryker, "Transgender Studies: Queer Theory's Evil Twin," *GLQ: A Journal of Lesbian and Gay Studies,* 10.2 (2004), 213.
7. Jaime Cortez, *Sexile/Sexilio* (New York: The Institute for Gay Men's Health, 2004), vii.
8. Oxford Latin Dictionary, second edi-

tion, volume II, ed. by P.G.W. Glare (Oxford: Oxford University Press, 2012).

9. Scholarship in this area is steadily increasing. See for example Patricia Gherovici's book, *Please Select Your Gender: From the Invention of Hysteria to the Democratizing of Transgenderism* (New York: Routledge, 2010); David Valentine's, *Imagining Transgender: An Ethnography of a Category* (Durham: Duke University Press, 2007); and Laura Erickson-Schroth's, *Trans Bodies, Trans Selves: A Resource for the Transgender Community* (Oxford: Oxford University Press, 2014).

10. In its 2013 report on hate violence, key findings from the National Coalition of Anti-Violence Programs (NCAVP) reveal that "transgender people of color" who survived violent attacks were "2.7 times more likely to experience police violence and 6 times more likely to experience physical violence from the police compared to White cisgender survivors and victims." Homicide rates for transgender people of color were also markedly higher. Refer to report at: http://www.avp.org/resources/avp-resources/315

11. Viviane Namaste, "Undoing Theory: The 'Transgender Question' and the Epistemic Violence of Anglo-American Feminist Theory," *Hypatia*, 24.3 (Summer 2009), 20.

12. *Ibid.*, 16–17.

13. Jean Bobby Noble, *Masculinities without Men? Female Masculinity in Twentieth-Century Fictions* (Vancouver: UBC Press, 2004), xi.

14. Susan Stryker, "(De) Subjugated Knowledges: An Introduction to Transgender Studies," in *The Transgender Studies Reader*, ed. by Susan Stryker and Stephen Whittle (London: Routledge, 2006), 1–2.

15. Janice G. Raymond, "Sappho by Surgery: The Transsexually Constructed Lesbian-Feminist," in *The Transgender Studies Reader*, ed. by Susan Stryker and Stephen Whittle (London: Routledge, 2006), 134.

16. Zachary I. Nataf, selections from "Lesbians Talk Transgender," in *The Transgender Studies Reader*, ed. by Susan Stryker and Stephen Whittle (London: Routledge, 2006), 442.

17. Gabriel Arkles, "Safety and Solidarity Across Gender Lines: Rethinking Segregation of Transgender People in Detention," *Temple Political & Civil Rights Law Review*, 18.2 (2008) (p. 547). Arkles notes that under the Eighth Amendment, prison officials could be held accountable if they "exhibit deliberate indifference to excessive risks to the health or safety of prisoners" (p. 547). (See also Christine Peek's extensive discussion of this same issue in her essay,

"Breaking out of the Prison Hierarchy: Transgender Prisoners, Rape, and the Eighth Amendment").

18. Aimee Wodda and Vanessa R. Panfil, "'Don't Talk to Me About Deception': The Necessary Erosion of the Trans Panic Defense," *Albany Law Review*, 78 (2014/2015), 933.

19. *Ibid.*, 935.

20. Theresa M. Tensuan, "Crossing the Lines: Graphic (Life) Narratives and Co-Laborative Political Transformations," *Biography* (Honolulu), 32.1 (Winter 2009), 175.

21. *Ibid.* (Note: As I have done in previous chapters, I use the terms "comics" and "graphic narratives" interchangeably, primarily because of the common structural and spatiotemporal elements they share).

22. Judith Butler, "Doing Justice to Someone: Sex Reassignment and Allegories of Transsexuality," *GLQ*, 7.4 (2001), 622.

23. Talia Mae Bettcher, "Evil Deceivers and Make-Believers: On Transphobic Violence and the Politics of Illusion," *Hypatia*, 22 (Summer 2007), 48.

24. Katrina C. Rose, "When is an attempted rape *NOT* an attempted rape? When the victim is a transsexual," *American University Journal of Gender, Social Policy & the Law*, 9 (2001), 505 (n.2).

25. *Ibid.*

26. See also Jay Prosser's *Second Skins: The Body Narratives of Transsexuality* (New York: Columbia University Press, 1998), specifically the chapter "No Place Like Home," where he alternately refers to transgender as a "container" and "umbrella" term. His definition of the term is in line with previously mentioned scholars, although he frames the debate from a slightly different viewpoint.

27. Paisley Currah, "Gender Pluralisms under the Transgender Umbrella," in *Transgender Rights*, ed. by Paisley Currah, Richard M. Juang, and Shannon Price Minter (Minneapolis: University of Minnesota Press, 2006), 6–7.

28. *Ibid.*

29. Judith Halberstam, *In a Queer Time and Place: Transgender Bodies, Subcultural Lives* (New York: New York University Press, 2005), 49.

30. Cristan Williams, "Transgender," *Transgender Studies Quarterly*, 1 (May 2014), 234.

31. *Ibid.*

32. See for example Judith Butler's work (*Gender Trouble* and *Undoing Gender*) for a broader treatment of how sex/gender is displaced and re-signified in trans contexts.

33. An extensive research project undertaken

by *The Miami Herald/El Nuevo Herald* over a five-month period resulted in the creation of a database listing the names of 130,000 Cuban refugees arriving in America between April and September of 1980 on 1,600 vessels. Coast Guard records that were previously thought to be unavailable or non-existent were uncovered. Yet in spite of this impressive collection of data, the list was always a work in progress, relying in part on "Marielitos" who had made the journey coming forward to add their details to the database. This might explain why neither the "Lynn Marie," nor Jorge Antonio Vázquez's name, could be located on the passenger manifests. (Also refer to Aileen S. Yoo and Glenn Garvin's respective articles regarding Fidel Castro's alleged intentional release of criminals and the mentally ill. Depending upon the political bent of the newspaper, the number of criminals and mentally ill patients released from Cuba's prisons and institutions vary widely). See articles: http://www.washingtonpost.com/wp-srv/inatl/longterm/cuba/mariel_port.htm; http://www.latinamericanstudies.org/mariel/fallout.htm

34. Cortez, *Sexile*, vii.

35. *Ibid.*

36. Refer to Michele Carlson's January 28, 2013 interview with Jaime Cortez at http://www.artpractical.com/feature/in_the_artists_studio_part_3_jaime_cortez/

37. On April 1, 1980, Hector Sanyustiz, an unemployed bus driver, drove a bus through the gates of the Peruvian Embassy in Cuba. He was accompanied by Radamés Gomez, Francisco Molina Díaz, Maria Antonia Martínez and her 12-year-old stepson, as well as Arturo Quevedo, Hector Sanyustiz's 18-year-old stepson. (Refer to the critical account in *Florida and the Mariel Boatlift of 1980: The First Twenty Days*). In a fit of pique over the Peruvian government's refusal to turn these people over to the Cuban authorities, Fidel Castro ordered the gates around the Embassy to be torn down. He let it be known that those who wanted to leave Cuba could do so by gathering at the Embassy, and within a matter of days, upwards of ten thousand people swarmed the Embassy grounds. Refer to Susana Peña's essay, "'Obvious Gays' and the State Gaze: Cuban Gay Visibility and U.S. Immigration Policy during the 1980 Mariel Boatlift," *Journal of the History of Sexuality*, 16.3 (July 2007) (pp. 484–485). These Cuban exiles came to be known as "Marielitos."

38. Accounts vary relevant to the number of vessels sailing back and forth between Cuba and Florida, as well as on the total number of Cubans arriving in Florida from April 1980 to September/October 1980. For the sake of consistency, any further data included in this chapter is based on Coast Guard reports.

39. Most accounts of the Mariel Boatlift leave out several key events preceding Hector Sanyustiz and others driving a bus through the gates of the Peruvian Embassy. Gay Nemeti, a researcher for the *Miami Herald*, compiled a chronology that began on 30 January 1980 with the hijacking of a sand dredger from Varadero, Cuba. It took thirty-two hours for sixty-six Cubans to reach Miami, where they were granted asylum. Approximately sixteen days later, Cuban stowaways on a Liberian freighter hijacked the boat and sailed it to Key West, Florida. And on February 26, 1980, twenty-six Cubans (using two rusty revolvers) commandeered a government-owned pleasure craft and set sail for the Florida Keys. The chronology ends in 1985, five years after the official end of the boatlift. Refer to: http://www.latinamericanstudies.org/mariel/mariel-chronology.htm

40. Two years after Fidel Castro came to power on the back of the Cuban Revolution of 1959, President-elect John F. Kennedy was briefed by the CIA relevant to carrying forward Dwight D. Eisenhower's plan to overthrow Castro's government. The failed mission came to be known as the Bay of Pigs, or in Latin America as *La Batalla de Girón*. Refer to http://www.jfklibrary.org/JFK/JFK-in-History/The-Bay-of-Pigs.aspx

41. Cortez, *Sexile*, 50.

42. *Ibid.*, iv.

43. It was not until 1982 that the name of the disease was officially announced as Human Immunodeficiency Virus Infection/Acquired Immunodeficiency Syndrome(HIV/AIDS). Refer to Mirko D. Grmek's *History of AIDS: Emergence and Origin of a Modern Pandemic* (Princeton: Princeton University Press, 1990), 13.

44. Refer to reports produced by the Center for Disease Control (CDC), http://www.cdc.gov/mmwr/preview/mmwrhtml/mm5021a2.htm. See also the 'Diagnosis of HIV Infection in the United States and Dependent Areas, 2012,' report from the Centers for Disease Control, http://www.cdc.gov/hiv/library/reports/surveillance/2012/surveillance_Report_vol_24.html

45. Refer to https://www.aids.gov/hiv-aids-basics/hiv-aids-101/statistics/

46. Refer again to https://www.aids.gov/hiv-aids-basics/hiv-aids-101/statistics/

47. San Francisco Department of Health HIV Epidemiology Annual Report 2013. (San Francisco: San Francisco Department of Health, 2013), 52.

48. Michael J. Green and MK Czerwiec, "Graphic Medicine: The Best of 2016," *JAMA*, 316 (December 2016), 2580.

49. Pramod K. Nayar, "Communicable Diseases: Graphic Medicine and the Extreme," *Journal of Creative Communications*, 10 (2015).

50. *Ibid.*, 163.

51. Excerpt from Maureen Burdock's paper, "Desire Paths: PathoGraphics and Transgenerational Trauma," to be published in the forthcoming book by Penn State University Press, *PathoGraphics: Narrative, Aesthetics, Contention, Community.*

52. *Ibid.*, unpaginated.

53. *Ibid.*

54. Cortez, *Sexile*, vii.

55. *Ibid.*, 3.

56. "Timeline: Key events in Fidel Castro's life," *Reuters*, February 20, 2008, https://www.reuters.com/article/us-cuba-castro-chronology/timeline-key-events-in-fidel-castros-life-idUSN1922589220080220

57. Cortez, *Sexile*, 4.

58. *Ibid.*

59. *Ibid.*, 10.

60. *Ibid.*

61. *Ibid.*

62. Califia, *Sex Changes,* 89.

63. *Ibid.*

64. *Ibid.*, 90.

65. Silvia Pedraza, "Los Marielitos of 1980: Race, Class, Gender, and Sexuality," in *Cuba in Transition,* 14 (August 2004), p. 97. Note: Pedraza's paper was presented at the annual conference of The Association for the Study of the Cuban Economy (ASCE), from 5–7 August 2004, at the Wyndham Grand Bay Hotel in Miami, Florida.

66. *Ibid.*

67. Cortez, *Sexile*, 8.

68. *Ibid.*

69. Susana Peña, "Gender and Sexuality in Latina/o Miami: Documenting Latina Transsexual Activists," *Gender & History*, 22.3 (November 2010), 755.

70. Roger N. Lancaster, "Subject Honor and Object Shame: The Construction of Male Homosexuality and Stigma in Nicaragua," *Ethnology*, 27.2 (April 1988), 113.

71. *Ibid.*

72. *Ibid.*

73. *Ibid.*

74. Cortez, *Sexile*, 9.

75. R.W. Connell, "A Very Straight Gay: Masculinity, Homosexual Experience, and the Dynamics of Gender," *American Sociological Review,* 57.6 (December 1992), 736.

76. Cortez, *Sexile*, 6.

77. Karen Kopelson, "Dis/Integrating the Gay/Queer Binary: "Reconstructed Identity Politics" for a Performative Pedagogy," *College English*, 65.1 (September 2002), 20.

78. Cortez, *Sexile*, 6.

79. *Ibid.*, 9.

80. *Ibid.*, 10.

81. *Ibid.*

82. Bettcher, "Evil Deceivers and Make-Believers," 47.

83. Cortez, *Sexile*, 10.

84. Scott McCloud, *Understanding Comics: The Invisible Art* (New York: HarperCollins, 1993), 63.

85. *Ibid.*

86. Kopelson, "Dis/Integrating the Gay/Queer Binary," 20.

87. *Ibid.*, 20.

88. Kopelson, 'Dis/Integrating the Gay/Queer Binary,' 19.

89. Cortez, *Sexile*, 11.

90. *Ibid.*

91. *Ibid.*, 12.

92. Two significant events significantly changed the narrative in American politics. The first was the repeal in September 2011 of the "Don't Ask, Don't Tell" policy that prevented LGBT people from openly serving in the United States Armed Forces. The second was the June 2015 United States Supreme Court decision striking down the marriage ban for same-sex couples. While these victories do not guarantee across-the-board equality for LGBT people, they are nevertheless a clarion call to those who still seek meaningful legal relief from the tyranny of other forms of injustice.

93. Cortez, *Sexile*, 15.

94. *Ibid.*, 16.

95. *Ibid.*, 19.

96. Toril Moi, *What is a Woman? And Other Essays* (Oxford: Oxford University Press, 1999), 113.

97. Cortez, *Sexile*, 22.

98. *Ibid.*

99. *Ibid.*, 23.

100. See for example the article at: http://www.theguardian.com/world/2014/jan/03/cuba-classic-car-streets-rule-change-new-purchase; and also the article at http://www.nytimes.com/2004/10/27/automobiles/27MILL.html?_r=0

101. Cortez, *Sexile*, 34.

102. *Ibid.*

103. *Ibid.*, 35.

104. *Ibid.*, 36.

105. Ramona F. Oswald, Katherine A. Kuvalanka, Libby B. Blume, and Dana Berkowitz, "Queering 'The Family,'" in *Handbook of Feminist*

Theory and Family Studies, ed. by Sally A. Lloyd,
April L. Few, and Katharine R. Allen (Thousand
Oaks: Sage Publications, Inc., 2009), 43.
106. Cortez, *Sexile,* 8.
107. *Ibid.,* 36.
108. *Ibid.,* 40.
109. *Ibid.*
110. *Ibid.,* 42.
111. *Ibid.*
112. *Ibid.,* 45.
113. Hortense J. Spillers, "Mama's Baby,
Papa's Maybe: An American Grammar Book,"
Diacritics, 17.2 (Summer, 1987), 65.
114. Cortez, *Sexile,* 45.
115. Henry Louis Gates, Jr., *The Signifying
Monkey: A Theory of African-American Literary
Criticism* (Oxford: Oxford University Press,
1988), xx.
116. *Ibid.*
117. James V. Morrison, *Homeric Misdirection: False Predictions in the Iliad* (Ann Arbor:
The University of Michigan Press, 1992), 7.
118. *Ibid.,* 51.
119. Cortez, *Sexile,* 34.
120. *Ibid.,* 35.
121. *Ibid.*
122. Morrison, *Homeric Misdirection,* 3.
123. Refer to Michele Carlson's "Inside the
Artist's Studio, Part 3: Jaime Cortez," http://
www.artpractical.com/feature/in_the_artists_
studio_part_3_jaime_cortez/
124. Ralowe T. Ampu, "What I Learned
From Being G Minus in the World of Homohop
Commerce," in *Nobody Passes: Rejecting the
Rules of Gender and Conformity,* ed. by Matt
Bernstein Sycamore (Berkeley: Seal Press,
2006), 126.
125. Eithne Luibhéid, "Queer/Migration: An
Unruly Body of Scholarship," *GLQ: A Journal of
Lesbian and Gay Studies,* 14.2/3 (2008), 174.
126. Sandy Stone, "The Empire Strikes Back:
A Postranssexual Manifesto," in *The Transgender
Studies Reader,* ed. by Susan Stryker and Stephen
Whittle (London: Routledge, 2006), 230.
127. Heike Bauer, "Literary Sexualities," in
*The Cambridge Companion to the Body in Lit-
erature,* ed. by David Hillman and Ulrika Maude
(Cambridge: Cambridge University Press, 2015),
102.
128. Gayle Rubin, "Of Catamites and Kings:
Reflections on Butch, Gender, and Boundaries,"
in Susan Stryker and Stephen Whittle, eds, *The
Transgender Studies Reader* (London: Routledge,
2006), 478.
129. Cortez, *Sexile,* 60.
130. *Ibid.,* 48.
131. *Ibid.,* 57.
132. *Ibid.*
133. *Ibid.*
134. C. Riley Snorton, "Passing for White,
Passing for Man: Johnson's *The Autobiography of
an Ex-Colored Man* as Transgender Narrative" in
*Trans/Gender Migrations: Bodies, Borders, and
the Politics of Gender Crossing,* ed. by Trystan T.
Cotton (Oxon: Routledge, 2011), 111.
135. Cortez, *Sexile,* 59.
136. *Ibid.,* 58.
137. *Ibid.*
138. *Ibid.*
139. *Ibid.*
140. *Ibid.,* 61.
141. Snorton, "Passing for White, Passing for
Man," 109.
142. Karen Cronacher, "Unmasking the Minstrel Mask's Black Magic in Ntozake Shange's *spell
#7*," *Theatre Journal,* 44.2 (May 1992), 178.
143. *Ibid.,* 180.
144. *Ibid.,* 178.
145. Cortez, *Sexile,* 62.
146. *Ibid.*
147. *Ibid.*
148. Will Eisner, *Comics and Sequential Art:
Principles and Practices from the Legendary Cartoonist* (London: W.W. Norton, 2008), 90.
149. Cortez, *Sexile,* 64.
150. *Ibid.*
151. Cortez, *Sexile,* vii.

Chapter 7

1. To avoid confusion I refer to the author
by her given name or as "author" and to her
character as the "narrator."
2. "Interview with a Raw Talent: Beldan
Sezen—Cartoonist," *Sable LitMag,* 9 (November
2012), http://beldansezen.squarespace.com/dis
play/ShowImage?imageUrl=/storage/61-raw-
talent-extract.jpg?__SQUARESPACE_CACHE
VERSION=1323010087106
3. Sanam Naraghi Anderlini and John Tirman, "Resisting the New Conservatism: Women's
campaigns for rights, peace and participation in
Turkey," *International Civil Society Action Network,* Brief 12 (Winter 2015), 4.
4. *Ibid.,* 5.
5. *Ibid.*
6. Jackie Stacey, "'If You Don't Play, You
Can't Win': *Desert Hearts* and the lesbian romance film," in *Immortal, Invisible: Lesbians and
the moving image,* ed. Tamsin Wilton (London:
Routledge, 1995), 70.
7. Beldan Sezen, *Snapshots of a Girl* (Vancouver: Arsenal Pulp Press, 2015), 46.

8. Stacey, "'If You Don't Play, You Can't Win,'" 77.

9. There are numerous examples of comic book illustrators utilizing this technique to breach the imaginary wall between readers and comic book characters. In 2015 Grant Morrison and Doug Mahnke created "Ultra Comics," where the technique was used to great effect. This technique was also used in 2005's "Infinite Crisis," where Superboy-Prime crosses over into the real world to troll message boards and even take aim at DC Comics. Refer to Nigel Mitchell's 2017 article at: https://www.cbr.com/16-comic-book-characters-who-broke-the-fourth-wall/

10. Tamsin Wilton, "On Not Being Lady Macbeth: Some (troubled) thoughts on lesbian spectatorship," in Immortal, Invisible: Lesbians and the moving image, ed. Tamsin Wilton (London: Routledge, 1995), 116.

11. Anne Friedberg, "Urban mobility and cinematic visuality: the screens of Los Angeles—endless cinema or private telematics," Journal of Visual Culture, 1 (2002), 188.

12. Elizabeth Freeman, Time Binds: Queer Temporalities, Queer Histories (Durham: Duke University Press, 2010), xviii.

13. Sabine Hake, "The Filmic Gaze," H-Net Reviews in the Humanities & Social Sciences (August 2009), 2.

14. Sezen, Snapshots, 8.

15. Ibid., 10.

16. Jewel Daney, "Family Banishments: Understanding Honor Crimes in the United States," in Femininities, Masculinities, and the Politics of Sexual Difference(s), eds. Dorothy Sue Cobble, Beth Hutchison, and Amanda B. Chaloupka (New Jersey: Institute for Research on Women, 2004), 38.

17. Refer to Eric Wong's article, "Breaking the Silence: How Comics Visualize Sound," Sequart Organization, December 31, 2014, http://sequart.org/magazine/53486/how-comics-visualize-sound/

18. Anne Magnussen, "The Semiotics of C.S. Peirce as a Theoretical Framework for the Understanding of Comics," in Comics & Culture: Analytical and Theoretical Approaches to Comics, ed. by Anne Magnussen and Hans-Christian Christiansen (Denmark: Museum Tusculanum Press, 2000), 203.

19. Feyza Burak Adli, "The Veiled Periphery: Rural Kurdish Women in Turkey and the Taboo of Sexuality," Student Anthropologist, 3.1 (2012).

20. Eve S. Sedgwick, "The Character in the Veil: Imagery of the Surface in the Gothic Novel," PMLA, 96.2 (March 1981), 256.

21. Ibid.

22. Sezen, Snapshots, 8.

23. Ibid. Refer also to Alice Walker's, In Search of Our Mothers' Gardens: Womanist Prose, for full quote.

24. Sezen, Snapshots, 27.

25. Sara Ahmed, Queer Phenomenology: Orientations, Objects, Others (Durham NC: Duke University Press, 2006), 79.

26. William R. Freudenburg and Margarita Alario, "Weapons of Mass Distraction: Magicianship, Misdirection, and the Dark Side of Legitimation," Sociological Forum, 22.2 (June 2007).

27. This is a reference to Sara Ahmed's discussion of Frantz Fanon's reflection on the intra-psychic stratification manifested through the simple act of a black man reaching for a cigarette, when the act of reaching itself is dictated by the limits of one's surroundings and place in the world, and certainly by the internalization of the hostility communicated through white gaze.

28. Anderlini and Tirman, "Resisting the New Conservatism," 1.

29. Feride Acar and Gübanu Altunok, "The 'politics of intimate' at the intersection of neoliberalism and neo-conservatism in contemporary Turkey," Women's Studies International Forum, 41 (2013), 16.

30. Ibid.

31. See in general Freudenburg and Alario, "Weapons of Mass Distraction."

32. Sezen, Snapshots, 14.

33. Ibid.

34. Ibid., 16.

35. Antwaun Sargent, "An Artist is Deconstructing Comics into Grids in Order to Challenge Power Structures," Creators, 9 February 2017, https://creators.vice.com/en_us/article/8qdwyz/an-artist-deconstructs-comic-books-to-explore-race-and-sexuality

36. Sezen, Snapshots, 50–52.

37. Ibid., 54.

38. Ibid., 55.

39. Gill Valentine, Tracey Skelton, and Ruth Butler, "Coming out and outcomes: negotiating gay and lesbian identities with, and in, the family," Environment and Planning D: Society and Space, 21 (2003), 480.

40. Justin Vela, "'Abortions are like Air Strikes on Civilians': Turkish PM Recep Tayyip Ergodan's Rant Sparks Women's Rage," Independent, 30 May 2012, http://www.independent.co.uk/life-style/health-and-families/health-news/abortions-are-like-air-strikes-on-civilians-turkish-pm-recep-tayyip-erdogans-rant-sparks-womens-rage-7800939.html

41. H. Burcu Baba, "The Construction of

Heteropatriarchal Family and Dissident Sexualities in Turkey," *Fe Dergi 3*, 1 (2011), 56.

42. *Ibid.*

43. Trevor A. Le V. Harris, *Maupassant in the Hall of Mirrors: Ironies of Repetition in the Work of Guy de Maupassant* (New York: Palgrave Macmillan, 1990), 54.

44. Samuel Osborne and Chris Baynes, "Turkey bans all LGBT events in capital to 'protect public security,'" *Independent*, 19 November 2017, http://www.independent.co.uk/news/world/europe/lgbt-events-banned-turkey-ankara-protect-public-security-governors-office-health-and-morality-a8063526.html.

45. See for example Evan Ettinghoff's article, "Outed at School: Student Privacy Rights and Preventing Unwanted Disclosures of Sexual Orientation," *Loyola of Los Angeles Law Review*, 47 (27 October 2014). See also Mary Lou Rasmussen's "The Problem of Coming Out," *Theory into Practice*, 43 (Spring 2004). Also refer to Jason Ritchie's "How Do You Say 'Come Out of the Closet' in Arabic?" *GLQ: A Journal of Lesbian and Gay Studies*, 16 (2010).

46. Prior to passage of the "Don't Ask, Don't Tell" policy in 1994, LGBT soldiers lived in fear of being discovered and discharged from military service. Caught in a legalistic limbo, they were prohibited from coming out or being asked questions about their sexual orientation. In 2011, the Obama administration repealed "Don't Ask, Don't Tell," but the current attack on transgender soldiers by the Trump administration once again shines a light on the precariousness of legal protections for LGBT people.

47. Richard T. Liu and Brian Mustanski, "Suicidal Ideation and Self-Harm in Lesbian, Gay, Bisexual, and Transgender Youth," *American Journal of Preventive Medicine*, 42 (2012), 226.

48. Sezen, *Snapshots*, 73–74.

49. *Ibid.*, 116.

50. *Ibid.*, 117. The anthology referred to by Sezen was published in 1999 by Blue Moon Press. The full title of the book is *Talking Home: Heimat aus unserer eigenen Feder: Frauen of Color in Deutschland.*

51. *Ibid.*, 116.

52. This term describes feelings, thoughts, and states of mind in comics.

53. Sezen, *Snapshots*, 118.

54. Martha J. Cutter, *Unruly Tongue: Identity and Voice in American Women's Writing, 1850–1930* (Jackson: University Press of Mississippi, 1999), unpaginated.

55. Sezen, *Snapshots*, 118.

56. *Ibid.*, 119.

57. *Ibid.*, 118.

58. *Ibid.*, 63.

59. From 1984 to 1989, Eberhard Diepgen served as the Mayor of West Berlin. In 1991, under a unified Germany, he was elected Mayor of Berlin. I could find no information that suggested he was gay. However, Klaus Wowereit, Diepgen's successor, was elected as the first openly gay Mayor of Berlin. His term ended in December 2014 amid controversy over repeated delays and cost overruns on Berlin's new airport.

60. *Ibid.*, 98.

61. Michiel Dehaene and Lieven De Cauter, *Heterotopia and the City: Public space in a post-civil society*, eds. Michiel Dehaene and Lieven De Cauter (London: Routledge, 2008), 3.

62. *Ibid.*, 3–4.

63. *Ibid.*, 4.

64. Sezen, *Snapshots*, 116.

65. Cristina Delgado-Garcia, "Invisible Spaces for the 'Impossible' State: National Identity and the Production of Space in Joe Sacco's *Palestine*," *ImageText: Interdisciplinary Comics Studies*, 8 (2015), unpaginated.

66. Sezen, *Snapshots*, 132.

67. *Ibid.*

68. Kevin G. Barnhurst, "Visibility as Paradox: Representation and Simultaneous Contrast," in *Media/Queered: Visibility and Its Discontents*, ed. Kevin G. Barnhurst (New York: Peter Lang, 2007), 4.

69. *Ibid.*

70. *Ibid.*

71. Sezen, *Snapshots*, 133.

72. *Ibid.*

73. *Ibid.*

Chapter 8

1. Paul Tillich, *The Eternal Now* (New York: Charles Scribner's Sons, 1963), 5.

2. Susan Sontag, *Reborn: Journals and Notebooks, 1947–1963* (New York: Farrar Straus Giroux, 2008), 303.

3. *Ibid.*, 137.

4. Daphne Merkin, "The Dark Lady of the Intellectuals," *New York Times*, October 29, 2000, http://www.nytimes.com/2000/10/29/books/the-dark-lady-of-the-intellectuals.html.

5. Noelle Leslie Dela Cruz, "Surviving Hiroshima: An Hermeneutical Phenomenology of *Barefoot Gen* by Keiji Nakazawa," from a paper Dela Cruz presented in 2015 at the National Conference of the Philosophical Association of the Philippines.

6. Refer to Carlos Kong's "SuperQueeros— Our LGBTI Comic Book Heroes and Heroines," *Contemporaneity: Historical Presence in Visual Culture*, 5.1 (2016); Donald E. Hall's *Reading Sexualities—Hermeneutic Theory and the Future of Queer Studies* (New York: Routledge, 2009); and Karin Kukkonen's *Contemporary Comics Storytelling* (Lincoln: University of Nebraska Press, 2013)

7. Dela Cruz, "Surviving Hiroshima," 3.

8. Annemie Halsema, "The Time of the Self: A Feminist Reflection on Ricoeur's Notion of Narrative Identity," in *Time in Feminist Phenomenology*, eds. Christina Schües, Dorothea E, Olkowski, and Helen A. Fielding (Bloomington: Indiana University Press, 2011), 116.

9. Chris Kincaid explains the colored lines that drop over a character's face as situational and representative of various emotions depending upon their color and shape. The cruciform popping veins are represented by a symbol typically appearing on the forehead or a clenched fist. See "Anime's Visual Language" at: https://www.japanpowered.com/japan-culture/animes-visual-language

10. Dela Cruz developed two versions of the matrix; the first appeared in a paper presented in 2015 at the National Conference of the Philosophical Association of the Philippines, and the second in 2016 for the *Polish Journal of Aesthetics*. The second version added a third axis to the matrix.

11. Paul Ricoeur, "The Task of Hermeneutics," *Philosophy Today*, 17 (Summer 1973), 112.

12. Valérie Angenot, Semiotics and Hermeneutics," in *A Companion to Ancient Egyptian Art*, ed. Melinda K. Hartwig (Massachusetts: John Wiley & Sons Ltd, 2015), 108.

13. Ingrida Vaňková, "Life as a Story—Self as a Text," *English Matters* (2010), 54. http://www.pulib.sk/elpub2/FHPV/Kacmaroval/

14. Kathleen O'Dwyer, "Paul Ricoeur: The Intersection Between Solitude and Connection," *Lyceum* XI (Fall 2009), 6.

15. *Ibid.*

16. Vaňková, "Life as a Story," 56.

17. *Ibid.*

18. *Ibid.*

19. *Ibid.*, 57.

20. *Ibid.*, 56.

21. This is the Japanese word for hermeneutics. Refer to Jay Goulding's article, "*Chushingura's* Innovation: From Kaishaku (Execution) to Kaishakugaku (Hermeneutics)," *JSAC: Japan Studies Association of Canada* (2014), 9.

22. Nicholas Davey, "The hermeneutics of seeing," in *Interpreting Visual Culture: Explo-*

rations in the Hermeneutics of the Visual, eds. Ian Heywood and Barry Sandywell (London: Routledge, 1999), 9.

23. *Ibid.*,10.

24. *Ibid.*

25. *Ibid.*, 10–11.

26. Susan Sontag, *Styles of Radical Will* (London: Penguin Classics, 1969), 9.

27. *Ibid.*, 32.

28. Neil Cohn and Sean Ehly, "The vocabulary of manga: Visual morphology in dialects of Japanese Visual Language," *Journal of Pragmatics* 92 (2016), 19.

29. Monica Chiu, *Drawing New Color Lines: Transnational Asian American Graphic Narratives*, ed. Monica Chiu (Hong Kong: Hong Kong University Press, 2015), 4. It should also be noted that the term "culturally odourless" was coined by Koichi Iwacuchi, a well-known scholar in media and cultural studies.

30. *Ibid.*

31. Terry Kawashima, "Seeing Faces, Making Races: Challenging Visual Tropes of Racial Difference," *Meridians: feminism, race, transnationalism*, 3.1 (2002), 161

32. *Ibid.*

33. Olga Antononoka, "Blond is the new Japanese: Transcending race in shojo manga," *Mutual Images*, 1 (2016), 23.

34. Sophie Brickman, "The History of the Ramen Noodle," *The New Yorker*, May 21, 2014, https://www.newyorker.com/culture/culture-desk/the-history-of-the-ramen-noodle.

35. Mio Bryce, Jason Davis, and Christie Barber, "The Cultural Biographies and Social Lives of *Manga*: Lessons from the *Mangaverse*," *Scan Journal of Media Arts Culture*, 5 (September 2008), 5.

36. Trinh T. Minh-Ha, *When the Moon Waxes Red: Representation, Gender and Cultural Politics* (New York: Routledge, 1991), 149.

37. Sandra Annett, "Imagining Transcultural Fandom: Animation and Global Media Communities," *English & Film Studies Faculty Publications* (2011), 166.

38. John Russell, "Race and Reflexivity: The Black Other in Contemporary Japanese Mass Culture," in *Rereading Cultural Anthropology*, ed. George E. Marcus (Durham: Duke University Press, 1992), 298.

39. Annett, "Imagining Transcultural Fandom," 173.

40. *Ibid.*, 171.

41. Nina Cornyetz, "Fetishized Blackness: Hip Hop and Racial Desire in Contemporary Japan," *Social Text*, 41 (Winter 1994), 114.

42. Minh-Ha, *When the Moon Waxes Red*, 156.

43. Will Eisner, *Comics and Sequential Art: Principles and Practices from the Legendary Cartoonist* (New York: W.W. Norton & Company, 1985), 103.

44. Annett, "Imagining Transcultural Fandom," 173.

45. Robin E. Brenner, *Understanding Manga and Anime* (Connecticut: Libraries Unlimited, 2007), 40.

46. *Ibid.*

47. Brenner, *Understanding Manga*, 44.

48. *Ibid.*, 28.

49. Emily Jane Wakeling, "Girls are dancin'": shōjo culture and feminism in contemporary Japanese art," *New Voices*, 5 (2011), 130.

50. *Ibid.*, 132.

51. Nana Iro, "Isolate, Slow Faults: My Lesbian Experience with Loneliness," https://nanairocosmos.wordpress.com/2017/02/21/my-lesbian-experience-with-loneliness/

52. Tim MH Li and Paul WC Wong, "Youth social withdrawal behaviour (hikikomori): A systematic review of qualitative and quantitative studies," *Australian & New Zealand Journal of Psychiatry* 49 (2015), 596.

53. Patrick Corrigan, "How Stigma Interferes with Mental Health Care," *American Psychologist*, 59 (2004), 618.

54. Shuntaro Ando et al., "Review of mental-health-related stigma in Japan," *Psychiatry and Clinical Neurosciences*, 67 (2013), 476.

55. Kabi Nagata, *My Lesbian Experience with Loneliness* (Los Angeles: Seven Seas Entertainment, 2017), 19.

56. *Ibid.*, 20.

57. Translated, *Sabishisugite Rezu Fūzoku Ikimashita Repo* means *The Private Report on My Lesbian Experience with Loneliness*.

58. The visual symbols I point out here are by no means an exhaustive list.

59. Nagata, *My Lesbian Experience*, 4.

60. Sarah Chaplin, *Japanese Love Hotels: A Cultural History* (New York: Routledge, 2007), 1.

61. National Institute of Population and Social Security Research, "Marriage Process and Fertility of Married Couples Attitudes Toward Marriage and Family among Japanese Singles," (2017), 6.

62. See in general Richard Ronald and Yosuke Hirayama's "Home alone: the individualization of young, urban Japanese singles," *Environment and Planning*, 41 (2009).

63. Nagata, *My Lesbian Experience*, 5.

64. *Ibid.*

65. Nelson Ernesto Coelho, Jr., and Luis Claudio Figueiredo, "Patterns of Intersubjectivity in the Constitution of Subjectivity: Dimen-

sions of Otherness," *Culture & Psychology*, 9 (September 2003), 203.

66. Phil Schulte, "Holding in Mind: Intersubjectivity, Subject Relations and the Group," *Group Analysis*, 33 (December 2000), 534–535.

67. *Ibid.*, 535.

68. Nagata, *My Lesbian Experience*, 9.

69. *Ibid.*

70. *Ibid.*

71. *Ibid.*

72. *Ibid.*, 11.

73. *Ibid.*, 12.

74. See in general the article by Jose M. Valderas, et al., "Defining Comorbidity: Implications for Understanding Health and Health Services," *Annals of Family Medicine*, 7 (July/August 2009).

75. Michela Gatta, et al., "Alexithymia, impulsiveness, and psychopathology in nonsuicidal self-injured adolescents," *Neuropsychiatric Disease and Treatment* (September 2016), 2308.

76. Nagata, *My Lesbian Experience*, 13.

77. *Ibid.*

78. Donald E. Greydanus and Daniel Shek, "Deliberate Self-harm and Suicide in Adolescents," *The Keio Journal of Medicine*, 58 (2009), 147.

79. Nagata, *My Lesbian Experience*, 13.

80. George H. Mead, "What Social Objects Must Psychology Presuppose?" *The Journal of Philosophy, Psychology and Scientific Methods*, 7 (March 1910), 178.

81. Nagata, *My Lesbian Experience*, 22.

82. *Ibid.*

83. *Ibid.*

84. O'Dwyer, "Paul Ricoeur: The Intersection Between Solitude and Connection," 2.

85. *Ibid.*, 12.

86. *Ibid.*, 14.

87. Nagata, *My Lesbian Experience*, 15.

88. *Ibid.*, 18.

89. *Ibid.*

90. George H. Mead, "Wundt and the Concept of the Gesture," in *The Language of Gestures*, ed. by George H. Mead, et al. (The Hague & Paris: Mouton, 1973), 22.

91. *Ibid.*

92. See in general Jennifer H. Barnett and Jordan W. Smoller, "The Genetics of Bipolar Disorder," *Neuroscience*, 164 (November 24, 2009).

93. *Ibid.*

94. Nagata, *My Lesbian Experience* 24.

95. *Ibid.*

96. *PixieVision*, "Being a manga artist was my calling—interview with Kabi Nagata," 31 December 2016, https://www.pixivision.net/en/a/2026.

97. Nagata, *My Lesbian Experience*, 38.
98. *Ibid.*, 42.
99. *Ibid.*, 46.
100. *Ibid.*, 48.
101. *Ibid.*, 47.
102. In a letter written to Ethel Smyth on 19 August 1930, Virginia Woolf wrote: "It is true that I only want to show off to women. Women alone stir my imagination."
103. Patricia Morgne Cramer, "Virginia Woolf: Liberating Lesbian Readings from Heterosexual Bias," University of Connecticut DigitalCommons@UConn, *Articles, Papers and Presentations* (2010), 3.
104. *Ibid.*, 2.
105. *Ibid.*
106. Chris Kincaid, "Sex in Anime and Manga," *Japan Powered*, 26 March 2017, https://www.japanpowered.com/anime-articles/sex-in-anime-and-manga.
107. *Ibid.*
108. Nagata, *My Lesbian Experience*, 53.
109. *Ibid.*
110. It is only in passing that Kabi Nagata mentions having had a therapist. The focus of the therapy was her need to be held, but as seemed to be the case throughout most of the book, crucial pieces of information were either completely missing or touched on only superficially.
111. Nagata, *My Lesbian Experience*, 60.
112. *Ibid.*, 64.

113. Cassandra Avenatti and Eliza Jones, "Kinks and shrinks: The therapeutic value of queer sex work," in *Queer Sex Work*, eds. Mary Laing, Katy Pilcher and Nicola Smith (New York: Routledge, 2015), 88.
114. *Ibid.*
115. Nagata, *My Lesbian Experience*, 66.
116. *Ibid.*
117. *Ibid.*, 67.
118. *Ibid.*, 68.
119. *Ibid.*
120. *Ibid.*, 72.
121. *Ibid.*, 74.
122. *Ibid.*
123. *Ibid.*, 71.
124. *Ibid.*, 52.
125. *Ibid.*, 84.
126. *Ibid.*
127. *Ibid.*, 88.
128. *Ibid.*, 90.
129. *Ibid.*, 95.
130. *Ibid.*
131. *Ibid.*, 104.
132. There are two excellent resources that explain the history of Boys' Love manga in great detail. The first is *Boys Love Manga and Beyond: History, Culture, and Community in Japan* (2015), edited by Mark McLelland, Kazumi Nagaike, Katsuhiko Suganuma, and James Welker. The second is a 2013 editorial by Dru Pagliassotti, Kazumi Nagaike, and Mark McHarry in the *Journal of Graphic Novels and Comics*.

Bibliography

Acar, Feride, and Gübanu Altunok, "The 'politics of intimate' at the intersection of neo-liberalism and neo-conservatism in contemporary Turkey," *Women's Studies International Forum*, 41 (2013), 14–23.

Adli, Feyza Burak, "The Veiled Periphery: Rural Kurdish Women in Turkey and the Taboo of Sexuality," *Student Anthropologist*, 3.1 (2012), 47–62.

Ahmed, Sara, *Queer Phenomenology: Orientations, Objects, Others* (Durham, NC: Duke University Press, 2006).

AIDS.gov <https://www.aids.gov/hiv-aids-basics/hiv-aids-101/statistics/>

Aldrich, Robert, "Homosexuality and the City: An Historical Overview" in *Urban Studies*, 41.9 (August 2004), 1719–1737.

Alexander, Amy, *Fifty Black Women Who Changed America* (New York: Birch Lane Press, 1999).

Allen, Ernest, Jr., "Ever Feeling One's Twoness: 'Double Ideals' and Double Consciousness' in The Souls of Black Folk," *Contributions in Black Studies*, 9 (1992), 55–69.

Allen, Jafari S., "Black/Queer/Diaspora at the Current Conjuncture," *GLQ*, 18 (2012), 211–248.

Alverson, Brigid, "Defining Yuri Manga: Q&A with Erica Friedman," https://www.barnesandnoble.com/blog/sci-fi-fantasy/defining-yuri-manga-qa-erica-friedman/.

Ampu, Ralowe T., "What I Learned From Being G Minus in the World of Homohop Commerce," in Matt Bernstein Sycamore, ed., *Nobody Passes: Rejecting the Rules of Gender and Conformity* (Berkeley: Seal Press, 2006), 112–126.

Anderlini, Sanam N., and John Tirman, "Resisting the New Conservatism: Women's campaigns for rights, peace and participation in Turkey," *International Civil Society Action Network*, Brief 12 (Winter 2015), 1–12.

Anderson, Pamela S., and Beverley Clack, eds., *Feminist Philosophy of Religion: Critical Readings* (London: Routledge, 2004).

Ando, Shuntaro, et al., "Review of mental-health-related stigma in Japan," *Psychiatry and Clinical Neurosciences*, 67 (September 2013), 471–482.

Andrea, Heidi, "Queer Latina Punk Artist Cristy C. Road: The Interview," *Autostraddle* (2003) <http://www.autostraddle.com/queer-latina-punk-artist-cristy-c-road-the-interview/>

Angenot, Valérie, "Semiotics and Hermeneutics," in *A Companion to Ancient Egyptian Art*, ed. Melinda K. Hartwig (Massachusetts: John Wiley & Sons Ltd, 2015), 98–119.

Annett, Sandra, "Imagining Transcultural Fandom: Animation and Global Media Communities," *English & Film Studies Faculty Publications* (2011), 164–188.

Antononoka, Olga, "Blond is the new Japanese: Transcending race in shojo manga," *Mutual Images*, 1 (2016), 22–46.

Anzaldúa, Gloria, *Borderlands/La Frontera: The New Mestiza*, 3rd ed. (San Francisco: Aunt Lute Books, 2007).

Aoláin, Fionnuala Ní, "Women, Security, and the Patriarchy of Internationalized Transitional Justice," *Human Rights Quarterly*, 31.4 (2009), 1055–1085.

Arkles, Gabriel, "Safety and Solidarity Across Gender Lines: Rethinking Segregation of Transgender People in Detention," *Temple Political & Civil Rights Law Review*, 18.2 (2008), 515–560.

Arredondo, Gabriela F., and others, eds., *Chicana Feminisms: A Critical Reader* (Durham, NC: Duke University Press, 2003).

Arthos, John Jr., "The shaman-trickster's art of misdirection: The rhetoric of Farrakhan and the million men," *Quarterly Journal of Speech*, 87.1 (June 2009), 41–60.

Atoe, Osa, *Shotgun Seamstress: a zine by and for*

black punks (Tacoma: Mend My Dress Press, 2012).

Avenatti, Cassandra, and Eliza Jones, "Kinks and shrinks: The therapeutic value of queer sex work," in *Queer Sex Work,* eds. Mary Laing, Katy Pilcher and Nicola Smith (New York: Routledge, 2015), 88–94.

Baba, H. Burcu, "The Construction of Heteropatriarchal Family and Dissident Sexualities in Turkey," *Fe Dergi 3,* 1 (2011), 56–64.

Bacchetta, Paola, Fatima El-Tayeb, and Jin Haritaworn, "Queer of colour formations and translocal spaces in Europe," *Environment and Planning D: Society and Space,* 33 (2015), 769–778.

Bakhtin, Mikhail, M., *The Dialogic Imagination: Four Essays by M.M. Bakhtin,* ed. by Michael Holquist, trans. by Caryl Emerson and Michael Holquist (Austin: University of Texas Press, 1981).

Barnett, Jennifer H., and Jordan W. Smoller, "The Genetics of Bipolar Disorder," *Neuroscience,* 164 (November 24, 2009), 331–343.

Barnhurst, Kevin G., "Visibility as Paradox: Representation and Simultaneous Contrast," in *Media/Queered: Visibility and its Discontents,* ed. Kevin G. Barnhurst (New York: Peter Lang, 2007), 1–22.

Bauer, Heike, "Graphic Lesbian Continuum," in *Graphic Details: Jewish Women's Confessional Comics in Essays and Interviews,* ed. by Sarah Lightman (North Carolina: McFarland, 2014), 98–109.

_____, "Literary Sexualities," in *The Cambridge Companion to the Body in Literature,* ed. by David Hillman and Ulrika Maude (Cambridge: Cambridge University Press, 2015), 101–115.

Bechdel, Alison, *Fun Home* (London: Jonathan Cape, 2006).

Bennett, Michael, and Vanessa D. Dickerson, eds, *Recovering the Black Female Body: Self-Representations by African American Women* (New Brunswick: Rutgers University Press, 2001).

Bergman, Mike, "A Foundational Mindset: Firstness, Secondness, Thirdness," http://www.mkbergman.com/1932/a-foundational-mindset-firstness-secondness-thirdness.

Berlatsky, Noah, "Racism and Comics: Good Intentions are Not Enough," *The Atlantic,* December 2, 2013, https://www.theatlantic.com/entertainment/archive/2013/12/racism-and-comics-good-intentions-arent-enough/281966/.

Berube, Allan, "How Gay Stays White and What Kind of White It Stays," in *The Making and Unmaking of Whiteness* (Durham, NC: Duke University Press, 2001), 234–265.

Bettcher, Talia Mae, "Evil Deceivers and Make-Believers: On Transphobic Violence and the Politics of Illusion," *Hypatia,* 22.3 (Summer 2007), 43–65.

Bhabha, Homi K., "Signs Taken for Wonders: Questions of Ambivalence and Authority under a Tree outside Delhi, May 1817," *Critical Inquiry,* 12 (Autumn 1985), 144–165.

Black, Marc, "Fanon and DuBoisian Double Consciousness," *Human Architecture: Journal of the Sociology of Self-Knowledge,* 5.3 (Summer 2007), 393–404.

Blackmon, Douglas A., *Slavery By Another Name: The Re-Enslavement of Black Americans from the Civil War to World War II* (New York: Anchor Books, 2008).

Blunt, Alison, and Gillian Rose, eds., *Writing, Women and Space: Colonial and Postcolonial Geographies* (New York: Guilford Press, 1994).

Brenner, Robin E., *Understanding Manga and Anime* (Connecticut: Libraries Unlimited, 2007).

Breslin, James, "Gertrude Stein and the Problems of Autobiography," *The Georgia Review,* 33 (Winter 1979), 901–913.

Brickman, Sophie, "The History of the Ramen Noodle," *The New Yorker,* May 21, 2014, https://www.newyorker.com/culture/culture-desk/the-history-of-the-ramen-noodle.

Brody, Jennifer DeVere, *Impossible Purities: Blackness, Femininity, and Victorian Culture* (Durham: Duke University Press, 1998).

Brox, Ali, "'Every age has the vampire it needs': Octavia Butler's Vampiric Vision in Fledging," 19 (2008), 391–409.

Bryant, Cedric Gael, "The Soul Has Bandaged Moments: Reading the African American Gothic in Wright's 'Big Boy Leaves Home,' Morrison's 'Beloved,' and Gomez's 'Gilda,'" *African American Review,* 39 (2005), 541–553.

Bryce, Mio, Jason Davis, and Christie Barber, "The Cultural Biographies and Social Lives of *Manga*: Lessons from the *Manga*verse," *Scan Journal of Media Arts Culture,* 5 (September 2008), 1–13.

Burdock, Maureen, excerpt from "Desire Paths: PathoGraphics and Transgenerational Trauma," to be published in the forthcoming book by Penn State University Press, *Patho-Graphics: Narrative, Aesthetics, Contention, Community.*

Burns, R.E., "The Irish Penal Code and Some of Its Historians," *The Review of Politics,* 21 (January 1959), 276–299.

Butler, Judith, "Critically Queer," *GLQ*, 1 (1993), 17–32.

———, "Doing Justice to Someone: Sex Reassignment and Allegories of Transsexuality," *GLQ*, 7 (2001), 621–636.

———, *Frames of War: When is Life Grievable?* (London: Verso, 2009).

———, *Gender Trouble: Feminism and the Subversion of Identity* (New York: Routledge, 1990).

———, "Withholding the name: translating gender in Cather's 'On the Gull's Road,'" in *Modernist Sexualities*, ed. by Hugh Stevens and Caroline Howlett (Manchester: Manchester University Press, 2000), 56–71.

Califia, Pat, *Sex Changes: The Politics of Transgenderism* (San Francisco: Cleis Press, 1997).

Caminero-Santangelo, Marta, *The Madwoman Can't Speak: Or Why Insanity is Not Subversive* (Ithaca: Cornell University Press, 1998).

Carlson, Michele, "Inside the Artist's Studio, Part 3: Jaime Cortez," http://www.artpractical. com/feature/in_the_artists_studio_part_3_ jaime_cor tez/.

Cawley, Stephanie, "Postcolonial Feminism and Comics," *The Stockton Postcolonial Studies Project* at https://blogs.stockton.edu/postcolonialstudies/postcolonial-feminism-and-comics/.

Center for Disease Control, "Diagnosis of HIV Infection in the United States and Dependent Areas, 2012," <http://www.cdc.gov/hiv/pdf/ statistics_2012_HIV_Surveillance_Report_ vol_24.pdf>

———, "HIV and AIDS—United States, 1981–2000," <http://www.cdc.gov/mmwr/preview/ mmwrhtml/mm5021a2.htm>

Chandler, Daniel, *Semiotics: The Basics* (New York: Routledge, 2017).

Chaney, Michael A., "Introduction," in Michael A. Chaney, ed., *Graphic Subjects: Critical Essays on Autobiography and Graphic Novels* (Madison: The University of Wisconsin Press, 2011), 3–9.

———, "Slave Cyborgs and the Black Infovirus: Ishmael Reed's Cybernetic Aesthetics," *MFS Modern Fiction Studies*, 49 (2003), 261–283.

Chaplin, Sarah, *Japanese Love Hotels: A Cultural History* (New York: Routledge, 2007).

Chidgey, Red, "Riot Grrrl Writing," in Nadine Monem, ed., *Riot Grrrl: Revolution Girl Style Now!* (London: Black Dog Publishing, 2007), 100–141.

Chiu, Monica, ed., *Drawing New Color Lines: Transnational Asian American Graphic Narratives* (Hong Kong: Hong Kong University Press, 2014).

Chute, Hillary, *Graphic Women: Life Narrative and Contemporary Comics* (New York: Columbia University Press, 2010).

Chute, Hillary, and Marianne DeKoven, "Introduction: Graphic Narrative," *MFS Modern Fiction Studies*, 52 (2006), 767–782.

Cixous, Hélène, "The Laugh of the Medusa," in *Feminisms: An Anthology of Literary Theory and Criticism*, rev. by Robyn R. Warhol and Diane P. Herndl (Hampshire, England: Macmillan Press, 1997), 347–362.

Coelho, Nelson Ernesto, Jr., and Luis Claudio Figueiredo, "Patterns of Intersubjectivity in the Constitution of Subjectivity: Dimensions of Otherness," *Culture & Psychology*, 9 (September 2003), 193–208.

Cohn, Neil, "The limits of time and transitions: challenges to theories of sequential image comprehension," *Studies in Comics*, 1 (2010), 127–148.

———, "Un-Defining 'comics': Separating the cultural from the structural in 'comics,'" *International Journal of Comic Art*, 7 (October 2005), 1–11.

Cohn, Neil, and Sean Ehly, "The vocabulary of manga: Visual morphology in dialects of Japanese Visual Language," *Journal of Pragmatics* 92 (2016), 17–29.

Collins, Patricia Hill, *Black Feminist Thought: Knowledge, Consciousness, and the Politics of Empowerment*, 2nd ed. (London: Routledge, [1990] 2000).

———, *Black Sexual Politics: African Americans, Gender, and the New Racism* (London: Routledge, 2005).

Connell, R.W., "A Very Straight Gay: Masculinity, Homosexual Experience, and the Dynamics of Gender," *American Sociological Review*, 57 (December 1992), 735–751.

Cornyetz, Nina, "Fetishized Blackness: Hip Hop and Racial Desire in Contemporary Japan," *Social Text*, 41 (Winter 1994), 113–139.

Corrigan, Patrick, "How Stigma Interferes with Mental Health Care," *American Psychologist*, 59 (2004), 614–625.

Cortez, Jaime, *Sexile/Sexilio* (New York: The Institute for Gay Men's Health, 2004).

Cramer, Patricia Morgne, "Virginia Woolf: Liberating Lesbian Readings from Heterosexual Bias," University of Connecticut DigitalCommons@UConn, *Articles, Papers and Presentations* (2010), 1–12.

Cronacher, Karen, "Unmasking the Minstrel Mask's Black Magic in Ntozake Shange's *spell #7*," *Theatre Journal*, 44 (May 1992), 177–193.

Currah, Paisley, "Gender Pluralisms under the Transgender Umbrella," in Paisley Currah,

Richard M. Juang, and Shannon Price Minter, eds, *Transgender Rights* (Minneapolis: University of Minnesota Press, 2006), 3–31.

Cutter, Martha J., "Sliding Significations: Passing as a Narrative and Textual Strategy in Nella Larsen's Fiction," in *Passing and the Fictions of Identity*, ed. by Elaine K. Ginsberg (Durham: Duke University Press, 1996), 75–100.

_____, *Unruly Tongue: Identity and Voice in American Women's Writing, 1850–1930* (Jackson: University Press of Mississippi, 1999), unpaginated.

Cvetkovich, Ann, *An Archive of Feelings: Trauma, Sexuality, and Lesbian Public Cultures* (Durham, NC: Duke University Press, 2003).

Daney, Jewel, "Family Banishments: Understanding Honor Crimes in the United States," in *Femininities, Masculinities, and the Politics of Sexual Difference(s)*, eds. Dorothy Sue Cobble, Beth Hutchison, and Amanda B. Chaloupka (New Jersey: Institute for Research on Women, 2004), 37–40.

Davey, Nicholas, "The hermeneutics of seeing," in *Interpreting Visual Culture: Explorations in the Hermeneutics of the Visual*, eds. Ian Heywood and Barry Sandywell (London: Routledge, 1999), 3–29.

Decena, Carlos Ulises, *Tacit Subjects: Belonging and Same-Sex Desire Among Dominican Immigrant Men* (Durham, NC: Duke University Press, 2011).

Dehaene, Michiel, and Lieven De Cauter, *Heterotopia and the City: Public space in a postcivil society*, eds. Michiel Dehaene and Lieven De Cauter (London: Routledge, 2008).

Dela Cruz, Noelle L., "Surviving Hiroshima: An Hermeneutical Phenomenology of *Barefoot Gen* by Keiji Nakazawa," from a paper Dela Cruz presented in 2015 at the National Conference of the Philosophical Association of the Philippines.

DeLamotte, Eugenia, "White Terror, Black Dreams: Gothic Constructions of Race in the Nineteenth Century," in Ruth Bienstock Anolik and Douglas L. Howard, eds, *The Gothic Other: Racial and Social Constructions in the Literary Imagination* (North Carolina: McFarland, 2004), 17–31.

Delgado-Garcia, Cristina, "Invisible Spaces for the 'Impossible' State: National Identity and the Production of Space in Joe Sacco's *Palestine, ImageText: Interdisciplinary Comics Studies*, 8 (2015), unpaginated.

Dely, Carole, "Jacques Derrida: the 'perchance' of a coming of the otherwoman: the deconstruction of 'phallocentrism' from duel to

duo," *Sens Public Revue Web* (31 October 2007) <http://sens-public.org/spip.php?article312& lang=fr>

Denson, Shane, Christina Meyer, and Daniel Stein, "Intersections: Comics and transnationalism—transnationalism and comics," eds., in *Transnational Perspectives on Graphic Narratives: Comics at the Crossroads* (London: Bloomsbury, 2013), 1–14.

Department of English and Comparative Literature, "Black Women and Their Fictions in the Twentieth Century," at < http://english. columbia.edu/black-women-and-their-fictions-twentieth-century>

Dickerson, Vanessa D., "Summoning Somebody: The Flesh Made Word in Toni Morrison's Fiction," in Michael Bennett and Vanessa D. Dickerson, eds, *Recovering the Black Female Body: Self-Representations by African American Women* (New Brunswick: Rutgers University Press, 2001), 195–218.

Downes, Julia, "Riot Grrrl: The Legacy and Contemporary Landscape of DIY Feminist Cultural Activism," in Nadine Monem, ed., *Riot Grrrl: Revolution Girl Style Now!* (London: Black Dog Publishing, 2007), 12–49.

Doyle, Laura, "'These Emotions of the Body': Intercorporeal Narrative in *To the Lighthouse*," *Twentieth Century Literature*, 40 (Spring 1994), 42–71.

DuBois, W.E.B., *Darkwater: Voices from Within the Veil* (New York: Dover Publications, 1999).

Dulanto, Andrea, "On Feminism, Identity & Latinas in Arts and Literature," *The WIP* (2013) http://thewip.net/2013/04/17/on-feminism-identity-latinas-in-arts-and-literature-an-interview-with-cristy-c-road.

Duncan, Nancy, "Renegotiating Gender and Sexuality in Public and Private Spaces," in *Bodyspace: Destabilizing geographies of gender and sexuality*, ed. by Nancy Duncan (London: Routledge, 1996), 127–145.

Duncombe, Stephen, and Maxwell Tremblay, *White Riot: Punk Rock and the Politics of Race*, ed. by Stephen Duncombe and Maxwell Tremblay (London: Verso, 2011).

Eisner, Will, *Comics and Sequential Art: Principles and Practices from the Legendary Cartoonist Will Eisner Instructional Books* (London: W.W. Norton, 2008).

El Refaie, Elisabeth, *Autobiographical Comics: Life Writing in Pictures* (Mississippi: University Press of Mississippi, 2012).

Erikson-Schroth, Laura, *Trans Bodies, Trans Selves: A Resource for the Transgender Community* (Oxford: Oxford University Press, 2014).

Esquibel, Catrióna Rueda, *With Her Machete in Her Hand: Reading Chicana Lesbians* (Austin: University of Texas Press, 2006).

Ettinghoff, Evan, "Outed at School: Student Privacy Rights and Preventing Unwanted Disclosures of Sexual Orientation," *Loyola of Los Angeles Law Review,* 47 (October 2014).

Fearnley, Andrew M., "Primitive Madness: Re-Writing the History of Mental Illness and Race," *Journal of the History of Medicine and Allied Sciences,* 63 (April 2008), 245–257.

Felman, Shoshana, "Women and Madness: The Critical Phallacy," *Diacritics,* 5 (1975), 2–10.

Feyersinger, Erwin, "Diegetic Short Circuits: Metalepsis in Animation," *Animation: An Interdisciplinary Journal,* 5 (2010), 279–294.

Filler, Nathan, *The Shock and the Fall* (London: The Borough Press, 2014).

Foley, Neil, *The White Scourge: Mexicans, Blacks, and Poor Whites in Texas Cotton Culture* (Berkeley: University of California Press, 1997).

Freedman, Ariela, "'Sorting through My Grief and Putting It into Boxes,'" in *Knowledge and Pain,* ed. by Esther Cohen, Leona Toker, Manuela Consonni, and Otniel E. Dror (Amsterdam: Rodopi, 2012), 381–399.

Freeman, Elizabeth, *Time Binds: Queer Temporalities, Queer Histories* (Durham: Duke University Press, 2010).

Freudenburg, William R., and Margarita Alario, "Weapons of Mass Distraction: Magicianship, Misdirection, and the Dark Side of Legitimation," *Sociological Forum,* 22 (June 2007), 146–173.

Friedberg, Anne, "Urban mobility and cinematic visuality: the screens of Los Angeles—endless cinema or private telematics," *Journal of Visual Culture,* 1 (2002), 183–204.

Gallop, Jane, *Reading Lacan* (Ithaca: Cornell University Press, 1985).

Garvin, Glenn, "Storey's fallout was felt for decades," http://www.latinamericanstudies.org/mariel/fallout.htm.

Garza, Elisa A., "Chicana Lesbianism and the Multigenre Text," in Lourdes Torres and Inmaculada Pertusa, eds, *Tortilleras: Hispanic and U.S. Latina Lesbian Expression* (Philadelphia: Temple University Press, 2003), 196–212.

Gates, Henry Louis, Jr., "'The "Blackness of Blackness': A Critique of the Sign and the Signifying Monkey," *Critical Inquiry,* 9 (June 1983), 685–723.

———, *The Signifying Monkey: A Theory of African-American Literary Criticism* (Oxford: Oxford University Press, 1988).

Gateward, Frances, and John Jennings, eds, *The*

Blacker the Ink: Constructions of Black Identity in Comics and Sequential Art* (New Brunswick: Rutgers University Press, 2015).

Gatta, Michela, et al., "Alexithymia, impulsiveness, and psychopathology in nonsuicidal self-injured adolescents," *Neuropsychiatric Disease and Treatment* (September 2016), 2307–2317.

Gavey, Nicola, *Just Sex?: The Cultural Scaffolding of Rape* (East Sussex: Routledge, 2005).

Gentile, John, "Interviews: Rad Women Who Make Rad Art #5: Cristy Road," *Punknews.org* (2013) http://www.punknews.org/article/53472/interviews-rad-women-who-make-rad-art-5-cristy-road.

Gherovici, Patricia, *Please Select Your Gender: From the Invention of Hysteria to the Democratizing of Transgenderism* (New York: Routledge, 2010).

Gillespie, Carmen, *Critical Companion to Toni Morrison: A Literary Reference to Her Life and Work* (New York: Facts on File, 2008).

Gillman, Melanie, "As the Crow Flies" comic strip, <http://www.melaniegillman.com/?page_id=14>

Gilmore, Leigh, *Autobiographics: A Feminist Theory of Women's Self-Representation* (Ithaca: Cornell University Press, 1994).

Gilroy, Paul, *Against Race: Imagining Political Culture Beyond the Color Line* (Cambridge: Harvard University Press, 2000).

Giovanni, Nikki, *My House* (New York: Harper-Perennial, 1974).

Goodwin, Michele Cammers, "The Black Woman in the Attic: Law, Metaphor and Madness in *Jane Eyre*," *Rutgers Law Journal,* 30 (1998–1999), 597–682.

Goulding, Jay, "*Chushingura's* Innovation: From Kaishaku (Execution) to Kaishakugaku (Hermeneutics)," *JSAC: Japan Studies Association of Canada,* 2014 (2014), 8–18.

Green, Christopher, "Fluid Frames: The Hybrid Art of Michael Nicoll Yahgulanaas," *Art in America,* November 2, 2017, https://www.artinamericamagazine.com/news-features/news/fluid-frames-the-hybrid-art-of-michael-nicoll-yahgulanaas/.

Green, Michael J., and MK Czerwiec, "Graphic Medicine: The Best of 2016," *JAMA,* 316 (December 2016), 2580–2581.

Greenhill, Pauline, "'The Snow Queen': Queer Coding in Male Directors' Films," *Marvels & Tales,* 29 (2015), 110–134.

Gregory, Chase, "In the Gutter: Comix Theory," *Studies in Comics,* 3 (2012), 107–128.

Greydanus, Donald E., and Daniel Shek, "Deliberate Self-harm and Suicide in Adolescents," *The Keio Journal of Medicine*, 58 (2009), 144–151.

Grmek, Mirko D., *History of AIDS: Emergence and Origin of a Modern Pandemic* (Princeton: Princeton University Press, 1990).

Groensteen, Thierry, *The System of Comics*, trans. by Bart Beaty and Nick Nguyen (Jackson: University Press of Mississippi, 2007).

Gruzinski, Serge, *The Mestizo Mind: the intellectual dynamics of colonization and globalization* (New York: Routledge, 2002).

Hake, Sabine, "The Filmic Gaze," *H-Net Reviews in the Humanities & Social Sciences* (August 2009), 1–2.

Halberstam, Judith, *In a Queer Time and Place: Transgender Bodies, Subcultural Lives* (New York: New York University Press, 2005).

Hall, Donald E., *Reading Sexualities—Hermeneutic Theory and the Future of Queer Studies* (New York: Routledge, 2009).

Hall, Stuart, "Race, Articulation, and Societies Structured in Dominance," in *Black British Cultural Studies: A Reader*, ed. by Houston A. Baker, Jr., Manthia Diawara, and Ruth H. Lindeborg (Chicago: The University of Chicago Press, 1996), 16–60.

Halsema, Annemie, "The Time of the Self: A Feminist Reflection on Ricoeur's Notion of Narrative Identity," in *Time in Feminist Phenomenology*, eds. Christina Schües, Dorothea E, Olkowski, and Helen A. Fielding (Bloomington: Indiana University Press, 2011), 111–134.

Hamer, Diane, "Significant Others: Lesbianism and Psychoanalytic Theory," *Feminist Review*, 34 (Spring 1990), 134–151.

Hammonds, Evelyn, "Black (w)holes and the Geometry of Black Female Sexuality," in *The Black Studies Reader*, ed. by Jacqueline Bobo, Cynthia.

Haraway, Donna J., *Simians, Cyborgs, and Women: The Reinvention of Nature* (London: Free Association Books, 1991).

Hardack, Richard, "'A Music Seeking Its Words': Double-Timing and Double Consciousness in Toni Morrison's Jazz," *Callaloo*, 18 (1995), 451–471.

Harris, Angela P., "Race and Essentialism in Feminist Legal Theory," in *Critical Race Feminism: A Reader*, ed. by Adrien Katherine Wing (New York: New York University Press, 1997), 11–18.

Harris, Trevor A. Le V., *Maupassant in the Hall of Mirrors: Ironies of Repetition in the Work of Guy de Maupassant* (New York: Palgrave Macmillan, 1990).

Harris, Trudier, "African American Protest Po-

etry" at http://nationalhumanitiescenter.org/tserve/freedom/1917beyond/essays/aaprot estpoetry.htm.

Harrison, Richard, "Seeing and Nothingness: Michael Nicoll Yahgulanaas, Haida Manga, and a Critique of the Gutter," *Canadian Review of Comparative Literature*, 43 (March 2016), 51–74.

Harrison-Kahan, Lori, "Her 'Nig': Returning the Gaze of Nella Larsen's 'Passing,'" *Modern Language Studies*, 32 (Autumn 2002), 109–138.

Hart, Francis R., "Notes for an Anatomy of Modern Autobiography," *New Literary History*, 1 (Spring 1970), 485–511.

Hawk, Kate Dupes, Ron Villella, and Adolfo Leyva de Varona, *Florida and the Mariel Boatlift of 1980: The First Twenty Days* (Tuscaloosa: The University of Alabama Press, 2014).

Hebdige, Dick, "Bleached Roots: Punks and White Ethnicity," in Stephen Duncombe and Maxwell Tremblay, eds, *White Riot: Punk Rock and the Politics of Race* (London: Verso, 2011), 38–43.

_____, *Subculture: The Meaning of Style* (New York: Methuen & Co Ltd, 1979).

Henderson, Mae Gwendolyn, "Speaking in Tongues: Dialogics, Dialectics, and the Black Woman Writer's Literary Tradition," in *Changing Our Own Words: Essays on Criticism, Theory, and Writing by Black Women*, ed. by Cheryl A. Wall (London: Routledge, 1989), 16–37.

Hernández, Ellie, "Chronotope of Desire: Emma Pérez's *Gulf Dreams*," in *Chicana Feminisms: A Critical Reader*, ed. by Gabriela F. Arredondo, and others (Durham, NC: Duke University Press, 2003), 155–177.

Higgins, Kathleen Marie, "Double Consciousness and Second Sight," in *Critical Affinities: Nietzsche and African American Thought*, ed. by Jacqueline Scott and A. Todd Franklin (New York: State University of New York Press, 2006).

Hirsch, Marianne, "Editor's Column: Collateral Damage," *PMLA*, 119 (2004), 1209–1215.

Hirsch, Paul, "'This Is Our Enemy': The Writers' War Board and Representations of Race in Comic Books, 1942–1945," *Pacific Historical Review*, 83 (2014), 448–486.

Holland, Sharon Patricia, *The Erotic Life of Racism* (Durham, NC: Duke University Press, 2012).

Home, Stewart, *Cranked Up Really High: Genre Theory and Punk Rock* (Hove: CodeX, 1995).

The Homewreckers, "What the Hell?" *The Homewreckers* (2013) http://www.the-homewreckers.com/info.htm.

hooks, bell, *Ain't I A Woman: Black Women and Feminism* (London: Pluto Press, 1982).

_____, *Black Looks: Race and Representation,* New edition (Oxon: Routledge, 2015).

_____, "Whiteness and the Black Imagination," in Ruth Frankenberg, ed., *Displacing Whiteness: Essays in Social and Cultural Criticism* (Durham: Duke University Press, 1997), 165–179.

Hooper, M. Clay, "'It is Good to Be Shifty': William Wells Brown's Trickster Critique of Black Autobiography," *Modern Language Studies,* 38 (Winter 2009), 28–45.

Howard, Sheena C., *Black Queer Identity Matrix: Towards An Integrated Queer of Color Framework* (New York: Peter Lang Publishing, 2014).

Howes, Franny, "Imagining a Multiplicity of Visual Rhetorical Traditions: Comics Lessons from Rhetoric Histories," *ImageText: Interdisciplinary Comics Studies,* 5 (2010), 1–12. Hudley, and Claudine Michel (New York: Routledge, 2004), 301–314.

Hull, Gloria T., and Barbara Smith, "Introduction" in *All the Women are White, All the Blacks are Men, But Some of Us are Brave: Black Women's Studies,* ed. by Gloria T. Hull, Patricia Bell Scott, and Barbara Smith (New York: The Feminist Press, 1982), xvii-xxxii.

Huntington, Patricia, "Fragmentation, Race, and Gender," in *Existence in Black: An Anthology of Black Existential Philosophy,* ed. by Lewis R. Gordon (London: Routledge, 1997), 185–202.

Hutchinson, George, "Nella Larsen and the Veil of Race," *American Literary Journal,* 9 (Summer 1997), 329–349.

Ignatiev, Noel, *How the Irish Became White* (Oxon: Routledge, 1995).

Ingram, Penelope, *The Signifying Body: Toward an Ethics of Sexual and Racial Difference* (Albany: State University of New York Press, 2008).

Irigaray, Luce, *This Sex Which Is Not One,* 1st ed., trans. by Catherine Porter and Carolyn Burke (Ithaca: Cornell University Press, 1985).

Iro, Nana, "Isolate, Slow Faults: My Lesbian Experience with Loneliness," https://nanairocosmos.wordpress.com/2017/02/21/my-lesbian-experience-with-loneliness/.

Jantzen, Grace M., *Becoming Divine: Towards a Feminist Philosophy of Religion* (Manchester: Manchester University Press, 1998).

Johnson, Thomas H., ed., *The Complete Poems of Emily Dickenson* (London: Faber & Faber Limited, 1970).

Kawashima, Terry, "Seeing Faces, Making Races: Challenging Visual Tropes of Racia

Difference," *Meridians: feminism, race, transnationalism,* 3.1 (2002), 161–190.

Keating, AnaLouise, "From Borderlands and New Mestizas to Nepantlas and Nepantleras: Anzaldúan Theories for Social Change," *Human Architecture: Journal of the Sociology of Self-Knowledge,* 4 (2006), 5–16.

Kemp, Jonathan, "'Her Lips are Slightly Parted': The Ineffability of Erotic Sociality in Muriel Spark's *The Driver's Seat," Modern Fiction Studies,* 54 (Fall 2008), 544–557.

Keniston, Ann, and Jeanne Follansbee Quinn, eds, "Introduction: Representing 9/11: Literature and Resistance," in *Literature after 9/11* (New York: Routledge, 2008), 1–18.

Khair, Tabish, *The Gothic, Postcolonialism and Otherness: Ghosts from Elsewhere* (London: Palgrave Macmillan, 2009).

Kincaid, Chris, "Anime's Visual Language" at: https://www.japanpowered.com/japanculture/animes-visual-language.

_____, "Sex in Anime and Manga," *Japan Powered,* 26 March 2017, https://www.japanpowered.com/anime-articles/sex-in-anime-and-manga.

Kong, Carlos, "SuperQueeros—Our LGBTI Comic Book Heroes and Heroines," *Contemporaneity: Historical Presence in Visual Culture,* 5.1 (2016).

Kopelson, Karen, "Dis/Integrating the Gay/ Queer Binary: 'Reconstructed Identity Politics' for a Performative Pedagogy," *College English,* 65 (September 2002), 17–35.

Koven, Seth, *Slumming: Sexual and Social Politics in Victorian London* (Princeton: Princeton University Press, 2004).

Kristeva, Julia, *Revolution in Poetic Language,* trans. by Margaret Walker (New York: Columbia University Press, 1941; repr. 1984).

Kuhn, Gustav, and Luis M. Martinez, "Misdirection—Past, Present, and the Future," *Frontiers in Human Neuroscience,* 5 (2011), unpaginated.

Kukkonen, Karin, "Comics as a Test Case for Transmedial Narratology," *SubStance,* 40 (Issue 124), 34–52.

_____, *Contemporary Comics Storytelling* (Lincoln: University of Nebraska Press, 2013).

_____, "Metalepsis in Popular Culture: An Introduction," in *Metalepsis in Popular Culture,* ed. by Karin Kukkonen and Sonja Klimek (Berlin: Walter de Gruyter & Co., 2011), 1–21.

LaBruzza, Anthony L., and Jose Méndez-Villarubia, *Using DSM-IV: A Clinician's Guide to Psychiatric Diagnosis* (New Jersey: Jason Aronson, Inc., 1994).

Lancaster, Roger N., "Subject Honor and Object

Shame: The Construction of Male Homosexuality and Stigma in Nicaragua," *Ethnology,* 27 (April 1988), 111–125.

Lander, Ben, "Graphic Novels as History: Representing and Reliving the Past," *Left History,* 10 (Fall 2005), 113–114.

Leblanc, Lauraine, *Pretty in Punk: Girls' Gender Resistance in a Boys' Subculture* (New Brunswick: Rutgers University Press, 1999).

Lee, Carol D., *Signifying as a Scaffold for Literary Interpretation: The Pedagogical Implications of an African American Discourse Genre* (Urbana, IL: National Council of Teachers of English, 1993).

Lefèvre, Pascal, "The Construction of Space in Comics," in *A Comics Studies Reader,* ed. by Jeet Heer and Kent Worcester (Jackson: University of Mississippi Press, 2009).

Levinson, Jerrold, "Autographic and Allographic Art Revisited," *Philosophical Studies,* 38 (1980), 367–383.

Li, Tim MH, and Paul WC Wong, "Youth social withdrawal behaviour (hikikomori): A systematic review of qualitative and quantitative studies," *Australian & New Zealand Journal of Psychiatry* 49 (2015), 595–609.

Licona, Adela C., "(B)orderlands' Rhetorics and Representations: The Transformative Potential of Feminist Third-Space Scholarship and Zines," *NWSA Journal,* 17 (2005), 104–129.

Liu, Richard T., and Brian Mustanski, "Suicidal Ideation and Self-Harm in Lesbian, Gay, Bisexual, and Transgender Youth," *American Journal of Preventive Medicine,* 42 (2012), 221–228.

Lorde, Audre, *The New York Head Shop and Museum* (Chicago: Broadside Press, 1974).

Luibhéid, Eithne, "Queer/Migration: An Unruly Body of Scholarship," *GLQ: A Journal of Lesbian and Gay Studies,* 14 (2008), 169–190.

MacDonald, Ann-Marie, *Fall on Your Knees* (London: Vintage, 1997).

Machera, Mumbi, "Opening a Can of Worms: A Debate on Female Sexuality in the Lecture Theatre," in *Re-thinking Sexualities in Africa,* ed. by Signe Arnfred (Sweden: Almqvist & Wiksell Tryckeri AB, 2005), 157–172.

Magnussen, Anne, "The Semiotics of C.S. Peirce as a Theoretical Framework for the Understanding of Comics," in *Comics & Culture: Analytical and Theoretical Approaches to Comics,* ed. by Anne Magnussen and Hans-Christian Christiansen (Denmark: Museum Tusculanum Press, 2000).

Mahn, Churnjeet Kaur, "The Queer Limits of Pratibha Parmar's *Nina's Heavenly Delights,*" *Journal of Lesbian Studies,* 17 (2013), 317–328.

Manchester, Ashley, "Teaching Critical Looking: Pedagogical Approaches to Using Comics as Queer Theory," *SANE Journal: Sequential Art Narrative in Education,* 2 (April 2017), 1–23.

Manibo, Devyn, "Sm{art}: Diggin' Deep with Cristy C. Road," *BitchMedia* (2009) http://bitchmagazine.org/post/smart-diggin-deep-with-cristy-c-road-art-queer-poc-zines-feminist-magazine-books-music.

Marshall, Annecka, "From sexual denigration to self-respect: resisting images of Black female sexuality," in *Reconstructing Womanhood, Reconstructing Feminism: Writings on Black Women,* ed. by Delia Jarrett-Macauley (London: Routledge, 1996), 5–35.

Marshall, Elizabeth, and Leigh Gilmore, "Girlhood in the Gutter: Feminist Graphic Knowledge and the Visualization of Sexual Precarity," *Women's Studies Quarterly,* 43 (Spring/Summer 2015), 95–114.

Martin, Bronwen, and Felizitas Ringham, *Dictionary of Semiotics* (London: Cassell, 2000).

Martin, Douglas, "A Village Dies, A Park is Born," *New York Times,* January 31, 1997, http://www.nytimes.com/1997/01/31/arts/a-village-dies-a-park-is-born.html.

Martin, Francis, Jr., "To Ignore is to Deny: E. W. Kemble's Racial Caricature as Popular Art," in *The Journal of Popular Culture* (July 2007), https://onlinelibrary.wiley.com/doi/abs/10.1111/j.1540-5931.2007.00429.x.

McCloud, Scott, *Understanding Comics: The Invisible Art* (New York: HarperCollins, 1993).

McLelland, Mark, Kazumi Nagaike, Katsuhiko Suganuma, and James Welker, eds. *Boys Love Manga and Beyond: History, Culture, and Community in Japan* (Mississippi: University Press of Mississippi, 2015).

Mead, George H., "What Social Objects Must Psychology Presuppose?" *The Journal of Philosophy, Psychology and Scientific Methods,* 7 (March 1910), 174–180.

——, "Wundt and the Concept of the Gesture," in *The Language of Gestures,* ed. by George H. Mead, et al. (The Hague & Paris: Mouton, 1973), 20–29.

Merkin, Daphne, "The Dark Lady of the Intellectuals," *New York Times,* October 29, 2000, http://www.nytimes.com/2000/10/29/books/the-dark-lady-of-the-intellectuals.html.

Metzl, Jonathan M., *The Protest Psychosis: How Schizophrenia Became a Black Disease* (Boston: Beacon Press, 2010).

Millet, Kate, *The Loony-Bin Trip* (New York: Simon & Schuster, 1990).

Mills, Charles W., *The Racial Contract* (Ithaca: Cornell University Press, 1997).

Minh-Ha, Trinh, T., *When the Moon Waxes Red: Representation, Gender and Cultural Politics* (New York: Routledge, 1991).

Mitchell-Kernan, Claudia, "Signifying, Loud Talking and Marking," in *Signifyin(g), Sanctifyin,' and Slam Dunking: A Reader in African American Expressive Culture*, ed. by Gena Dagel Caponi (Amherst: University of Massachusetts Press, 1999), 309–330.

Moi, Toril, *What is a Woman? And Other Essays* (Oxford: Oxford University Press, 1999).

Montgomery, Maxine Lavon, ed., *Conversations with Gloria Naylor* (Jackson: University Press of Mississippi, 2004).

Morgan, Marcyliena, *Language, Discourse and Power in African American Culture* (Cambridge: Cambridge University Press, 2002).

Morris, Susana M., "More Than Human: Black Feminisms of the Future in Jewelle Gomez's The Gilda Stories," *The Black Scholar*, 46 (April 2016), 33–45.

Morrison, James V., *Homeric Misdirection: False Predictions in the Iliad* (Ann Arbor: The University of Michigan Press, 1992).

Morrison, Toni, *Paradise* (London: Vintage, 1999).

———, *Playing in the Dark: Whiteness and the Literary Imagination* (New York: Vintage Books, 1993).

Morrison, Toni, and Nellie McKay, "An Interview with Toni Morrison," *Contemporary Literature*, 24.4 (1983), 413–429.

Nagata, Kabi, *My Lesbian Experience with Loneliness* (Los Angeles: Seven Seas Entertainment, 2017).

Namaste, Viviane, "Undoing Theory: The 'Transgender Question' and the Epistemic Violence of Anglo-American Feminist Theory," *Hypatia*, 24 (Summer 2009), 11–32.

Nataf, Zachary I., "Selection from Lesbians Talk Transgender," in *The Transgender Studies Reader*, ed. by Susan Stryker and Stephen Whittle (London: Routledge, 2006), 439–448.

National Coalition of Anti-Violence Programs, "Lesbian, Gay, Bisexual, Transgender, Queer, and HIV-Affected Hate Violence in 2013," *The New York City Anti-Violence Project* (2014) <http://www.avp.org/resources/avp-resources/315> [3 January 2014].

National Institute of Population and Social Security Research, "Marriage Process and Fertility of Married Couples Attitudes Toward Marriage and Family among Japanese Singles," (2017).

Nayak, Anoop, "'Pale warriors': skinhead culture and the embodiment of white masculinities," in *Children's Cultural Worlds*, ed. by Mary

Jane Kehily and Joan Swann (Chichester: John Wiley & Sons, 2003), 256–270.

Nayar, Pramod K., "Communicable Diseases: Graphic Medicine and the Extreme," *Journal of Creative Communications*, 10 (2015), 161–175.

———, "The Rhetoric of Silence/ing: Hush," *Margins: A Journal of Literature and Culture*, 3 (2013), 32–44.

Naylor, Gloria, *The Women of Brewster Place* (London: Vintage, 1982; repr. 1999).

Nemeti, Gay, <http://www.latinamericanstudies.org/mariel/mariel-chronology.htm>

Newbold, Leah, "On Class, Punk, Organizing and Anti-Affluence Activism," in *Shotgun Seamstress: Zine Collection*, ed. by Osa Atoe (Tacoma: Mend My Dress Press, 2012), 96–97.

Ngô, Fiona I.B., and Elizabeth A. Stinson, "Introduction: Threads and Omissions," *Women & Performance: A Journal of Feminist Theory*, 22 (2012), 165–171.

Nguyen, Mimi Thi, "Queer Cyborgs and New Mutants: Race, Sexuality, and Prosthetic Sociality in Digital Space," in *American Studies: An Anthology*, ed. by Janice A. Radway and others (Chichester: Wiley-Blackwell, 2009), 372–384.

Noble, Jean Bobby, *Masculinities without Men? Female Masculinity in Twentieth-Century Fictions* (Vancouver: UBC Press, 2004).

Nomous, Otto, "Race, Anarchy and Punk Rock: The Impact of Cultural Boundaries Within the Anarchist Movement," in *White Riot: Punk Rock and the Politics of Race*, ed. by Stephen Duncombe and Maxwell Tremblay (London: Verso, 2011), 202–205.

Nyong'o, Tavia, "Do You Want Queer Theory (or Do You want the Truth)? Intersections of Punk and Queer in the 1970s," *Radical History Review*, 100 (2008), 103–119.

O'Brien, Lucy, "The Woman Punk Made Me," in *Punk Rock: So What? The Cultural Legacy of Punk*, ed. by Roger Sabin (London: Routledge, 1999), 186–198.

O'Dea, Gregory, "Framing the Frame: Embedded Narratives, Enabling Texts, and *Frankenstein*," *Romanticism on the Net*, 31 (2003), 1–34.

O'Dwyer, Kathleen, "Paul Ricoeur: The Intersection Between Solitude and Connection," *Lyceum* XI (Fall 2009), 1–30.

O'Flaherty, Eamon, "Ecclesiastical Politics and the Dismantling of the Penal Laws in Ireland, 1774–82," *Irish Historical Studies*, 26 (May 1998), 33–50.

Omi, Michael, "(E)racism: Emerging Practices

of Antiracist Organizations," in *The Making and Unmaking of Whiteness*, ed. by Birgit Brander Rasmussen, and others (Durham, NC: Duke University Press, 2001), 266–293.

Ortiz, Fernando, *Cuban Counterpart: Tobacco and Sugar*, trans. by Harriet De Onis (Durham, NC: Duke University Press, 1995).

Osborne, Samuel, and Chris Baynes, "Turkey bans all LGBT events in capital to 'protect public security,'" *Independent*, 19 November 2017, http://www.independent.co.uk/news/world/europe/lgbt-events-banned-turkey-ankara-protect-public-security-governors-office-health-and-morality-a8063526.html.

Oswald, Ramona F., and others, "Queering 'The Family,'" in *Handbook of Feminist Theory and Family Studies*, ed. by Sally A. Lloyd, April L. Few, and Katharine R. Allen (Thousand Oaks: Sage Publications, 2009), 43–55.

Pagliassotti, Dru, Kazumi Nagaike, and Mark McHarry (2013) Editorial: Boys' Love manga special section, Journal of Graphic Novels and Comics, 4:1, 1–8, DOI: 10.1080/21504857.2013.793207.

Palmer, Paulina, *Lesbian Gothic: Transgressive Fictions* (London: Cassell, 1999).

Pateman, Carol, *The Sexual Contract* (Oxford: Blackwell Publishers, 1988).

Pateman, Carol, and Charles W. Mills, *Contract & Domination* (Cambridge: Polity Press, 2007).

Pedraza, Silvia, "*Los Marielitos* of 1980: Race, Class, Gender, and Sexuality," *Cuba in Transition*, 14 (August 2004), 89–102.

Peek, Christine, "Breaking out of the Prison Hierarchy: Transgender Prisoners, rape, and the Eight Amendment," *Santa Clara Law Review*, 44 (2003), 1211–1248.

Peña, Susana, "Gender and Sexuality in Latina/o Miami: Documenting Latina Transsexual Activists," *Gender & History*, 22 (2010), 755–772.

———, "'Obvious Gays' and the State Gaze: Cuban Gay Visibility and U.S. Immigration Policy during the 1980 Mariel Boatlift," *Journal of the History of Sexuality*, 16 (July 2007), 482–514.

Pérez, Emma, *The Decolonial Imaginary: Writing Chicanas into History* (Bloomington: Indiana University Press, 1999).

———, *Gulf Dreams*, 2nd ed. (San Francisco: Aunt Lute Books, 1996).

———, "Queering the Borderlands: The Challenges of Excavating the Invisible and Unheard," *Frontiers: A Journal of Women Studies*, 24 (2003), 122–131.

———, "Sexuality and Discourse: Notes from a Chicana Survivor," in *Chicana Lesbians: The Girls Our Mothers Warned Us About*, ed. by Carla Trujillo (Berkeley: Third Woman Press, 1991), 159–184.

———, "Staking the Claim: Introducing Applied Chicana/o Cultural Studies," in *The Chicana/o Cultural Studies Forum: Critical and Ethnographic Practices*, ed. by Angie Chabram-Dernersesian (New York: New York University Press, 2007), 121–124.

Pérez-Sánchez, Gema, "Reading, Writing, and the Love That Dares Not Speak Its Name: Eloquent Silences in Ana María Moix's *Julia*," in *Tortilleras: Hispanic and U.S. Latina Lesbian Expression*, ed. by Lourdes Torres and Immaculada Pertusa (Philadelphia: Temple University Press, 2003), 91–117.

Pérez-Torres, Rafael, *Mestizaje: Critical Uses of Race in Chicano Culture* (Minneapolis: University of Minnesota Press, 2006).

Phillips, Layli, and Maria R. Stewart, "I Am Just So Glad You Are Alive: New Perspectives on Non-Traditional, Non-Conforming, and Transgressive Expressions of Gender, Sexuality, and Race Among African Americans," *Journal of African American Studies*, 12 (2008), 378–400.

Porter, Roy, *A Social History of Madness: Stories of the Insane* (London: Phoenix Giants, 1987).

Price, Patricia L., "Cohering Culture on *Calle Ocho*: The Pause and Flow of *Latinidad*," *Globalizations*, 4 (2007), 81–99.

Prosser, Jay, *Second Skins: The Body Narratives of Transsexuality* (New York: Columbia University Press, 1998).

Puar, Jasbir K, "Queer Times, Queer Assemblages," *Social Text*, 23 (Fall-Winter 2005), 121–139.

———, *Terrorist Assemblages: Homonationalism in Queer Times* (Durham, NC: Duke University Press, 2007).

Purdue-Vaughns, Valerie, and Richard P. Eibach, "Intersectional Invisibility: The distinctive advantages and disadvantages of multiple subordinate-group identities," *Sex Roles*, 59 (2008), 377–391.

Quehl, Nadine J., "Queering 'Madness': Possibilities of Performativity Theory," *Alternate Routes: A Journal of Critical Social Research*, 20 (2004), 107–131.

Quiroga, Jose, *Tropics of Desire: Interventions from Queer Latino Desire* (New York: New York University Press, 2000).

Randle, Gloria T., "Between the Rock and the Hard Place: Mediating Spaces in Harriet Jacobs's *Incidents in the Life of a Slave Girl*," *African American Review*, 33 (Spring, 1999), 43–56.

Rasmussen, Birgit Brander, and others, eds., *The*

Making and Unmaking of Whiteness (Durham, NC: Duke University Press, 2001).

Rasmussen, Mary Lou, "The Problem of Coming Out," *Theory into Practice*, 43 (Spring 2004).

Raymond, Janice G., "Sappho by Surgery: The Transsexually Constructed Lesbian-Feminist," in *The Transgender Studies Reader*, ed. by Susan Stryker and Stephen Whittle (London: Routledge, 2006), 131–143.

Razack, Sherene, *Looking White People in the Eye: Gender, Race, and Culture in Courtrooms and Classrooms* (Toronto: University of Toronto Press, 2001).

Reid-Pharr, Robert F., "Tearing the Goat's Flesh: Homosexuality, Abjection and the Production of a Late Twentieth-Century Black Masculinity," *Studies in the Novel*, 28 (1996), 372–394.

Rich, Adrienne, "Compulsory Heterosexuality and Lesbian Experience," *Journal of Women's History*, 15.3 (Autumn 2003), 11–48.

Richardson, Matt, *The Queer Limit of Black Memory: Black Lesbian Literature and Irresolution* (Columbus: Ohio State University, 2013).

Ricoeur, Paul, "The Task of Hermeneutics," *Philosophy Today*, 17 (Summer 1973), 112–128.

Ritchie, Jason, "How Do You Say 'Come Out of the Closet' in Arabic?" *GLQ: A Journal of Lesbian and Gay Studies*, 16 (2010).

Road, Cristy C., *Bad Habits* (Brooklyn: Soft Skull Press, 2008).

Rodriguez, Richard T., "Imagine a Brown Queer: Inscribing Sexuality in Chicano/a-Latino/a Literary and Cultural Studies," *American Quarterly*, 59 (June 2007), 493–501.

Ronald, Richard, and Yosuke Hirayama's, "Home alone: the individualization of young, urban Japanese singles," *Environment and Planning*, 41 (2009), 2836–2854.

Ronen, Ruth, *Possible Worlds in Literary Theory* (Cambridge: Cambridge University Press, 1994).

Rose, Katrina C., "When is an attempted rape NOT an attempted rape? When the victim is a transsexual," *American University Journal of Gender, Social Policy & the Law*, 9 (2001), 505–540.

Roses, Lorraine Elena, and Ruth Elizabeth Randolph, *Harlem Renaissance and Beyond: Literary Biographies of 100 Black Women Writers 1900–1945* (Boston: G.K. Hall & Co., 1990).

Roth, Benita, *Separate Roads to Feminism: Black, Chicana, and White Feminist Movements in America's Second Wave* (Cambridge: Cambridge University Press, 2004).

Round, Julia, *The Gothic in Comics and Graphic Novels: A Critical Approach* (North Carolina: McFarland, 2014).

Royal, Derek P., "Foreword; Or Reading within the Gutter," in *Multicultural Comics: From Zap to Blue Beetle*, ed. by Frederick Luis Aldama (Austin: University of Texas Press, 2010).

Rubin, Gayle, "Of Catamites and Kings: Reflections on Butch, Gender, and Boundaries," in *The Transgender Studies Reader*, ed. by Susan Stryker and Stephen Whittle (London: Routledge, 2006), 471–481.

Russell, John, "Race and Reflexivity: The Black Other in Contemporary Japanese Mass Culture," in *Rereading Cultural Anthropology*, ed. George E. Marcus (Durham: Duke University Press, 1992), 296–318.

Russell, Rachel, and Melissa Tyler, "Branding and Bricolage: Gender, consumption and transition," *Childhood*, 12.2 (May 2005), 221–237.

Sabin, Roger, "I Won't Let That Dago By: Rethinking Punk and Racism," in *White Riot: Punk Rock and the Politics of Race*, ed. by Stephen Duncombe and Maxwell Tremblay (London: Verso, 2011), 57–67.

Sady, Cleo, *Nothing to Hide* (self-published, 2012).

Salah, Trish, "What Memory Wants: Broken Tongue, Stranger Fugue in Fall on Your Knees," *Canadian Review of American Studies*, 35 (2005), 231–249.

Samuel, Henry, "Jews pressured into adopting 'French-sounding' surnames fight to change them back," *Telegraph* (2010) http://www.telegraph.co.uk/news/ worldnews/europe/france/7898978/Jews-pressured-into-adopting-French-sounding-surnames-fight-to-change-them-back.html.

San Francisco Department of Public Health, "HIV Epidemiology Annual Report 2013," (San Francisco: San Francisco Department of Health, 2013), i-67.

Sandoval, Chela, "U.S. Third World Feminism: The Theory and Method of Oppositional Consciousness in the Postmodern World," *Gender* 10 (1991), 1–24.

Saraceni, Mario, *The Language of Comics* (London: Routledge, 2003).

Sargent, Antwaun, "An Artist is Deconstructing Comics into Grids in Order to Challenge Power Structures," *Creators*, 9 February 2017, https://creators.vice.com/en_us/article/8qdwyz/an-artist-deconstructs-comic-books-to-explore-race-and-sexuality.

Scherer, Burkhard, ed., *Queering Paradigms* (Switzerland: Peter Lang AG, 2010).

Schulte, Phil, "Holding in Mind: Intersubjectivity, Subject Relations and the Group," *Group Analysis*, 33 (December 2000), 531–544.

Schwartz, Adria E., *Sexual Subjects: Lesbians, Gender, and Psychoanalysis* (London: Routledge, 1998).

Schweid, Richard, *The Cockroach Papers: A Compendium of History and Lore* (Chicago: University of Chicago Press, 1999).

Scott, Cord A., *Comics and Conflict: Patriotism and Propaganda from WWII Through Operation Iraqi Freedom* (Annapolis: Naval Institute Press, 2014).

Seawell, Sophia, "An Interview with Cristy C. Road: On Zines, Publishing, and Capitalism," *Bluestockings Magazine*, 2014, http://bluestockingsmag.com/ 2014/03/28/an-interview-with-cristy-c-road-on-zines-publishing-and-capitalism-part-1-of-3/.

Sedgwick, Eve K., "The Character in the Veil: Imagery of the Surface in the Gothic Novel," *PMLA*, 96 (March 1981), 255–270.

_____, "Introduction," in *Between Men: English Literature and Male Homosocial Desire* (New York: Columbia University Press, 1985).

_____, *Tendencies* (Durham, NC: Duke University Press, 1993).

Segret, Mab, "Exalted on the Ward 'Mary Roberts,' the Georgia State Sanitarium, and the Psychiatric 'Specialty' of Race," *American Quarterly*, 66 (March 2014), 69–94.

Sezen, Beldan, *Snapshots of a Girl* (Vancouver: Arsenal Pulp Press, 2015).

Shelley, Percy B., *Shelley: A Defence of Poetry*, ed. by F.B. Pinion and M.A. Cantab (London: James Brodie Ltd., [1821] 1955), 16–56.

Shinn, Thelma J., *Women Shapeshifters: Transforming the Contemporary Novel* (Connecticut: Greenwood Press, 1996).

Showalter, Elaine, *The Female Malady: Women, Madness and English Culture, 1830–1980* (London: Virago Press, 1987).

Simpkins, Scott, "Tricksterism in the Gothic Novel," *The American Journal of Semiotics*, 14 (Winter 1998), 11–23.

Smethurst, James, "Invented by Horror: The Gothic and African American Literary Ideology in Native Son," *African American Review*, 35 (Spring 2001), 29–40.

Smith, Barbara, "The Truth That Never Hurts: Black Lesbians in Fiction in the 1980s," in *Third World Women and The Politics of Feminism*, ed. by Chandra Talpade Mohanty, Ann Russo, and Lourdes Torres (Bloomington: Indiana University Press, 1991), 101–129.

Smith, Jeanne R., *Writing Tricksters: Mythic Gambols in American Ethnic Literature* (Berkeley: University of California Press, 1997).

Smith, Lois M., and Alfred Padula, *Sex and Revolution: Women in Socialist Cuba* (New York: Oxford University Press, 1996).

Smith, Sidonie, and Julia Watson, *Reading Autobiography: A Guide for Interpreting Life Narratives*, 2nd ed. (Minnesota: Regents of the University of Minnesota, 2010).

Snorton, Riley, C., "Passing for White, Passing for Man: Johnson's *The Autobiography of an Ex-Colored Man* as Transgender Narrative," in *Trans/Gender Migrations: Bodies, Borders, and the Politics of Gender Crossing*, ed. by Trystan T. Cotton (Oxon: Routledge, 2012), 107–118.

Softskull Press, "Bad Habits: A Love Story," *Softskull Press* (2008) http://softskull.com/bad-habits-a-love-story-2/.

Sontag, Susan, *Reborn: Journals and Notebooks, 1947–1963* (New York: Farrar Straus Giroux, 2008).

_____, "Regarding the Torture of Others," http://www.nytimes.com/2004/05/23/magazine/regarding-the-torture-of-others.html?_r=0.

_____, *Styles of Radical Will* (London: Penguin Classics, 1969).

Spillers, Hortense J., "Mama's Baby, Papa's Maybe: An American Grammar Book," *Diacritics*, 17 (Summer, 1987), 64–81.

_____, "The Permanent Obliquity," in *Changing Our Own Words: Essays on Criticism, Theory, and Writing by Black Women*, ed. by Cheryl A. Wall (London: Routledge, 1990), 127–149.

Spinks, C.W., "Trickster: Cultural Boundaries and Semiosis," *The American Journal of Semiotics*, 14 (Winter 1997), 3–7.

Spivak, Gayatri Chakravorty, "Three Women's Texts and a Critique of Imperialism," *Critical Inquiry*, 12 (Autumn 1985), 243–261.

Stacey, Jackie, "'If You Don't Play, You Can't Win': *Desert Hearts* and the lesbian romance film," in *Immortal, Invisible: Lesbians and the moving image*, ed. Tamsin Wilton (London: Routledge, 1995), 67–87.

Staels, Hilde, "Embracing Difference in Ann-Marie Macdonald's Fall on Your Knees," *Orbis Litterarum*, 64 (2009), 324–338.

Stein, Pippa, *Multimodal Pedagogies in Diverse Classrooms: Representation, rights and resources* (London: Routledge, 2008).

Stoker, Bram, *Dracula* (London: Puffin Books, [1897] 1986).

Stone, Sandy, "The Empire Strikes Back: A Posttranssexual Manifesto," in *The Transgender Studies Reader*, ed. by Susan Stryker and Stephen Whittle (London: Routledge, 2006), 221–235.

Stramskas, Arnoldas, "Making Sense of Punk Subcultures in the Neoliberal United States," *Groups and Environments,* 3 (2013), 115–129.

Stryker, Susan, "(De) Subjugated Knowledges: An Introduction to Transgender Studies," in *The Transgender Studies Reader*, ed. by Susan Stryker and Stephen Whittle (London: Routledge, 2006), 1–18.

———, "Transgender Studies: Queer Theory's Evil Twin," *GLQ: A Journal of Lesbian and Gay Studies*, 10 (2004), 212–215.

Sugg, Katherine, "The Ultimate Rebellion: Chicana Narratives of Sexuality and Community," *Meridians: feminism, race, transnationalism*, 3 (2003), 139–170.

Tannen, Ricki Stefanie, *The Female Trickster: the mask that reveals Post-Jungian and Postmodern Psychological Perspectives on Women in Contemporary Culture* (East Sussex: Routledge, 2007).

Taylor, Jodie Louise, "Spewing Out of the Closet: Musicology on Queer Punk," in *Musical Islands: Exploring Connections Between Music, Place and Research*, ed. by Elizabeth Mackinlay, Brydie-Leigh Bartleet, and Katelyn Barney (Newcastle Upon Tyne: Cambridge Scholars Press, 2009), 221–241.

Taylor-Stone, Charlene, "Afrofuturism: where space, pyramids and politics collide," https://www.theguardian.com/science/political-science/2014/jan/07/afrofuturism-where-space-pyramids-and-politics-collide.

Tensuan, Theresa M., "Crossing the Lines: Graphic (Life) Narratives and Co-Laborative Political Transformations," *Biography* (Honolulu), 32 (Winter 2009), 173–189.

Terry, Jennifer, "Theorizing Deviant Historiography," *A Journal of feminist cultural studies*, 3 (1991), 276–303.

Tewksbury, Richard, "Cruising for Sex in Public Places: the structure and language of men's hidden, erotic worlds," *Deviant Behavior*, 17 (January–March 1996), 1–19.

Tillich, Paul, *The Eternal Now* (New York: Charles Scribner's Sons, 1963).

Tomes, Nancy, "Feminist Histories of Psychiatry," in *Discovering the History of Psychiatry*, ed. by Mark S. Micale and Roy Porter (Oxford: Oxford University Press, 1994), 348–383.

Tongson, Karen, "Queer Fundamentalism," *Social Text 121*, 32 (Winter 2014), 117–123.

Traber, Daniel S., "L.A.'s 'White Minority': Punk and the Contradictions of Self-Marginalization," *Cultural Critique*, 48 (Spring 2001), 30–64.

Treviño, A. Javier, Michelle A. Harris, and Derron Wallace, "What's so critical about critical race theory?," *Contemporary Justice Review*, 11 (March 2008), 7–10.

Ussher, Jane M., *Women's Madness: Misogyny or Illness?* (Hertfordshire: Harvester Wheatsheaf, 1991).

Valderas, Jose M., et al., "Defining Comorbidity: Implications for Understanding Health and Health Services," *Annals of Family Medicine*, 7 (July/August 2009), 357–363.

Valentine, David, *Imagining Transgender: An Ethnography of a Category* (Durham: Duke University Press, 2007).

Valentine, Gill, "(RE) Negotiating the "Heterosexual Street": Lesbian Productions of Space," in *Bodyspace: destabilizing geographies of gender and sexuality*, ed. by Nancy Duncan (London: Routledge, 1996), 146–155.

Valentine, Gill, Tracey Skelton, and Ruth Butler, "Coming out and outcomes: negotiating gay and lesbian identities with, and in, the family," *Environment and Planning D: Society and Space*, 21 (2003), 479–499.

Vaňková, Ingrida "Life as a Story—Self as a Text," *English Matters* (2010), 54. http://www.pulib.sk/elpub2/FHPV/Kacmaroval/.

Van Leeuwen, Theo, *Introducing Social Semiotics* (London: Routledge, 2005).

———, "Semiotics and Iconography," in *Handbook of Visual Analysis*, ed. by Theo van Leeuwen and Carey Jewitt (London: Sage Publications, 2001), 92–118.

Vasquez, Tina, "The queer punk rock author presents unique challenges in a Cuban family," *Curve Magazine* (2013) http://www.curvemag.com/Curve-Magazine/Web-Articles-2013/Page-Turner-Christy-C-Road/.

Vela, Justin, "Abortions are like Air Strikes on Civilians': Turkish PM Recep Tayyip Ergodan's Rant Sparks Women's Rage," *Independent*, 30 May 2012, http://www.independent.co.uk/life-style/health-and-families/health-news/abortions-are-like-air-strikes-on-civilians-turkish-pm-recep-tayyip-erdogans-rant-sparks-womens-rage-7800939.html.

Vickroy, Laurie, *Trauma and Survival in Contemporary Fiction* (Charlottesville: University of Virginia Press, 2002).

Wakeling, Emily Jane, "Girls are dancin'": shōjo culture and feminism in contemporary Japanese art," *New Voices*, 5 (2011), 130–146.

Walker, Alice, *In Search of Our Mothers' Gardens: Womanist Prose* (Orlando: A Harvest Book, Harcourt Inc., 1983).

Walker, Mort, *The Lexicon of Comicana* (Lincoln, NE: iUniverse.com, 1980).

Warhol, Robin R., "The Space Between: A Narrative Approach to Alison Bechdel's "'Fun Home,'" *College Literature*, 38 (Summer 2011), 1–20.

Weeks, Jeffrey, "The Value of Difference," in

Identity: Community, Culture, Difference, ed. by Jonathan Rutherford (London: Lawrence & Wishart, 1990), 88–100.

Weiner, Stephen, *Faster Than a Speeding Bullet: The Rise of the Graphic Novel* (New York: Nantier, Beall, Minoustchine, 2003).

Whaley, Deborah Elizabeth, *Black Women in Sequence: Re-inking Comics, Graphic Novels, and Anime* (Seattle: University of Washington Press, 2016).

Whitlock, Gillian, "Autographics: The Seeing 'I' of the Comics," *Modern Fiction Studies,* 52 (Winter 2006), 965–979.

Whitlock, Gillian, and Anna Poletti, "Self-Regarding Art," *Biography* (Honolulu), 31 (Winter 2008), v-xxiii.

Whitted, Qiana, "'And the Negro thinks in hieroglyphics': comics, visual metonymy, and the spectacle of blackness," *Journal of Graphic Novels and Comics* (2014), 79–100.

Williams, Cristan, "Transgender," *Transgender Studies Quarterly,* 1 (May 2014), 232–234.

Wilton, Tamsin, "On Not Being Lady Macbeth: Some (troubled) thoughts on lesbian spectatorship," in *Immortal, Invisible: Lesbians and the moving image,* ed. Tamsin Wilton (London: Routledge, 1995), 113–130.

Wisner, William H., "The Perilous Self: Loren Eiseley and the Reticence of Autobiography," *The Sewanee Review,* 113 (Winter 2005), 84–95.

Wodda, Aimee, and Vanessa R. Panfil, "'Don't Talk to Me About Deception': The Necessary Erosion of the Trans Panic Defense," *Albany Law Review,* 78 (2014/2015), 927–971.

Wong, Eric, "Breaking the Silence: How Comics Visualize Sound," *Sequart Organization,* December 31, 2014, http://sequart.org/magazine/53486/how-comics-visualize-sound/.

Woodhead, Linda, "Feminism and the Sociology of Religion: From Gender-blindness to Gendered Difference," in *The Blackwell Companion to Sociology of Religion,* ed.by Richard K. Fenn (Massachusetts: Blackwell Publishing Ltd., 2001), 67–84.

Yoo, Aileen S., "The Mariel Boatlift," <http://www.washingtonpost.com/wp-srv/inatl/longterm/cuba/mariel_port.htm>

Younge, Gary, "The Serena cartoon debate: calling out racism is not 'censorship,'" *The Guardian,* 13 September 2018, https://www.theguardian.com/commentisfree/2018/sep/13/serena-williams-cartoon-racism-censorship-mark-knight-herald-sun.

Zepeda, Susy, "Mapping Queer of Color Methodology," *GLQ: A Journal of Lesbian and Gay Studies,* 15 (2009), 622–623.

Zin, Maxine Baca, and Bonnie Thornton Dill, "Theorizing Difference from Multiracial Feminism," *Feminist Studies,* 22 (Summer 1996), 321–331.

Index

Numbers in **bold italics** indicate pages with illustrations